FAITH, POLITICS, AND SEXUAL DIVERSITY IN CANADA AND THE UNITED STATES

FAITH, POLITICS, AND SEXUAL DIVERSITY IN CANADA AND THE UNITED STATES

Edited by David Rayside and Clyde Wilcox

UBCPress · Vancouver · Toronto

20 19 18 17 16 15 14 13 12 11   5 4 3 2 1

Printed in Canada on FSC-certified ancient-forest-free paper
(100% post-consumer recycled) that is processed chlorine- and acid-free.

Library and Archives Canada Cataloguing in Publication

Faith, politics, and sexual diversity in Canada and the United States /
edited by David Rayside and Clyde Wilcox.

Includes bibliographical references and index.
ISBN 978-0-7748-2009-7 (bound); ISBN 978-0-7748-2010-3 (pbk.)

    1. Gay rights – Canada – Religious aspects. 2. Gay rights – United States – Religious aspects. 3. Same-sex marriage – Canada – Religious aspects. 4. Same-sex marriage – United States – Religious aspects. 5. Gay rights – Canada – Public opinion. 6. Gay rights – United States – Public opinion. 7. Homosexuality – Religious aspects. 8. Public opinion – Canada. 9. Public opinion – United States. I. Rayside, David M. (David Morton), 1947- II. Wilcox, Clyde, 1953-

HQ76.3.C3F34 2011	323.3'2640971	C2010-907163-8

e-book ISBNs: 978-0-7748-2011-0 (pdf); 978-0-7748-2012-7 (epub)

Canadä

UBC Press gratefully acknowledges the financial support for our publishing program of the Government of Canada (through the Canada Book Fund), the Canada Council for the Arts, and the British Columbia Arts Council.

This book has been published with the help of a grant from the Canadian Federation for the Humanities and Social Sciences, through the Aid to Scholarly Publications Program, using funds provided by the Social Sciences and Humanities Research Council of Canada.

Printed and bound in Canada by Freisens
Set in Futura Condensed and Warnock by Artegraphica Design Co. Ltd.
Text design: Irma Rodriguez
Copy editor: Joanne Richardson
Proofreader: Dallas Harrison

UBC Press
The University of British Columbia
2029 West Mall
Vancouver, BC V6T 1Z2
www.ubcpress.ca

Dedicated to those who build bridges at the intersections of faith and sexual diversity

Contents

Evangelicals / 67

Mainline Protestants / 166

Conclusion / 355

Appendices

Figures and Tables

Figures

Tables

Preface

Each of us comes to the ideas contained in this volume through a distinct and personal path.

Clyde's roots in rural West Virginia included a family life deeply imbued with evangelical faith and a community shaped by traditional religiously based values. They were kind and generous people, even if their conservatism included opposition to gay rights. But Clyde was also strongly influenced by the social and political activism of the 1960s and 1970s, and he wanted his own children to learn respect for diversity. In the process of blending these two currents, he has tried to write respectfully about the role of evangelical Christianity in American politics and to argue against over-simplification in characterizing the political beliefs of born-again Christians. He has also taken seriously the political claims of sexual minorities and sought to write about them knowledgeably at a time when few political scientists were doing so.

David's roots lie in the urbanized and largely secularized anglo-Montreal of the decades after the Second World War. Like Clyde, David was politically shaped by the social and political activism of the 1960s and 1970s, in his case during the dramatic period of Quebec's "Quiet Revolution," when religious traditions were being challenged at every turn. It took some time for him to come to terms with being a gay man, but by the mid-1980s he was deeply engaged in community activism on lesbian/gay rights and was beginning to teach and write in the area. His extensive work on sexual diversity since then has required understanding religiously based opposition to lesbian/gay/bisexual/transgender (LGBT) rights claims in Canada, the United States, and Europe, eventually leading to the introduction of a new undergraduate course on religion and politics.

We each knew of the other's work but first encountered one another through David's contribution of an article to a book co-edited by Clyde on gay rights politics in the United States. Then, in January 2007, Clyde served as the F. Ross Johnson Visitor to the University of Toronto's Centre for the Study of the United States. At the core of his intensive two-week stay was his participation in a conference entitled "Religion, Sexuality, and Politics in Canada and the United States," organized by David and principally sponsored by the Mark S. Bonham Centre for Sexual Diversity Studies, which David directed at the time.

During that visit we agreed that Canada and the United States were ripe for more comparative treatment of these issues and that an edited collection drawing from several of the contributions to the conference and additional submissions would help to stimulate interest in that comparison. The collection is predicated on the belief that the comparison between the United States and Canada inevitably points to instructive differences but has suffered from some exaggeration of contrasts. Sweeping claims portray the United States as dominated by religious conservatism and Canada as untouched by it. These claims imply that the United States is resistant to LGBT claims, while Canada has undergone a political and legal revolution and now embraces them fully. They are all misleading. These two countries are distinct, to be sure, but there are also more parallels than is widely appreciated. Each covers a large territory in which regional variations are important. In each we see complex questions about the way in which faith and religious diversity can and should be accommodated. And in each we continue to see conflict over the extent to which sexual diversity should be publicly recognized.

We are both committed to moving beyond stereotypes in assessing political claims based on sexual diversity and faith, recognizing that they are often in conflict but often are not. Each of us knows of religious leaders who have been strong advocates of LGBT rights or who are genuinely struggling over the reconciliation of their faith with a respect for sexual diversity.

Communities of deep religious commitment are often little understood from the outside, just as sexual minorities are still subject to stereotype or oversimplified generalization. We also realize that, in societies built upon multicultural realities, the accommodation of difference often requires new approaches and potentially uncomfortable compromises.

Both of us recognize the importance of the borders that separate populations from one another. Americans and Canadians have many similarities, but the 49th parallel separates out distinct patterns of religiosity, politics, culture, and the public play of sexual diversity. Within each of these countries, regional borders also count. And within every state or province and locality, there are important segments of the population that live in worlds that are starkly differentiated along lines of religion and sexuality.

And yet we also recognize important similarities between Canadian and American patterns as well as across regions. We also see growing signs of bridges being built between people of faith and members of sexual minorities and indications that acceptance of sexual difference is expanding even among those who embrace relatively traditional forms of religious belief.

We have much to be thankful for in the completion of this volume. We first acknowledge the thoughtfulness and work of our many contributors, who showed great patience in travelling the long road with us since early 2007.

The original conference benefited from the support of several academic units at the University of Toronto and especially the Centre for the Study of the United States (directed by Elspeth Brown), the Department of Political Science (chaired successively by Rob Vipond and David Cameron), the Office of the Provost, the Faculty of Arts and Science, and the School of Public Policy. Dr. Richard Isaac, a good friend of the Bonham Centre, provided additional support. Robbie Morgan was inimitable and indispensable throughout all stages of conference planning.

Since that time, the preparation of this book has benefited from the assistance and cooperation of Patrick Carr, Michael Cobb, Anthony Collins, Pam Klassen, Jason Klocek, Matt Malone, Jon Mummolo, Andrew Phillips, and Erica Rosenfield. The people at UBC Press have been wonderful to work with, especially our extraordinary editor Emily Andrew. We benefited enormously from anonymous reviewers who took great care in their evaluation of all parts of the large manuscript.

We are happy to acknowledge that this book is published with the help of a grant from the Canadian Federation for the Humanities and Social Sciences, through the Aid to Scholarly Publications Program, using funds provided by the Social Sciences and Humanities Research Council of Canada.

And finally, we thank those who have to live most closely to and continuously with the kind of work patterns that get projects like this completed. To Elizabeth, Elaine, Neil, and Gerry we say, once again, the warmest possible thank you.

David Rayside, Toronto
Clyde Wilcox, Washington, DC

INTRODUCTION

The Difference that a Border Makes
The Political Intersection of Sexuality and Religion in Canada and the United States

DAVID RAYSIDE AND CLYDE WILCOX

Religion and sexual diversity issues are intertwined. Any discussion of homosexuality or gender identity will inevitably evoke a response from religious conservatives. Debates over the relationship between religion and the public square frequently settle on sexuality issues as critical tests.

The contentiousness of lesbian and gay marriage in recent American elections demonstrates the extent to which religion and sexuality are entangled. In the 2008 election, when the urgency of other issues swept almost all else aside, four states had anti-gay ballot measures, and in California only the presidential race garnered more resources and visibility than did the referendum to roll back same-sex marriage.

And yet, within six months, the number of states that had extended civil marriage to same-sex couples jumped from two to five. A few additional states established full or partial domestic partnership regimes, bringing to seventeen the number of states that wholly or partially, directly or indirectly, recognized same-sex relationships. And, beyond that, such couples had secured at least partial parenting rights in close to half of the American states at a time when European governments were just beginning to grapple with the issues associated with lesbians and gays having children.

Both presidential campaigns featured regular avowals of Christian faith – on the Republican side through the campaigning of Sarah Palin, on the Democratic side through Barack Obama's repeated professions of faith. And yet we are also seeing evidence of young evangelical Christians' growing dis-illusionment with their elders' preoccupations with anti-gay campaigning.

Canada, too, had a national election in the fall of 2008, but religion played a very different role there than it did in the United States. No major party leader in recent history has made more than passing reference to a personal faith. Even Stephen Harper, current leader of the Conservative Party and an evangelical Christian, has remained largely silent on his reli-gious beliefs.

And while the legalization of same-sex marriage had been hotly debated only three years before, when the Conservatives angrily denounced it and threatened to overturn it, there was now nothing being said about it. The party that had succeeded in attracting more religiously conservative votes than any other party in recent Canadian history was disciplining its local candidates to avoid discussing morally conservative issues on the grounds that such issues were electorally hazardous.

How could these neighbouring systems, with so much shared economic life and so many shared social patterns, display such different political pat-terns? And are the contrasts as great as these electoral snapshots would sug-gest? When we take a broad comparative view, are we more struck by the difference the border makes or by the power of bridging connections that sustain similarities?

There are important similarities across the international border in the claims pressed against state authority on religious and sexual issues. In Can-ada as well as in the United States, the 1970s marked a dramatic increase in the visibility of political demands based on one or another form of queer sexuality. In both countries, in part as a response to gains secured by lesbian, gay, and feminist activists, social and religious conservatives mobilized large-scale resources for political intervention in defence of what was argued to be "traditional family values." In both countries, such mobilization led the adherents of such values to shift towards major parties of the right – the Republicans and the Conservatives, respectively.

All this was occurring in the midst of continuing uncertainties in the public at large regarding where and how faith and political action inter-sected. These uncertainties were bitterly fought out in courts, in legislatures, and in the mass media. And yet, at the same time, we find dramatic shifts in popular beliefs towards more acceptance of sexual diversity, even among those who attach importance to their faith. In looking at each of these coun-tries, then, are we most drawn to political opposition across deep cultural and social chasms or to indications of bridge building?

For all these similarities, cross-border differences still leap out. Questions about religion and the public square have been posed more unrelentingly and contentiously in the United States than in Canada. In so many respects, the American case is an unusual one – in the resources marshalled for Christian advocacy, in the strength of religious conservatism and its organizational presence, and in the persistence of raucous debate over the role of faith in the public arena. For decades, the front line of what some would call a culture war is defined by debates over public recognition of sexual diversity.

Canada seems so different from the United States on these fronts. Despite major controversies over three decades, many claims to public recognition of sexual minorities have been politically settled. All parties at the federal level have essentially turned the page even on marriage – that most contentious of issues. On questions about religion and the public sphere, there continue to be flare-ups, for example over state support for religious schools or the "accommodation" of religious differences. But these tend not to persist as elements in a continuing struggle over core political or constitutional principles.

An exploration of similarities and differences between Canada and the United States in how such issues and debates get played out requires nuance. The Canada-US comparison is so obvious and yet so often neglected. Stereotypes abound, of course, on both sides of the border – either about how completely alike the two societies are or about how completely different they are. More careful observation reveals similarities in areas where most casual observers most notice contrasts, and contrasts in areas where they most notice similarities.

Speaking to Broader Analyses of Canadian-American Differences

An exploration of politics at the intersection of religion and sexual diversity gets to the heart of debates over the extent of cross-border contrast in values and policies. In fact, the character of political struggles over such issues as lesbian/gay rights, abortion, and the death penalty, or the policy outcomes of those debates, are frequently cited in the media of both countries as key illustrations of a growing divide between the two countries or as symptoms of American exceptionalism.

There are roughly three schools of thought on what, if anything, differentiates the Canadian and American cases. The first is that there are sharp differences in values and political outcomes across a wide range of issues. Seymour Martin Lipset (1990) was the most enduring proponent of the argument that

there are major distinctions in the core political cultures of the two countries and that those differences are congealed at crucial foundational mo-
ments (Hartz 1964). The United States was born of revolution and of an
intense individualism suspicious of state authority. It was also born with a
population of fervent Christians, most of whom rejected the idea of an established church but still took their faith very seriously and viewed the new
republic in moralistic terms. Canada (both English and French) was founded on counter-revolutionary principles, more focused on public order than
on individual freedom, more dependent on an interventionist state than on
a less regulatory one, more open to group rights than to individual rights,
more likely to adhere to traditional religious denominations than to non-
traditional ones, less fervent in both religion and politics than its southern
neighbour, and more mosaic than melting pot.

A variant of this approach is just as emphatic with regard to socio-cultural-
political contrasts but is less focused on explaining them through origins.
Here we might place Michael Adams (2003), who uses survey data to argue
that there is a growing divergence in values, particularly on questions of
morality, gender, and family, and that this is driven, in part, by religious differences and by lower levels of social anxiety in Canada than in the United
States.

Another variant of the argument for contrast is one that emphasizes not
so much differences in public beliefs as the role of political and legal institutions, which creates more room in Canada than in the United States for the
advocacy of minority rights. This argument is most clearly advanced by
Miriam Smith (2008), but it is also evident in those parts of Alexander
Smith and Raymond Tatalovich's analysis of moral conflicts that point to
contrasting outcomes (2003; see also Tatalovich 1997).

On the other side are analyses that emphasize similarities and, in some
cases, convergence. Comparative political economy usually places Canada
and the United States in the same category, sharply distinguishing the two
cases from the more state-interventionist welfare states of Europe (Hall and
Soskice 2001; Coates 2005). Canadian writers in this vein usually emphasize
the pressures towards neoliberal convergence that operate on a Canadian
economy already so tightly connected to the American economy (Brodie
2003; Bashevkin 1998). On social and cultural fronts, any visitor to Canada
and the United States from far away is invariably struck by the economic,
social, and cultural similarities between the two countries. After all, most
Canadians buy merchandise or obtain services from American-owned companies. Anglophones are more likely to watch American film and television

drama than Canadian, and they are much more likely to tune in to CNN than in to CBC's news channel during times of crisis. In broad cultural terms, Quebec and the American South are justifiably seen as somewhat apart, though perceptive observers will often comment on just how distinctly North American they are.

As to political values, Neil Nevitte (1996) has directly challenged the Lipset view by pointing to similarities in public beliefs on such core values as deference. His more recent work with Chris Cochrane and Steve White challenges the view that "post-industrialism" leads to value convergence, but it still shows strong similarities between the Canadian and American cases, for example in the relationship between religious faith and attitudes towards moral issues (Nevitte and Cochrane 2006). Fletcher, Russell, and Sniderman (1996) also show as many similarities as differences in Canadian and American beliefs on questions of individual rights. Jeff Reitz and Raymond Breton (1994), exploring the experience of immigrant groups and policies towards them, challenge the "illusion of difference" between the two countries, a point also made by Tamara Palmer Seiler (2008). Donley Studlar's (2002) work on tobacco regulation points to more parallel than divergence in policy evolution, despite important contextual differences.

We find ourselves drawing from all these analytical threads, weaving a portrayal of responses to debates over religious and sexuality rights that points both to sharp differences and sometimes to surprising similarities. Whether born of foundational principles or more recent circumstances, there are indeed value differences across the border, even taking into account the variations within each of these vast and regionalized countries. Crucial to these differences is the unusually strong religious faith in the United States and the exceptional strength of evangelical Protestantism. In the United States, this in itself produces more continuous political combat over even the most basic of rights for sexual minorities than occurs in Canada. The stakes in American struggles over these issues are raised by highly politicized debates over the appropriate degrees of separation between church and state.

But we also know that contrasts across the international border are not uniform. Yes, on lesbian/gay marriage, there is a major difference – with 55 to 60 percent of Canadians and 40 to 45 percent of Americans supportive of the inclusive position. About 60 percent of Canadians view homosexual behaviour as morally acceptable; about 40 percent of Americans do so. However, when asked if they support protections against discrimination in employment, Canadians and Americans are about equally (and overwhelmingly) in support, and when asked about adoption rights they are about equally (and evenly) divided. There is almost no survey evidence on attitudes towards transgender issues, but we suspect that there would not be major differences in the views of Canadians and Americans and that popular responses would display considerable anxieties about identities and behaviours that cross gender lines.

In both countries, LGBT minorities are highly visible, and, increasingly, people of faith – especially young ones – know friends, work associates, or family members who are part of those communities. Contact with minorities does not invariably lead to tolerance or full acceptance, but with sexual minorities the evidence points in that direction. More and more religious communities are struggling collectively towards a more positive attitude towards sexual minorities, with strong parallels across the border. For these and other reasons, we are not convinced that the United States is nearly as beset by a "culture war" as is often argued by observers both inside and beyond American borders.

As to the role of political and legal institutions, here, too, we find mixed evidence. The complexity of the US political system privileges the status quo and reduces the likelihood of sweeping change. Populist mechanisms such as referenda also create openings for Christian right opponents to enact barriers to LGBT rights, further slowing the pace of change towards inclusion for sexual minorities. Contributing to further distinguishing the two systems are the constitutional provisions governing rights protection – affording more robust protections for both sexual and religious minorities in Canada than in the United States.

The institutionalist argument, though, can be easily overdone. Very different institutional orders have produced some strikingly similar policies, as Studlar (2002) shows in respect to tobacco regulation and Smith and Tatalovich (2003) report on abortion – a "morality" policy area where we would expect to see contrast. One reason for the similarities lies in the role of courts in regulating conflict over religion and sexual diversity. These are two very similar countries in the extent to which courts have the right to review legislative acts (in Canada more recently than in the United States). And while the national constitutional frameworks in which courts operate have crucial differences, particularly with respect to LGBT rights, many US state courts have moved in much the same direction as have Canadian courts in responding to relationship and parenting claims by same-sex partners (Pierceson 2005; Rayside 2008). The "exceptional" American institutional setting, in other words, has allowed for more change than is generally appreciated by comparative analysts.

The two national party systems used to be categorically different in the extent to which the major parties differed on questions related to either religion or sexuality. There is still very strong pressure towards centrism for national parties in Canada, particularly on these issues, but party realignment in Canada over the past decade has narrowed the gap between the party systems.

To what extent are debates over sexuality and religion part of a distinct category of "moral" conflicts? We are not sure how useful this category is. No doubt, the public recognition of rights claims based on religious faith, sexual orientation, and gender identity elicits strong assertions of "deep-seated moral codes" (Smith 1975; Mooney 1999, 2000; Smith and Tatalovich 2003). They are generally not focused on material distribution or redistribution, and, for some writers, this entails a form of "post-materialist" politics centred on issues of recognition that do not easily admit of compromise (Inglehart 1977; Gutmann 1992; Fraser 2003; Taylor 1992). Christopher Mooney (1999) argues that, because they are based on core principles, they are highly salient to the general public.

But these are slippery categories, and, even if there are particular issues that are framed by some protagonists as tied to core moral principles, they are open to very different frames (e.g., about equality). Political battles over redistributive issues like taxation and social welfare have often enough had strong moral currents. Policy initiatives once framed largely in moral terms (liquor regulation, heterosexual marriage, and divorce) have moved towards more utilitarian considerations. And, as for salience, issues related to the public recognition of either religion or sexual diversity vary enormously over time in their salience. Even in the United States, public ratings of high-priority political issues rarely include same-sex marriage – that most controversial of current issues related to sexual diversity.

Some writers argue that, because morality policy, especially in North America, is so often left to the courts, decisions are regularly out of tune with majority sentiment (Morton and Knopff 2000; Smith and Tatalovich 2003). We believe that there is no evidence that systematically differentiates the proportion of "majoritarian" outcomes on moral issues from those in other policy realms (Fletcher and Howe 2000, 2001).

We therefore do not believe that we are helped much or at all by treating the issues at stake here as part of a distinct policy category. As a result, we believe that the comparative lessons to be drawn from an examination of the intersecting politics of religion and sexuality have broad application, complicating important currents of received wisdom about each country.

In laying the foundation for a more detailed comparative exploration of the political debates over religion and sexual diversity, we begin with a comparison of the religious landscapes of the two countries and the patterns of mobilization around issues of faith and sexuality. We then return to a discussion of the crucial constitutional and institutional contexts within which political action occurs in Canada and the United States.

Religious Landscapes

The fact that the relationship between religion and politics is so continuously debated in the United States derives significantly from the large numbers of Americans who consider religion important, the high proportion of them with traditional or literalist interpretations of scripture, and the size of the groups representing conservative moral positions in policy debates. These characteristics distinguish the American case from the Canadian case, but they also distinguish it from almost all cases in the liberal democratic West.

Of the 50 percent of the US population that is Protestant, 20 percent belong to evangelical denominations, 19 percent to mainline denominations (some of which are evangelical), and 11 percent to black Protestant churches (most of them being evangelical). Twenty-five percent of Americans are Roman Catholic, 2 percent Mormon, 3 percent Jewish, between 1 and 2 percent Muslim, and 2 to 3 percent other religions, the rest mostly declaring no religion. Many more white Americans than Canadians belong to conservative evangelical Protestant denominations, and, in their conservative approach to sexuality, they have many allies in mainline Protestant denominations among Roman Catholics (Latino/as and others), African Americans, and other faiths. Mormons constitute only 2 percent of the population, but their capacity to mobilize and raise money to oppose gay rights was dramatically influential in the campaign against same-sex marriage in the California election of 2008.

In the United States, most evangelical Christians disapprove of homosexuality and strongly oppose same-sex marriage, even if we can see important shifts away from categorical rejection of all rights claims based on sexual diversity. Despite such change, most religious right groups have white evangelical Protestants as their largest core constituency, and they constitute the vanguard of political opposition to LGBT advocates. Though bridges between white evangelical Protestantism and African-American churches have been difficult to build, the strength of opposition to lesbian/gay marriage is similar in both sets of faith communities (Boykin 2005; Cohen 1999; Jones and Cox, this volume).

Mainline Protestant churches in the United States have slowly moved towards a more positive view of sexual diversity but often only in small steps and with much conflict. Of the major denominations, the United Church of Christ has moved the furthest on such issues as ordination and blessing of same-sex unions. Some Episcopal dioceses or archdioceses have taken similar steps but in the face of even stronger resistance from within the American faith community and the broader Anglican communion. American Catholics in general are not distinctly conservative on questions of sexuality, though the Latina/os among them are somewhat more so than is the average American. Non-Christian faith communities have not been highly visible in public policy debates over sexual diversity, but survey evidence indicates that Jewish Americans strongly support LGBT rights claims (Wald, this volume). Most Muslims and adherents of other faiths oppose them, though they generally do not ally themselves with evangelical Protestant groups on other issue fronts.

Canada has far fewer evangelical Protestants than does the United States, fewer in separate evangelical churches, and their views on a range of public policy issues are at least a little less conservative than are those of their counterparts in the United States. By any of the several measures used to gauge the strength of religious conservatism among Protestants, the proportion of evangelicals in Canada is less than half that in the United States. In the whole population, religion is seen as important among half as many Canadians as Americans, and both regular church attendance and biblical literalism are half as prevalent (Reimer 2003; Stackhouse 2000; Hoover 1997; Hoover et al. 2002; see also Bibby 2002).

The influence of Catholic voices in Canadian public debate is not as strong as their numbers (43 percent of the population) would suggest. This is partly a result of the distinctiveness of Quebec. Catholics constitute an overwhelming majority in that province but rarely attend church; anticlericalism is noticeably stronger in Quebec than in other provinces; and the church's political influence is negligible (Lefebvre and Breton, this volume). The strong stand taken by Canadian bishops against lesbian/gay marriage appears to have only modest impact on Catholics in the English-dominated provinces and much less in Quebec.

As in the United States, most mainline Protestant denominations in Canada have taken up sexuality issues and have moved towards more inclusive positions. Here there are striking similarities between the path taken by the United Church of Canada (the largest of the mainline denominations) and the United Church of Christ and by the Anglican Church of Canada and its American Episcopal counterpart. In both countries, Jewish minorities have stood out as adopting policies and supporting measures inclusive of sexual minorities. Muslim organizations have more recently acquired a political profile, and, while most are preoccupied with challenging Islamophobic stereotypes, the largest Canadian Muslim groups echo a conservative approach that rejects the public recognition of sexual diversity (Hussain and Rahman, this volume).

In both the United States and Canada, substantial "social justice" currents exist within most faith communities, though they are less visible than are religious conservative interveners in political debate. Conservative organizations are larger, and media coverage regularly pits LGBT advocates against conservative faith-based groups who frame their claims as representing all believers. Equity claims in some sense return the favour, rarely encouraging the use of religious frames in their calls for inclusion. Even in Canada, where there have been such strong voices of social justice coming from Catholicism and Protestantism (including evangelicism), religiously based political activity is widely assumed to be conservative on issues related to gender and sexuality.

Political Advocacy

It is no surprise that faith-based political intervention in the United States is dominated by a conservative chorus, with evangelical Protestants the dominant voices within. In Canada, religious conservatism is more fragmented, in part because of the smaller numbers of evangelical Protestants and the larger proportion of conservative Catholics in the religious right.

In the United States, political mobilization by conservative evangelicals became more prominent in the 1970s, largely as a result of legal and policy gains secured by pro-choice feminists and gay rights advocates (Adam 1995). Their strength was enhanced not only by the high rates of church attendance and the availability of congregations attentive to the delivery of mobilizational messages but also by the wide reach of conservative media. Gay rights issues, particularly same-sex marriage, have provided religious conservatives with a wedge that has energized their evangelical base and created bridges to other moral conservatives.

Canadian religious conservatives did not have nearly the numerical strength of their American counterparts, nor did they have the incentives to mobilize continuously. Until the mid-1980s, groups representing evangelical Protestantism were small, with a very modest national presence in either the media or the federal political system. Their visibility increased somewhat in the late 1980s, in response to gains by feminists and lesbian/ gay rights advocates, and then more so in the early 2000s, when same-sex marriage moved to the front burner (Stackhouse 2000; Malloy, this volume). The patterns of mobilization, and the arguments used, have been heavily influenced by American evangelical Protestant groups. Many English-speaking conservative Christians also have ready access to American religious broadcasting. Still, none of the political intervention in Canada has been on the scale that has become routine for the American Christian right, and none of it has had any lasting visibility. At points where major claims by lesbian and gay advocates were prominently debated, conservative Catholic voices joined in the campaigning against challenges to traditional family values, but this never produced a sustained alliance with evangelical Protestants.

Queer activism is markedly similar in Canada and the United States – in the timing of surges, the development of policy agendas, the strategies deployed, and the frames used to articulate claims (Adam 1995; Rayside 1998, 2008). In both countries, the 1970s witnessed a significant wave of activism and a broadening of the agenda for change. The 1980s spread of AIDS and the emergence of a "baby boom" among same-sex couples (particularly lesbians) were major stimuli to a new wave of activism and to the inclusion of relationship issues in the agenda. The late 1980s and early 1990s also created new openings in national and regional politics on both sides of the border, reinforcing the development of skills and resources applicable to mainstream political intervention.

In both countries, the 1990s saw an important increase in activism focused on transgender rights, with uneven success in broadening the agenda of mainstream groups ostensibly committed to full inclusion. Much energy was focused on health care issues and on the right to have changes made to official documentation registering gender. The relative fragility of the organizations making transgender political claims has been especially marked on the Canadian side, where national and provincial groups of any sort are harder to maintain; however, on both sides of the border the social and economic marginality of trans-constituencies has represented a major challenge to collective LGBT mobilization.

The growth of mainstream organizations focused on sexual orientation has been on radically different scales in the two countries. LGBT groups in the United States have far greater access to resources than do their Canadian counterparts as well as much stronger incentives to organize continuously. Egale Canada remains on its own at the national level, with a permanent staff varying from between two and five. Provincial groups, where they exist at all, rely almost entirely on volunteers. In contrast, the Human Rights Campaign in Washington, DC, has over 140 permanent staff working out of its handsome Washington headquarters.

Substantial advocacy for LGBT equality in both countries has taken place within faith communities. For decades, networks and formalized groups have developed among Roman Catholics, all of the mainline Protestant denominations, some evangelical churches, each of the major currents in Judaism, and, more recently, Muslim communities. This work has often been isolated from other parts of the queer activist movement, which has tended towards highly secular language. But it has contributed importantly to shifts in popular response to homosexuality and (perhaps) to claims based on gender identity.

Constitutional Framework

The constitutional framework governing the role of religion in the public square and the place of sexuality in equality rights law is quite different in Canada than it is in the United States. These differences have widened the cross-border contrast in public recognition of sexual diversity since a good deal of that recognition has been boosted by court rulings. Courts have played extremely important roles in both countries, but from the 1990s onward they were especially critical in shifting public policy towards greater acceptance of lesbian/gay rights, narrowing the capacity of religious conservatives to roll back the clock (see Appendix A and Appendix B).

Both the US and the Canadian constitutions guarantee freedom of religion. The American Constitution's First Amendment stipulates that "Congress shall make no law respecting an establishment of religion, or prohibiting the free exercise thereof." The guarantee of "free exercise" is broadly similar to that in Canada, though more regularly contested. Canadian non-Christian minorities may well have been more successful than their American counterparts in securing accommodation of their religious practices (Moon 2008). In 1990, the US Supreme Court seemed to narrow the constitutional reading of "free exercise" in disallowing the religiously grounded use of a hallucinogenic substance (*Employment Division v. Smith*), though it did not give governments free rein to interfere with faith practices that cause no harm or to favour one religion over another. In the protections offered to faith practices, much is left to federal and state law and to state courts (Greenawalt 2006).

Where there seem to be sharper differences are in current and historical treatments of the question of "separation." In the United States, the "establishment" clause has been interpreted in a variety of ways, seen by some as a clear stipulation that church and state must be completely separate, by others as a declaration that the state cannot privilege just one faith or denomination (Jelen 2000; Wald and Calhoun-Brown 2006; Wilcox and Larson 2006). In some rulings, the court has seemed to lean towards the first interpretation, but in others it has allowed for the display of faith in public institutions – not least in the retention of "in God we trust" on coins. Political and legal challenges regularly arise to assert the full range of positions on these questions.

The Canadian Charter of Rights and Freedoms, in section 2, sets out "freedom of conscience and religion" as fundamental, alongside freedom of thought and belief, peaceful assembly, and association. In addition, section 15 of the Charter includes "religion" in its declaration of non-discrimination rights. The Canadian political system was not forged by a strong current of anti-clericalism or disestablishmentarianism (Lipset 1990). In what is now Quebec, the Roman Catholic Church long benefited from state support, and elsewhere in Canada Protestant and, to some extent, Catholic churches enjoyed various forms of state recognition. Gradually (and much later in Quebec), most visible forms of state recognition receded, though Catholic school funding remained in place in several provinces, as did tax concessions to other religious schools. Quebec – that most anti-clerical of provinces – has now reorganized its schools along language rather than religious lines, but it continues to provide supports to faith-based and other private schools. A crucifix still hangs over the Speaker's chair in the National Assembly – this in a province with extremely low rates of church attendance. Across the country, then, discussions of the public role of faith and the intersection of state and religious authority occur within a history of fluid compromise.

Constitutionally based challenges have been directed at Canadian public institutions privileging a single faith (e.g., by opening council meetings with the Lord's Prayer). The courts, however, have leaned towards a view that official recognition of religious belief is possible as long as it does not

discriminate between faiths. At the same time, they have provided no opening for a challenge to the provision of state funding to Catholic schools
since guarantees for at least some such support are embedded in the
Constitution.

The constitutional treatment of sexual diversity seems to mark out the
United States as clearly distinct from Canada and, some would say, from
most of the Western liberal democratic world. The latter claim is most surely exaggerated, but there are in fact strong contrasts with Canada (Smith
2008; Richards 2005; Pierceson 2005; Anderson 2005; Pinello 2003; Mezey
2007). Section 15 of the Charter lays out specific grounds on which discrimination is prohibited, but it does so with open-ended language. So while
sexual orientation is not named, the courts have now declared unequivocally that it is an "equity" ground fully analogous to those named and is therefore covered. This interpretative clarity emerged gradually through several
judgments in the 1990s, ending with the 1999 *M. v. H.* declaration that
same-sex couples could not be denied rights extended to heterosexual
couples (Smith 2008).

None of these decisions touched on parenting, but by the mid-1990s it
had been the subject of an influential court ruling in Ontario, which ruled
against discrimination. Restrictions based on marriage had long been removed, allowing individuals and de facto heterosexual couples to adopt
across the country. With the *M. v. H.* ruling, no one doubted that discrimination against same-sex de facto couples would fail to survive constitutional
scrutiny. *M. v. H.* did not address marriage; however, starting in 2003, appeal courts in one province after another ruled that civil marriage rights had
to be extended to lesbian and gay couples.

The public recognition of individual civil rights for lesbians and gay men,
and of family-related rights for same-sex couples, "took off" during the
1990s, widening the gap in policy and law between Canada and the United
States (Rayside 2008). Section 15 has not yet been interpreted definitively to
cover transgender rights, though some rulings by lower courts and human
rights tribunals have accepted claims under the "gender" rubric. Provinces
have their own human rights codes, but they are tightly bound to court interpretation of the Charter, which effectively requires the inclusion of sexual
orientation in such codes across the country.

The "equal protection" clause of the American Constitution's Fourteenth
Amendment has not been interpreted to create anything like the protective
umbrella created for lesbian and gay rights in Canada. Racial discrimination

has been unequivocally prohibited, as, to a substantial extent, has gender; but sexual orientation and gender identity claims have been less positively and consistently embraced. There have been important victories in the US Supreme Court, most notably in the 1996 ruling on *Romer v. Evans* (on an anti-gay ballot measure in Colorado) and in the 2003 decision in *Lawrence v. Texas* (striking down that state's sodomy law), but largely on grounds other than gender identity or sexual orientation (e.g., privacy). Transgender claimants have won some cases in the federal court system, but they have done so under the gender rubric (e.g., in cases related to harassment).

On the other hand, American states have constitutions, and state court systems have more autonomy than do their Canadian counterparts. In the absence of unambiguous direction from the US Supreme Court that discrimination based on sexual orientation or gender identity warrants higher levels of constitutional "scrutiny" than it has so far received, state courts have room to move in quite varied directions and are the ultimate arbiters of state constitutions. In some cases, they are able to rely on state constitutional prohibitions on anti-gay discrimination or on expansive jurisprudence on "equal protection" provisions. In several states this has opened up space for claims from lesbian and gay couples seeking recognition for either their relationships or their parenting rights. Particularly striking is the success of parenting claims by lesbian and gay couples in courtrooms across about half of the states. In Massachusetts, Connecticut, and Iowa, courts have ruled in favour of same-sex marriage (in Iowa, the ruling was unanimous).

Policy Legacies

There is a long history of Canadian state provision of supports to religious institutions – as part of a legacy of blurriness in church-state relations – and little invocation of language equivalent to the Jeffersonian "wall of separation" except, to some degree, in Quebec. Some provinces have in practice moved substantially towards full secularism, for example in school policy, yet have also encouraged a discussion of religious diversity in the name of multiculturalism.

Exaggerated contrasts are routinely drawn between the Canadian cultural "mosaic" and the American "melting pot" – exaggerated because each country has important elements of the characteristic associated with the other (Reitz and Breton 1994). Nevertheless, the official federal Canadian policy on multiculturalism does seem to have provided an important rhetorical framework for the acceptance of religious diversity. The slow but steady incorporation of multiculturalism into English Canadian identity – and, to some extent, into Québécois identity – is at least partially rooted in the decades-long formal policy commitment to the recognition of difference. The incorporation of ethnic diversity into national identity has also, to some extent, spilled over into the recognition of sexual diversity.

Quebec has some distinctiveness in policy approach and public response to questions of the recognition of religious minorities. Policy recognition is more likely to be framed as "interculturalism" than as "multiculturalism," with explicit expectations laid out for immigrants to integrate into Quebec society (and to adopt French as their lingua franca). There is also more public antipathy in Quebec than in English Canada to the recognition of minority faith practices. Still, the actual differences in public policy are subtle, where they exist at all, and the daily accommodation practices by state and private institutions are not dramatically different in Quebec than elsewhere in Canada in most arenas.

In daily American practice, there is much institutional recognition of multiculturalism, but there are still more heated public debates than in Canada over, for example, school instruction in languages other than English. There are also highly visible claims that the United States is a Christian country and that public policy should reflect that. Across the country there is debate and conflict over what degree of state recognition of religion is appropriate, most of this pitting Christian activists against those defending the separationist view. In the United States, then, multicultural arguments over the recognition of religious difference regularly get swamped by more basic culture wars.

The depth of the racial division in American society, and the dreadful history of slavery associated with it, shape more general debates about equity and rights. The long struggle over civil rights led to important gains in public policy and constitutional interpretation, and it provided inspiration to claimants who focused on other rights questions. On the other hand, the specific legacies around racial struggles, and the continuing depth of social and economic divisions based on race, contribute to a treatment of African-American civil rights claims as distinct. This may well limit the transportability of rights frameworks from race to other issues. The race-based fears and anxieties that permeate American political life may also fuel opposition to all human rights claims. In Canada, no single set of rights claims rises so prominently above the others or provides a master frame. Gains on one front, therefore, are more likely to encourage gains on others.

Much research has pointed to the importance of an orderly progression of rights associated with sexual minorities – namely, to the potential for early gains on fundamental rights to provide a platform for later gains (Wintemute and Andenaes 2001; Waaldijk and Bonini-Baraldi 2006; Wald, Button, and Rienzo 1996). The decriminalization of homosexual activity eases arguments about the legitimacy of prohibiting discrimination in the workplace. The acquisition of individual rights protections then eases claims based on relationships, and, if those are successful, parenting rights flow more readily. Much of this literature is aimed at explaining variations across American states, but it has some relevance cross-nationally. The fact that the criminal law in Canada was amended in 1969 to partially decriminalize homosexual activity helped prepare the ground for later rights claims, which were then successful first on individual claims and then on relational ones. In the United States, most criminal law is lodged within state jurisdiction, with the result that decriminalization of homosexual activity had to proceed state by state. Several reforms were enacted at around the time of the change in Canada's criminal code, but it took the 2003 US Supreme Court ruling in *Lawrence v. Texas* to complete the job.

Another area in which historical legacy distinguishes the two countries is in family policy. As much as in any Western liberal democratic country, Canadian public policy and law have provided recognition to and support of de facto conjugal relationships (Rayside 2008). From the 1970s until the mid-1990s, Canada and most of its provinces substantially narrowed the differential treatment of formal marriage and heterosexual cohabitation. This contrast arguably reduced the resistance to according gay and lesbian couples the right to marriage, especially after cohabiting same-sex couples had gained policy equality in comparison to de facto heterosexual couples in 1999.

There are jurisdictions in the United States, particularly on the west coast, in which legislators and courts have shifted towards a recognition of cohabitational rights, and this no doubt helped ease the way for same-sex claimants. However, the gap between marriage and cohabitation has not been narrowed anywhere in the United States as much as it has been in Canada.

Political Institutions

In the United States, the complexities of the legal environment in which religious and sexual rights are debated are matched by the complexity of the political structure. It was designed to fragment political authority and to

impede radical change. The federal system splits jurisdiction over issues relating to both religion and sexuality between national and state governments. Executive leverage over the legislature is regularly compromised,
and, within the legislature, party leaders have far less control over the policy
agenda than do their counterparts in parliamentary systems. This fragmentation translates into a comparatively permeable political system, though
one that privileges social movements and interests willing and able to play
the complex tunes associated with mainstream politics. By providing so
many veto points, the political system also advantages advocates of the
status quo. It provides unparalleled opportunities and incentives for social
movements and interest groups to intervene continuously, but it also presents huge challenges to effecting major change.

The Canadian system concentrates much more agenda-setting power in
the hands of the executive at the federal and provincial levels and, specifically, in the hands of the prime ministers or premiers. Few regimes in the
Western liberal democratic world give heads of government as much control as does Canada to federal and provincial first ministers. This provides
social movement groups with only occasional opportunities to exercise influence, which is entirely a function of the specific policy openness of the
party in power. Major leverage may be possible with the right party and
leadership in power, perhaps even with modest mobilizational resources,
but otherwise it is next to impossible. And, if the governing party at one
level or another wishes to duck an issue by letting courts take the lead, as is
so often the case on religious and "moral" issues, this avoidance is hard for
opponents to challenge.

Party Systems

During the 1980s the American party system became more polarized on
religious and sexual issues. Christian conservatives established themselves
as a crucial element in the Republican coalition, increasing their influence
over state parties in the 1980s and 1990s (Wald and Calhoun-Brown 2006;
Wilcox and Larson 2006). This has reinforced anti-gay positions on a range
of issues in the national party and most state parties. The 2004 platform of
the Texas Republican Party offers a particularly dramatic illustration in the
following passage:

> The Party believes that the practice of sodomy tears at the fabric of society,
> contributes to the breakdown of the family unit, and leads to the spread of
> dangerous, communicable diseases. Homosexual behavior is contrary to

the fundamental, unchanging truths that have been ordained by God, recognized by our country's founders, and shared by the majority of Texans.

There are countervailing pressures. Another important Republican constituency is made up of business representatives and their allies, who advocate lower taxes and other corporate-friendly policies. Many of these advocates are either indifferent to the moral agenda of religious conservatives or fearful that it will distract policy makers from more important issues. There are also well-educated and youthful voters whom the party must attract, and many of them would be deterred by an overemphasis on such issues as abortion and gay rights. Sarah Palin was not shy about her faith and her opposition to same-sex marriage during the 2008 election campaign, but she still spoke in favour of equality on fronts other than marriage during the vice-presidential debate.

The long-term impact of evangelical Christians on public policy during periods when Republicans have been in power is open to debate, even during the administration of George W. Bush. The rhetorical commitment to conservative Christian positions was clear and was backed by policies enacted on, for example, abstinence-only education and international AIDS funding. But the policy legacy of the Bush administration fell significantly short of the expectations of many Christian right leaders, and the same is true in many states in which Republicans have ruled.

The Democrats gradually moved towards an embrace of LGBT claims from the 1980s on, though at every step there was a vocal minority objecting. Marriage remains a major stumbling block at the federal level and in most state parties, largely due to the weakness of popular support. And Democrats know full well that Republican strategists remain eager to exploit their division or to play on the most insidious stereotypes in campaigning against Democrats who support LGBT equality on other fronts. Further complicating the Democratic commitment on these issues is the fact that the party has recurrently pitched appeals to the Christian faithful – no more so than in the campaigning of Barack Obama.

Both parties are "federalized." National election campaigns have been more and more centred on the presidential candidates, but for both Republicans and Democrats relatively autonomous state parties still constitute important organizational foundations. This produces important variations across regions in the way that issues of sexuality and faith are taken up by each party during national campaigns and, even more so, in state-level policy debates.

Still, the Democrats and Republicans as a whole do represent distinct religious constituencies, and though there are signs of a shift among some Republicans on issues apart from marriage, the two parties do represent very different positions on sexual diversity. There is a readiness for election campaigners at the national level, and in most states, to present pitches to their core electorates that are more starkly contrasted than we could find in the vast majority of elections in recent Canadian history.

The Canadian party system is even more federalized than the American, with party systems in several provinces being entirely distinct from the federal level. The federal party system has also undergone a radical shift in the past two decades. Until the 1990s, the political landscape was dominated by two "catch-all," or "brokerage," parties – the Progressive Conservatives (centre-right) and the Liberals (centrist or centre-left) – alongside a smaller social democratic New Democratic Party (NDP). Now there is a Conservative Party that is more clearly on the right; a Liberal Party that is much the same as before but somewhat reduced in size; a sovereigntist Bloc Québécois; and the NDP. Like the Republicans, Conservatives are driven primarily by a neoliberal critique of the interventionist state. Moral traditionalists are an important constituency and are more prominent than ever, but their views are downplayed in the party's platform and, to some extent, in its policy making within government.

The Liberals came to support gay rights positions at least as slowly as did the US Democrats, during the 1990s and 2000s. Ultimately, they supported lesbian/gay marriage but only after the courts made it clear that not doing so violated the Charter. The NDP has a longer history of support for equity and has made a difference in a couple of provinces when it has been in power. The sovereigntist Bloc Québécois has strong progressive currents, and like its provincial counterpart, the Parti Québécois, it developed a commitment to equity comparatively early on.

At the provincial level, there are still brokerage-style parties on the centre-right and others more clearly dominated by neoliberalism. Most do not make explicit appeals to Christian right constituencies, except (at times) for the Conservatives in Alberta. When in power, parties on the right have not kicked up too much fuss when courts have ruled in favour of gay rights claims.

At present, then, all major Canadian political parties avoid taking high-profile positions on issues of sexual diversity. They also avoid questions related to religious diversity or faith in general. This has not prevented electoral appeals specifically targeting faith communities, but they are kept as quiet as possible. Declarations of personal religious belief remain largely out of the partisan mainstream.

An Outline of the Book

Comparative political analysis frequently positions Canada between the United States and northwestern Europe – whether the focus is on social policy, economic management, political parties, or media culture. An exploration of the politics of religion and sexuality may well position Canada somewhat closer to the European pattern, but the contributors to this volume, taken together, warn against any overgeneralized view.

Public opinion is surveyed in the first major section of the book, and it includes two contributions, both of which remind us of important increases in popular acceptance of diversity. In Chapter 2, Shauna Shames, Didi Kuo, and Catherine Levine challenge some elements of the claim that the United States is deeply riven by a culture war. In Chapter 3, Amy Langstaff's historical treatment of Canadian public response to homosexuality provides an especially dramatic view of how much has changed in twenty years – a point that could be made with equal strength in the United States.

Evangelical Protestantism is the subject of five contributions in the next section, which indicates the central role that this constituency has played in opposing rights claims from sexual minorities. In Chapter 4, Samuel Reimer points to similarities between Canadian and American evangelicals as well as to differences in outlook and intensity of feeling around sexuality issues. In Chapter 5, Tina Fetner and Carrie Sanders compare the historical foundations of Christian right political organizing in the United States and Canada, pointing to a variety of factors impelling American conservatives to establish the kind of autonomous institutions that facilitated later political mobilizing. In Chapter 6, Clyde Wilcox and Rentaro Iida acknowledge the conservatism of US evangelical Christians but point out signs of dramatic shifts towards moderate views – particularly among the young. In Chapter 7, Robert Jones and Daniel Cox take a closer look at African Americans, who respond to most sexuality issues in ways similar to white evangelicals, even though they are not allies on other fronts. In Chapter 8, Jonathan Malloy acknowledges the considerable resources and alliances built up by Canadian religious conservatives during the time when the same-sex marriage debate was at its most intense, but he sees this as a temporary phenomenon and not one indicative of a longer-term convergence between Canadian and American patterns.

In the next section, the struggles over sexual orientation issues within mainline Protestant denominations are examined in three contributions. In Chapter 9, Pamela Dickey Young, one of several writers in this volume who focus on the debate over same-sex marriage, unearths core elements in the deliberations of Canada's largest Protestant denomination. In Chapter 10, Roger Hutchinson explores difficult debates over sexual orientation also within the United Church of Canada, detecting in them the possibility that those adopting contrasting positions on same-sex marriage might find common ground. In Chapter 11, Laura Olson, Paul Djupe, and Wendy Cadge marshal a variety of data (including those tapping the attitudes of clergy) to analyze struggles over this kind of issue within American mainline Protestant churches.

Roman Catholic responses to sexual diversity are the subject of two chapters. In Chapter 12, Ted Jelen points to important contrasts between the US Catholic hierarchy's position on these issues and the views of parishioners, particularly on issues like marriage. A similar point could be made about disconnection among Catholics in Canada, and, in Chapter 13, Solange Lefebvre and Jean-François Breton argue that this is even more starkly true in Quebec, where religious practice has dropped to dramatically low levels.

The following section deals with non-Christian responses to LGBT rights claims. In Chapter 14, Kenneth Wald examines American Jewish attitudes to lesbian/gay rights claims and leads us through an explanation of the persistence of positive responses to them. Much of what he claims about the US case could be applied to the Canadian Jewish community. Deciphering Muslim community reaction to such claims is harder, both because there is less survey evidence on them and because there have been fewer public debates within either Canadian or American Muslim communities about sexuality issues. In Chapter 15, Momin Rahman and Amir Hussain do draw from a range of sources to set out the challenges in taking up rights claims by sexual minorities, including those within their own communities.

The next section focuses on political parties, elections, and activist mobilization. In Chapter 16, David Rayside's analysis of the Canadian Conservative Party highlights the contradictory pressures faced by party leaders when dealing with sexuality issues within a national political setting in which such issues are increasingly difficult to campaign on. In Chapter 17, John Green mines data on both the general public and delegates to national party conventions at the time of the 2004 election in order to examine US

Republican and Democratic responses to the issue of same-sex marriage. These data show how alluring a strongly conservative position on the issue was for the Republicans but how difficult it was for the Democrats.

The next section focuses on rights claiming, and it features contributions by Richard Moon (Chapter 19) and Jason Pierceson (Chapter 20), which examine the distinctive features of the constitutional frameworks within which sexual minorities and religious groups have made legal claims. Moon focuses on issues in which claims from both sides have been at stake and finds an inconsistent response from the Canadian courts. Pierceson focuses on court responses to sexual diversity and, in doing so, flags some of the distinct features of US court readings of the relationship between church and state.

We find in these chapters evidence of divergence, convergence, and both simultaneously. Both countries show evidence of unresolved struggles over the way in which, or the degree to which, faith should influence political deliberation as well as over whether the state should support any particular faith, all faiths, or none. We also find continuing debates over the recognition of sexual diversity, admittedly fiercer in the United States than in Canada. These struggles often pit people of faith against LGBT activists, but, increasingly, they occur among people of faith. Courts, legislators, and officials navigate through these dangerous waters with a mixture of backgrounds, stereotypes, opportunistic instincts, and occasional wisdom.

PUBLIC OPINION

By showing broad trends in public opinion, the chapters in this section help set the overall context for the rest of the book. In Chapter 2, Shauna Shames, Didi Kuo, and Katherine Levine show a trend towards acceptance of sexual difference in the United States. They show variations across religious groups and regions but also that all religious groups have become more supportive of equality policies in the United States, a point to which a few authors in later sections return. Shames and her colleagues point to the need for more research on attitudes towards transgendered citizens, and we would argue that the same is true for bisexuality.

In Chapter 3, Amy Langstaff draws on proprietary survey data to show a dramatic liberalization of Canadian attitudes between 1987 and 2008. As in the United States, the public has become more accepting of sexual diversity over time, and differences in attitudes towards LGBT rights issues have become more partisan. She shows that recent immigrants are more conservative on these issues, especially marriage, a finding that undoubtedly has parallels in the United States.

Both chapters suggest that policy progress is enabled by changing attitudes as well as that changing policies help to create more egalitarian attitudes, though the relationship between court decisions, legislative action, and public opinion is complex. The lessons from Canada are that, even in a setting in which courts have played an important role in advancing equality rights for sexual minorities, judges have not been notably out of tune with public opinion on questions of sexual diversity. What we draw from the US case is that the slow spread of legal and policy inclusiveness has, in general terms, been lagging behind the dramatic shifts across religious communities in attitudes towards sexual diversity.

Culture War?
A Closer Look at the Role of Religion, Denomination, and Religiosity in US Public Opinion on Multiple Sexualities

SHAUNA L. SHAMES, DIDI KUO, AND
KATHERINE LEVINE

Even in 2010, it still appears that the United States is in the middle of a culture war over public recognition of multiple sexualities. The justices of several state supreme courts (including Massachusetts, Vermont, California, Connecticut, Iowa, and, to some extent, New Jersey)[1] have legalized or paved the way for same-sex marriages, while in other states (including New Hampshire, Vermont, and the District of Columbia) the state legislatures have legalized the practice. In some states, including California and Maine, courts or legislatures have approved the extension of marriage rights, only to have their attempts overturned by voter initiatives. In others, such as Washington, Oregon, and Nevada, governors or state legislatures have extended to same-sex couples all the rights of marriage without the name. Beyond the six (Massachusetts, Vermont, New Hampshire, Connecticut, Iowa, and the District of Columbia) with full marriage, two recognize marriages in other states, and five have comprehensive recognitions of domestic partnerships, making a total of thirteen. At the same time, thirty-eight states have added provisions to their constitutions to prevent same-sex marriages or have enacted prohibitory statutory restrictions. Many of these amendments and laws reach beyond marriage to deny official recognition for civil unions. The conventional wisdom, as in the mainstream media hype over "values voting" in recent national elections, suggests that the divide is between religious and secular voters. In this chapter we present evidence to dispute, at least in part, such a claim. To fully understand the complexity of the current situation, we must go beyond a religious/secular divide and instead look more closely at the positions of people from various religions, denominations, and levels of religiosity and scriptural traditionalism.

The United States is an extremely diverse country religiously, with hundreds of active religions and denominations. Moreover, Americans are more religiously active than are citizens of most comparable countries. Thus, unsurprisingly, despite constitutional provisions enshrining religious freedom and non-establishment, US public opinion and policy are inevitably affected by the deep religiosity of the American people.

Writing in 1835, Alexis de Tocqueville (2005) noted that, "upon my arrival in the United States, the religious aspect of the country was the first thing that struck my attention." This legacy continues: over 40 percent say they go to weekly religious services, over 60 percent say they belong to a church or synagogue, and 54 percent say religion is "very important" in their lives, with another 26 percent calling it "fairly important" (Gallup 2009). Similarly, the World Values Survey (2009) reports that 36 percent of Americans surveyed report attending church or synagogue once or more a week. These numbers are vastly higher than self-reports of weekly church attendance in such countries as Australia (14 percent), Great Britain (17 percent), Spain (16 percent), Canada (25 percent), Sweden (3 percent), Japan (3 percent), France (7 percent), and the Netherlands (12 percent).

It is important to note that researchers have found that church attendance reports in the United States are exaggerated, although they disagree as to the extent of the "attendance gap," and no evidence seriously discredits the high ranking of Americans in overall religiosity compared to citizens of other Western industrialized countries (see Hout and Greeley 1987, 1998; Hadaway, Marler, and Chaves 1993; and Marler and Hadaway 1999). This tendency to exaggerate church attendance highlights the social pressure in the United States to be, or to appear to be, religious.

If religion is a dominant factor shaping political beliefs, are the divisions between secular and religious Americans or among religions and religious denominations? We explore these questions here using the lens of US public opinion regarding multiple sexualities and the laws concerning them and – when possible – looking at how this opinion has changed in the past several decades. Support for moral issues – as well as the strength of such support – may vary among religious denominations in ways that the literature on public opinion has just begun to explore more fully (see Campbell and

Robinson 2007). Following the trend of recent literature, we investigate not only individuals' self-identified religion and denomination (what Wald and Glover 2007 call "official religion") but also their levels of religious traditionalism (Campbell and Robinson 2007) and levels of religiosity, such as frequency of Bible reading and church attendance. Throughout, our focus is on the *impact of religion, denomination, and religiosity* in creating or modifying public sentiment about the public policies relating to homosexuality and other sexualities. Using recent survey data and maps of religious denominational support, we find that denomination and religiosity are often overlooked factors that are deeply important in shaping the attitudes of religious Americans.

Public Opinion: Homosexuality, Gays and Lesbians, and Civil Rights

Our initial task in this section is to establish the overall liberalizing trends within public opinion regarding homosexuality and other "morality"/social issues over the past several decades. Subsequently, we use individual-level survey data and mapping to investigate specifically the role of religion in these and other trends within public opinion.

Americans have been more supportive of granting rights and non-discrimination laws to gays and lesbians than they have been of accepting them morally. Questions framed in terms of morality or religion may elicit a very different response from people than a question couched in the language of laws and rights. Polling evidence suggests that public opinion about same-sex marriage, for example, is highly susceptible to change based on the framing of the question (Wilcox et al. 2007). This also holds for placement and context matter: in a report from 2007, Gallup noted that, when its question about supporting gay marriage follows a number of questions about other homosexual rights, it found a higher level of support than it did when the gay-marriage question was asked on its own. This suggests that public opinion on these issues remains malleable, shifting in a more conservative direction if respondents think about homosexuality within a morality frame and in a more liberal direction if they think about it within a legal rights and equality frame.

Let us first examine some basic data on public opinion concerning the morality of homosexuality and opinions about gays and lesbians themselves. Although many of the questions and issues have changed over time, a few national surveys have asked the same question about homosexuality with the same wording for decades. Since 1982, Gallup has asked respondents

FIGURE 2.1

Should homosexuality be considered an "acceptable alternative lifestyle?" Survey of general population, 1982-2008

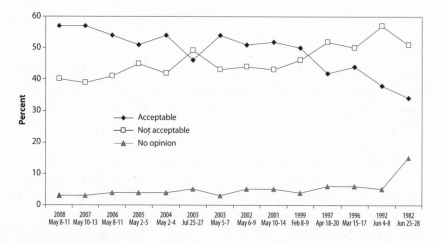

Note: N for each Gallup poll is 1,000.
Source: Gallup (2009).

whether or not "homosexuality should be considered an acceptable alternative lifestyle" (Gallup 2009). As Figure 2.1 shows, in 1982 only 34 percent of people said homosexuality should be an acceptable alternative lifestyle, with 51 percent calling it not acceptable and 15 percent registering no opinion. By 2007, 57 percent called it acceptable as an alternative lifestyle.

Not so long ago, in 2001, when asked directly if they considered homosexuality to be "morally acceptable" or "morally wrong," 53 percent said "wrong" and 40 percent said "acceptable" (Gallup 2009). In the past few years, however, this 13-point gap has narrowed significantly, and, by 2007, the numbers were roughly even, with 47 percent choosing "acceptable" and 49 percent choosing "wrong." This was the first year that a majority of Americans had not characterized homosexual relations as morally wrong in Gallup polling.

This trend is in line with a liberalizing of American moral attitudes more generally. Homosexuality now occupies something of a moral middle ground between the negatively viewed acts of adultery and polygamy and the increasingly acceptable acts of having sex or a baby outside of marriage. Divorce, viewed until relatively recently as a sin or perhaps even a necessary evil, is now regarded as morally acceptable by 70 percent of Americans (Gallup 2009).

Other related questions have also shown great movement over time. Since 1977, Gallup has asked this question: "In your view, is homosexuality something a person is born with, or is homosexuality due to factors such as upbringing and environment?" The over-time trend shows a steady increase in the number of Americans who view homosexuality as genetic, which most likely relates to the increased acceptance of gays and lesbians (intuitively, it's easier to blame someone for a "choice" than for an immutable, genetic feature). There has also been a sharp increase in the number of Americans who say that someone close to them is gay, another factor that seems to be changing public opinion – or at least correlating with that change. In 1985, the *Los Angeles Times* poll reported that 54 percent of people said they had no friends, family members, or co-workers who were gay or lesbian; by 2004, this figure had dropped to 27 percent, suggesting that a vast majority of respondents did know someone who was gay or lesbian. In 2009, Gallup reported that 58 percent of the population said they have friends, relatives, or co-workers who have personally told the respondent that they are gay or lesbian. In the 2008 American National Election Studies poll, half of respondents reported that they knew someone gay, lesbian, or bisexual "among [their] immediate family members, relatives, neighbors, co-workers, or close friends." These polls suggest that between half and three-quarters of Americans are close to someone whom they think or know is gay or lesbian.[2]

From these data, we cannot tell if the liberalization in attitudes towards gays, lesbians, and homosexuality is a cause or a consequence of Americans knowing more out-gay/lesbian friends and family. It could be that personally knowing more gays and lesbians is having an impact on how people view homosexuality; conversely, it is also possible that, as people become more liberal, their gay and lesbian friends and family members feel more comfortable coming out to them. Or perhaps these two factors are both at work, in a kind of virtuous circle, with each leading to the other as attitudes liberalize and more people personally know gays/lesbians. Previous studies by Overby and Barth (2002) and Herek and Capitanio (1996) have shown that people who come into contact with homosexuals – especially those who count gays and lesbians as close friends – are much more likely to support gay rights.

There is more support for lesbian and gay issues when survey questions ask about laws and rights rather than about morality. Starting in 1977, Gallup began asking respondents this question: "Do you think homosexual relations

FIGURE 2.2

Do you favour or oppose laws protecting homosexuals against employment discrimination?
Survey results by selected religious traditions, 2000 and 2004

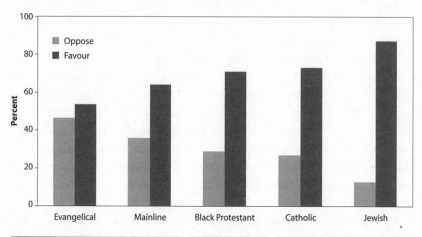

Note: Question wording: "Do you FAVOR or OPPOSE laws to protect homosexuals against job discrimination?" Percentages displayed are proportions of those who answered that they either favoured or opposed the policy (with those answering "don't know" eliminated from this analysis). Denomination classification is from Layman (2001). *N*s are as follows: evangelical = 1,038; mainline = 1,069; black Protestant = 354; Catholic = 1,482; Jewish = 132.
Source: ANES Cumulative Data File, results aggregated from 2000 and 2004 ANES surveys.

between consenting adults should or should not be legal?," and the proportion of Americans saying they should be legal jumped from 43 percent in 1977 to 56 percent in 2009. Public attitudes about employment discrimination offer another clear view of the liberalizing trend. Between 1992 and 2005, Gallup measured Americans' opinions on whether homosexuals should be hired as salespersons, military personnel, doctors, clergy, elementary and high school teachers, and members of the president's cabinet. For several jobs, the change in opinion is drastic, including an increase of 25 percentage points in public acceptance of homosexuals as doctors and a nearly 20-point jump in acceptance of gays/lesbians in the armed forces. And, despite the media story about a "culture war," relatively strong public support for civil rights protections persists across religious traditions and denominations, despite their adherents' differing levels of opposition to homosexuality. As Figure 2.2 shows, large proportions of religious people favour the implementation of laws to protect homosexuals from discrimination on the job.

Even among evangelical Christians, the group least likely to support such protections, 54 percent favour a non-discrimination law.[3]

Survey Data: Religion and US Public Opinion

To begin to pull apart the effects of religious affiliation, denomination, and measures of religiosity, we examine data from the 2004 and 2008 American National Election Studies (ANES), which contain a battery of items that test for public opinion on homosexuality and rights for gays and lesbians, and the ANES Cumulative Data File, which contains survey data from 1948 to the present.

As a first cut, we start by comparing adherents of different religious traditions with respect to their attitudes towards homosexuality and rights for gays/lesbians. One easy way to determine a group of people's attitudes towards gays and lesbians is to look at their average "feeling thermometer" rating. Since 1984, the ANES has asked respondents to rate homosexuals on a feeling thermometer scale, with a maximum rating of 100 (meaning strong positive feeling) and a minimum of 0 (meaning intense dislike). Figure 2.3 plots the average ratings of members of three religious traditions (Catholics, Protestants, and Jews) on the feeling thermometers in the ANES from 1984 to 2004, also plotting data on mainline versus evangelical versus black Protestants. Although the number of Jews in the samples for each year is quite small, we still see some major differences.

Two conclusions are quickly apparent from this figure: first, Protestants, and in particular evangelicals, generally give gays and lesbians the lowest thermometer ratings, with mainline Protestants, black Protestants, and Catholics giving relatively mid-level ratings and Jews giving the highest ratings. Interestingly, black Protestant respondents gave thermometer scores similar to those given by Catholics and white mainline Protestants from 1988 to 1998, but afterwards their mean scores decline until, by 2004-08, they come close to the mean scores given by evangelicals. Yet even Protestants' feeling thermometer scores had risen by 2008 to a score of around 45 across denominations, far higher than just a decade or two earlier. Across all groups, the general over-time trend shows an increase in warmth.

Even negative feelings, however, frequently coincide with supports for civil rights protections. Among those evangelicals and Catholics who rate homosexuals less than a 50 on the feeling thermometer, majorities still support policies to protect gays and lesbians from job discrimination. Of all those across religions and denominations who rate homosexuals less than a

FIGURE 2.3

Feeling thermometer scores on homosexuals by selected religious traditions, 1988-2008

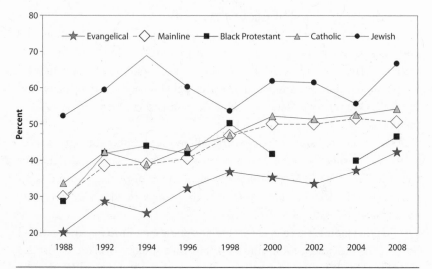

Note: Classification scheme for religions/denominations from Layman (2001). *N*s are as follows for all years aggregated: evangelical = 2,498; mainline = 2,304; black Protestant = 922; Catholic = 3,469; Jewish = 256. The *N* of black Protestants in 2002 was extremely small (9), and the results of this analysis for that year were far out of line with the general trend, so we exclude that clearly unrepresentative data point. Thermometer scores range from a very cold zero (negative) to very warm (positive) of 100 degrees.
Source: ANES Cumulative Data File.

30 on the thermometer, nearly half favour laws to protect against job discrimination (48.5 percent) and believe gays and lesbians should be able to serve in the military (50.2 percent) (ANES Complete Data File).

Figure 2.4 displays differences across denominations in the levels of opposition to gay marriage, gays in the military, protections against job discrimination, and gay adoption. Higher response values indicate higher levels of opposition: on gay adoption, for example, responses received a 1 if gays should be allowed to adopt and a 5 if they shouldn't. Generally, members of the religions/denominations tested were supportive of gays and lesbians in the military and of policies to protect against job discrimination, with evangelicals being slightly less supportive and Jews being most supportive. Turning to the family-related issues, we see more dispersion in the responses, with evangelicals least likely and Jews most likely to support same sex marriage or adoption, and Catholics, mainline, and black Protestants in the

FIGURE 2.4

Opposition to homosexual rights by selected religious traditions, 2004 and 2008

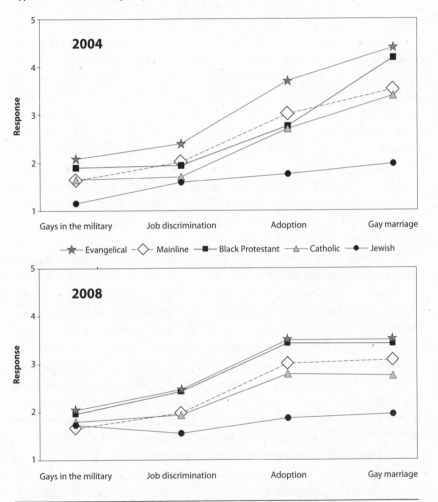

Note: Charts give the means for each religion/denomination in each year. A response of 1 indicates approval for the policy in question, and a response of 5 indicates opposition. For the gay marriage question only, a response of 1 indicates that gays should be allowed to marry, 3 indicates that gays should be allowed to enter civil unions, and 5 indicates that gays should not be allowed to marry. For 2008, note that religious measures are approximate because, as of this publication, the full religious codes have yet to be released. *N*s for 2004 (average across the four questions) are as follows: evangelical = 169; mainline = 127; black Protestant = 70; Catholic = 257; Jewish = 29. *N*s for 2008 (average across the four questions) are as follows: evangelical = 605; mainline = 266; black Protestant = 366; Catholic = 509; Jewish = 23. *Source:* ANES (2004, 2008).

middle. Yet by 2008, resistance to all gay rights issues, even marriage and adoption, had dropped somewhat across all denominations except black Protestants (where opposition remained fairly constant) and Jews (where opposition had been the lowest and stayed low).

The push for anti-gay legislation has been strongly supported by evangelical denominations such as the Southern Baptist Convention. Not surprisingly, then, evangelicals are more likely than are mainline Protestants to support bans on gay marriage (with a mean of 4.1 versus 3.6 in the 2004 ANES and a mean of 3.4 versus 2.8 in the 2008 ANES). Evangelicals were also much more likely to oppose gay adoption and laws protecting homosexuals from job discrimination. By 2008, attitudes had become slightly more tolerant. For example, fewer members of all denominations prefer outright bans on gay marriage and gay adoption. However, there does not seem to be much more tolerance across the board. There has not been a shift towards general favour of gays in the military or laws to protect homosexuals from job discrimination.

When we tested to see whether demographic factors that might blur the relationship between denomination and moral values were at play, regression results consistently showed a significant relationship between evangelicalism and opposition to gay rights.[4] Being older and married decreased support for gay marriage but not nearly to the same extent as did evangelicalism. Even when controlling for church attendance, affiliation with an evangelical denomination was still significantly correlated with greater opposition to gay marriage. Jews remain the most supportive of gay rights, and Catholics are somewhat more tolerant than are their Protestant counterparts. Evangelicals still display more intolerant attitudes but seem to have softened: in 2008, evangelicals supported some laws to protect gays against job discrimination and were just as likely to support either gay marriage or civil unions as they were to oppose gay marriage.

Evangelicalism alone is not driving all variation in public attitudes towards homosexuals and gay/lesbian rights. A closer look at religiosity variables reveals important intra-denominational differences in such attitudes based on church attendance, frequency of prayer, and frequency of Bible reading. Frequent churchgoing corresponds with lower average feeling thermometer scores, though mean scores for weekly attendees increased from the mid-20s in 1984 to nearly 40 by 2004. Those who attend church less than monthly rose to just above the 50 threshold by 2004. The increase over time is strongest for those who rarely or never attend worship services, while those who attend every week continue to give the lowest average ratings. As of 2008, frequent churchgoers and those who pray daily prefer bans on gay marriage, whereas less religious people are much more likely to support legalizing gay marriage. Religiosity therefore continues to be an important factor determining tolerant attitudes.

Frequency of Bible reading and tendency to view the Bible as the word of God (not the work of humans) also have important effects on people's attitudes. Figure 2.5 shows that over one-third of respondents said the Bible was the word of God and should be taken literally. These respondents were the most opposed to marriage/union rights for homosexuals and were far more likely to support full governmental bans on both same-sex marriage and gay adoption. Those who believe the Bible is the word of God but should not always be taken literally were more supportive of civil unions, while those who believe the Bible is the word of man and should not be taken literally exhibited the most liberal attitudes towards public recognition of homosexual partnerships. These are dramatic differences, and their significance withstands all controls.

Results from the 2008 ANES indicate some convergence towards low-level tolerance of gay rights. Whereas in 2004 many people who thought the Bible was the word of God wanted bans on gay marriage and gay adoption, by 2008 they felt more moderate – supporting civil unions, for example. Those who do not take the Bible literally have become more tolerant regarding issues of gay marriage and gay adoption. Overall, however, those who take the Bible literally showed somewhat *less* tolerance in that the means of their responses were all above 2 (as opposed to what they were in 2004, when they were frequently between 1 and 2).

Those who prayed several times a day were far more likely than were those who did not to support banning gay marriage and gay adoption, although they generally supported gays in the military and anti-discrimination laws. Respondents who prayed once a day were only slightly more liberal: they still showed support for banning both gay marriage and gay adoption. Evangelical Protestants are more likely to take the Bible literally, to pray several times a day, and to view religion as an important guide in everyday life than are their mainline counterparts. Yet, as we have already seen, there are large within-group contrasts in attitudes towards gays and lesbians. While 41 percent of evangelicals oppose job discrimination protections for gays and lesbians, fully 25 percent support such protections (with the remainder either not being asked the question or answering "don't know").

FIGURE 2.5

Policy positions by belief in divine authorship of Bible, 2004 and 2008

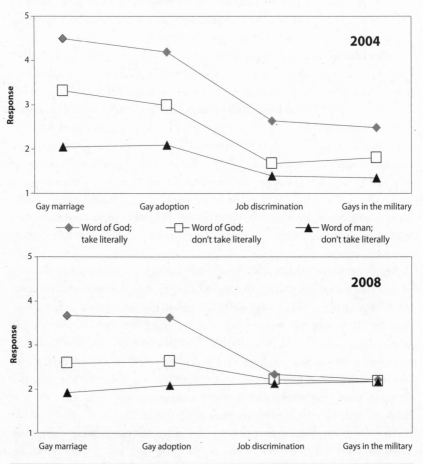

Note: Question wording for belief in divine authorship of Bible: "Which of these statements comes closest to describing your feelings about the Bible?" Three responses were as follows: (1) "The Bible is the actual word of God and is to be taken literally, word for word"; (2) "The Bible is the word of God but not everything in it should be taken literally, word for word"; and (3) "The Bible is a book written by men and is not the word of God." For policy positions, means indicate level of opposition to expanding the rights of gays/lesbians, with 1 indicating low opposition and 5 indicating high opposition. *N*s for 2004 are as follows: Word of God, take literally = 1,541; Word of God, don't take literally = 1,976; Word of man, don't take literally = 678. *N*s for 2008 are as follows: Word of God, take literally = 955; Word of God, don't take literally = 897; Word of man, don't take literally = 309.
Source: ANES (2004, 2008).

Devotional and scriptural differences within other faith communities are even more pronounced and coincide with very different views of homosexuality (ANES Complete Data File). In most cases, therefore, intra-denominational variations in religiosity and religious traditionalism account for more differences on gay rights than does denomination.[5] Recent controversies within the Episcopalian church highlight this fact. The denomination's official stance on homosexuality currently threatens a worldwide rift that may divide the American church from the rest of the worldwide Anglican Communion. The recent ordination of a gay bishop in the United States sparked an outcry from conservative and influential bishops in the global South, causing the Anglican Communion to threaten to expel the US church and the bishops in the United States to declare a moratorium on ordaining gay or lesbian bishops.

Mapping Religious Variables and Same-Sex Partnership Policies across the States

One way to grasp the aggregate relationship between religion and same-sex legislation is through mapping. While maps cannot prove causality or describe individual-level behaviour, they can offer an overview of important regional variations. For example, if we were to look at a map illustrating percentage of Christian adherents by state, we would quickly see that the United States is an overwhelmingly Christian nation. Indeed, in no state does the percentage of self-identified Christian adherent dip below 30 percent (Glenmary Research Center 2000). Figure 2.6 plots states in which more than 25 percent of the population is either evangelical Protestant (coloured in black) or Catholic (grey). This map demonstrates that evangelical Protestants are clustered in a group of southern states, while heavily Catholic states are predominantly found in the Northeast, Southwest, and Upper Midwest.

As a comparison, Figure 2.7 displays state same-sex marriage legislation in 2008. For ease of representation, several categories of legislation were necessarily lumped together. Thus, states with constitutional bans, defence of marriage acts, or something similar are coloured black. Similarly, states with civil unions or domestic partnerships are coloured grey. States with legalized gay marriage are coloured white, and states lacking either an allowance or a ban are striped. Before analyzing this map, it is important to remember that this figure represents a snapshot of *contemporary* legislation and that laws – even constitutions – are mutable.

FIGURE 2.6

Percentage of Catholics and evangelical Protestants by state, 2008

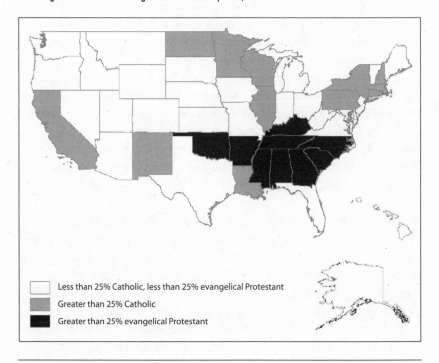

Less than 25% Catholic, less than 25% evangelical Protestant

Greater than 25% Catholic

Greater than 25% evangelical Protestant

Source: Map constructed by authors, based on data from the Association of Religion Data Archives (2008).

Figure 2.7 reveals the stunning extent to which same-sex marriage has been rejected by state legislatures nationwide. A majority of states in a wide swath of regions have constitutional bans on same-sex marriage or defence of marriage acts (DOMAs). The only two regions in which there appears to be some pocket of legislative tolerance for same-sex unions are the Northeast and the Northwest. In the Northeast, Massachusetts, Vermont, New Hampshire, Rhode Island, New York, and New Jersey have all legalized some form of same-sex union. On the opposite end of the country, Washington and Oregon offer same-sex domestic partnerships.

Comparing this map to the religious affiliations illustrated in Figure 2.6, we can see that every single state with a substantial cluster of evangelical Protestants has a constitutional ban on gay marriage or a DOMA. The

FIGURE 2.7

Same-sex marriage legislation by state, 2009

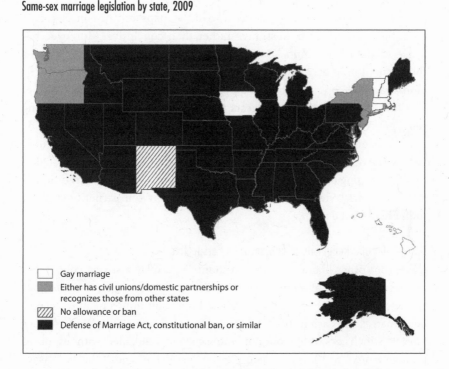

- Gay marriage
- Either has civil unions/domestic partnerships or recognizes those from other states
- No allowance or ban
- Defense of Marriage Act, constitutional ban, or similar

Source: Map constructed by authors, based on data from National Public Radio (2009).

impact of evangelical affiliation on attitudes towards homosexuality has been widely documented. Such affiliation is substantial across US regions, but mapping shows how strong the clustering is in the southern states.

While the official positions taken by the Roman Catholic hierarchy lead some observers to believe that formally adherent Catholics are more conservative on issues like abortion and homosexuality than are other Americans, survey evidence rarely if ever suggests that this is the case – a fact hinted at by the heavy concentration of Catholics in the Northeast, where tolerance for homosexuality appears greater than it does in other areas. Indeed, Catholics constitute more than 25 percent of the population in several of the states that permit same-sex marriages, civil unions, or domestic partnerships. And, as the survey data above have shown, Catholics tend to express more liberal attitudes than do Protestants (particularly evangelicals) on measures of gay/lesbian rights and approval.

It is worth emphasizing that, because of the maps' reliance on aggregate data, these findings are illustrative rather than conclusive. Moreover, because of data constraints, these maps only examine the ethnoreligious thesis and do not delve into a second crucial tenet of the literature on religion and public opinion: the "religious restructuring" perspective (Guth et al. 1997, 225). This theory suggests that the most salient division among religious Americans is between orthodox and progressive factions (ibid., 226; Howse 2005; see also Campbell and Robinson 2007). Thus, according to this line of thought, the most important determinant of the role religion plays in shaping public attitudes is whether an individual holds traditionalist or secularist views, a conclusion supported by our earlier analysis of individual-level data.[6]

US Opinion and Religiosity in Comparative Perspective

Data from other liberal democratic countries display a strong connection between religiosity and rejection of homosexuality, though a few countries provide examples of faith acting as a less important impediment to acceptance than is the case in the United States. Here we use the World Values Survey (which asks whether or not homosexuality is justified, with responses ranging from 1 to 10, with 1 being "never justifiable" and 10 being "always justifiable").

Figure 2.8 shows the same pattern across all nations tested that we found in the ANES data: the less they attend church, the more likely respondents are to find homosexuality justifiable. Across this sample of developed democratic countries, based on frequency of church attendance, the relationship between churchgoing and support for homosexuality is direct and mostly linear. Although the Roman Catholic hierarchy has stood firmly against any formal recognition of same-sex relationships and adoption rights, the attitudes of nominal Catholics within those European countries with majorities nominally adherent to the Roman Catholic Church are significantly more egalitarian than are the attitudes of Americans. One reason for this is that churchgoing in most of Europe and other Western and predominantly Christian countries is much less frequent than it is in the United States. So, while churchgoing still serves as a strong predictor of attitudes towards homosexuality, the numbers of those who do attend church regularly are low.

FIGURE 2.8

Is homosexuality "justifiable?" Survey results by church attendance, 2005-09

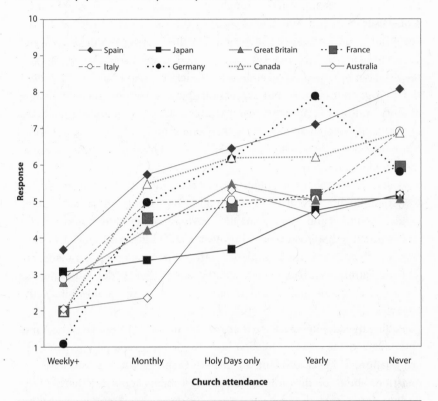

Note: Higher values on the *y*-axis indicate greater acceptance of homosexuality. Question wording: "Please tell me for each of the following statements whether you think it can be justified, never be justified, or something in between: ... Homosexuality" (scale of 1 to 10, with 1 signifying "never justifiable" and 10 signifying "always justifiable." *N*s are as follows: Spain = 1,106; Japan = 971; Great Britain = 925; France = 992; Italy = 924; Germany = 1,923; Canada = 1,998; Australia = 1,373; Sweden = 977.
Source: World Values Surveys (2005-09).

Transgenderism, Transsexuality, and Bisexuality: Emerging Issues

Transgenderism, transsexualism, and bisexuality have not enjoyed such widespread support or attention as has homosexuality/lesbianism, despite a growing movement for public recognition.[7] The national survey data we have from the 1970s through to today do not ask about transgendered, transsexual, or bisexual people and their rights; questions on national surveys are phrased in terms of "homosexuals" or "gays and lesbians." However, the recent congressional debate over the 2007 Employment Non-Discrimination Act (ENDA) seems to have hastened the explicit incorporation of transgender advocacy into the broader national gay rights platform. An article by the *Advocate*, an LGBT news source, suggests that the decision by Congress's Democratic leaders to strip ENDA of its protections for gender identity and expression spurred "an unprecedented show of unity" among gay rights activists (Minter 2007). Within forty-eight hours of the congressional action, more than one hundred LGBT organizations came together to form United ENDA, "a grassroots campaign to pass only the original, unified bill."

Conservative religious lobbies such as the Family Research Council, the Christian Coalition, and the Traditional Values Coalition say little about gender identities and other sexualities beyond condemning homosexuality and embracing heterosexuality; however, the Traditional Values Coalition (2008) website states the group's belief that "nobody is born a transsexual," and the Family Research Council (2008) states that it "does not consider homosexuality, bisexuality, and transgenderism as acceptable, alternative lifestyles."

Polling by Lake Research Partners has found that 61 percent of respondents believed the country needed laws to protect trans people from discrimination, a lower level of affirmative response than was elicited by questions about job discrimination against lesbians and gays. There cannot be any doubt that evangelicals, other "traditionalists," and those within other denominations who attend church frequently are substantially less likely than that to support anti-discrimination legislation. In the general population, 67 percent agreed that "it is possible for a person to be born as one sex but inside feel like another sex," and here we would anticipate even more contrast between evangelicals and church-attendees than others, given the long-standing denial of biological origins for sexual diversity among conservative religious groups (HRC 2002). The general public's opinion, however, won out in the enactment of the Hate Crimes Prevention Act, 2009, which added to existing US hate crimes legislation protection for crimes based on the "actual or perceived race, color, religion, national origin, gender, sexual orientation, gender identity, or disability of the victim." Meanwhile, as this book was going to print, Congress was still debating the inclusion of transgender protections in ENDA.

Discussion

While gay rights have been on the American political agenda for decades, only recently have they been at the forefront of national politics. Political strategists and post-election analysts alike proclaimed that the 2004 presidential election had ushered in a new era of "moral values-based" voting among the public. Gay marriage in particular became inextricably tied to the voting agenda when more than one-fifth of states included gay marriage bans on their ballots. The common wisdom following the election was that religious Americans held strong beliefs about the sanctity of marriage between a man and a woman and that they tended to care more about moral issues on the public agenda than did their secular counterparts. Much debate ensued about the role of moral values in voter decisions, and the influence of the marriage debate in particular, but few could doubt that the debate over lesbian and gay family rights and obligations had moved to centre stage. The 2006 and 2008 elections brought yet more successful statewide referenda prohibiting same-sex unions and/or marriages, and the fight reached a fever pitch in the battle over Proposition 8 in California, which was approved by a narrow margin of voters in November 2008 and which reversed the state's judicial legalizing of same-sex marriage. Yet again, the media stories were rife with suggestions of a culture war between religious and secular people.

Our chapter suggests that there is a complex truth to some elements of the conventional wisdom. States with majorities of evangelicals have all banned gay marriage, and surveys show that, regardless of other demographic factors, evangelical Protestants are not only more likely to be opposed to abortion, gay marriage, and gay adoption than are other denominations but also more likely to feel more strongly about these issues. Across the whole population, religious traditionalism and regular adherence to church rituals play an even stronger role than does denomination.

Evangelicals aside, the fact that variations *within* denominations can loom larger than those *between* denominations indicates that practising Christians are often quite tolerant or accepting of gays and lesbians. For some, this comes from a belief in the separation of church and state, a view echoed historically by the Roman Catholic hierarchy in the United States and by mainline Protestant denominations. For some, too, it comes from a readiness to accord rights even to unpopular minorities. And for others, it reflects the steady increase in numbers of Americans who know someone who is lesbian, gay, bisexual, or transgendered.

This chapter has explored the links between religion, religiosity, and public opinion on sexuality issues, taking as its starting point the assumption that religion, or even denomination, alone cannot explain individuals' divergent opinions on gay rights. Over the past few decades, Americans have become more tolerant of gays and lesbians overall: they count homosexuals as friends, family members, and co-workers, increasingly consider homosexuality to be an acceptable lifestyle, and are increasingly likely to view homosexuality as a genetic trait rather than as a personal choice. Over time, Americans have also become more likely to support legal rights for gays and lesbians, such as protections from workplace discrimination. Issues that seem particularly linked to the private rather than to the public sphere – such as those concerning gay couples as parents or spouses – remain controversial among Americans. This controversy, however, should not be called a religious-secular divide; rather, we must examine carefully the impact of denomination, religiosity, and scriptural traditionalism in order to understand the many factors that shape US public opinion about public recognition of multiple sexualities.

3

A Twenty-Year Survey of Canadian Attitudes towards Homosexuality and Gay Rights

AMY LANGSTAFF

The past two decades have seen tremendously rapid change in the rights accorded to lesbians and gay men in Canada. The country decriminalized homosexuality in 1967, a legal step that was accompanied by one of the more famous rhetorical flourishes in Canadian politics: Justice Minister Pierre Trudeau's declaration that there was no place for the state in the bedrooms of the nation. A decade later (1977), Quebec became the first province to name sexual orientation in its human rights act. In the late 1980s, the march of gay and lesbian rights accelerated; provincial human rights documents were amended in fairly brisk succession to include sexual orientation as a protected class, beginning with Ontario (1986) and Manitoba (1987) and ending with Newfoundland (1997) and Prince Edward Island (1998). In 1995, the Supreme Court of Canada ruled in *Egan v. Canada* that sexual orientation should be read into section 15 of the Charter of Rights and Freedoms (even if, on other grounds, the court rejected the challenge to old age pension legislation).

As laws were changed to grant gays and lesbians protection from discrimination as individuals, recognition of same-sex relationships also spread. In 1999, the Supreme Court of Canada ruled in *M v. H* (a case in which a woman sued her former female partner for spousal support payments) that same-sex unions warranted the same rights and obligations as did opposite-sex common-law unions. The federal government responded the following year with its Modernization of Benefits and Obligations Act, which amended sixty-eight federal statutes to extend all spousal rights (short of marriage) to same-sex couples. Between 2003 and 2005, courts in eight provinces ruled in favour of same-sex marriage, calling the restriction of marriage to hetero-sexual couples unconstitutional. In July 2005, under Paul Martin's Liberal government, Bill C-38, the Civil Marriage Act, was signed into law, legaliz-ing same-sex marriage across Canada. A coda to this legislative process played out quietly in December 2006, when Stephen Harper's Conservative government (elected the previous January) delivered its promised free vote on the question of whether to revisit the marriage issue. Parliament voted 175 to 123 against reopening the marriage debate.

Where was Canadian public opinion as these legal machinations took place? What we find is a steady, and in some cases remarkable, shift towards more accepting attitudes, even on the incendiary topic of marriage. There has been important change in the United States, too, although growing ac-ceptance in Canada has been evident on a wider range of issues, including gender roles and family structure. Change is evident even in the kinds of questions pollsters ask and in the questions they no longer see fit to pose. This does not mean that opposition to gay rights has disappeared: there re-mains adamant opposition in some quarters to all gay rights as well as to homosexuality itself. There is no doubt, however, which major changes in public policy and law have been mirrored in deep shifts in public attitudes.

The Questions Asked

Survey questions about homosexuality and gay rights tend to fall into three broad strains. The first invites judgment of homosexuality itself, asking, for example, whether homosexuality is moral or immoral or whether the re-spondent personally approves or disapproves of same-sex relationships. The second probes the extent to which respondents see homosexuality as some-thing that, in the most general sense, society should tolerate. The third probes public attitudes about specific legal rights for gays and lesbians, from discrimination protections to civil unions, marriage, and adoption rights.

Environics first began polling Canadians on their attitudes towards homosexuality and gay rights in 1987. In our earliest surveys on sexuality, the questions are sometimes more striking than the answers. Changes in Canadians' answers to survey questions over time quantify shifts in public opinion, but the fact that some of the queries that appeared in our earliest polls could scarcely be asked today is arguably a more meaningful sign of how much public attitudes have changed in two decades.

In that first year of polling, for example, Canadians were asked to estimate the likelihood of various consequences if "homosexual rights" were
protected by law. Among the possibilities listed were that "child molesters
[would] have free access to our children" (with 33 percent of respondents
agreeing that this was at least somewhat likely) and that "AIDS [would]
spread more rapidly (with 62 percent responding "likely"). Questions
about adoption and marriage were not even on the polling agenda. The
first time Environics polled Canadians about same-sex "spousal" benefits
was in 1996.

A wide range of rights questions has been posed more consistently in the
United States, largely because so many of those questions are still under
active policy debate in large parts of that country, including the most basic
rights protections. Those in the United States who oppose the public recognition of sexual diversity fight persistently to roll back gains made at the
state and local levels even as they fight to ensure that new rights measures
are not adopted. As a result, particular questions no longer posed in Canada
"live" longer south of the border and, thus, continue to inspire polling.

Approval and Disapproval

Over the past two decades, acceptance of homosexuality itself has increased
dramatically in Canada. Over the past twenty years, for example, Environics
has asked Canadians this question: "Do you personally strongly approve,
somewhat approve, somewhat disapprove, or strongly disapprove of homosexuality?"[1] At first measure, in 1987, just 10 percent of Canadians expressed
approval of homosexuality, with 55 percent disapproving and 34 percent
neutral (see Figure 3.1). In its most recent survey, in 2004, the proportion
approving of homosexuality had grown to nearly half the population: 48
percent (36 percent disapproved, and 14 percent were neutral). Among
those under thirty, approval was 68 percent.

Americans moved considerably towards approval over this same period,
but a 10 to 20 percent Canada/US gap has remained on most questions related to this dimension (Rayside and Bowler 1988; Nevitte 1996; Inglehart et
al. 2004). In World Values Surveys for 1990, for example, 24 percent of US
respondents scored 8, 9, or 10 on a 10-point scale, where 10 meant that
homosexuality was "never justified," while only 13 percent of Canadians did
so. A 2007 Pew Center survey found that 70 percent of Canadians and 49
percent of Americans agreed that "homosexuality should be accepted by
society" (Pew 2007).

FIGURE 3.1

Approval of homosexuality compared to support for various gay rights initiatives, 1987-2005

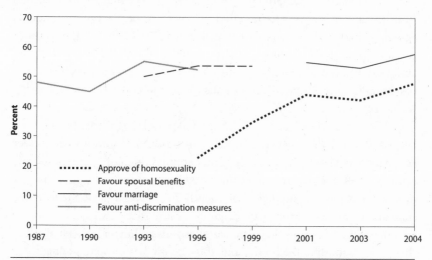

Source: Environics Research Group, Focus Canada (various years).

Lesbian/Gay Rights

Along with acceptance of homosexuality itself, support for gay rights has also increased notably in the past two decades. Because polling is generally carried out on the policy issues of the day, there is no gay legal rights question on which Canadian attitudes have been tracked consistently over the past two decades. The policy issues under debate have changed, and the polling questions have changed to match. But looking at public attitudes over time on a changing slate of issues gives a picture of growing support for lesbian and gay rights in general.

In the late 1980s and early 1990s, the rights issues most actively discussed revolved around the protection of individual gays and lesbians from discrimination. In the polling of the day, about half of the Canadian general public expressed support for such protections; in 1987, 48 percent of Canadians believed that the Canadian Bill of Rights should prohibit discrimination against homosexuals.[2] By 1996, a year after *Egan v. Canada*, support for constitutional protections for gays and lesbians had crept up 4 points to 52 percent.[3] This was a modest change, but, significantly, the proportion of Canadians who favoured protecting gays and lesbians against discrimination was 30 points higher than was the proportion of Canadians (22 percent) who expressed personal approval of homosexuality.

As sexual orientation was legally incorporated into human rights frameworks, debates around constitutional protections for lesbian and gay individuals subsided, and discussions of same-sex partnerships emerged as the next major issue. It is in this area that we see the most dramatic changes in public attitudes, starting in the late 1990s. In 1996, when Environics began polling Canadians on the extension of spousal benefits to same-sex partners, 53 percent expressed support.[4] Support held at this level through 1999, the year of *M v. H.*[5] By the time the federal Parliament extended spousal benefits and obligations to same-sex couples in 2000, the legislature was in step with a slim but growing majority of Canadians.

As for the question of same-sex marriage, polling in the 1990s showed only minority support, but a 2001 Environics poll showed a remarkable shift to majority support (55 percent).[6] Support for same-sex marriage reached 58 percent in 2004, just prior to the legalization of lesbian and gay unions in the summer of 2005.

The fact that a majority of Canadians expressed support for same-sex marriage is noteworthy for a couple of reasons. First, although gay rights had been on the public agenda on and off for a number of years, it was only in 2003 that an Ontario Superior Court decision (and subsequent decisions in British Columbia [2003] and Quebec [2004]) sparked intensive debate on the matter at the federal level. The mobilization of opposition to the recognition of same-sex marriage was intense from that period on through the next two years. Such mobilization did result in some short-term slippage in support for gay and lesbian marriage, but the medium- and longer-term trends continued along a trajectory towards stronger support. The fact that support was widespread for a legal step that was radical by international standards at the time suggests that considerable openness to gay rights among the Canadian public preceded the legal shifts of the early 2000s. Remarkably, public support registered barely a hiccup as the survey questions shifted from one of spousal benefits short of marriage to full, equal marriage for same-sex couples.

Majority support for same-sex marriage in Canada contrasts markedly to attitudes in the United States, where positive responses to marriage questions ranged from the low 30s to the low 40s during the same period. Canadian/American contrasts on other lesbian/gay rights questions are much smaller than this, and very large majorities of Americans support prohibitions on discrimination in employment and housing. Nevertheless, the stubborn cross-border disparity on a central issue like marriage lends support to Michael Adams' (2003) contention that social values in the two countries exhibit some important differences – not least on issues related to gender, family, and sexuality.

The shifting centre of gravity for Canadians on gay rights issues was evident in the language of the debate on same-sex marriage. It was not uncommon, for example, to hear opponents of same-sex marriage say that they did not wish for gays and lesbians to be discriminated against in general – and that they might even support same-sex civil unions – but that they "drew the line" at marriage, which they saw as having special symbolic importance that would be undermined by gay and lesbian participation in the institution. In other words, the contentious issues of the past were taken as settled (and the outcomes more or less acceptable). And, as Figure 3.1 shows, a significant proportion of the population believed in granting legal protections to a minority group of which they personally disapproved.

Canada is not unique in having support for gay rights traditionally exceed acceptance of homosexuality. In 1989, the General Social Survey of the United States found 74 percent of Americans declaring that "sexual relations between two adults of the same sex" are "always wrong." In the same year, however, Gallup found 71 percent of Americans agreeing that "homosexuals should have equal rights in terms of job opportunities."[7]

Changing Definitions of Family

Canadian attitudes towards what constitutes a family are obviously related to their beliefs about sexuality. Opponents of gay rights frequently claim that legal recognition of same-sex unions will undermine the family (the family, in this analysis, being understood as a married heterosexual couple who produce children), while proponents of gay rights claim that same-sex couples, with or without children, are effectively families and deserve recognition as such.

In 1992, Environics began asking whether a variety of living arrangements constituted families.[8] At that time, as today, Canadians universally (99 percent) classified two married opposite-sex adults *with children* as a family. The same year, when acceptance of homosexuality was less than one in five (inferring from 1987 and 1996 data), only about one-quarter of Canadians believed that two lesbians (24 percent) or two gay men (23 percent) committed to one another and living together constituted a family (see Table 3.1).

From 1992 to 2007, however, Canadians' attitudes about family changed significantly. Most striking was the change in attitudes towards gay and lesbian couples, whose acceptance as families doubled in a decade and a half.

TABLE 3.1

Definitions of family: Survey results, 1992, 1999, and 2007

	1992	1999	2007	Change from 1992
Married man and woman, kids	99	99	99	–
Unmarried man and woman, kids	89	89	93	+6
Single woman, kids	83	84	91	+8
Married man and woman, no kids	81	79	81	–
Unmarried man and woman	64	65	70	+6
Two lesbians	24	31	50	+26
Two gay men	23	31	49	+26

Note: Question wording: "We have heard a lot these days about the changing of the family. I'd like to know your opinion on what a family is. For each of the following types of living arrangements, please tell me whether you would definitely call it a family or definitely would not call it a family."
Source: Environics Research Group, Focus Canada (various years).

Increasingly flexible definitions of family are driven by major trends that have unfolded over the past several decades. Growing secularism has softened public attitudes regarding the propriety or impropriety of various arrangements outside of heterosexual marriage, including single parenthood, common-law unions, and same-sex partnerships. Increased divorce rates have further contributed to the view of marriage itself as a "companionate" contract rather than as a lifelong relationship shaped by timeless religious precepts.

Canadians are still markedly more likely to view as families households that include children, but they express growing openness to a variety of parenting arrangements. As early as 1992, an Environics survey showed that over eight in ten Canadians saw a single mother with children (83 percent) and an unmarried couple with children (89 percent) as families. As of 2007, the proportion of Canadians who see an unmarried man and woman with children as a family (93 percent) is only 6 points behind the "rating" of a married couple with children but a full 23 points higher than the proportion who see a childless unmarried couple as a family (70 percent). This suggests that, for most Canadians, the presence of children is a more salient factor in family formation than is marriage.

In 2003, Reginald Bibby (2004) drew on data from a survey commissioned by the Vanier Institute of the Family to present a somewhat different portrait. When asked what constituted a family, only 68 percent of

Canadians responded affirmatively when asked about an unmarried man and woman with at least one child, compared to 96 percent who said a married man and woman with at least one child constituted a family. Forty-six percent of Canadians saw a same-sex couple *with children* as a family.

Even if traditional conceptions of the family remain widespread in Canada, comparative evidence suggests that Canadians adhere less strongly to traditional family models than do Americans. Although Canadian and American data are not precisely comparable, in 1992 and 1999, Roper surveyed Americans using the same question Environics employed in the same years, naming various domestic arrangements and asking whether they constituted families.[9] Canadians were more likely to attach the name "family" to groupings other than a heterosexual married couple with children. In 1999, 89 percent of Canadians said a heterosexual cohabiting couple with children counted as a family; the formality of marriage made a 10-point difference (99 percent). In the same year, south of the border, Americans almost universally (98 percent) saw a married heterosexual couple with children as a family. However, if the couple were described as "committed (but not married) to each other and living together" with their children, then the proportion of Americans who saw them as a family fell to 75 percent. Just as Americans were less likely to accord family status to unmarried heterosexual couples, so too they were less likely to see same-sex couples as families. In 1999, only about one in five Americans saw same-sex couples living together as families (21 percent for lesbians, 20 percent for gay men), compared to 31 percent of Canadians.

When same-sex couples were described as having children, the proportion of Americans seeing them as families grew to 26 percent for gay men and 29 percent for lesbians. The 2003 Bibby survey found less willingness (24 percent) than did the Environics survey (31 percent) to use the term "family" for same-sex couples without children; this is likely because the Bibby survey specified childlessness and the Environics survey did not. On the other hand, the presence of children notably increased – to 46 percent – Canadians' willingness to use the family label for households led by same-sex couples. Intriguingly, the presence of children seemed to make a greater difference for Canadians than for Americans in their assessments of "family" status even when the couples in question were heterosexual. In 1999, 86 percent of Americans saw married heterosexual couples without children as family compared to 79 percent of Canadians.

The emergence of more inclusive attitudes towards sexual minorities, and particularly those in relationships, is related to important changes in

FIGURE 3.2

Position on same-sex marriage by attitude towards homosexuality, 2004

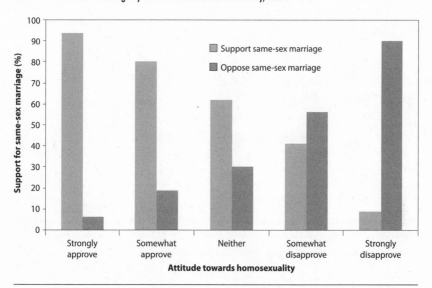

Source: Environics Research Group, Focus Canada (2004).

opinions about roles within the family. There has been, for example, a sharp decline in deference to patriarchal frameworks of family structure. In 1983, 42 percent of Canadians agreed that "the father of the family must be master in his own house." By 2005, that proportion had declined to 18 percent, although it appears to have plateaued, generally hovering in the low 20s since its 2005 low.[10] Along with a more egalitarian sensibility as to how families should be organized and governed, Canadians have adopted more flexible attitudes regarding the kinds of relationships (biological and legal) that must be present in order for a group of people living in the same home to constitute a family.

The Adamantly Opposed One-Third

In Canada, disapproval of homosexuality and support for the gay legal rights issue of the day are becoming less likely to coexist. In 2004, support for same-sex marriage exceeded acceptance of homosexuality by only 10 points, and, as Figure 3.2 indicates, the two positions are correlated more strongly than the analogous items could have been in 1987.

In fact, increased approval of homosexuality in Canada comes largely from a reduction in the ranks of those who had previously expressed neutrality

FIGURE 3.3

Trends regarding neutrality towards homosexuality, 1987-2005

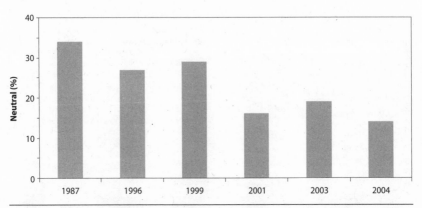

Note: Question wording: "Do you personally strongly approve, somewhat approve, somewhat disapprove, or strongly disapprove of homosexuality?" [1987 wording: "... of homosexuals?"]

Source: Environics Research Group, Focus Canada (various years).

FIGURE 3.4

Disapproval of homosexuality: The adamant one-third, 2004-06

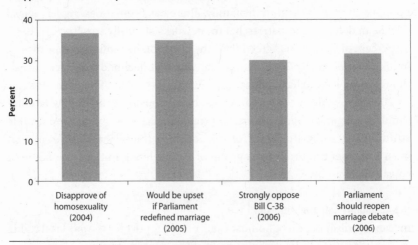

Source: Environics Research Group, Focus Canada (2004-06).

on the subject. This diminished neutrality reflects increased public awareness of the issues during various periods of public controversy and the enhanced visibility of sexual minorities. Gay rights advocates and opponents
have devoted considerable resources to moving Canadian opinion to their

side; the net result seems to be that more Canadians have switched from neutral to accepting views, but those who object to gay legal rights have hardened in their opposition.

For the time being, opposition to both homosexuality and gay rights, in steady decline for two decades, is holding firm. Although there is no quantitative evidence to suggest a backlash among the Canadian public against the advancement of gay rights, an examination of various survey results in concert gives the impression that a fairly stable minority of about one-third of Canadians are profoundly dismayed by growing social acceptance of homosexuality – particularly the legalization of same-sex marriage. At last measure of approval or disapproval of homosexuality per se in 2004, 36 percent of Canadians disapproved. A 2005 Environics survey asked Canadians whether they would be upset if the parliamentary vote on same-sex marriage produced a result contrary to their own position: 35 percent reported that they would be upset if the legislation passed. A 2006 survey of public opinion on same-sex marriage showed that a lingering 30 percent still strongly opposed Bill C-38. Thirty-two percent of Canadians were so dissatisfied with the success of the same-sex marriage legislation in the summer of 2005 that they favoured a return to the issue in Parliament in 2006.

The fact that the size of this group of strong gay rights opponents has remained fairly stable during the past several years likely reflects the impact of intense mobilization of gay rights opponents through publicity campaigns and religious networks. This has produced a core constituency of opposition resistant to accommodating the kind of legal change that, in the past, opened the way to opinion shifts. High levels of immigration from source countries in which gay legal rights are not on the public agenda may also have a dampening effect on the erosion of anti-gay rights attitudes, although polling data suggest that the attitudes of foreign-born Canadians are evolving alongside the attitudes of the Canadian-born.[11] It is also possible that the high profile of gay rights issues in the media during the past several years led to a short-term backlash against homosexuality and gay rights or at least to a stiffening of opposition.

In the United States, there remains an adamant core of opposition to homosexuality as such and to rights advancement: there is evidence (particularly from surveys that measure disapproval) to suggest that this adamant core is noticeably larger than in Canada, perhaps 50 percent larger. On the other hand, some portion of the strong disapprovers (a larger proportion than in Canada) are still prepared to support basic non-discrimination rights in employment and housing (which are supported by 85 to 90 percent of Americans). There is also a larger population in the United States than in Canada of those with a mixture of positive and negative views on rights issues. Marriage consistently inspires the strongest opposition of any rights issue – stronger even than adoption rights. A 2007 CNN/Opinion Research Corporation poll found support for same-sex marriage at 40 percent, much lower than the 57 percent who supported adoption.[12] On marriage specifically, the proportion of Americans who find homosexuality per se acceptable and the proportion who support same-sex marriage are now roughly aligned. And, as Egan, Persily, and Wallsten (2008) have observed in the United States, periods of intense media coverage can lead to upsurges in anti-gay sentiment as well as to the polarization of views on gay rights, even if attitudes tend to resume their previous shape and movement within a few years of major controversy.

Religion and Partisanship

Environics surveys indicate that Canadians who attend religious services at least monthly are more than twice as likely (68 percent) as are those who do not (30 percent) to oppose same-sex marriage. In 2004, among those who never attended religious services, 67 percent supported same-sex marriage, while 30 percent were opposed.

Reginald Bibby's 2004 survey for the Vanier Institute asked respondents if they agreed or disagreed that government should give high priority to ensuring that same-sex families received the same benefits as other families. Only 37 percent of weekly-plus attendees agreed, as compared to 76 percent of those who attended less frequently (Bibby 2004, chap. 3). When the subject turned to whether same-sex couples should be allowed to marry, the contrast was even sharper: only 21 percent of weekly-plus attendees agreed, as compared to 74 percent of those who attended less often. And then even greater contrasts emerged when the subject turned to the sexual or relational activity of "children" (ibid., chap. 2). The proportion of respondents who would disapprove and not accept their children's informing them that they were gay or lesbian was 29 percent among weekly-plus attendees, more than four times the 9 percent among those who attended less often. As for children engaging in homosexual activity, 71 percent of weekly-plus attendees would disapprove and not accept, four times the 18 percent of those who attended less often.

In addition to religious attendance, religious affiliation plays a role in shaping Canadian attitudes. In 2004, before Bill C-38 was introduced, seven in ten Canadians who claim no religious affiliation (69 percent) favoured the legalization of same-sex marriage. At 42 percent, Protestants were the least likely to support full marriage rights, while Catholics and those who claimed a non-Catholic, non-Protestant religious affiliation fell in between (55 percent each). In 2006, when Canadians were asked whether the marriage debate should be reopened,[13] Protestants were most likely (44 percent) to say the issue should be revisited. Those with no religious affiliation were least likely (18 percent) to desire a return to the marriage debate, while, again, Catholics (32 percent) and those in the "Other religion" category (35 percent) fell in between.

Sam Reimer, in his contribution to this volume, points to important shifts in the attitudes of Canadian evangelical Christians over the past twenty years but sees very little change regarding questions like whether sexual activity between two adults of the same sex is "always wrong." Among church-attending evangelicals, disapproval was 87 percent in 2005, contrasted with 27 percent among non-evangelicals. Disapproval among Canadian evangelicals is only slightly less than it is among American evangelicals, though there is a much higher level of disapproval among American non-evangelicals (50 percent) than among their Canadian counterparts.

Party realignment in the 1990s and early 2000s produced dramatic polarization on sexuality issues, a phenomenon not unrelated to the religious-conservative core constituency that was one of the building blocks of the Reform and Alliance parties. Conservative Party supporters are nearly twice as likely (59 percent) as Liberal Party supporters (35 percent) to oppose same-sex marriage and nearly three times as likely as Canadians who say they will support the Bloc (22 percent) or the NDP (20 percent) in the next federal election. Approval of homosexuality also varies widely, from 31 percent among Conservative supporters, to 48 percent among Liberals, to 69 percent among New Democrats.

These partisan contrasts are a fairly new phenomenon. Back in 1987, there was remarkably little variation across parties in attitudes towards homosexuality and gay rights. In the three major federal parties of the time (Liberal, Progressive Conservative, and NDP), disapproval of homosexuality ranged from 50 to 60 percent, and approval hovered around 10 percent. Similarly, on the legal question of the day (whether gays and lesbians should be protected from discrimination), pluralities in all three parties supported gay rights, with smaller proportions opposing discrimination protections or declining to state an opinion. The changes since then include a sharp decline of disapproval of homosexuality among Liberals (down 21 points) and NDP

FIGURE 3.5

Approval levels for homosexuality by political party, 1987-2004

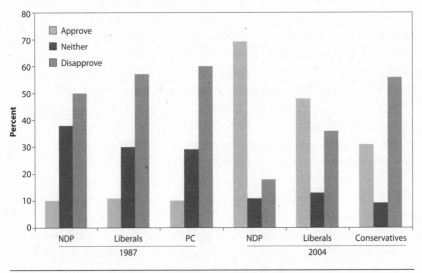

Source: Environics Research Group, Focus Canada (various years).

supporters (down 32 points) but an almost imperceptible change among supporters of the new Conservative (formerly Progressive Conservative) Party, where disapproval declined only 4 percent from 1987 to 2004.

Region and community size matter but much less than religion and party preference. Alberta, and the two other prairie provinces (Saskatchewan and Manitoba), have the highest levels of objection to same-sex marriage (50 and 48 percent, respectively). Opposition is 42 percent in British Columbia, 39 percent in Ontario and the Atlantic provinces, and 37 percent in Quebec. Canadians in small towns and rural areas are markedly more likely than are those in larger communities to oppose same-sex marriage. Half of those living in towns of fewer than 5,000 residents (49 percent) express opposition, as compared to 44 percent of those in towns with populations of 5,000 to 100,000 and 36 percent of those in cities of 100,000 or more.

Age differences are pronounced. The most recent Environics data show that Canadians over the age of 60 are about twice as likely (52 percent) as those between the ages of 18 and 29 (27 percent) to oppose same-sex marriage. Bibby's 2003 survey showed 64 percent support for gay marriage among 18-34 year olds and only 24 percent among those 55 and over (Bibby

2004, chap. 3). Similar contrasts show up in questions about approving or disapproving homosexuality. In the youngest cohort, 68 percent approved of homosexuality (20 points higher than the national average).

These differences suggest that the longer-term future will see a significant increase in overall acceptance of homosexuality and the public recognition of rights and obligations associated with sexual diversity. For the time being, however, despite these intergenerational patterns, core opposition remains stable in Canada. One reason for this could well be the intensity of belief among religious conservatives, which is reinforced by the political mobilization on such issues as marriage. Another possibility, already alluded to, is the very high rate of immigration to Canada, much of it from source countries in which gay rights are not addressed.

Attitudes of Newcomers

Newcomers to Western countries such as Canada are often assumed to exert a conservative influence over public opinion on social issues – especially in the areas of gender and sexuality. In early 2005, as Stephen Harper sought to expand support for the Conservative Party from its rural, western base into central and suburban Canada, he began to court urban immigrant voters with socially conservative messages – most notably on same-sex marriage.

Canada consistently has one of the highest immigration rates in the world and currently has the second highest foreign-born population (19 percent) after Australia (22 percent).[14] As of 2005, the top four source countries of newcomers to Canada were China, India, the Philippines, and Pakistan, countries where relatively little policy recognition of gay rights has been achieved (although India decriminalized homosexuality in 2009, and several anti-discrimination measures have been submitted [not passed] in the Philippines).[15] Ronald Inglehart and others have argued that equal rights for women and such minority groups as gays and lesbians are often ignored or rejected in societies where survival is uncertain and basic material needs are often unmet (Inglehart and Baker 2000). Given that newcomers to Canada arrive primarily from societies in which survival values are strong, some political strategists have speculated that, after several decades of increasingly liberal approaches to matters of sexuality, Canada's political centre may begin to shift towards greater traditionalism as immigrants gain influence in Canadian public life.

On the other hand, it is not clear that the Harper Conservatives' attempt to attract immigrant votes with a socially conservative message was an important contributor to the party's electoral gains in January 2006. At the very least, the Conservative approach did not result in increased support from urban ridings with high concentrations of immigrants. The Conservatives did gain some urban ground in the 2008 election, and there is anecdotal evidence that the party has made further progress among immigrants since then, but this ground has been gained at a time when same-sex marriage is no longer much in public discourse; perceived Liberal neglect may be more salient than shared social conservatism.

Social values data indicate that, although foreign-born Canadians are generally less supportive of gay rights than the national average, this issue might not have been a sufficiently powerful wedge in 2006 to induce immigrants to abandon their traditional allegiance to the Liberal Party. Immigrants on average share more common ground with core Liberal supporters than with core Conservative supporters on matters such as the environment, the welfare state, and Canadian identity. Family-related and sexuality issues stand out as the only values issues on which immigrants more closely resemble Conservative supporters (see Adams and Langstaff 2005). But even here polling indicates that the differences are not vast. Forty-one percent of non-European immigrants express disapproval of homosexuality, compared to 36 percent of all Canadians (with 47 percent of European immigrants disapproving). Differences on marriage have been sharper: 43 percent of non-European immigrants are strongly opposed to same-sex marriage, as are 37 percent of European immigrants (as compared to 30 percent of all Canadians). The gap was smaller on the question (posed in 2006) of whether Parliament should reopen debate on the same-sex marriage legislation passed in 2005, with 40 percent of non-European immigrants wanting to revisit the question, 33 percent of European immigrants, and 32 percent of all Canadians.

Moreover, a look at the attitudes of immigrants over time indicates that immigrants' views on homosexuality and gay rights are changing in much the same way – and at much the same rate – as are the views of the Canadian average (see Figure 3.6). In part, this is probably a consequence of cultural assimilation or adaptation, especially among younger immigrants (immigrants tend to be younger on average than other Canadians). Canada's immigration system also focuses on attracting highly educated, highly skilled immigrants. According to Citizenship and Immigration Canada (2005), the proportion of immigrants arriving in Canada with university degrees rose from 17 percent in 1986 to 36 percent between 1996 and 2001. As of 2001, 60 percent of newcomers to Canada, as compared to 43 percent

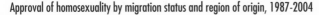

FIGURE 3.6

Approval of homosexuality by migration status and region of origin, 1987-2004

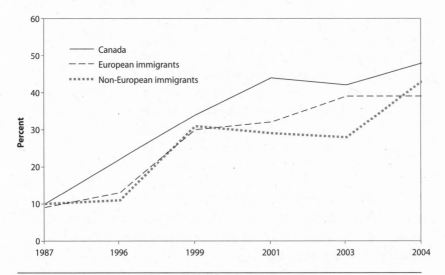

Note: Question wording: "Do you personally approve, somewhat approve, somewhat disapprove, or strongly disapprove of homosexuality?" [1987 wording: "... of homosexuals?"]. Note also that the sample of immigrants is small, and results should be interpreted with caution.
Source: Environics Research Group, Focus Canada (various years).

of the population at large, had completed some kind of postsecondary education. Since acceptance of homosexuality and support for gay rights tend to correlate with high levels of education, it may be that an increasing proportion of newcomers to Canada are already tolerant of sexual difference upon their arrival.

Conclusion

The past twenty years have witnessed a dramatic shift in public opinion on questions related to sexual difference. The decline in disapproval of homosexuality and opposition to the public recognition of gay and lesbian relationships is remarkable by any measure. Although not all issues show stark contrasts in Canadian and American attitudes, there are some issues – including moral disapproval of homosexuality and rejection of same-sex marriage – on which Canadians and Americans continue to differ sharply. A major contributor to this divergence is the relative weakness of religious conservatism north of the border.

The shift towards more accepting attitudes has persisted despite an influx of immigrants whom some Canadians might have assumed would represent more conservative moral values than those prevailing among native-born Canadians. On some issues related to sexuality, there is indeed a tendency for immigrants to express stronger disapproval of difference. The differences between the Canadian-born and the foreign-born, however, are not stark and seem susceptible to the same strong intergenerational contrasts that we see among other Canadians.

There remains, still, a core of opposition to homosexuality itself and to the public recognition of same-sex marriage. This "adamant" one-third has remained stable for the past few years and may well increasingly coincide with the persistent minority of the population practising a conservative strain of any faith. With changes in public policy and law reflecting values of greater inclusiveness, and an LGBT population of growing visibility, even that core of opposition may slowly decline as religious communities move to positions of tolerance in a bid to remain relevant to members whose attitudes are evolving over time.

EVANGELICALS

In the United States and Canada, the most intense opposition to egalitarian policies towards sexual minorities (and especially towards marriage rights) has come from evangelical Protestants. The chapters in this section point to similarities across the border in evangelical spirituality and in attitudes towards questions of sexual difference. However, there are also significant Canada/US differences in those attitudes as well as in the institutional development of evangelicism and the political resources that can be marshalled.

In Chapter 4, Sam Reimer discusses differences in attitudes between US and Canadian evangelicals on sexual diversity issues, noting that many evangelicals (especially in Canada) have adopted a "civility without compromise" approach to key issues such as marriage. He shows the diversity of approaches within the evangelical community and helps to explain why Canadian evangelicals are less antagonistic and more tolerant towards gays and lesbians than are many of their American co-religionists.

In Chapter 5, Tina Fetner and Carrie Sanders show that contrasts in the development of faith-related political institutions account for some but not all of the differences between Canadian and American evangelicals. The latter have long been mobilized outside of denominational boundaries and have been more prone than their Canadian counterparts to form large coalitional bodies. More Canadian evangelicals have remained organized within already-established denominations and, in this and other ways, have been less inclined (or able) to create a sustained set of segregated institutions. This naturally weakened their capacity to intervene politically.

In Chapter 6, Clyde Wilcox and Rentaro Iida show that the simplest explanation of policy differences between the United States and Canada – that the former has more evangelicals and that the conservative wing of this faith tradition is far better organized in the United States than it is in Canada – is true and partially explains policy differences. Yet the authors also show that this is an oversimplified explanation. They show that the trends highlighted by Shames, Kuo, and Levine (this volume) for the whole population hold for white evangelicals as well: younger cohorts are far more liberal, and all age groups have become more egalitarian over time.

In Chapter 7, Robert Jones and Daniel Cox explore the attitudes of African-American Protestants, nearly all of whom hold evangelical doctrinal views and practise evangelical-style worship. Drawing on a unique set of focus groups with progressive African-American pastors as well as national surveys that include many African-American evangelicals, they point out the blend of liberationist theology and moral conservatism with regard to sexual diversity that is so characteristic of black churches in the United States. We believe that there are some echoes of this pattern in Canadian black churches, though this question has yet to receive sustained analytical treatment in Canada.

In Chapter 8, Jonathan Malloy discusses the mobilization of Canadian evangelicals on the marriage issue and the limitations of that mobilization. He argues that this issue provided a vehicle for unprecedented public profile and alliance building among religious opponents of gay/lesbian marriage, but that this newly found strength failed to stop full legalization. This period of intense activism represented a high-water mark for Christian evangelical political mobilization and did not signal a sustained enhancement of its capacity to shape public policy. Later in this volume, David Rayside returns to some of these themes.

"Civility without Compromise"
Evangelical Attitudes towards Same-Sex Issues in Comparative Context

SAMUEL REIMER

In early November 2006, Ted Haggard, then president of the National Association of Evangelicals (NAE) and pastor of the fourteen-thousand-member New Life Church in Colorado Springs, admitted to "sexual immorality." He was promptly dismissed from his pastoral position and resigned as NAE's president. The scandal was brought to light by a former male prostitute, Mike Jones, who claimed he had a three-year relationship with Haggard (the accusations also included the purchase and use of crystal methamphetamine). How would evangelicals react towards issues of homosexuality when it involved one of their own?

In the heated political climate that surrounded same-sex marriage legislation in both North American countries at the time, prominent evangelicals were quick to reiterate their position that sex outside of a heterosexual, monogamous marriage relationship is morally wrong. Missing from the publicized evangelical reactions to the Haggard scandal was any reasoned debate about or re-evaluation of issues related to sexual orientation.[1] Typical of responses from evangelical spokespersons was that of Reverend Leith Anderson, who replaced Haggard as president of the NAE: "I honestly don't think there is significant rethinking on evangelical positions on homosexuality, but I think there may be greater compassion" (Banerjee 2004). The common message was civility without compromise.

These recent events once again put the spotlight squarely on the sexual attitudes of evangelicals, who are known for their anti-gay views. So is there good reason to expect more positive regard towards homosexuals within the evangelical fold? On the one hand, evangelicals tend to hold uncompromising positions towards homosexuality because they are related to their defence of traditional family values, which is central to their identity and political agenda; on the other hand, evangelicals (especially those in Canada) resemble most North Americans in that they embrace values of diversity, tolerance, and individual rights. A growing positive regard for homosexuality, among other things, may pressure evangelicals towards more civil responses. This chapter examines Canadian and American evangelical attitudes towards homosexuality. These attitudes are contextualized both by comparing them to other family/sexuality issues and by looking for change over time. Two research questions frame this chapter. First, is there evidence for increased civility towards homosexuals, and if so is the trend towards greater civility more pronounced in Canada than it is in the United States? Second, does a shift towards greater civility correspond with more accommodating attitudes towards sexual activity in either country?

For the purposes of this chapter, evangelicals are defined as those who affiliate with a conservative Protestant denomination. This includes most Baptist groups, Pentecostals, Mennonites, Nazarenes, the Christian and Missionary Alliance, and many others. About 8 percent of Canadians and about 25 percent of Americans fit this definition of evangelicals, accounting for roughly 80 million North Americans. While most evangelicals hold strong negative views of homosexuality, a group of this size is likely to be somewhat diverse.

Limited Diversity within the Evangelical Camp

Even on issues as salient as homosexuality, evangelicals are not monolithic. If one listens closely, at least three evangelical positions can be deciphered: (1) homosexuality is not a choice, (2) homosexuality is a choice, and (3) homosexuality is dangerous. These three positions do not have clear boundaries, and one could argue that evangelical positions on homosexuality form not so much distinct groups as a continuum. Whatever the case, the point is that there is a range of opinions, although largely on the conservative end of the broader range of views within North America.

The least antipathy comes from the "homosexuality is not a choice" camp, led by Tony Campolo, a prominent evangelical, sociologist, and Baptist pastor. For the past twenty years, he has been outspoken in his contempt for the way some evangelicals have treated homosexuals, chastising them

for their hate-mongering. He told the *New York Times* that, since the Haggard scandal, "we're seeing ... a growing awareness among evangelicals that
they have oversimplified, made false judgments and been very, very mean
to the gay and lesbian community" (Banerjee 2004). He publicly supports
adoptions by same-sex couples, but he is against sexual relations outside of
heterosexual marriage.[2] While there are many who agree that homosexuality is not a choice and that evangelicals should be compassionate towards
homosexuals (Jantz 1999), Campolo represents a minority opinion and has
been severely criticized by many within the evangelical camp.

Possibly the largest group within evangelicalism is the "homosexuality is
a choice" group, the majority of whom promote compassionate responses
to homosexuals as individuals, even if they hope to reform them. The best-
known spokesperson here is James Dobson, psychologist and founder of
Focus on the Family. He argues that homosexuals can find "healing" through
his "Love Won (One) Out" campaign, which promotes therapeutic treatments to help people out of homosexuality. Apostolidis (2001, 1) suggests
that the "'Love Won Out' conferences typify a broader recasting of homophobic discourse by important segments of the Christian Right toward the
theme of compassion," a theme that has been evident in their discourse
since the 1990s.[3] Similarly, many rank-and-file evangelicals view LGBT
orientations as (sinful) personal choices that can be changed through personal conversion, even if individuals with these orientations should be treated civilly.

Focus on the Family also promotes sexual abstinence outside of hetero-
sexual, monogamous marriage and actively campaigns against same-sex
marriage. Dobson's (2004, 84-85) book, *Marriage under Fire: Why We Must
Win This Battle*, states that there is "no issue today that is more significant
to our culture than the defense of the [traditional] family." Focus on the
Family may be the greatest single influence on American (and even North
American) evangelical sexual attitudes, and Dobson tops recent lists of the
United States' most influential evangelicals (Crowley 2004; Little 2005).

The late fundamentalist Jerry Falwell may be the best representative of
the "homosexuality is dangerous" group.[4] Falwell viewed homosexuality as
physically and emotionally harmful, and he stated that homosexuals cannot
go to heaven unless they confess their sin and repent. Those who hold this
position tend to see homosexuals and pro-gay groups as well organized
and powerful, partly because they have formed alliances with other politically "left" groups (environmentalists, atheists, etc.) bent on undermining

traditional values. For some, pro-gay groups are dangerous because they spread diseases like AIDS, promote pedophilia and promiscuity, and actively recruit young people for their cause (Green 2000; Herman 2000).

In light of the latter two positions, it is not surprising that LGBT evangelicals have difficulty finding acceptance and struggle to find compatibility between their sexual and evangelical identities (Thumma 1991). Indeed, many evangelicals would see the term "gay evangelical" as an oxymoron.

Yet, one wonders if the Haggard scandal or a call for greater compassion from limited sectors within evangelicalism is pushing evangelicals towards a more positive regard for homosexuals. Previous research suggests that rank-and-file evangelicals (in both countries) value civility and are eager to distance themselves from the narrow-minded intolerance with which they are often labelled (C. Smith 2000, Reimer 2003). Add to this the external society pressures towards tolerance and acceptance of diversity – especially in Canada – and there is reason to expect greater positive regard, at least north of the border.

Similarities and Differences in North American Evangelicalism

Canadian evangelicals are often hidden under the shadow of their southern co-religionists, making comparative studies all the more important. While it is true that Canadian evangelicals are more like US evangelicals than they are like fellow Canadians (at least in their theological and moral views), there is reason to believe that evangelicalism takes on some "local colour" (Hexham and Poewe 1997) based on national differences. Assuming that national factors affect evangelical attitudes, there are demographic, historical, political, and cultural reasons to predict a more civil, or irenic (gentle, moderate), brand of evangelicalism in Canada.

A leading voice in Canada/US differences is Seymour Martin Lipset (1990, 1996). He argues that, because of its unique history (particularly its revolutionary genesis), the United States evinces an ideology that makes it distinctive and exceptional. The United States is marked, among other things, by meritocratic individualism, a preference for small government, and a traditional moralism that spawns regular reform movements. Lipset implicates the powerful influence of Protestant sectarianism, or evangelicalism, south of the border for its moral conservatism (Hoover et al. 2002). If Lipset is right, one would predict more traditional attitudes towards homosexuality among evangelical and non-evangelical Americans.

Demographically, Canadian evangelicals form a much smaller percentage of the population than do American evangelicals and, thus, are unable to wield the political and cultural force of the latter. Furthermore, Canadian evangelicals have higher proportions of Mennonites and lower proportions of independent and fundamentalist groups (Stackhouse 1993), which Simpson and MacLeod (1985, 228) argue undercuts the probability of a "politics of moral causes" in Canada.

Historically, Canada lacks the compelling civil religious myths (Blumstock 1993) that fuel the "culture wars" in the United States (Hunter 1991). The religious climate is one of greater deference to inherited religious institutions, along with a greater commitment to peaceful coexistence, in contrast to greater competition, innovation, and aggressive proselytism in the United States (Bibby 1987, 2002). Religiosity shows few signs of waning in the United States, whereas Canada has seen a significant decline in religious participation over the past half century.

Politically, evangelicals in Canada do not align with conservative politics to the same degree as do US evangelicals (Rawlyk 1994). Canadian evangelicalism has significant historical roots in the political left. Furthermore, the "political opportunity structure" in Canada, which involves the concentration of power in the hands of political elites, is not conducive to the aggressive populist tactics of special interest groups. Religious groups try to exercise power through "insider" influences and avoid drawing attention to sources of authority (like the Bible) that are unique to them. Add to this government control over religious broadcasting (which, south of the border, acts as a means of raising funds and consciousness), and the result is a more irenic tone in Canadian evangelical politics (Hoover 1997). For Noll (1997, 17), all these factors, along with other important historical differences, have the effect of "moderating the political extremes" of Canada's evangelicalism.

Cultural differences between the two countries include a greater emphasis on multiculturalism, pluralism, and tolerance of differences in Canada. Pluralism was enshrined by the Official Languages Act, 1969; the Multiculturalism Act, 1988; and the 1982 Charter of Rights and Freedoms (Bibby 2006). Diversity is to be celebrated in the Canadian "mosaic," a virtue that is assumed to distinguish Canada from the American "melting pot." This would seem to predict less antipathy towards homosexuals among Canadian evangelicals.

This focus on national differences does not mean that regional differences are unimportant. Indeed, the Mason-Dixon line serves as an important religious and cultural divide, and Canadian regionalism may be even more pronounced (see Grabb and Curtis 2005). However, when comparing evangelical attitudes, research suggests that national differences are more significant than are regional differences (Reimer 2003).

National differences result in a more civil tone in Canada's politicized sexual debates, but this does not necessarily mean that Canadian evangelicals will evince more moderate sexual attitudes. This is because conservative sexual ethics are central to evangelical identity and boundary maintenance. "Loose" sexual morals are seen as corrosive to the traditional family. Sexual ethics have become a litmus test for orthodoxy. The protection of the traditional family is central to evangelical goals in both countries because evangelicalism has the institutional base and cultural production necessary to form a pervasive subculture with strong identity and clear boundaries (Reimer 2003). Distinctive sexual attitudes strengthen subcultural boundaries and create tension with the "world." In spite of Hunter's (1987) and Quebedeaux's (1978) claims to the contrary, recent research shows little evidence that evangelical groups are accommodating to secularizing forces (Smidt and Penning 2002; Reimer 2003); rather, it shows that, among evangelicals, homosexuals are the least-liked group – more disliked than atheists, communists, or other ethnic and religious groups. For example, evangelicals in the United States are less willing to grant civil liberties to homosexuals than they are to any other disliked group, and they are less likely to want homosexuals as neighbours. Not surprisingly, it follows that they are more likely to feel "far" or "very far" from homosexuals than they are from other disliked groups (Reimer and Park 2001; C. Smith 2000). This suggests the importance of sexual ethics to evangelical sectarian tension and boundaries.

Why sexual ethics became central to evangelical subcultural boundaries poses another interesting question. Simpson (1994) argues that the "politics of the body" (i.e., abortion, pornography, homosexuality, etc.) in late capitalism stems from several factors, including the move away from manual labour, the visual stimulation in advertising, and the breakdown of the traditional family. As the economy moved past industrial capitalism, work became more mental and less physical, leaving the body less controlled. With consumer capitalism came "the requirement that desire be stimulated in order to encourage the consumption of goods and services" (9), and this included the stimulation of sexual desires. Finally, the breakdown of patriarchal nuclear families, with clearly defined gender roles, was also instrumental in placing the body in the centre of a bitter conflict. These forces provide a frame within which the politics associated with sexual ethics can be understood.

For North American evangelicals, the rapid changes in sexual ethics heightened the salience of issues associated with the politics of the body. Conservatives felt the moral foundations of the country were crumbling, a fear that was heightened by civil religious myths south of the border. Furthermore, the "deceptions of sexual freedom" were infiltrating the schools, churches, and mass media, ultimately leading to liberal sexual attitudes and practices among youth, even those within the evangelical fold. Evangelical spokespersons sounded the warning, and evangelicals retrenched in an attempt to protect orthodoxy and the traditional family, while other religious groups, to varying degrees, accommodated changes to sexual ethics. As a result, sexual ethics became a foil to distinguish fellow conservatives from liberals.

This act of "distinguishing" those who are "in" the evangelical fold from those who are "out" is something evangelicals do very well. Active evangelicals across North America not only share a religious identity but also have surprisingly similar group boundaries. They agree on the criteria for distinguishing an evangelical (a true "Christian") from a non-evangelical, including a conversion ("born-again") experience, a high view of scripture, and the centrality of the salvific work of Christ (Hunter 1983, 1987). In addition, active evangelicals can locate themselves in socio-religious space vis-à-vis other groups and can identify those groups to which they feel close and those to which they do not. Active evangelicals in the United States and Canada share warm regard for fellow evangelicals, like Pentecostals and Southern Baptists; they are ambivalent towards Catholics, Jews, and Episcopalians; and they feel far from "secular humanists," the New Age movement, and homosexuals (Reimer 2003). Their agreement with and recognition of certain "ingroups" and "outgroups" (Conover 1988, 54) are indicative of their distinctive subculture.

Clarity and agreement regarding subcultural boundaries allows evangelical spokespersons to mobilize some constituents by vilifying certain outgroups and defining their actions as threatening (e.g., those who seek to undercut biblical authority, the traditional family, or religious freedoms). These issues become symbolic in the sense that, through them, evangelicals "flag" their conservative position in socio-religious space, and they become litmus tests for whether or not one is an evangelical.

In spite of their shared identity and subcultural boundaries, evangelicals as a whole are not unified in political action because they do not agree on the appropriate means to meet their group goals. One roadblock to aggressive political action is the commitment of many rank-and-file evangelicals to pluralism, tolerance, religious freedom, and civility (C. Smith 2000, Bibby 2002). To maintain civility towards individuals while maintaining tension with society means that evangelicals can have strong negative reactions to certain "political" groups (like homosexuals, pro-choice activists, the American Civil Liberties Union), while showing a more positive regard for individuals who may identify with such groups. It may also mean that evangelicals will "flag" their conservatism with uncompromising views on sexual ethics but will evince warmer feelings towards homosexuals themselves.

Data

In Canada, data are drawn from Bibby's Project Canada Survey Series (1975-2005); in the United States, they are drawn from the combined 1972-2004 General Social Survey (GSS) and the 1974-2004 American National Election Studies (ANES) cumulative file. The data sources have a limited set of matching items over a thirty-year period.[5] These datasets include questions on denominational affiliation, by which conservative Protestants, or evangelicals, are distinguished from non-conservative Protestants, matching Bibby's (1975-2005) and Steensland et al.'s (2000) definitional strategies. Attending evangelicals (those who attend "nearly every week" or more) are analyzed because those active in the subculture best represent the attitudes proliferated therein.

In order to contextualize the changing attitudes towards homosexuals, I present changes in attitudes towards other groups in Table 4.1. The ProCan data ask respondents what their immediate reaction would be – (1) at ease, (2) a bit uneasy, (3) very uneasy – if they were to meet a broad array of people. Averages (ranging from 1 to 3) are given for three groups in Table 4.1: attending conservative Protestants (ACP); all conservative Protestants (CP); and all non-conservative Protestants (Non), in both Canada and the United States.

Canadian respondents were asked how they would feel meeting an alcoholic, mental patient, drug user, drug addict, or ex-convict. In general, Canadians feel uneasy towards such groups, and, in most cases, this dis-ease increases slightly over time, perhaps because any threat they pose is perceived to be more prevalent or immediate.[6] There is very little difference between evangelicals and non-evangelicals in their comfort when meeting individuals in such groups. Typical here are the attitudes towards alcoholics, which are presented in the table.

TABLE 4.1

Attitudes towards selected groups in Canada and the US, 1980-2005

		1980 (N = 97)	1985 (N = 81)	1990 (N = 92)	1995 (N = 89)	2000 (N = 72)	2005 (N = 140)
Canada averages: "What would be your immediate reaction if you were to meet ..." 1 (at ease), 2 (a bit uneasy), 3 (very uneasy)							
An alcoholic	ACP	1.81	1.71	1.60	2.03	1.88	1.96
	CP	1.80	1.67	1.62	2.03	1.93	1.93
	Non	1.65	1.62	1.68	1.76	1.84	1.88
A black	ACP	1.25	1.10	1.02	1.14	1.04	1.05
	CP	1.18	1.11	1.06	1.11	1.08	1.06
	Non	1.12	1.13	1.11	1.12	1.10	1.09
A male homosexual	ACP	2.44	2.33	2.08	2.05	1.68	1.64
	CP	2.17	2.12	1.91	1.93	1.58	1.62
	Non	1.93	1.87	1.81	1.55	1.43	1.34
A female homosexual	ACP	2.31	2.18	1.98	1.99	1.71	1.64
	CP	2.13	2.07	1.88	1.85	1.59	1.54
	Non	1.86	1.86	1.72	1.50	1.34	1.27
		1980	1984	1992	1996	2000	2004
US averages: Feeling thermometers range from 0 (coldest) to 100 (warmest)							
Catholics	ACP	–	57.82	61.00	–	66.15	67.82
	CP	–	58.01	60.73	–	65.04	66.85
	Non	–	64.43	66.52	–	67.78	68.65
Blacks	ACP	62.98	63.57	69.56	72.71	71.07	75.55
	CP	60.84	62.46	68.83	69.69	68.79	74.34
	Non	64.55	64.25	63.06	63.95	66.49	70.76
Women's feminist liberation movement	ACP	37.10	40.23	54.84	56.75	57.69	53.97
	CP	43.43	49.98	59.71	61.66	61.16	54.37
	Non	55.87	59.59	62.83	63.16	62.73	56.81
Gays and lesbians	ACP	–	11.40	25.74	27.59	32.14	31.93
	CP	–	18.38	29.42	31.30	35.88	37.70
	Non	–	32.64	41.59	43.43	51.10	52.30

Note: ACP = attending conservative Protestant; CP = conservative Protestant; Non = all other Canadians and Americans (non-conservative Protestants).

Source: Project Canada Series and American National Election Studies Series (various years).

Nearly all Canadians feel at ease meeting racial and religious minorities – Jews, blacks, Orientals, East Indians/Pakistanis, Aboriginal people, and Muslims – and Canadians evince slightly higher levels of comfort towards such groups over time. Predictably, Canadians show high levels of ethnic/racial civility. Evangelicals are not, on the whole, less comfortable meeting individuals in such groups, which is consistent with previous research (Reimer 2000). In fact, they are slightly more comfortable meeting people in these groups, as is shown in their attitudes towards blacks in Table 4.1.

The contrast between the above and attitudes towards gays and lesbians is sharp. Evangelicals distinguish themselves from most Canadians by being less comfortable meeting homosexuals, and this difference increases with church attendance. While the positive change in evangelical attitudes matches the rate of change for all Canadians, the gap is not narrowing over time (according to slope estimates). Evangelicals, then, are uniquely uncomfortable with homosexuals but not with other groups of people.

American data present a similar story. Comparative data are based on the "feeling thermometers" from the ANES, in which respondents are asked to rate how "warm" they feel towards the group on a scale of 0 to 100 (responses closer to 100 are more favourable). American evangelicals and attending evangelicals rate Catholics and blacks at least as warmly as do non-evangelicals, further supporting the contention that evangelicals are not less irenic overall. Evangelicals are surprisingly warm towards feminists, with scores that, in 2004, are not significantly different from those of non-evangelicals. Regarding feelings towards gays and lesbians, evangelical ratings are substantially and significantly colder.

While evangelicals continue to distinguish themselves through their discomfort with homosexuals, the rate of change in these attitudes is noteworthy. That is, discomfort with gays and lesbians is decreasing at a much faster rate than is discomfort with any other group in the survey. This change is made clear when we look at the percentage of Canadians and Americans who give homosexuals the lowest rating possible. Table 4.2 shows the percentage of Canadians who feel "very uneasy" meeting a homosexual and the percentage of Americans who give gays and lesbians a zero (0) on the feeling thermometers. By 2005, only about one in ten evangelicals in Canada feel very uncomfortable meeting a homosexual, and over half claim that they would be "at ease" meeting a homosexual. Overall, the percentages in 2005 are only about one-fifth of what they were in 1980.

While the US data show a general decline in negative feelings towards gays and lesbians, the pattern is somewhat different from the Canadian one.

TABLE 4.2

Change in antipathy towards homosexuals in Canada and the US, 1980-2005

Canada	1980	1985	1990	1995	2000	2005
Percent "very uneasy" meeting a lesbian						
ACP	46.9	37.3	28.6	30.8	14.6	10.1
CP	36.3	32.1	21.1	22.7	11.1	9.4
Non	24.7	25.5	19.0	12.5	6.1	5.2
Percent "very uneasy" meeting a male homosexual						
ACP	52.4	44.2	38.6	30.2	15.0	12.4
CP	36.2	37.5	26.1	24.7	11.1	11.6
Non	29.5	25.9	24.7	14.8	9.7	8.4

US		1984	1992	1996	2000	2004
Percent giving a "0" to gays and lesbians on a 0-100 feeling thermometer						
ACP		–	58.9	38.9	38.8	26.7	33.6
CP		–	48.4	34.4	32.2	22.7	24.9
Non		–	26.3	17.4	14.9	8.4	9.7

Note: ACP = attending conservative Protestant; CP = conservative Protestant; Non = all other Canadians and Americans (non-conservative Protestants).

Source: Project Canada Series and American National Election Studies Series (various years).

There is a rapid drop in negative valuations between 1984 and 1992, and then some levelling among CPs. As a result of the levelling after 1992, American CPs seem to have greater antipathy for homosexuals than do their Canadian counterparts in recent years, although the data are not directly comparable. American CPs are also in sharper contrast with non-CPs than their Canadian counterparts are with most Canadians. The difference between CPs and non-CPs is greater in the United States than in Canada, in spite of the fact that non-CP Americans are more conservative than are their Canadian counterparts. Furthermore, Canadian attitudes seem to be changing a bit more rapidly, although differences are not large.

To the degree that these questions tap increasing civility, it shows support for the claim that North Americans are rapidly becoming more civil towards homosexuals. Why the rapid change? Three factors come into play. First, the shifting depiction of homosexuals in the media likely plays a role (Wilcox and Wolpert 2000). In the 1990s, television shows like *Roseanne* and *Melrose Place* and movies like *Philadelphia* presented homosexuals in positive ways, while talk show hosts Ellen DeGeneres and Rosie O'Donnell normalized same-sex relationships. Second, increased personal contact with openly LGBT individuals likely decreases negative attitudes towards them (Wilcox and Wolpert 2000). Third, court decisions that framed same-sex marriage as a human right likely increased the legitimacy of homosexuality. This is particularly true in Canada, argues Matthews (2005), where the Supreme Court decision seemed to promote broad acceptance of both the human-rights framing of the issue and the final decision of the courts and legislature, culminating in the same-sex marriage law on 20 July 2005. For evangelicals, these external social influences[7] are coupled with some evangelicals, like Tony Campolo, who are calling for greater civility towards homosexuals, and the total effect is clearly a decreasing antipathy.

In sum, evangelicals are claiming warmer feelings towards homosexuals, although these feelings are not as warm as are those of non-evangelicals. All this, of course, says nothing about attitudes towards diverse sexual acts and conjugal arrangements. It may be that attitudes towards issues like homosexual sex and same-sex marriage are not changing in the same way as are attitudes towards individuals. I look first at the limited data available on same-sex marriage.

While there are no matching items related to same-sex marriage across the two countries in the datasets, the GSS does ask if respondents agree or disagree that "homosexuals should have the right to marry." In the United States, fewer than 4 percent of ACPs and 10 percent of CPs agree with the statement, as compared to 25 percent of non-evangelicals in the United States. Comparable numbers from the 2005 ProCan data show that 1 percent of ACPs, 13 percent of CPs, and 51 percent of non-evangelical Canadians approve of same-sex marriage.[8] It is clear from the data that evangelicals distinguish themselves in their rejection of same-sex marriage and that differences between evangelicals in the two countries are small. The contrast between the two countries in support for gay marriage comes almost entirely from the much higher levels of support among non-evangelicals in Canada.

In spite of their opposition to same-sex marriage, Canadian evangelicals resemble other Canadians in fully embracing values of diversity and individual rights. For example, 84.5 percent of ACPs and 80.5 percent of CPs agree that "racial and cultural diversity is a good thing for Canada" (82.5 percent of non-evangelicals agree). Further, 94.1 percent of ACPs and 95.4 percent of CPs agree that "I am willing to at least tolerate how other people choose to live their lives," which is equal to non-evangelicals (94.0 percent). The majority of evangelicals even agree that "homosexuals are entitled to the same rights as other Canadians" (ACP 61.9 percent, CP 68.4 percent), although they fall below national levels on this item (82.1 percent for non-evangelicals), which is likely related to their opposition to same-sex marriage. Evidently, for evangelicals, rejection of same-sex marriage is not incompatible with certain pluralistic values (this tension is discussed in greater detail below).

GSS and ProCan ask respondents about their attitudes towards homosexual, premarital, and extramarital sex (with almost identical wording).[9] Table 4.3 shows not only the percentages across selected years of the surveys but also the slope and the grand mean across all the years of the survey.

TABLE 4.3

Attitudes towards sexual issues in Canada and the US, 1975-2005

ProCan (1975-2005)	1975	1985	1995	2005	Grand mean	Slope
Same-sex adults having sex "always wrong" (%)						
ACP	97.2	98.0	96.2	86.5	3.87	−.006
CP	80.5	89.7	75.3	70.6	3.53	−.009
Non	61.1	60.2	41.7	27.4	2.76***	−.040
Premarital sex "always wrong" (%)						
ACP	72.2	66.0	83.0	74.7	3.55	.001
CP	48.3	48.7	53.4	51.4	2.82	−.004
Non	16.8	13.0	9.2	8.5	1.76***	−.015
GSS (1974-2004)	1974	1985	1996	2004		
Same-sex adults having sex "always wrong" (%)						
ACP	86.5	96.8	95.5	90.2	3.87	−.002
CP	86.0	89.9	82.8	78.4	3.65	−.009***
Non	69.1	69.5	52.4	49.6	3.10***	−.022***
Premarital sex "always wrong" (%)						
ACP	65.0	67.6	69.7	66.1	3.41	.000
CP	49.4	44.8	44.2	51.9	2.82	−.006***
Non	28.3	22.1	17.3	17.6	2.09***	−.013***

Note: ACP = attending conservative Protestant; CP = conservative Protestant; Non = all other Canadians and Americans (non-conservative Protestants). Significance: *.05 **.01 ***.001. Significance in the "grand mean" column indicates a significant difference between Canadian and US averages. Significance in the "slope" column in the US indicates that the change over time is statistically significant.

Source: Project Canada Series and the General Social Surveys (various years).

The means are based on scales that range from 1 (never wrong) to 4 (always wrong), and the slope is the average yearly change in the mean. Looking at the first row, we see that ACPs in Canada are almost unanimous in their conviction that homosexual sex is always wrong, with a minor decrease in this unanimity in recent years, as the slight negative slope indicates (−.006). The ACP means are identical in Canada and the United States (3.87). CPs are softening their views on homosexual sex at a slightly higher rate (slope of −.009), but this change is insubstantial compared to the change among non-CPs (−.040). Thus, among CPs, the rapid change in attitudes towards homosexual *individuals* does not correspond to a similar change in attitudes towards sexual *issues*. For non-CPs, there is rapid change towards both issues and individuals. Similar patterns are evident in conservative Protestant attitudes toward extramarital sex and abortion.[10]

The story in the United States is surprisingly similar for ACPs and CPs. The means and the slopes are very similar. However, non-CP Canadians are consistently less conservative than are non-CP Americans, mainly because they have liberalized more quickly. Overall, the main point is that the rapidly changing evangelical attitudes towards homosexual *individuals* are not matched by changes in attitudes towards sexual *issues*.

Three other conclusions can be drawn from this table. First, note that there are only minor differences between evangelicals in the two countries. If evangelicals take their queues from their national context, then we should see a more liberal Canadian brand of evangelicalism, but this is not the case here. The data show continuity between evangelicals in the two countries, both in means and slopes.

Second, there is a general pattern of evangelical stability and non-evangelical liberalization towards homosexual and premarital sex. While evangelical attitudes towards homosexual sex have changed slightly over time, these slopes are not substantial even if they reach significance due to large samples. Again, the magnitude of the (non-evangelical) change in attitudes towards homosexual relations dwarfs other changes in the table.

Third and finally, the gap between evangelicals and non-evangelicals is increasing in both countries, but it is doing so much more quickly in Canada. In recent years, the gap between Canadian evangelicals and non-evangelicals has been consistently larger than the comparable gap in the United States. Based on the size of the gap alone, one would predict greater tension between evangelicals and non-evangelicals in Canada than in the United States, which brings the religious and political climate in the two countries into sharper contrast.

Discussion

The move towards "civility without compromise" among rank-and-file evangelicals in Canada (and the United States) started long before news broke of the Haggard scandal. Greater civility towards homosexuals is part of a twenty-five-year trend. Discomfort with homosexual individuals is plummeting – much faster than is discomfort with other types of individuals, and it is doing so at the same rate for evangelicals as for most other Canadians. Yet, evangelicals remain fairly unyielding in their strictures against same-sex sexual practice and same-sex marriage.[11] American evangelicals follow the same trends as do Canadian evangelicals, although they are warming to homosexuals at a slower rate. I think these incompatible findings are best understood as a pragmatic solution to the tension that exists between competing identities.

On the one hand, Canadian evangelicals, as Canadians, embrace values of diversity, pluralism, and individual rights; on the other hand, as evangelicals, they hold to sexual strictures and the protection of the traditional family. The easiest way to balance these competing identities seems to be a pragmatic one: evincing civility towards individuals with same-sex orientations, while rejecting same-sex marriage and non-heteronormative sexual practices. I think a similar argument could be made in the United States, even if there is less pressure to embrace pluralism and to celebrate diversity there than there is in Canada.

Sexual attitudes, particularly views on homosexuality and same-sex marriage, are symbolic for evangelicals. An uncompromising stance on sexual issues is a way of publicly confirming one's evangelicalism, even if the idiosyncrasies of life are not as black and white. There is plenty of evidence for what New Paradigm thinkers have called a "loose coupling" between rhetoric and actual practice in all types of institutions (Powell and DiMaggio 1991), including evangelical ones. For example, Chaves (1997) argues that a denomination's position on women's ordination has less to do with theological differences than with siding with like-minded conservative denominations. Women's ordination is a symbolic issue through which conservative groups identify themselves in relation to other conservative groups. Another example is the lip service paid to male headship, alongside a pragmatic egalitarianism that exists in evangelical marriages (Gallagher 2003; Bartkowski 2001; Wilcox 2004). Similarly, evangelicals consider themselves strongly pro-life, even if they think women should be permitted legal abortions in certain circumstances. A strong stance on such issues can be seen as an example of symbolic orthodoxy, used by evangelicals to affirm subcultural boundaries and to "flag" their position on the conservative side of socio-religious space. If this tendency can be applied to views on homosexuality, practical responses may be more civil than US publicized rhetoric suggests. Thus, we see a pragmatic "loose coupling" in attitudes towards *issues* and *individuals*. By holding conservative positions on issues, evangelicals "flag" their position in socio-religious space and reconfirm their evangelical identity. They may even support politically active groups that seek to preserve the traditional family. Yet, they seem to opt for compassion, or at least for civil interaction, with individuals.

What of the future? There are some signs that it is difficult for evangelicals to avoid compromise on sexual issues. While there is not enough evidence yet to suggest a clear trend, Table 4.3 gives some evidence of weakening strictures towards homosexual relations after the year 2000. One wonders if this boundary will erode in light of the growing scientific literature that refutes the notion that homosexuality is a personal choice.[12] However, the gap between evangelicals and non-evangelicals on sexual issues is growing in both countries, so it is undoubtedly premature to predict the end of political conflicts over sexual issues.

5

The Pro-Family Movement in Canada and the United States
Institutional Histories and Barriers to Diffusion

TINA FETNER AND CARRIE B. SANDERS

The US pro-family movement has achieved outstanding success. It has great influence in politics, education, culture, and law, and it has inserted a religious frame into political discourse, in a country in which one of the founding principles is the separation of church and state. As a result of the activism of the pro-family movement, Americans have limited access to abortion, limits on adoption and foster care by lesbians and gay men, restrictions on access to birth control, and constraints on the sexual education curriculum that exceed controls in Canada, Australia, and parts of Western Europe. There has also been widespread refusal by states and the federal government to legally recognize same-sex marriage or partnerships, with only a few states granting full marriage rights to same-sex couples. The pro-family movement in the United States is a well-oiled machine, highly integrated with the Republican Party (Wilcox 1992).

The pro-family movement in Canada has not reached the powerful heights of its counterpart in the United States. Although pro-family organizations exist in Canada and are actively mobilizing for conservative social change, they have not yet produced much policy success. Is it possible that this change is on Canada's horizon? Will the pro-family movement in Canada find strength, perhaps using some of the massive resources of its American counterpart, to achieve the same socially conservative policies that have been set in place in the United States?

We argue that the Canadian pro-family movement is significantly different from the American movement and that it is unlikely to gain a great deal
of political influence in the near future. The institutional supports of the
pro-family movements in Canada and the United States are markedly different, with the American movement relying on an extensive and densely net-
worked set of organizations, and the Canadian movement relying on a set of
institutions that are smaller, have fewer resources, and are only loosely tied
together in networks. For Canada, this means more difficulty in reaching
constituents, in mobilizing action, and in communicating pro-family claims.
We argue that the roots of these institutional differences lie in the historical
institution-building projects of evangelical Christian communities in the
middle of the twentieth century. American evangelicals had a unique path of
community growth, which led to their great strength in supporting social
movements decades later.

To explain the difference in political influence, we first briefly present
Miriam Smith's (2007, 2008) argument regarding the greater resistance to
pro-family activism on the part of Canada's political institutions. While we
agree with Smith's conclusions, we argue that there are also differences in
the social movements themselves in these two countries – differences that
are not readily apparent from the activities of the movements today. Rather,
we argue that a historical analysis reveals that pro-family activists in Canada
have a much weaker institutional structure supporting their activism than
do American activists.

Turning our analytical attention to a historical period of peak growth in
evangelicalism in both Canada and the United States, 1920 to 1950, we demonstrate that the development of evangelical communities in Canada was
different from their development in the United States with regard to the
degree of *factionalism*, *withdrawal*, and *institution building*. These three
differences, we argue, are key for understanding why Canadian pro-family
movements, although adopting the same rhetoric, claims, collective identity, and issue frames as American evangelical Christians, have not been as
socially or politically strong as has the American pro-family movement.

Political Institutions: One Key Difference

Smith (2007, 2008) argues convincingly that the political institutions in
Canada are more resistant to socially conservative activism than are those in
the United States. While the parliamentary system in Canada makes room
for ideological diversity by including multiple political parties, controversies within parties are for the most part suppressed, especially when policy

votes are taken. In contrast, the United States' two-party political system creates more opportunities for controversy within parties. Party legislators are allowed to vote as individuals, and the power within parties is distributed throughout the fifty states. This creates points of entry for activists wishing to influence party politics, and, in fact, it was through state parties that pro-family activists got their foothold in the Republican Party in the late 1980s and early 1990s.

Smith goes on to argue that Canada's Charter of Rights and Freedoms has created impediments for pro-family activism by extending rights to lesbians and gay men as a group (Smith 2005b). The focus of the Charter, Smith points out, was to quell conflict between Quebec and anglophone Canada. This set the stage for a language of inclusion and equality for all. Although the Charter does not refer to lesbian and gay people directly, its human rights guarantees have set the stage for Canadian courts to consistently rule in favour of granting equal rights to this group. In the United States, constitutional rights jurisprudence has a more erratic pattern when it comes to issues such as lesbian and gay rights, creating more openings for Christian right interveners.

Another major explanation for Canadian-American contrasts in political influence is the drastic difference in the proportion of each population that is conservative evangelical. The far greater institutional strength of the movement organizations in the United States, however, goes beyond the explanatory power of factors associated with religiosity or with the institutional factors discussed to this point. To an important extent, this strength is rooted in the resource base built up over decades by communities that support pro-family activism.

In the United States, conservative evangelical churches, para-church organizations, and the networks that connect them are massive, and the largest organizations bring in revenue streams that are far beyond the capacity of similar Canadian organizations. American pro-family organizations reach millions of constituents and have large budgets. For example, Focus on the Family has revenues of around $120 million annually, and its flagship radio program, featuring James Dobson, reaches tens of millions of listeners (Preslar 2006). Concerned Women of America reports revenues of $10 million annually (PFAW 2006). And Pat Robertson's media conglomerate, the Christian Broadcast Network, brought in revenues of $230 million as far back as 1986 (Oldfield 1996, 99). In contrast, the Evangelical Fellowship of Canada reported a budget of $3.5 million in 1997 (Feiguth 2004). A major source of the differences in both size and strength of pro-family organizations in the

United States and Canada can be traced to the formation of conservative evangelical organizations in the early and middle decades of the twentieth century.

Twentieth-Century Evangelicalism in the United States and Canada

In the United States, theological disputes led to a high degree of factionalism among evangelicals from the early twentieth century. One of the key disputes was over how churches dealt with changes associated with modernity, especially scientific advances that challenged a literal reading of the Bible. Among Protestants in the United States, feuds erupted, and anti-modernist groups split off from mainline denominations. In other cases, fundamentalists were rejected by mainlines. For example, in 1933, the Presbyterian Church USA expelled a group of fundamentalists, who formed new churches, including the Bible Presbyterian Church, led by Reverend Carl McIntyre, a prominent leader of the anti-modern fundamentalist movement. In this major rift, there emerged a wave of new churches that rejected modern science and insisted that biblical literalism was a necessary part of the Christian faith. These new groups included the Moody Bible Institute, the Bible Institute of Los Angeles, Youth for Christ, and many others (Carpenter 1980). These churches not only rejected mainline Protestant denominations but also the secular world more generally. Attempts to repair the factionalism in evangelical Christianity while supporting its separation from the secular sphere led to the establishment of para-church organizations, an institution-building project that was not intended to support secular political activism but that, decades later, did just that. For example, theological institutes like Bob Jones University and the Dallas Theological Seminary were founded to train anti-modernist evangelical clergy (Diamond 1995, 93). These fundamentalist groups faced public scorn, which may have contributed to their separatist goals.

Unlike their mainline Protestant counterparts, fundamentalist churches flourished in the period between the First World War and the Second World War, through the Great Depression. Some historians argue that this popularity was partly a product of fundamentalists' vision of the rapture, which, for true believers, was to provide relief from the End Times, which were understood to be close at hand (Sandeen 1970). This core belief produced an emphasis on individual morality and personal salvation as a way out of the dire material circumstances of the day. At the same time, this emphasis encouraged fundamentalists to avoid temptation in the secular world.

Among Canadian evangelicals, there was a much smaller and less successful movement to reject modernity, which led to there being less factionalism among evangelicals in Canada than in the United States. The institution building that resulted in the Canadian evangelical community was tied more closely to denominations and to the secular sphere. While Canadian para-church organizations play an important role within the evangelical community today, they do not provide an institutional infrastructure for the pro-family movement that is comparable to the massive apparatus that supports that movement in the United States. Below, we discuss the differences between these institution-building projects with regard to factionalism, withdrawal, and institution building.

Factionalism

Changes in the modern world created a schism in the American Protestant church, which grew greatly in the 1920s. Sweeping demographic changes in the United States, such as the influx of Roman Catholic and Jewish immigrants from southern and eastern Europe, pushed diverse religious views into American life (Smith 1998). Biblical criticism and liberal theologies began to challenge orthodoxies. Scientific advances such as the theory of evolution challenged a literal interpretation of the Bible, and the scientific community began to reject the integration of biblical teachings with scientific theory. While mainline Protestant denominations generally adapted to this changing world, moving away from biblical literalism and embracing scientific discovery, some conservative Protestants decided to fight these changes both in the church and in secular society. Around the turn of the century, these resisters became known as fundamentalists, the name deriving from a tract entitled *The Fundamentals* (Smith 1998). At first, fundamentalists focused their challenge on the Protestant church, attempting to replace existing leaders. When these efforts failed, many fundamentalists decided to break off from what became known as mainline American Protestantism to form their own churches.

Rather than come together to create a conservative, anti-modern denomination, American fundamentalists' obsession with doctrinal purity and their refusal to work together with those whose biblical interpretations differed from their own led to innumerable stand-alone, neighbourhood churches that belonged to no denomination whatsoever. Major disputes included beliefs in dispensation (rapture) and embodied worship practices such as speaking in tongues. Additional factionalism was caused by different beliefs in prophecies about the timing of Armageddon and interpretations of natural disasters (Wuthnow 1993). While some fundamentalist leaders rejected dancing, drinking, and card playing, others were less concerned with these issues. Single preachers in neighbourhood churches routinely determined the theocratic direction of their congregations. This factionalism did not hamper the growth of fundamentalism in the United States. Indeed, throughout the 1930s, independent fundamentalist churches proliferated.

As Robert A. Wright (1990) notes, Canadian Protestants also went through a period of disruption in this era. Between 1921 and 1941, mainline Protestant organizations shrank while evangelical churches, such as Pentecostals and independent fundamentalists, grew (140-41). This break was largely along class lines, with the greatest amount of support for breakaway churches coming from the "slightly lower than average socio-economic strata of Canadian society" (158; see also Christie and Gauvreau 1996). There was a good deal of immigration from the United States to Canada, and especially to the Canadian Prairies, and some of the growth in Canadian evangelicalism is the result of Americans moving north. Robert Burkinshaw (1995, 318) notes that, in 1911, 22 percent of Albertans were from the United States, and that number had grown to 50 percent by the 1920s.

The major Protestant denominations (Anglican, Methodist, Presbyterian, and Baptist) in Canada during the late nineteenth and early twentieth centuries had considerable intellectual, social, and cultural influence, but they grew too "large, bureaucratic and ill-equipped to cope with the accelerated change. As a result, Protestant church life in Canada in the years between the Wars was marked by considerable stress and fragmentation" – divided not only by theology but also by religion, class, and ethnicity (Wright 1990, 139; Airhart 1990, 131).

These similarities in the religious concerns of Canadians and Americans might cause one to expect a similar process of disintegration and factionalism in Canada. However, this was not the case. Instead of splitting apart from each other, Canadian Protestant leaders responded to this crisis of modernity by mobbing in the opposite direction, consolidating several of their denominations into a single, larger church. Years of collaboration to resolve or minimize theological disputes resulted in the formation of the United Church of Canada in 1925, combining two-thirds of Presbyterian congregations, most Methodists, as well as smaller denominations and more independent Protestant churches, and accounting for about 20 percent of the Canadian population (Wright 1990).

The United Church was theologically open-minded, placed emphasis on Christian unity, and became a vehicle for international fellowship and peace advocacy (see Airhart 1990; Wright 1990). Like Wright (1990), we argue that the United Church of Canada reorganized mainline Protestantism in a way that may have mitigated some of the disillusionment with Protestantism that fundamentalists in the United States were feeling. This effort, we argue, demonstrated a uniquely Canadian spirit of moderation, rejecting the extremes of conservative evangelicalism while creating room for conservative views in mainline Protestantism. The United Church of Canada's ecumenical make-up can be interpreted as a demonstration of the tolerance for diversity and the distaste for factionalism in Canadian Protestantism during this era (Reimer 2003).

This Canadian preference for cooperation and moderation may well have been in response to the factionalism of American fundamentalist leaders at the time. As Nancy Christie and Michael Gauvreau (1996, 18) point out, the debates about social reform and Christianity that were most important to Canadians took place in the context of similar debates in the United States and Britain. Where individualistic approaches to church formation in the United States led pastors to emphasize theological disputes and differences between churches, Canadian approaches to evangelicalism were decidedly more community oriented. This revealed itself in Canadian evangelicals' adherence to denominations and their focus on building a broad Protestant community. It was also demonstrated by the Canadians' more liberal vision of evangelicalism, focusing less on individual salvation and more on Christian principles of social reform, including poverty relief, education, and brotherhood. The voices of social progressives were much louder in Canada, and their views prevailed when it came time to reorganize and re-energize evangelical Christians. Whereas the most conservative views inspired a mass following among American evangelicals, it was the more moderate and socially progressive views that working-class Canadian evangelicals responded to most positively at this time of transition and economic hardship.

Seymour Martin Lipset (1964) might have included this difference as one more example of the parting of the ways of American and Canadian culture caused by the American Revolution. From Lipset's perspective, the American Revolution set the cultural values for the United States as centring on independence and mistrust of authority. Canada's ongoing relationship with the British created a culture that was less extremely individualistic and more focused on community (for dissenting views, see Baer, Grabb, and Johnston 1990, 1993). Given that theological leaders of both conservative and progressive bents were present in both countries, and that Americans flocked to the former while Canadians followed the latter, this example supports Lipset's view about Canadian and American cultures. Whatever the reason for this difference, however, it resulted in very different paths of community development and institution building among evangelicals in Canada and those in the United States.

Withdrawal

In the United States, while conservative fundamentalists split off from Protestant denominations, they also retreated from the secular world more generally. American fundamentalist leaders were wary of secular culture, warning of the sinful character of, for example, popular music. Many leaders also claimed that popular culture was an avenue for communist infiltration (Wilcox 1987). Fundamentalists in this era were so emphatic about doctrinal purity that they rejected not only liberal theology but also association with anyone who subscribed to such theology. This led to rather extreme efforts at isolation from other Protestant denominations as well as from the larger society. Christian Smith (1998, 9) characterizes American fundamentalists in this era as "reclusive and defensive," suspicious of much both inside Protestantism and in the larger culture. Their preoccupation was individual virtue and morality.

A few Canadian fundamentalist leaders certainly denounced the culture of the day as sinful. However, while some leaders urged followers to refrain from dancing and playing card games, for the most part Canadian fundamentalists wanted to change the world around them rather than withdraw from it (Stackhouse 1993, 1994, 1997). This engagement took the form of missionary work, social activism, and electoral politics (see Burkinshaw 1994, 1995; Wright 1990). The personal and emotional experiences of religion were integrated with a social evangelism that combined conversion with service to the community. The willingness of Canadian mainline denominations to personalize the religious experience while retaining a social focus meant that they were able to retain a broader range of adherents than were their American counterparts (Wright 1990).

One Canadian figure who encouraged Canadian evangelicals to withdraw from secular life was Thomas Todhunter (T.T.) Shields, a passionate advocate of abstaining from "worldly amusements" (Stackhouse 1993, 1997). Shields was one of the first Canadians to lead fundamentalists out of the Baptist Convention of Ontario and Quebec in the 1920s and to establish and build two mainstream evangelical institutions: the Toronto Baptist

Seminary, which served as the denomination's training school, and the Canadian Protestant League, which acted to spread the doctrines and principles of the Protestant Reformation (Stackhouse 1993, 29). Although Shields' efforts seemed successful at first – in 1941 the Canadian Protestant League had over eighteen hundred members – this effort failed after a few years. In 1949, Shields was forced out of the presidency and withdrew from his church (Stackhouse 1993). By 1950, Shields found himself isolated throughout Canadian religious affairs. This spoke to Canadian evangelicals' preference for engagement with the secular world.

A prominent proponent of Christian evangelicals' political engagement was William Aberhart, founder of the Prophetic Bible Institute. Aberhart launched a Calgary radio broadcast of his sermons in 1929 that rapidly expanded to five hours of Sunday broadcasting to stations across Alberta, with an estimated listening audience of 350,000 (Stackhouse 1993, 39). Although Aberhart characterized his church as "extreme fundamentalist," he did not follow the American path of retreating from the public sphere. In fact, Aberhart's political aspirations led him to form the Social Credit Party, which won the 1935 provincial election, making him premier of Alberta. He won a second election in 1940 and remained in office for the rest of his life, until 1943 (Barr 1974). Aberhart's political career was not supported by all in his church. Nonetheless, this criticism neither deterred his church's engagement with the secular political sphere nor affected his popularity to a great degree.

While there were Canadian evangelicals like Shields who wished to escape modernism, this was not the preoccupation that it was on the American side of the border. Because Canadian evangelicals did not demonize modernism to the same degree as did American evangelicals, the Canadian evangelical experience was not so beholden to the idea of separating from the secular world. Consequently, Canadian evangelicals did not need as many institutions to replace secular educational and cultural institutions as did American evangelicals (Reimer 2003).

Institution Building

During this period of retreat and isolationism, a movement emerged in the United States that sought to unite the various factions within American fundamentalist Christianity. Over the period between 1920 and 1950, a major institution-building project was undertaken by a set of reformers. These reformers called themselves neo-evangelicals, and their work sought to unite the conservative Christian community in the United States. They shared the fundamentalists' distrust of the corruptive effect of secular influences and sought common ground by ignoring the minutiae of theological interpretations. The neo-evangelicals built the foundation for what would become the American evangelical Christian community, bringing together leaders who had in the past fought each other over doctrinal issues. They sought common ground among various factions by emphasizing important similarities among them: a belief in biblical literalism and pre-millennial dispensationalism (the rapture) and its corresponding distrust of modernity. Over time, many new institutions were formed to support these conservative, evangelical Christian beliefs, allowing Christian communities to thrive apart from secular institutions in the realms of education, politics, and media.

Over several decades in the middle of the twentieth century, American neo-evangelicals created a wide variety of para-church organizations. They were not tied to any denomination and were unique in size and scope. Most remain active today, serving more constituents than similar denominational organizations (Apostolidis 2000; Carpenter 1984; Marsden 1980; Ostling 1984). For example, evangelical Christians have established missionary organizations, providing both young people and entire families with opportunities to travel, schools at every level from pre-kindergarten to postsecondary, and youth ministries that provide after-school evangelical education, summer camps, and Sunday school events (Carpenter 2000). Most of these institutions are self-sustaining, for-profit ventures. Because they are not limited by denomination, they can and do provide services to a wide array of evangelical Christians, regardless of the doctrinal theology of their particular congregation. These para-church institutions have formulated and entrenched a broadly defined Christian identity that is distinct from mainline Protestantism.

The National Association of Evangelicals (NAE), formed in 1942, embraced evangelical-leaning churches from a variety of denominations as well as non-denominational churches. The NAE created a very broad umbrella of conservative Christians, bringing together fundamentalists, Pentecostals, and Charismatics (Diamond 1995). Its membership included the Fundamentalist Baptist Fellowship, the General Association of Regular Baptist Churches, the Orthodox Presbyterian Church, the Bible Presbyterian Church, and the Independent Fundamental Churches of America. It created cohesion among a wide group of conservative Christians that, previously, had not existed (Carpenter 1984). The American neo-evangelicals believed, as fundamentalists did, that the secular world was sinful and corrupting, so they put much effort into building a variety of conservative Christian institutions to replace those in the secular sphere.

In addition to creating a network for conservative evangelical churches, the NAE advocated for its members by working to secure positions for evangelical chaplains in the military, providing support to missionaries overseas, and advocating for policy. This one institution created and maintained a network for evangelicals both inside and outside denominations, and it supported the development of specialized institutions to provide services and to build communities for conservative evangelicals. These ranged from Bible camps and family missionary trips to massive conferences for independent clergy. One of the biggest sets of institutions supported by the NAE was a wide variety of media organizations that independently produced and promoted information on numerous topics, all of which supported a literal reading of the Bible and a belief in the End Times. These sources of information combined to create a conservative, evangelical body of knowledge.

The growth of evangelical Christian media over the twentieth century was profound. Evangelical revivals were broadcast directly over the radio to rapidly growing audiences (Apostolidis 2000). In the 1920s and 1930s, radio evangelism expanded dramatically; stations could be found anywhere in the country and at just about any time of day. Here, too, institutionalization spread rapidly. The NAE established its official radio arm in 1944, the National Religious Broadcasters. By 1983, the National Religious Broadcasters had over nine hundred radio station members (Ostling 1984). Evangelical Christians also built extensive print production facilities for Christian pamphlets, magazines, and books, and Christian bookstores have provided outlets for these publications in a for-profit Christian print industry. These independent media organizations have often outpaced their denominational counterparts in terms of sales and readership. These include history, theological works, and popular fiction as well as Sunday school curricula. The Christian Booksellers Association, founded in 1950, has 2,055 member stores and reported revenues for Christian product sales of $4.63 billion in 2006 (CBA 2007). As for television, evangelical Christians have been wildly successful in creating popular shows and independent broadcasting networks. "Televangelism" was very popular by the 1970s, Billy Graham having set a precedent with his long-running *The Hour of Decision,* beginning in the early 1950s (Martin 1991).

The American evangelical Christians' large-scale development of church networks, Bible institutes, religious retreats, television and radio networks, videos, and a host of other Christian children's books, Bible study pamphlets, and so on, became the foundation for a strong pro-family movement (McAdam 1982; McCarthy and Zald 1977; Walsh 1981). From the beginning, in other words, the US pro-family movement had a solid organizational network, a distinctive Christian identity that imagined true Christians as outside the political and social mainstream, and a strongly held ideology of shared Christian values, such as a narrowly defined sexual morality, support for traditional gender hierarchies, and belief in the superiority of the male-headed nuclear family (Apostolidis 2000; Frankel 1998; Johnson 1998). In addition, American evangelicals had amassed incredible financial resources and membership numbers; they had also created wide information networks and an ideological consistency among their members that would turn out to serve their political ends very well (Diamond 1989).

By contrast, in Canada denominations remained central to the lives of fundamentalist Christians as well as to the establishment of para-church institutions. Rather than taking on the function of replacing denominations, as in the American case, the para-church institutions in Canada were supplementary, seeing themselves as bridges between denominations. Like their American counterparts, they were connected by a belief in "the evangelical basics," and they provided important services to the evangelical community, forming missionary societies, publishing houses, Sunday schools, and the like (Stackhouse 1993, 9). They were concerned with trans-denominational cooperation and sought to bring together Christians from different denominations.

The Toronto Bible College serves as a perfect example. It was first opened in 1894 and remained a prominent institution until 1964. It was Canada's largest Bible school east of the Prairies and was a major evangelical presence in Toronto. The college hosted a variety of missionary services that relied upon a trans-denominational, rather than an anti-denominational or a separatist, approach to evangelical practice (Stackhouse 1993, 10). It led the work of the Upper Canada Bible Society, the Upper Canada Tract Society, and the YMCA and the YWCA. It also played a significant role in the establishment of many social services and hospitals, such as the Home for Incurables (now known as Queen Elizabeth Hospital), the Haven for Fallen Women, and the Newsboys' Home (Stackhouse 1993, 54). The school's enrolment peaked in 1938 and 1939 with 380 students and remained strong through the mid-1950s (Stackhouse 1993, 66-67).

Canadian evangelical institution building focused largely on the provision of social services to the community at large rather than on creating an autonomous institutional sector. In particular, a number of voluntary societies emerged in the early to mid-twentieth century to provide trans-denominational cooperative action for evangelical Christians. There was some independent institution building. Canadian evangelical colleges and Bible schools were built to train preachers. However, according to Phyllis Airhart (1990), the school movement in evangelical Christianity was slower to develop in Canada than it was in the United States. A few media outlets were also created in this era. In addition to Aberhart's radio show mentioned above, the Christian Missionary Alliance's radio show was broadcast from Edmonton from 1927 until 1941 (Burkinshaw 1995). Other printing houses and, eventually, television shows emerged. The size and scope of these endeavours, however, was much more modest than in the United States.

Institutional Foundations of the Pro-Family Movement

In the United States, the rapid growth of fundamentalism and its corresponding factionalism, combined with a withdrawal from the secular world, set the stage for an intense project of institution building by evangelical Christians who wanted to unite like-minded, conservative Christians and create spaces separate from the modern world. This project laid the foundations of contemporary American evangelical Christianity. The vast network of para-church institutions created by American evangelicals may not have been intended to serve as an infrastructure for a political movement, but when the American pro-family movement emerged in the 1970s it certainly did serve that function (Fetner 2008). In contrast, the institutions built by Canadian evangelicals connected with both Protestant denominations and the political sphere, created a more moderate or even liberal-minded community of evangelical Christians, and were less suited to political mobilization by conservative Protestants (in particular).

Canadian evangelical networks are dominated by denominations that do not necessarily consider themselves part of the pro-family movement. In the United States, para-church networks are much more oriented to activism. In addition, the communications channels created by American evangelicals are much broader than in Canada, reaching a wide audience of readers, listeners, and viewers. In many cases, pro-family activists are welcomed on a wide variety of Christian media outlets to convey their messages. In other cases, the television and radio shows are themselves part of the pro-family movement. Although Canada has a rich tradition of Christian broadcast media, these media are both smaller and less tied to pro-family activism than are those in the United States.

Further, the difference in the strength of the pro-family movements in the United States and Canada is tied to important differences in the collective identities and social attitudes of the evangelical Christian communities in each nation. The Canadian ecumenical tradition has led to a less uniformly conservative Christian identity and more moderate social attitudes. While it is clear that there exists more variation in social attitudes among American evangelicals than pro-family activists would lead us to believe, overall the community does have more conservative attitudes and a strong Christian collective identity that reflects the stances of the pro-family movement.

Canadian pro-family activists, we argue, have faced a much more difficult road than have their American counterparts with regard to acquiring social change. This is because of (1) the divergent institutional foundations of American and Canadian pro-family movements, (2) the smaller proportion of evangelical Christians in the Canadian population, and (3) a set of political institutions that is more resistant to a conservative activist agenda. Thus, despite the diffusion of rhetoric, strategy, and organizations, the Canadian pro-family movement is in a weaker political position than is its American counterpart. Working in a more hostile political context, relying on a much weaker infrastructure, the Canadian pro-family movement has created much less policy change than one sees south of the border.

Evangelicals, the Christian Right, and Gay and Lesbian Rights in the United States
Simple and Complex Stories

CLYDE WILCOX AND RENTARO IIDA

In the 2008 US elections, voters in California, Arizona, and Florida amended their state constitutions to bar same-sex marriage. These votes were disappointing to GLBT activists in different ways: California allowed same-sex marriage for a short time and had a liberal electorate; Arizona, in 2006, had been the only state to ever defeat a marriage amendment; and Florida required a 60 percent threshold to adopt amendments. Most of the post-election coverage focused on California, where opposition to barring same-sex marriage had led in the polls. After the defeat of the California initiative, attention was focused on the voting behaviour of African Americans and the financial support of the Mormon Church.

However, in California, as in other states, the bigger story was the evangelical vote. The publicly released exit poll results showed that white evangelicals in California voted to bar same-sex marriage by 81 to 19, while the rest of the state voted to retain the marriage right by 52 to 48. In Arizona, the initiative to bar marriage won 83 percent of the votes of white evangelicals and 48 percent of the votes of the rest of the state combined. And, in Florida, the referendum carried overwhelmingly among white evangelicals but fell below the threshold with other voters. These exit polls underestimate the extent of evangelical support since many African-American and Latino(a) voters have evangelical theological views. One private poll commissioned after the California election showed that more than 75 percent of both African Americans and Latinos(as) identified as born-again.

Although same-sex marriage is largely a settled issue in Canada, it remains a matter of great controversy in the United States. Moreover, the United States lags behind Canada in enacting laws to bar employment and housing discrimination, to allow gays and lesbians to serve openly in the military, and to allow same-sex couples to adopt children. In order to explain the relatively conservative policies in the United States, many scholars point to the large number of evangelicals in that country and to the organized power of the Christian right (Bull and Gallagher 1996; Lunch 1995).

There is some truth to this simple story. Christian right groups are far more powerful in the United States than they are in Canada, and their target constituency – white evangelical Protestants – are three times more numerous in the former country than they are in the latter (see also Reimer, this volume). Christian right groups have mobilized strongly on same-sex marriage as well as on other sexual diversity issues. They amplify the voice of the most conservative evangelicals (Campbell and Robinson 2007; Wilcox 2000b).

Yet, like most simple explanations, this one overlooks a great deal. Religious coalitions on these issues are complex and diverse; for example, African-American and Latino(a) evangelicals do not support the Christian right, and same-sex marriage encounters opposition among some mainline Protestants, Catholics, Muslims, and, especially, Mormons. Moreover, evangelical Protestants hold diverse views on gay/lesbian/bisexual/transgender/queer (GLBTQ) issues: some support very restrictive policies, many more support some progressive policies, and some fully support equality.

In the end, it is again a simple story but a slightly different one from that commonly told. American public opinion has moved massively and quickly towards greater acceptance of sexual minorities, at a rate that is on par with earlier changes in racial and gender attitudes. And evangelicals are changing along with the rest of American society, although they began at a lower level of acceptance and retain that distinctiveness today. Moreover, the Christian right has never dominated American politics and is less powerful today than at any time in the past two decades. Recent defeats in the struggle for marriage equality are discouraging and make it seem that American policy is unchanging; yet, in the 1980s, political battles were over sodomy laws. That the United States is debating marriage rights for gays and lesbians is actually a sign of significant change in the politics of sexual diversity.

It's a Simple Story, Part 1: Evangelicals and the Christian Right Make the United States Distinctive

The United States has more conservative attitudes and policies towards sexual minorities than does Canada, in part because of the magnitude of the evangelical religious community. In the United States, white evangelicals constitute slightly more than a quarter of the population, African-American evangelicals add another 10 percent, and Latino(a) evangelicals perhaps another 2 percent. Moreover, many members of mainline Protestant denominations in the United States profess evangelical religious doctrine and attend congregations that would identify as evangelical (Wilcox 1986).

In the 1990s, evangelicalism had a similar impact on the attitudes of US and Canadian citizens towards GLBTQ rights, but, in recent years, American evangelicals have been more distinctively conservative than have those in Canada (Hoover et al. 2002). We can estimate the impact of the larger number of American evangelicals by simply weighting them to their portion in the Canadian population (Chandler et al. 1994). This procedure suggests that, if the United States had the same number of evangelicals as Canada, the three state constitutional amendments in 2008 would have been defeated, as would have several other state referenda in previous years.[1]

Not only does the United States have more evangelicals than Canada, but its most conservative evangelicals are also better organized. Christian right organizations have been active in US politics for thirty years, with considerable membership and money (Wilcox and Larson 2006). Surveys show that between 10 percent and 15 percent of the public have supported these organizations over time, although the number of active members is much lower. These organizations give extra voice to fundamentalist and Pentecostal evangelicals, and they help to frame the debate over sexual diversity issues for other religious populations, including observant mainline Protestants in the South and the Midwest and conservative Catholics nationwide.

Christian right publications regularly stoke fears of gays and lesbians among their members. In 1980, the Moral Majority mailed a "survey" to potential donors asking if they favoured forcing public schools that accepted federal funds to hire known, practising, and *soliciting* homosexual teachers.[2] In the 2008 elections, Focus on the Family posted on its website a hypothetical letter from the future to young evangelical voters, warning that the Obama presidency had created a world in which Boy Scouts were required to hire gay scoutmasters and to allow them to sleep in tents with young boys and in which Christian teachers were fired for not endorsing homosexuality in Grade 1. Another Christian right publication warned that the true agenda for gay rights groups was to "promote pedophiles as prophets of the new world order."

Christian right groups have sought to reframe equality claims by gays and lesbians, labelling efforts to end job discrimination as "special rights." When, in 2004, the Massachusetts state Supreme Court ruled that the state's constitution entitled same-sex couples to full marriage rights, Christian right groups quickly mobilized to frame the debate around the "defense of marriage." They worked to pass state initiatives to amend state constitutions, a move that has been highly successful (Campbell and Robinson 2007). Today, thirty states ban same-sex marriage in their constitutions (Shames, Kuo, and Levine, this volume).

Not surprisingly, surveys show that Christian right activists are hostile towards gays and lesbians and hold intolerant attitudes. In one survey in 2000, more than half of Christian right group members rated gays and lesbians at 0 degrees on a 100-point feeling thermometer – the coldest possible rating. And, although 60 percent of this highly educated activist population would allow gays and lesbians to demonstrate in their community, only 24 percent would allow them to teach in public schools (Wilcox 2010).[3] Fully 45 percent agreed with the statement that sodomy was a crime and that known homosexuals should be prosecuted.

There is, therefore, some truth in the common story of US GLBTQ rights policies. Evangelicals are more numerous in the United States than in Canada, and the Christian right is stronger and better organized. Yet, the story significantly oversimplifies the narrative of religious response to sexual diversity and of the diversity of response among evangelicals.

It's a Complex Story: Religious Coalitions and Evangelical Diversity

Diverse Religious Coalitions in the United States

Members of American evangelical denominations are not alone in opposing GLBTQ rights policies. Conservatives in other Christian denominations have joined evangelicals to lobby legislatures and to rally voters. Mormons have provided substantial financial resources to referenda opposing same-sex marriage, and Orthodox Jews and Muslims have also supported these efforts (Campbell and Robinson 2007).

For many years, white mainline Protestants dominated the political landscape, but in the United States, as in Canada, their congregations are aging and declining in numbers. In the United States, they are deeply divided on sexual diversity issues. The Episcopal Church has received the most attention, where breakaway congregations have aligned with a Nigerian bishop whose homophobic comments are only now being fully discussed in the United States. But Methodists, Presbyterians, and Lutherans are also divided over the ordination of gay or lesbian pastors as well as over doctrine on matters of sexual identity (see Olson, Djupe, and Cadge, this volume).

Many mainline churches in the South, the Midwest, and, especially in Appalachia preach evangelical doctrine, and these churches have higher attendance rates than do other mainline Protestant churches. The evangelically oriented among them are the ones most opposed to gay and lesbian rights. Among mainline Protestants who believe the Bible is inerrant, or literally true, and who attend church regularly, opposition to same-sex marriage is as high as it is among similar sets of evangelicals (although support is higher for anti-discrimination laws among the former than it is among the latter).

The Roman Catholic Church in the United States has endorsed laws that provide dignity and that bar discrimination against gays and lesbians, but it has also mobilized significant resources against same-sex marriage. In the United States, there is a considerable contingent of Catholics who have an evangelical worship style and even evangelical doctrine (Welch and Leege 1991). Among Catholics who attend infrequently and who do not have evangelical doctrinal beliefs, there is considerable support for gay rights; however, among the smaller subset who are observant and who endorse biblical literalism, opposition to GLBTQ equality is high. Latinos(as) constitute a rapidly growing portion of American Catholics, and they are especially conservative on gay and lesbian rights and especially likely to hold evangelical doctrinal views.

American Mormons constitute a relatively small portion of the electorate, but the church has mobilized effectively to support state constitutional amendments barring same-sex marriage, as they did earlier to block the national Equal Rights Amendment for women (Campbell and Monson 2007b). Mormon efforts in 2008 were probably critical in the passage of Proposition 8 in California, and some GLBTQ groups estimate that Mormons contributed more than $20 million to help fuel a late surge of advertising at a stage when the proposition trailed in the polls.

Finally, some non-Christian groups, including Muslims and Orthodox Jews, have mobilized their communities in opposition to various GLBT-friendly policies. The participation of these groups is sometimes obscured by the logic of internal coalitions: Muslims have generally not advertised their role in anti-marriage efforts because of friction with American evangelicals, but in some states they have played a key role (Campbell and Robinson 2007). Conservative Hindus have occasionally played a role as well.

These religious groups differ in their positions on many of the issues associated with homosexuality, and some favour anti-discrimination laws in housing. When the debate in the United States shifted rapidly to marriage, conservatives in every religious tradition worked together to pass laws and constitutional amendments. But some of these groups have sought to ban not only marriage but also civil unions and other legal protections, whereas others have focused on banning only marriage.

In each faith tradition, opposition to gay and lesbian rights is highest among those who attend church most frequently. It may be that moral conservatism leads to both higher rates of attendance and lower support for GLBT equality. Frequent attendance may also cause lower levels of support, especially among those who hear conservative messages about sexual minorities in their congregation. But there is also evidence that many younger Americans attend religious services less often because they perceive their church to be unfriendly to sexual minorities. In this way the causal relationship runs both ways – attendance may lead to conservative attitudes, but liberal attitudes combined with conservative sermons may lead to less attendance.

Diverse Evangelical Voices

American evangelicalism is a rich and diverse tradition that encompasses a variety of doctrinal and political positions. Evangelicalism includes a range of figures, from Pat Robertson to George W. Bush to Jimmy Carter to Jesse Jackson. Christian right groups support sharp reductions in spending on programs that benefit the poor, but liberal evangelicals like the Sojourners focus on biblical teachings that favour income redistribution (Wallis 1996). The National Association of Evangelicals has condemned torture of prisoners and policies that lead to global warming. Evangelicals are not a monolithic political bloc.

Evangelicals are united by a doctrine that the Bible is divinely inspired and without error. Nearly all evangelicals believe that sex outside of marriage is sinful. A substantial consensus exists among evangelicals that marriage is biblically ordained to be between one man and one woman, despite ample cases of polygamy in the Old Testament. Evangelical churches teach that sexual orientation is malleable and, thus, that gays and lesbians could choose to live as heterosexuals, while heterosexuals could similarly decide to engage in same-sex relationships.

Fundamentalist and Pentecostal churches take the stronger doctrinal view that the Bible is literally true, and they cite various passages of Leviticus in condemning GLBTQ sexual relationships. The Bible Baptist Fellowship proclaims this on its web page: "We believe that any form of homosexuality, lesbianism, bisexuality, bestiality, incest, fornication, adultery and pornography are sinful perversions of God's gift of sex." And it lists a variety of scriptural citations. The Assemblies of God position paper on homosexuality emphasizes the word *detestable,* and it devotes special attention to biblical accounts of attempted homosexual rape.[4]

In theory, most fundamentalists and Pentecostals believe that homosexuality is no different from adultery or fornication or any other form of sexuality outside of marriage. But many single it out for special condemnation. Some argue that God has specially punished societies that endorse sexual diversity, citing the story of Sodom and Gomorrah in Genesis.[5] Pat Robertson has repeatedly warned that natural disasters will be visited on gay-friendly cities and businesses. In part, fundamentalists emphasize homosexuality because, despite consistent and vehement denunciations, some of their children come out as gay or lesbian. If sexual orientation is voluntary and the church has repeatedly condemned sexual minorities, then this must mean that homosexuality is a powerfully attractive sin and that gays and lesbians seek to seduce young Christians (Wilcox and Larson 2006).

These doctrinal positions lead to opposition to gay and lesbian rights. The most conservative evangelicals oppose not only same-sex marriage and civil unions but also adoption rights and the right to serve openly in the military. They oppose laws protecting gays and lesbians from job discrimination, arguing that such laws would force evangelical small business owners to hire sinful employees.[6]

More moderate evangelicals focus on forgiveness and the possibility of change in sexual orientation, frequently citing the account of Jesus' forgiving an adulterous woman in the gospel of John. Some support various "ex-gay" ministries that try to turn the sexual orientations of sexual minorities towards heterosexuality (Erzen 2006). Others welcome sexual minorities to their services but not to membership in the congregation (at least not until they have renounced their "sinful lifestyle").

Most moderate and even liberal evangelicals maintain that homosexual sex is sinful, but many support various types of civil liberties for GLBTQ citizens, often distinguishing religious belief and public policy (Moore 2007; Wuthnow 2007). Liberal evangelicals such as Jim Wallis have long supported civil unions for same-sex couples, and former NAE vice-president Richard Cizik also publicly announced support for civil unions. Cizik's statement led to a firestorm of opposition from Christian right activists, and he resigned from his position in the organization. But his statement represents the position of increasing numbers of evangelicals who would reserve marriage for heterosexual couples but provide some form of recognition or protection for same-sex couples. Even among conservative evangelicals there is now growing support for equality in public life for gays and lesbians.

There are also ethnic divides among evangelicals. Although African-American evangelicals and white evangelicals share a common belief in the importance of scripture and regular worship, they construct the meaning of the Bible differently. African-American evangelicals are more supportive of women's social and political equality, and they have in the past been more supportive of anti-discrimination laws to protect sexual minorities (Thomas and Wilcox 1992). But African-American religious leaders have emphatically rejected comparisons between the GLBTQ movement and the civil rights movement that sought racial equality, and many have mobilized their churches in support of anti-marriage referenda (Campbell and Monson 2007a). Surveys have shown that Latino(a) evangelicals are quite conservative on issues such as marriage and adoption but less so on military service or anti-discrimination laws. All three groups are especially resistant to same-sex marriage.

In the pews, evangelicals struggle with reconciling a doctrine that condemns homosexuality with their personal experiences with GLBTQ family members, friends, and co-workers. This leads to a kind of "everyday theology" that is somewhat different from that preached in the pulpit (Moon 2004). As a consequence, many evangelicals attend churches that oppose gay rights policies but themselves hold views that are more moderate.

One indication of the changes in approach to sexual diversity can be found in Rick Warren's Saddleback Church. Before he was chosen to deliver a prayer at President Obama's inauguration, the church's website proclaimed the policy of welcoming members of sexual minorities to the congregation only when they have renounced their "sinful lifestyle." But this material was then removed, and assistant pastors have downplayed Warren's involvement in California's Proposition 8 campaign. More recently, Warren has denounced the actions of a former associate in Uganda, who has supported legislation that punishes homosexuality with life in prison or even death. Large evangelical mega-churches frequently avoid discussion of homosexuality since their well-educated and somewhat younger membership is divided, much like the membership of mainline Protestant churches.

The Complicated Story of Religion and Public Opinion

The complexity of religious coalitions and of evangelical attitudes is evident in data from public opinion surveys. Table 6.1 shows general orientations towards GLBTQ sexual activity and towards sexual minorities for members of different denominational traditions in the General Social Survey (2008) and the American National Election Studies (2008). Respondents are classified by denominational affiliation, with white evangelicals

TABLE 6.1

Basic orientations towards gays, lesbians, and sexual activity, by religious group and doctrinal view, 2008

	Gay sex always wrong (%)	Extramarital sex always wrong (%)	Know gays (%)	Rate homosexuals	
				0 degrees (%)	70+ degrees (%)
White evangelical	71	92	49	24	17
Attend regularly	87	96	44	29	14
Literal Bible	88	97	41	30	11
Black Protestant	74	87	45	19	24
Attend regularly	90	96	36	25	23
Literal Bible	80	92	38	21	24
White mainline	50	81	50	9	25
Attend regularly	65	89	45	8	31
Literal Bible	81	98	43	17	11
Catholic	46	82	53	9	29
Attend regularly	64	88	49	10	25
Literal Bible	69	93	48	18	23
Secular	23	66	56	9	29

Note: Thermometer scores range from a very cold zero (negative) to very warm (positive) of 100 degrees.

Source: General Social Survey and American National Election Studies (2008).

and black Protestants (most of whom are evangelicals) shown separately. For comparison, attitudes of white mainline Protestants, Catholics, and secular citizens (who list no religious affiliation) are also listed. Other religious traditions are not shown because there are too few cases in these data to reliably estimate attitudes.

The first line of data for each religious tradition shows all members. The next two lines for each group show attitudes for the subset of members who attend church regularly and for those who believe that the Bible is literally true, word for word.[7] The data show that a majority of Protestants and nearly half of Catholics think that sexual relations between two adults of the same sex are *always* wrong. Fewer than one-quarter of secular Americans share this view. But the second column shows that condemnation of extramarital sex for heterosexuals is much higher for every religious group. There is no doubt that, for many respondents, opposition to gay or lesbian sex is part of a more general opposition to sex outside of marriage; however, for many Americans, homosexual activity is seen as less morally problematic than are extramarital affairs.

White evangelicals and African-American Protestants are more likely to believe that same-sex activity is always wrong than are mainline Protestants and Catholics, and they are far more likely to do so than are seculars. This ordering holds among those who attend church regularly; however, white mainline Protestants who believe the Bible is literally true are as likely to oppose homosexual activity as are white evangelicals. Further analysis (not shown) suggests that, among mainline Protestants who do not hold evangelical theology, regular church attendance is not associated with more negative views of homosexuality. Among those who do believe that the Bible is literally true, more frequent attendance does lead to more negative views. Thus, regular attendance does not automatically lead to decreased support for equality; rather, it is attendance in congregations that proclaim the literal truth of scripture that does so.

There is little difference across religious groups in the percentage who say they have a close friend or family member who is gay. Among Protestants who believe the Bible is literally true, fewer know that they have a GLBTQ friend or family member, but many do have a personal contact who is GLBTQ.

Evangelicals frequently claim to love the sinner but hate the sin; however, this is not fully borne out by survey data. The ANES asked respondents to rate gays and lesbians (among other groups) on a feeling thermometer that ranges from 0 degrees to 100 degrees. The table shows those who rate gays

TABLE 6.2

Support for GLBT rights by religious group and doctrinal view, 2008

	Anti-discrimination laws (%)	Military service (%)	Adoption (%)	Same-sex marriage (%)	Civil unions (%)
White evangelical	66	73	40	25	25
Attend regularly	59	63	24	13	14
Literal Bible	60	69	28	13	22
Black Protestant	66	76	42	30	21
Attend regularly	60	69	28	16	22
Literal Bible	59	75	36	25	18
White mainline	76	79	49	31	32
Attend regularly	70	77	37	27	27
Literal Bible	68	63	27	14	25
Catholic	78	79	56	42	29
Attend regularly	76	74	47	28	29
Literal Bible	64	71	38	35	22
Secular	80	84	71	62	21

Source: American National Election Studies (2008).

and lesbians at 0 degrees (which is surely hating the sinner) and those who rate them at 70 degrees or more (not love but at least friendship). Here white evangelicals and African-American Protestants are distinctive in being among the high portion who rate gays and lesbians at 0 degree. Catholics, seculars, and mainline Protestants without fundamentalist theology are less hostile towards gays and lesbians and are more likely to rate them warmly.

But if evangelicals disapprove of homosexuality and rate gays and lesbians negatively, they also support at least some progressive policies. Table 6.2 shows that, in 2008, substantial majorities of all religious groups, regardless of attendance or doctrine, favoured banning employment discrimination and allowing gays and lesbians to openly serve in the military. The magnitude of this support is striking: nearly three in four of every religious group would allow gays and lesbians to serve openly in the military – a policy that was hotly disputed in 1992 when Bill Clinton sought to change military policy. Even among white evangelicals who believe the Bible is literally true, 60 percent support anti-discrimination laws.

Support for egalitarian family policy is lower for all religious groups, a pattern that exists for gender equality as well (Wilcox 1991). Only among Catholics and seculars is there majority support for allowing same-sex couples to adopt children. Support is lowest among regularly attending white and African-American evangelicals, though still around one-quarter of them support adoption (in 1992, only one in four of the entire country supported adoption). Support for marriage is even lower, with only one in eight frequently attending white evangelicals supporting marriage equality, and one in six frequently attending black Protestants doing so.

The ANES question also allowed respondents to indicate support for civil unions. Summing the last two numbers in each row shows the percentage that would permit some legal recognition of same-sex couples. More than 60 percent of white mainline Protestants support some sort of recognition of same-sex couples, as do half of white evangelicals and African-American Protestants. Among Catholics support increases to more than 70 percent, and among seculars it is more than 80 percent. For each religious group, support is lower among those who attend regularly or who believe the Bible is literally true, but even in these groups there are sizable minorities who favour some legal status for same-sex couples.

Evangelicals, then, are not a homogeneous bloc opposed to any protections for sexual minorities. There is very strong approval for equality for gays and lesbians in the public sphere and significant support for adoption and legal recognition of same-sex couples. This is true because of another underlying simple story: evangelicals live in a society in which attitudes are rapidly becoming more liberal.

The Simple Story, Part 2: A Rising Tide Lifts All Boats

Public support for gay and lesbian rights has increased dramatically over the past fifteen years. During this period there has been a remarkable increase in the number of Americans who realize that they know someone who is GLBTQ, and this enables them to understand the way these policy issues affect relatives, friends, and co-workers. In addition, the public has increasingly come to see sexual orientation as fixed, which makes discrimination difficult to justify (Wilcox, Merolla, and Beer 2007).

Since the 1990s, there has been a large overall shift in public attitudes towards gays and lesbians and towards homosexual activity. In 1988, fully 35 percent of Americans rated gays and lesbians at 0 on the 100-point feeling thermometer; in 2008, that figure was 13 percent. In 2008, more Americans

FIGURE 6.1

Changing support levels of religious groups on GLBT issues, 1988 and 2008

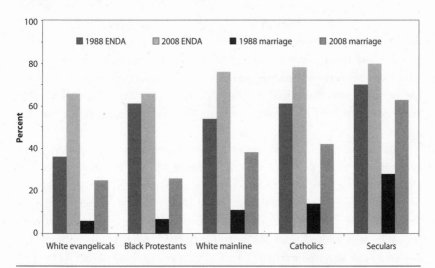

Source: American National Election Studies (1988, 2008); General Social Surveys (1988, 2008).

rated gays and lesbians at 85 degrees or more, indicating very warm feelings, than rated them at 0. A similar change has occurred in moral evaluations of gay and lesbian sex. In 1988, 76 percent of the public agreed that same-gender sexual activity was always wrong; in 2008, it was 51 percent. This change occurred during a period in which the public became even more negative towards extramarital sex, so it is not merely a liberalizing trend in sexual mores.

There has been remarkable change in attitudes on policy as well. Figure 6.1 shows the percentage of each religious tradition taking liberal positions on laws protecting sexual minorities from job discrimination and marriage discrimination.[8] Support for banning job discrimination has increased markedly among all groups except African-American Protestants, and the increase is largest for white evangelicals. Although support for marriage is far lower than for job equality, the change is in some ways more remarkable. White and African-American Protestants lag behind other religious communities in support for same-sex marriage in 2008, but both groups have experienced substantial increases in support over the past two decades. Similar trends exist for other policy issues, such as military service and adoption.

Younger Americans are much more likely than are those over sixty to say that they have several friends who are gay or lesbian; they are only half as likely as those over sixty to say that same-sex activity is always wrong; and they rate gays and lesbians more warmly on feeling thermometers. As the oldest and most conservative cohort dies off, it is being replaced by a cohort that is far more supportive of equality. Younger Americans are not markedly more permissive regarding extramarital sex, and they are less supportive of legal abortion than is the oldest cohort. So, once again, this generational pattern does not represent a general liberalization of sexual mores.

This generational divide exists among white and African-American evangelicals. The GSS data show that, compared to other Americans, the oldest evangelicals are least likely to know someone who is gay or lesbian, but the youngest evangelicals are more likely than are other Christian groups to have gay or lesbian friends or family members. Prominent evangelical leaders such as then NAE president Ted Haggard have publicly admitted to gay sex, and evangelical colleges now confront demands for gay and lesbian student organizations.[9]

The generation gap among young white evangelicals is perhaps best seen in feeling thermometer ratings of gays and lesbians. Among white evangelicals over sixty in the 2008 survey, 42 percent rate gays and lesbians at 0 degree, and only 7 percent rate them at 70 degrees or above. Among white evangelicals thirty or younger, only 8 percent rate gays and lesbians at 0, and more than 30 percent rate them at 70 or above. Moreover, nearly half of young white evangelicals in the 2008 GSS survey said that homosexual activity is *not* always wrong.

On policy issues, too, the coming generation of white evangelicals is markedly more liberal than is the cohort they are replacing. Table 6.3 shows combined data from the 2000-08 ANES surveys, broken down by religious tradition and age cohort. Combining the surveys allows for larger age cohorts in each tradition and therefore more reliable estimates. But it is important to remember that attitudes in 2008 are much more liberal than are those in 2000, so these averaged figures understate support for GLBTQ rights. What these data show is a pronounced generational gap on every issue. More than half of young white evangelicals over this period, for example, would allow same-sex couples to adopt (in the 2008 survey, this figure reaches nearly two-thirds).

Among young white evangelicals who say that their faith is important but who do not believe the Bible is literally true, attitudes are even more liberal

TABLE 6.3

Support for GLBT rights by religious group and age cohort, 2000-08

	Age	Anti-discrimination laws (%)	Military service (%)	Adoption (%)
White evangelicals	18-30	70	78	51
	31-45	61	74	37
	46-60	59	64	28
	61+	54	60	17
Black Protestants	18-30	65	79	46
	31-45	71	76	34
	46-60	71	68	31
	61+	62	54	21
White mainline	18-30	81	91	67
	31-45	72	87	63
	46-60	67	76	45
	61+	73	74	35
Catholics	18-30	79	80	63
	31-45	78	82	62
	46-60	80	85	54
	61+	74	75	39
Seculars	18-30	83	88	72
	31-45	81	84	66
	46-60	76	84	68
	61+	75	68	56

Source: American National Election Studies (2000-08).

than is seen in Table 6.3. These evangelicals are engaging issues of gay and lesbian rights inside their faith tradition, not outside it. More important, the liberalizing trends exist among white evangelicals who attend church weekly, among those who believe the Bible is inerrant, and among those who do both. This latter group is by far the least supportive of GLBTQ rights and the most hostile towards gays and lesbians. It is moving at a more glacial pace than the rest of the society, but it is moving. Even the most conservative evangelicals are increasingly aware that some family members are sexual minorities, and this creates the dissonance that allows for attitude change.

Generational differences are smaller for African-American Protestants than they are for white evangelicals. This is especially true regarding attitudes towards anti-discrimination laws, where blacks who came of age during the civil rights movement are far more supportive than are white evangelicals of the same age, but the pattern is reversed among the youngest cohort. In Table 6.3, the differences between the youngest white evangelicals and African-American Protestants are not great, but this is in part because the table averages across nearly a decade. In the 2008 survey, this gap widens, with significant liberalization among young white evangelicals but not among African Americans. The 2008 GSS and ANES do not have enough cases to confidently explain the source of this emerging racial gap among evangelicals, and additional surveys will be required to validate the trend. The data suggest that, although younger white evangelicals are increasingly likely to know gays and lesbians, this is not true of younger African-American Protestants. Those younger African-American Protestants who do not know gays and lesbians are especially negative in their evaluations of them.

Of course, this more egalitarian generation might change its attitudes as it ages or in response to period effects. All cohorts are now more conservative on abortion than they were twenty years ago, although the generations who came of age in the 1960s and after *Roe v. Wade* remain more supportive of abortion rights. Even the oldest cohorts have become more egalitarian in the past decade, so it seems unlikely that the youngest Americans, who have grown up with GLBTQ friends since high school or before, will suddenly reverse course. Generational replacement seems likely to move Americans towards more liberal attitudes.

Conclusion

The relationship between evangelicals and GLBTQ policy in the United States is both simple and complex. It is simple in that the large numbers of evangelicals help to explain conservative American policies and attitudes. The Christian right has served as a resonance chamber that amplifies the voices of the most doctrinally conservative. If the United States had fewer evangelicals and no large Christian right groups, it would almost certainly have more liberal policies.

Yet the story is more complex, for evangelical denominations are not the only source of opposition to progressive policies. Evangelically oriented mainline Protestants and conservative Catholics join them on some issues, especially marriage. Mormons provide funding for ballot measures, and

Orthodox Jews and Muslims also oppose many liberal policies. Evangelicals are not entirely responsible for conservative US policies.

And evangelicals themselves are a diverse group, with theological and ethnic divisions that matter when it comes to GLBTQ issues. More important, there is a generation gap among evangelicals that mirrors that in the rest of the society. Many younger evangelicals retain a commitment to their faith but have gay and lesbian friends, have warmer attitudes towards sexual minorities, and are more supportive of ending discrimination and even allowing adoption.

And this ties in with the larger simple story: over the past two decades, American attitudes have become far more liberal with regard to gay and lesbian rights. The magnitude of this change is striking, and generational differences in attitudes suggest that the trend will continue. The data show that white and African-American evangelicals are changing along with the rest of society; they are just starting from a more conservative position. Even the most doctrinally conservative and observant evangelicals are becoming more liberal regarding gay and lesbian rights, and they will continue to do so as younger cohorts replace those with far more conservative attitudes.

And thus the simple story that the Christian right has dominated American politics for the past two decades is wrong. Paradoxically, the Christian right has been successful in electoral politics but unsuccessful in changing American attitudes and policies. Public schools are more likely today than they were in 1978 to teach evolution in biology classes and to offer a full sex education curriculum. An increasing number of states reject federal government subsidies to teach abstinence as part of their sex education curriculum.[10] Abortion remains legal in the United States, although there are more restrictions than in Canada. Feminists have had far more success than have Christian conservatives in matters of gender equality, and today, in many top law and medical schools, a significant majority of students are women. Americans' attitudes towards gender equality have become significantly more liberal over the thirty years of Christian right mobilization.

More important, on issues of GLBTQ rights, the rhetorical efforts of the Christian right have failed, with the result that the public is far more liberal today than it was when the Moral Majority formed in 1978. The extent of the change was evident in the vice-presidential debate of 2008, in which Sarah Palin, a candidate enthusiastically backed by Christian right groups, spent several minutes supporting basic equality for gays and lesbians. In 1988, this would have been unthinkable.

In thirty years the civil rights movement and the feminist movement re-shaped American public life and politics. Students today can scarcely believe the discrimination based on race and gender that their professors describe from a few decades ago. The gay and lesbian rights movement has also made great strides. The Christian right did help the Republicans capture a major-ity in Congress in 1994, and it did help G.W. Bush win the White House in 2000 (Wilcox and Larson 2006). But this did not lead to the same kind of policy success as was achieved by earlier social movements.

These earlier movements sought to remove barriers to equality and to reshape attitudes towards their members. Fairness claims by workers in the 1900s, by African Americans in the 1960s, by women in the 1970s, and by gays and lesbians in the 1990s have swayed many Americans who were not themselves members of these groups. Where the Christian right has made fairness claims – for the right for religious groups to meet on school prop-erty or for religious students to read the Bible in study hall – they have also won. But the core agenda of the Christian right is different from that of other social movements. It asks that others live by its moral standards, an argument that is difficult to make in a libertarian culture. Although the movement perceives itself as defensive – protecting its families and children against moral decay – to the rest of the culture it appears to be imposing moral standards and depriving others of choices. The Christian right does not ask to be allowed to engage in heterosexual marriage; it asks that others be barred from same-sex marriage.[11]

Such movements can occasionally succeed. The United States did once amend the national Constitution to ban the sale of alcohol, although it soon sobered up and rescinded that amendment. But these kinds of movements face long odds. Republican policy makers can read public opinion polls, and they have been reluctant to press the Christian right's agenda on a public that has not been convinced. Republican leaders, to be sure, have played to that agenda in symbolic ways, such as in their vocal support of a national constitutional amendment prohibiting the recognition of same-sex mar-riage.[12] But they have not followed through with the kind of determination required to enact the policies that are at the forefront of that agenda.

The Christian right represents the oldest generation of evangelicals – one that is concentrated in fundamentalist and Pentecostal denominations and that feels threatened on every front. Christian right activists believe them-selves to be under siege by a liberal movement that threatens to overwhelm the United States. They decry cultural liberalism in schools and television because they fear that their children will lose their evangelical faith (Lienesch

1993). The leadership of this generation is rapidly aging: Jerry Falwell is dead, and Pat Robertson, James Dobson, and Beverely LaHaye have retired from active management of Christian right groups. For these groups to prosper, they will need to acknowledge changes in their target constituency.

The current generation of evangelical leaders is conservative, but it is also more confident of the resiliency of evangelical churches, which are growing and attracting many young members. They are strongly opposed to abortion but are now grappling with homosexuality in ways that resemble those seen in mainline Protestants a decade ago. These new leaders have a broader agenda, and they see the polarizing politics of the Christian right as damaging to the religious mission of evangelicalism. Rick Warren and Richard Cizik, along with Richard Land and others, are more moderate than the retiring generation of Christian right leaders.

Surveys show that the next generation of evangelicals has an even broader agenda, with strong interest in the environment, world poverty, and AIDS. They are engaged in discussions with Catholics, with liberal Protestants, and with other groups who might be allies on some issues and adversaries on others (Robinson 2008). They are more likely to have travelled abroad and to have diverse friendship networks. This makes them less hostile towards those who disagree with them and less likely to think of political issues in apocalyptic terms. This will give them greater odds for policy impact than the Christian right, but it also means that their actions will be tempered by deliberation.

The negative image of the Christian right has been at least partially responsible for a decline in religious affiliation among the young, who now report far higher rates of secular identity than was the case in past generations. Liberal mainline Protestants have moved away from religious affiliation as their churches have battled over gay rights, and surveys have shown that the single most common negative image that young people have of organized religion is that it is too homophobic (Kinnaman and Lyons 2007). As denominations and congregations struggle with issues of sexual orientation, they must have an eye to the next generation of members. This does not mean that evangelicals will embrace sexual diversity, but it does mean that fire-and-brimstone condemnations will cost them younger congregants.

If the Christian right has not succeeded, then why have so many states amended their constitutions to bar same-sex marriage? These setbacks have been very disappointing for activists, but it is important to recognize that, twenty years ago, none of these states permitted marriage or civil unions, and most activists did not imagine that marriage would be possible in their lifetimes. Over the past twenty years, the public debate has shifted from sodomy laws to allowing military service to marriage, and the public has become more liberal on each of these issues. But, unlike Canada, the United States does not have a tradition of full benefits for heterosexual couples who choose not to marry, and a large number of American marriages occur in churches as religious ceremonies. Thus marriage, in particular, has been a difficult issue for many religious Americans, whose religious beliefs support heterosexual norms and who have little experience with civil marriage.

But the rapidity of attitude change and the generational differences that are evident in all religious communities suggest that the day is not far off when a state will reverse one of these amendments. Evangelical churches will not perform these weddings, not in the next decade and perhaps not in our lifetimes. But there will be at least some young evangelicals in the audience when these ceremonies are performed.

7

Liberal, with Conservative "Vibrations"
African-American Protestants and the Struggle over Legal Rights for Gay and Lesbian Couples

ROBERT P. JONES AND DANIEL COX

> *There is a battle and a struggle within black religion itself ... On the one hand, they are very conservative. On the other hand, they are preaching liberation. And the two don't always coexist.*
>
> – African-American minister (AAMLC Focus Group 2005)[1]

While for the vast majority of American voters the issue of same-sex marriage ranks relatively low as an important voting issue, it nonetheless functions alongside abortion as a powerful symbolic issue in the so-called culture wars.[2] The issue of same-sex marriage entered the national stage when the Massachusetts Supreme Court legalized the practice in the state near the end of 2003. It played a particularly prominent role in the 2004 presidential election, and since then it has been a perennial issue in the public debate, where it has been kept alive through a series of statewide ballot initiatives. In many religious communities, the issue of same-sex marriage has taken on particular significance because it has been perceived as a direct challenge to some traditional moral teachings of the church. While much has been written about this issue among white evangelical Protestants, less is known about the way in which it has resonated among African-American Protestants.

African-American Protestants have struggled in unique ways with the issues of legal rights for gay and lesbian Americans, in part due to two competing currents that flow through African-American theology. On the one hand, African-American theology is founded on a prophetic vision emphasizing liberation and social justice; on the other hand, it emphasizes individual morality. These twin theological currents often compete with one another, with the prophetic vision pushing black Protestants in one direction and with the pietistic vision pushing them in another.

Issues concerning gay and lesbian equality – especially same-sex marriage, which explicitly evokes religious themes – accentuate the tensions between these two theological orientations. Our analysis provides key insights into how and why African-American clergy and congregants struggle with issues of gay and lesbian equality. Attending to the ways in which black clergy and congregants struggle with these cross-pressures also casts important light on the complex interplay of political ideology, race, and religion. We focus on attitudes about same-sex marriage among both African-American clergy and African-American Protestant congregants. For the clergy data, we draw on two sets of focus groups that we conducted with self-identified progressive African-American clergy in 2005 and 2006.[3] For the congregant data, we draw upon a wide range of recent public opinion data in which the sample size is sufficient to draw conclusions about black Protestants.

In addition to examining the importance of the interplay of the prophetic and pietistic theological orientations, we offer three key insights for understanding the implications of these orientations, especially for gay and lesbian issues. First, the tensions between these visions cannot accurately be characterized as a struggle between progressive political currents and conservative religious currents as conservative/liberal tensions run through each. Second, within the religious context, these tensions should not be understood as a battle between two distinct groups of churches (although there are clearly some who have cast their lot on both sides of these debates); rather, these competing theological visions most often coexist *within* particular churches. Third, there is also evidence that these competing visions are operative not only within particular churches but also within individuals. In other words, these competing orientations go all the way down: they are embodied in the institutions, the culture, and the worldviews of African-American Protestants. In certain circumstances and on certain issues, one orientation may be stronger than the other, but both are generally operative. The struggle and interplay of these orientations are critical for understanding black Protestant attitudes on same-sex marriage and gay and lesbian equality issues.

African-American Clergy and Same-Sex Marriage

The Black Church

The centrality of the church among African Americans is difficult to over-estimate. In the African-American community, in addition to its primary spiritual role, the church has often served as the hub of social, cultural, and political activity. According to Lincoln and Mamiya (1990, 8), "the black church has no challenger as the cultural womb of the black community. Not only did it give birth to new institutions such as schools, banks, insurance companies, and low income housing, it also provided an academy and an arena for political activities, and it nurtured young talent for musical, dramatic, and artistic development."[4]

For African Americans, the black church has been not only a central social institution that serves to reinforce cultural solidarity but also an important religious lens for viewing the world.[5] There are, however, at least two different collective theological orientations within black churches, and each has implications for how the church understands and responds to same-sex marriage and other issues regarding gay and lesbian rights (this view derived from the AAMLC Focus Group 2005). One orientation, which we call the "prophetic orientation," emphasizes communal religiosity, political engagement, and the role of the church in addressing economic and social injustice. The other orientation, which we call the "pietistic orientation," stresses private religiosity, rewards in the next life, and the priestly role of the church to help individuals live better moral and spiritual lives (Lincoln and Mamiya 1990).[6] While both have always been present in the black church, they lead to significantly different political orientations. Political scientist Melissa Harris-Lacewell (2004, 187) summarizes the differences in these orientations and their political implications as follows:

> When the black church offers a theology rooted in a social gospel tradition, emphasizing the alleviation of poverty, the advancement of racial and gender equality, and the promotion of peace as moral values, it leads to a progressive political agenda among African Americans. When black churches advance a pervasively individualistic conception of the gospel that breaks the link between moral reasoning and structural inequality, it leads to a conservative political agenda focused exclusively on private morality.

Liberal, with Conservative Vibrations: Tensions among African-American Clergy

These tensions within the black church and their complex political implications were a prominent theme in our focus groups with African-American ministers. When clergy addressed the issue of same-sex marriage, the countervailing pull of the prophetic and pietistic currents – what one minister described as "dangerous dichotomies" – became quickly evident.

> There is a battle and a struggle within black religion itself. On the one hand, they are very conservative. On the other hand, they are preaching liberation. And the two don't always coexist. So you have progressiveness and a willingness to advance the cause of civil rights, but a selected civil rights. On the race issue, we are with you. When you start talking about how women are treated, when you start talking about how gays and lesbians in the black church are treated, we are not going to touch that. Most of our mega-church preachers simply get their models from white evangelicalism, and they live with those dangerous dichotomies and don't reconcile them. And I think this is why they make easy inroads for conservatives too. (AAMLC Focus Group 2005)

Another minister captured this tension by describing himself as a "liberal" who also felt internalized "conservative vibrations" (AAMLC Focus Group 2005). This colourful way of describing his outlook elicited nearly unanimous agreement from the rest of the group. Although we were not talking about the issue of same-sex marriage at that point in the discussion, he used this issue to illustrate his own struggles with these competing theological currents:

> Well, I'm a liberal. I'm a black man with a mom and dad with a ninth-grade education, who came out of a black neighbourhood with nothing but black neighbours. And I'm not ashamed of my politics or who I am or what I am. But I'm still not a black man liberal that's for this gay marriage and stuff. But the thing is that I am a liberal, but then that's a traditional liberal issue. And so that's my conservative vibration right there. (AAMLC Focus Group 2005)

African-American Ministers' Responses to Same-Sex Marriage as a Political Issue

The legalization of same-sex marriages in Massachusetts changed the nature of the debate over homosexuality. It was no longer an argument about morality or theology but a question about rights: to what extent should society legally recognize or sanction relationships between same-sex couples? The consideration of same-sex marriage as a political issue accentuated the tensions within the black church because it set the prophetic vision (with its emphasis on justice and rights) against the pietistic vision (with its emphasis on individual morality).

In our focus groups with self-identified progressive African-American clergy, much of the discussion centred on the political implications of same-sex marriage. Three response strategies were prominent in the focus groups. First, virtually all participants felt strongly that this issue was being used by political conservatives as a wedge to divide the African-American community and therefore should be treated as a distraction from more important issues. Although a sizable minority were content to leave it at that, a majority of ministers in the focus groups believed that some direct engagement with the issue was necessary because it had been so effectively put on the table through mechanisms like ballot initiatives. Among these, response strategies fell along two distinct lines: (1) a majority who favoured an appeal to rights that emphasized human rights rather than civil rights or gay rights and (2) a minority who favoured a direct appeal to theology that emphasized being "a whosoever church."[7]

Strategy One. "Not Our Issue": Same-Sex Marriage as a Distraction
Virtually all the participants in the AAMLC focus groups noted with frustration that the issue of same-sex marriage had been used somewhat successfully by conservatives to divide the African-American community and distract it from what they believed were more pressing issues.

> It's a disguise. It's a disguise. And it's a disgrace how the conservative right has put issues on the table that are not our issues as black people. I mean our issues are not about how many men in our churches want to marry men. Why are we concentrating on that issue? That is not our issue. Our issue is basic needs in our community like health care, jobs, education, and those kinds of needs that we have. (AAMLC Focus Group 2005)

Another participant echoed these sentiments, noting how the 2004 Republican "values campaign" had influenced ministers to narrow their own conceptions of morality:

> They tried to talk about [same-sex marriage] in moralistic terms. And I think it's hypocritical because ... those same pastors in Detroit have never,

ever talked about the immorality of unemployment, the Iraq war, the lack
of health care. They have never talked about the racism, the economic divide as a moral question. So you take an issue of homosexuality, of gay marriage or whatever, or abortion, and then use that as your linchpin to try to
promote the conservative agenda and never talk about black folk in prison
and all those social issues, which I think are immoral. (AAMLC Focus
Group 2005)

While all agreed with naming the issue of same-sex marriage as a distraction, a minority were content to stop there. These ministers argued that the
best response would be to return to more traditional issues such as jobs and
economic issues, education, and health care. Moreover, several of these
ministers passionately cautioned that anyone advocating a strategy of pushing for full affirmation of same-sex marriage among African Americans had
underestimated the "conservative DNA" of the black church. The following
excerpt expresses this position clearly:

Political conservatives tapped into the DNA of the black church ... The
black church is *conservative*. We had a moment in history where we birthed
something that was glorious. I thank God for this moment, but at the same
time you are not going to change the DNA of the black church. They will
receive the right message to expand the definition of morality, but if you are
going to shove the sin of homosexuality down their throat, I guarantee you
[political conservatives] will have the White House and everything else
until Jesus comes back. (AAMLC Focus Group 2005)

It is important to note the limits this minister perceived regarding the
ability to engage black Protestants on gay and lesbian issues. On the one
hand, African-American clergy talked about the birth of the civil rights
movement, with its emphasis on the prophetic theological tradition, as
something "glorious"; on the other hand, they talked about the powerful
"conservative DNA" of the black church, with its emphasis on the pietistic
tradition and traditional teaching, which portrays homosexuality as sinful.
The minority of ministers who advocated the avoidance strategy were convinced of two things: (1) on a practical level, gay and lesbian issues were an
avoidable distraction from the more important economic justice issues
traditionally supported by the prophetic tradition; and (2) any direct engagement of gay and lesbian issues would inevitably evoke the dominance

of the pietistic tradition, threatening the influence of the prophetic tradition generally. Because of the power of the pietistic tradition, rather than
engaging gay and lesbian issues directly, these clergy sought to help congregants "expand the definition of morality." In other words, those clergy
who favoured the avoidance strategy hoped that, by avoiding gay and lesbian issues, they could enable their congregants to keep their focus on the
prophetic tradition and even to reinterpret the pietistic tradition to make it
more consistent with the demands of the former.

Strategy Two. Rights Talk: "Human Rights," Not "Gay Rights" or "Civil Rights"

In our focus groups, African-American ministers frequently evoked the language of rights to talk about same-sex marriage and rights for gay and lesbian Americans. There was near consensus in the groups that, while an
appeal to rights would be effective, the best way to talk about them was as
"human rights" rather than as "gay rights" or even "civil rights." One minister
articulated why he would not talk about "gay rights":

> So I think that where I come down clearly for myself is the issue of human
> rights and not gay rights. I wouldn't ever attend a gay rights anything. I
> would attend something dealing with human rights ... When gay [activists]
> start dealing with gay rights, then the evangelical, the Christian right, is go-
> ing to take the opposite view: "No, not gay rights." If you deal with human
> rights, then gay rights will just become a part of that because you're dealing
> with the fact that humans have certain rights that should not be violated.
> (AAMLC Focus Group 2005)

Similarly, African-American ministers in the focus groups resisted comparisons between legalizing same-sex marriage and the struggle for civil
rights, chiefly because of a widespread belief within the African-American
community that homosexuality is a choice. For example, 58 percent of African Americans say homosexuality is just the way some people prefer to live,
while just 40 percent of the general public feel this way (Pew Research Center for the People and the Press 2006). One minister, who clarified that these
were not his own views, expressed the problem this way:

> The majority of African Americans have been taught, we've been condi-
> tioned, we believe that you've got a choice in this matter. It ain't like being

black in the civil rights movement. You've got a choice. You can decide. You can wake up one morning and decide, "I'm not going to be gay anymore." (AAMLC Focus Group 2006)

Several prominent political leaders have stumbled in their relationships with the African-American community by failing to understand these distinctions. For example, Senator John Kerry blindly ran into this problem at a town hall meeting in Jackson, Mississippi, during the 2004 presidential campaign when he asserted that there were strong parallels between the movement to legalize same-sex marriage and the civil rights struggle. Following the meeting, the Democratic Congressional Black Caucus issued a public statement denouncing this comparison (Debose 2004).[8]

The African-American ministers in our focus groups also noted that another advantage of framing rights for gay and lesbian Americans as human rights is that it does not necessarily directly challenge traditional African-American views of homosexuality as sinful; rather, it allows black congregants to distinguish between homosexuality as a "spiritual issue" and human rights for gays and lesbians as a "political issue." As a spiritual issue, most African Americans see homosexuality as a sin, but participants argued that congregants were capable of separating this religious conviction from the political question of human rights, which includes rights for gays and lesbians.

> I think our congregants are not as myopic as we might try to paint them to be. They're not so shallow that they cannot separate the issues. I don't believe as a person that what you do with your sexual organs defines your civil rights. I think that you as a person deserve all of your civil rights because of the very nature of you being a person. And that's just the way I see it, and a lot of other folks see it, too. (AAMLC Focus Group 2005)[9]

Another minister in the extended focus groups echoed this sentiment:

> You can't be a homosexual unless you engage in a homosexual act. Okay. So it's about sin ... My congregation understands this. But they also understand that everybody in this country has a right to be in this country and a right to believe like they want to believe and a right to live like they want to live, as long as it does not infringe upon anyone else's rights. (AAMLC Focus Group 2006)

The strategy of appealing to human rights is one way of finessing the direct conflict between the competing prophetic and pietistic traditions. It gives the pietistic impulse its due in the private realm of the church because it does not challenge the theological evaluation of homosexual behaviour as sinful, and it taps a commitment to the separation of church and state because it allows the prophetic impulse that emphasizes justice and rights to function in the public sphere.

Strategy Three. A Direct Theological Appeal: Being a "Whosoever Church"

Because a substantial majority of black Protestants adopt a literal view of the Bible, and because there are a number of texts that, at least as traditionally interpreted in the black church, condemn homosexual acts, a fully supportive position on same-sex marriage has been a minority one, both among black Protestants and among black ministers. There have been some recent organizing efforts aimed at reconceiving black Protestant theology and sexual ethics, such as, beginning in 2006, the Black Church Summits hosted by the National Black Justice Coalition. These events have drawn the support of a number of well-known leaders, such as Reverend Al Sharpton, Reverend Jesse Jackson, and Reverend Peter Gomes, but their impact on rank-and-file African Americans has been modest.[10]

Similarly, only a small minority of African-American ministers in our focus groups had publicly expressed fully supportive positions on full inclusion and equal rights for gay and lesbian people, including same-sex marriage.[11] Among these ministers, one theme in particular was pronounced, and it was an appeal to one of the most cited verses in the New Testament for evangelical Christians: "For God so loved the world, that He gave His only begotten Son, that whosoever believed in Him should not perish, but have everlasting life" (John 3:16, KJV). These ministers talked of the resonance of "whosoever" and how it had challenged them to become "a whosoever church."

> [Minister 1] I do not get to choose whom I pastor. Whoever God sends, that's whom I have to pastor ... whether they are legal or illegal, whether they are gay, whether they're straight, whether they're black, whether they're white ... So I'm still evolving ... I don't hate like I used to. I don't use those labels like I used to. And I see that God is a God of love, and God is a God of compassion, that the church is a healing station, not a hurting

station. And that means that whosoever will, let him come. I do not get to
define what "whosoever will" is.

[Minister 2] The whole Bible is a narrative about the story of a God who is
so extravagant and so unbiased in God's love for humanity that God ex-
travagantly offers God's self as a sacrifice not just for some but for the whole
wide world. The whole story is that God so loved the world that *whosoever*
... That's got to reverberate and that's got to have deep religious and theological foundations in the psyche of the Christian body. (AAMLC Focus
Group 2006)

This theme of becoming a "whosoever church" has resonated widely
among the minority of African-American ministers who have worked for a
decidedly theological approach to addressing the issue of welcoming gays
and lesbians and for supporting a full range of rights, including marriage.[12]
The challenge of this approach, in terms of the twin theological impulses
within African-American Protestant theology, is that it demands either the
dominance of the prophetic orientation over the pietistic orientation or a
radical reinterpretation of the latter, moving it away from traditional teachings about the immorality of homosexual acts and relationships. The promise of this approach is that, if it is successful, it may provide a stable, long-
term solution because it moves these currents more into harmony with one
another.

These three approaches to the issues of gay and lesbian political rights –
avoidance, human rights, and the "whosoever church" – constitute the
range of strategic responses we heard from progressive African-American
ministers. A majority of ministers in our focus groups noted that, because of
how prominent the issue of same-sex marriage had become following the
2004 elections, the avoidance strategy was increasingly untenable. Most
were struggling, even if somewhat reluctantly, towards some form of a human rights approach or even towards a version of the "whosoever church"
approach.

African-American Protestants and Same-Sex Marriage: A Look at the Data

The qualitative data above paint a complex picture of the views of black Protestants on same-sex marriage, and the quantitative data paint a similarly
complex portrait. On the one hand, same-sex marriage ranks very low in
importance as a voting issue; on the other hand, in church, black Protestants

hear frequent negative messages about homosexuality, and a substantial majority oppose the legalization of same-sex marriage.

At the height of the same-sex marriage debate in 2004, 73 percent of black Protestants said they opposed same-sex marriage, but only 27 percent said the issue was "very important" in their vote for president (Pew Research Center for the People and the Press 2004b). This put it dead last on a list of almost a dozen issues. In contrast, nearly nine in ten black Protestants (87 percent) said that the issue of the economy was "very important" (Pew Research Center for the People and the Press 2004a). Four years later, fewer than three months before the 2008 presidential election, the salience of same-sex marriage had not budged (27 percent), and it still ranked much lower than most other concerns (Pew Research Center for the People and the Press 2008).

Despite the low significance of homosexuality as a voting issue, in the 2008 Faith and American Politics Survey, black Protestants reported that it was mentioned frequently and negatively in black churches. In 2008, more than two-thirds (67 percent) of black Protestants reported hearing about the issue in their place of worship. In fact, more black Protestants reported hearing their clergy discuss this issue than the issue of abortion (55 percent). Moreover, among those black Protestants who reported hearing about homosexuality in church, nearly two-thirds reported that clergy said homosexuality was something to be discouraged rather than accepted (Public Religion Research 2008).

Even as support for many gay rights policies is increasing in the general US population, a majority still oppose same-sex marriage, and this opposition has been particularly strong among black Protestants (Brewer 2003; Haeberle 1999; Wilcox and Norrander 2002; Yang 1997). In 2008, nearly two-thirds of black Protestants opposed same-sex marriage, compared to 52 percent of Americans overall. Among those who oppose same-sex marriage, more than six in ten (62 percent) say that they strongly oppose it. In 2004, and again in 2006, opposition to same-sex marriage spiked approximately 10 points among African Americans, perhaps as a result of the concerted emphasis on the issue in the national election campaigns in those years (Pew Research Center for the People and the Press 2008).[13]

A number of studies have demonstrated the importance of demographic factors like age, gender, and education as well as personal contact with lesbian or gay people, political ideology, and partisanship in shaping views about homosexuality (Brewer 2003; Herek and Glunt 1993; Herek 2002; Kite

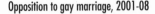

FIGURE 7.1

Opposition to gay marriage, 2001-08

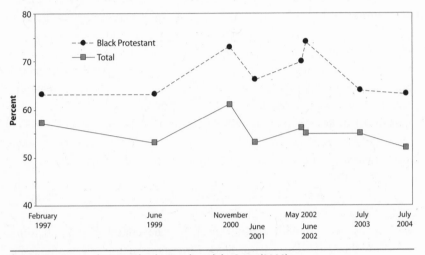

Source: Pew Research Center for the People and the Press (2008).

and Whitely 1996; Olson et al. 2006; Haeberle 1999; Wilcox and Norrander 2002). Other research has shown that religious affiliation and frequency of church attendance are powerful predictors of individual attitudes on gay and lesbian issues (Finlay and Walther 2003; Green 2000). Green (2000) argues that, historically, organized religion is the most potent source of opposition to gay rights, not least because many religious groups, based on a literalist reading of scripture, believe that homosexuality is morally wrong.

In the following sections, we examine a number of known factors associated with views on same-sex marriage among black Protestants. We examine measures of religious belief and engagement, views on other social issues, views about homosexual behaviour, and views on other gay and lesbian issues. On each of these, we find that black Protestants embrace views that are correlated with more conservative views on same-sex marriage. In a final section, we use two logistic regression models to assess the relative predictive power of demographic factors and key religious measures such as belief, behaviour, and affiliation on views of same-sex marriage.

High Religious Belief and Engagement

Even against the highly religious backdrop of the American public, black Protestants stand out for their traditional beliefs and high levels of engagement.

TABLE 7.1

Religious beliefs and behaviour of black Protestants and white evangelical Protestants, 2007

Beliefs/behaviour	Total population (%)	Black Protestants (%)	White evangelical Protestants (%)
Religious attendance			
At least once a week	40	59	64
Few times a month/year	33	30	25
Seldom/never	28	11	10
DK/ref.	1	*	1
Importance of religion			
Very important	58	85	83
Somewhat important	26	13	14
Not too/at all important	16	2	2
DK/ref.	1	*	*
Read the Bible (scripture)			
At least once a week	36	64	64
Few times a month/year	18	19	19
Seldom/never	45	17	17
DK/ref.	1	1	1
Frequency of prayer			
Several times a day	38	62	60
Daily/few times a week	34	28	34
Weekly/few times a month	9	4	3
Seldom/never	18	4	2
DK/ref.	2	2	1
View of the Bible			
Literal word of God	33	62	60
Word of God, not literal	30	22	26
Book written by men	28	9	5
Other/DK (vol.)	9	8	4

Note: Due to rounding, not all columns add to 100.

Source: Pew Forum on Religion and Public Life, Religious Landscape Survey (2007).

Six in ten black Protestants are biblical literalists, roughly the same as the number of white evangelicals who embrace a literal interpretation of scripture. Among the general population, only one-third agree with this view of the Bible. More than two-thirds (68 percent) of black Protestants say that they consider themselves born-again or evangelical Christians (Pew Forum on Religion and Public Life 2007). Finally, nearly half (44 percent) of black Protestants rely primarily on religious teachings to sort out matters of right and wrong, compared to 29 percent of the general public (ibid.).

On measures of engagement, such as frequency of religious attendance, frequency of prayer, and the perceived importance of religion, black Protestants also exhibit significantly higher levels of engagement than do most other religious groups and the public as a whole. Close to six in ten (59 percent) black Protestants attend religious services at least once a week, and nearly one-third (30 percent) attend more than once a week. Only about one in ten black Protestants say they seldom or never attend worship services, compared to 27 percent of the general population (Pew Forum on Religion and Public Life 2007).

More than six in ten (62 percent) of black Protestants say they pray several times a day, compared with only 38 percent of the general population. Similarly, more than six in ten (61 percent) of black Protestants say they read the Bible, outside of religious services, at least once a week, compared to 35 percent of the general population. When asked how important religion is in their lives, black Protestants overwhelmingly say that it is very important (85 percent). Only 2 percent of black Protestants say that religion is not important in their lives, compared to 16 percent in the general population (Pew Forum on Religion and Public Life 2007).

FIGURE 7.2

Religious engagement by faith group, 2007

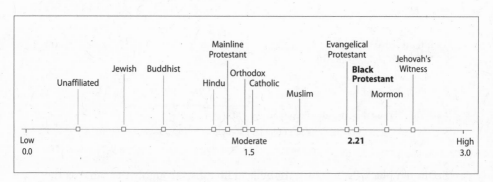

Note: Index, ranging from 0 to 3, is based on measures of church attendance, prayer, and importance of religion.

Source: Pew Forum on Religion and Public Life (2007).

On a composite scale of religious engagement created from three measures – attendance, prayer, and importance of religion – black Protestants
score higher than nearly every religious group, including white evangelical
Protestants. Only Mormons and Jehovah's Witnesses rank higher (Pew
Forum on Religion and Public Life 2007).[14]

Traditional Views on Social Issues

It is important to see the conservatism of black Protestants on gay and lesbian issues within the context of a more general social conservatism. Nearly
half (45 percent) of black Protestants say that premarital sex is always
wrong, a significantly greater number than one finds in the American public
overall (25 percent). Only half support physician-assisted suicide, while
more than two-thirds of the general population do so (GSS 2006). Only 37
percent, compared to nearly half (48 percent) of the general population,
agree that evolution is the best explanation for the origins of human life
(Pew Forum on Religion and Public Life 2007).

This conservative pattern, however, does not hold for all social issues. On
the issue of abortion, black Protestants are split (47-46 percent) between
those who believe it should be legal in all or most cases and those who believe it should be illegal in all or most cases. On this issue, black Protestants
are only slightly more conservative than is the general population, among
whom a bare majority (51 percent) favour keeping abortion legal in all or
most cases (Pew Forum on Religion and Public Life 2007). And, although
nearly three-quarters of the American public favour the death penalty for
persons convicted of murder, only half as many black Protestants (38 percent) do so (Pew Research Center for the People and the Press 2007a).

Negative Views about Homosexuality and Homosexual Behaviour

Black Protestants overwhelmingly oppose sexual relations between members of the same gender. Nearly eight in ten (77 percent) say that homosexual sex is always wrong, compared to slightly more than half (54 percent) of
the general public. Among black Protestants, men are more likely to disapprove of homosexual sex than are women, even though, by most measures,
women are more highly religiously engaged than men. Older black Protestants and those with a high school education or less are also more likely than
are younger black Protestants and those with at least some college education to say sexual relations between people of the same gender are wrong
(GSS 2006). The same patterns are evident in the population at large.

TABLE 7.2

Views on homosexuality by black Protestants when asked whether homosexuality should be accepted by society, 2007

Criteria		Total population (%)	Black Protestants (%)
All		50	39
Age	18-29	63	50
	30-49	51	37
	50-64	48	38
	65+	35	27
Gender	Male	45	33
	Female	55	42
Religious attendance	Weekly or more	33	31
	A few times a month/year	58	49
	Seldom/never	66	53
Biblical literalism	Literal, word of God	28	32
	Word of God, not literal	52	49
	Book written by men	76	67

Source: Pew Forum on Religion and Public Life, Religious Landscape Survey (2007).

Not surprisingly, religious attendance exhibits a powerful influence on views about homosexual relations. Eighty-six percent of black Protestants who attend religious services weekly or more, and an equal percentage (86 percent) of those who attend a few times a month, say that sex between adults of the same gender is always wrong. Among black Protestants who attend once a year or less, significantly fewer (59 percent) say that same-gender sex is always wrong, though only 28 percent say it is not wrong at all (GSS 2006).

Although half of the general population believes that homosexuality is a way of life that should be accepted, roughly four in ten (39 percent) black Protestants agree (Pew Forum on Religion and Public Life 2007). Compared to most other religious groups, black Protestants are much more likely to say homosexuality should be discouraged. Here again, age, gender, and education are significant factors in attitudes towards homosexuality. For example, while half of younger black Protestants (under age thirty) say that homosexuality should be accepted by society, only 27 percent of older black Protestants (age sixty-five and older) agree. However, even here there is a significant gap between young black Protestants and their younger generational peers in the general population, among whom 63 percent say homosexuality should be accepted (ibid.).

Interestingly, the relationship between religious attendance and attitudes towards homosexuality is somewhat different among black Protestants and the general public. Among the general public, religious attendance appears to have a more linear relationship to attitudes towards homosexuality, with those who frequently attend religious services being most likely to say homosexuality should be discouraged in society. While black Protestants who attend church most often are much less likely to believe homosexuality should be accepted, there is little difference between black Protestants in the other attendance categories: once or twice a month, a few times a year, seldom, or never (Pew Forum on Religion and Public Life 2007).

Opposition to Other Gay and Lesbian Issues
Black Protestants are more conservative than is the general population on virtually all issues concerning legal rights for gay and lesbian persons. On the issue of civil unions, black Protestants also demonstrate significantly lower support than does the general public. Only four in ten black Protestants support allowing gay or lesbian couples to enter into legal agreements that would give them many of the same rights as married couples. In contrast, a solid majority (54 percent) of Americans support civil unions for gay or lesbian couples. Slightly more than one-third (35 percent) of black Protestants favour allowing gays and lesbians to adopt children, significantly fewer than what is found in the population as a whole (46 percent) (Pew Research Center for the People and the Press 2008).

Sorting Out the Relationships between Black Protestants and Same-Sex Marriage
Much of the data presented thus far provides evidence to support the contention that, among black Protestants, there is an association between certain demographic characteristics, religious beliefs, and religious behaviours, on the one hand, and same-sex marriage, on the other. The relative strength of these factors and their independent influences, however, remain somewhat opaque. In order to sort out these complex relationships – particularly whether being a black Protestant remained a significant predictor of opposition to same-sex marriage when controlling for other factors – we conducted a multiple logistic regression analysis.

Data and Variables

To explore the power of religious engagement and other factors in shaping the attitudes of African-American Protestants towards same-sex marriage, we conducted a logistic regression analysis using an August 2007 Pew survey, which included 197 black Protestants among a total of 3,002 respondents. In the model we included a number of relevant demographic variables: age, education, gender, marital status, and political ideology. We also included two religious measures known to correlate strongly with views of same-sex marriage: religious attendance and biblical literalism. Finally, we included a variable for religious affiliation that separated people among a few major religious traditions to see if being a black Protestant remained a significant predictor of views on same-sex marriage even when controlling for all of the above variables.[15]

The descriptive statistics in Table 7.3 are unweighted; subsequent analysis is weighted to be representative of the general adult population in the United States. The data in Table 7.3 replicate findings we reported earlier: black Protestants are more likely to oppose gay marriage than is the general public (76 percent to 61 percent). They also have many characteristics known to correlate with opposition to same-sex marriage. Black Protestants have lower levels of educational attainment, more frequently attend religious services, and are much more likely to believe that the Bible is the literal word of God than is the general population. The goal of the logistic analysis was to sort out the independent influences of these factors.

The Pew survey asked respondents whether they strongly favour, favour, oppose, or strongly oppose allowing gays and lesbians to marry legally. In the multivariate analysis this variable was recoded as binary (favour/oppose) in order to simplify the analysis and focus on categorical opposition to same-sex marriage.

Logistic Regression Results

When controlling for other variables in the model, political ideology is seen to exert the greatest influence on views of same-sex marriage. Table 7.4 shows that the largest odds ratio (5.4) is for conservatives, with liberals as the reference group. Thus, political conservatives are more than five times more likely to oppose same-sex marriage than are self-identified liberals. After political ideology, religious affiliation is the most powerful independent predictor.

TABLE 7.3

Attitudes towards same-sex marriage, and descriptive data for independent variables used in logistic regression model, comparing black Protestants and the total US population, 2007

		Black Protestant N (%)		Total population N (%)	
Attitude towards same-sex marriage					
Strongly favour		12	(7%)	371	(13%)
Favour		30	(17%)	714	(26%)
Oppose		49	(28%)	698	(26%)
Strongly oppose		83	(48%)	957	(35%)
Independent variables					
Education	High school or less	91	(46%)	1,038	(35%)
	Some college	47	(24%)	719	(24%)
	College graduate	59	(30%)	1,219	(41%)
Gender	Male	69	(35%)	1,371	(46%)
	Female	128	(65%)	1,631	(54%)
Biblical literalism	Bible not literal word of God	75	(38%)	2,068	(69%)
	Bible literal word of God	122	(65%)	934	(31%)
Religious attendance	Seldom or never	22	(11%)	718	(24%)
	Monthly or yearly	55	(28%)	954	(32%)
	Weekly or more	119	(61%)	1,290	(44%)
Religious tradition	White evangelical	0		743	(26%)
	White mainline	0		640	(22%)
	Black Protestant	197	(100%)	197	(7%)
	Roman Catholic	0		644	(22%)
	Other Christian	0		188	(6%)
	Non-Christian	0		107	(4%)
	Unaffiliated			373	(13%)
Marital status	Married	79	(40%)	1,780	(59%)
	Not married	118	(60%)	1,222	(41%)
Political ideology	Conservative	64	(34%)	1,195	(42%)
	Moderate	82	(44%)	1,132	(39%)
	Liberal	40	(22%)	531	(19%)

Source: Pew Research Center for the People and the Press, August 2007.

TABLE 7.4

Logistic regression model predicting opposition to gay marriage

	Estimate	Std. error	Sig.	Odds ratio
Constant	1.062	0.263	0.000	2.89
Age	0.02	0.003	0.000	1.02
HS or less	0.665	0.119	0.000	1.94
Some college	0.438	0.137	0.001	1.55
College graduate	0*	–	–	
Female	−0.582	0.1	0.000	0.56
Male	0*	–	–	
Not married	−0.174	0.101	0.086	0.84
Married	0*	–	–	
Bible, not literal	−0.801	0.121	0.000	0.45
Bible, literal word of God	0*	–	–	
Attend (seldom/never)	−0.785	0.138	0.000	0.46
Attend (monthly/yearly)	−0.645	0.119	0.000	0.52
Attend (weekly or more)	0*	–	–	
White evangelical	1.334	0.191	0.000	3.80
White mainline	0.377	0.167	0.024	1.46
Black Protestant	0.965	0.225	0.000	2.62
Catholic	0.362	0.165	0.028	1.44
Other Christian	1.343	0.247	0.000	3.83
Non-Christian	−0.231	0.293	0.429	0.79
Unaffiliated	0*	–	–	
Conservative	1.687	0.139	0.000	5.40
Moderate	0.758	0.13	0.000	2.13
Liberal	0*	–	–	

* Denotes reference category.

Even when controlling for age, education, gender, marital status, biblical literalism, religious attendance, and political ideology, our model demonstrates that black Protestants are still two and one-half times as likely as are Americans without a religious affiliation to oppose same-sex marriage. Non-Christian, Catholic, and white mainline Protestant affiliations are also found to be independent predictors of opposition to same-sex marriage, although the effect sizes are much smaller. Black Protestant opposition to same-sex marriage is only surpassed by two groups: white evangelicals and other Christians (a category that includes Mormons, Orthodox Christians, and racial and ethnic Protestants), who are each nearly four times as likely to oppose same-sex marriage as are those without a religious affiliation.

Although their effects are less powerful than political ideology and religious affiliation, other religious factors, like worship attendance and biblical literalism, are also important independent predictors of opposition to same-sex marriage. Americans who have a literal interpretation of the Bible are more than twice as likely to oppose same-sex marriage as are those who do not view the text literally. The most frequently attending Americans (those who attend weekly or more) are twice as likely as are those who seldom or never attend to oppose same-sex marriage. Interestingly, there is relatively little difference between Americans who seldom or never attend religious services and those who attend once or twice a month or a few times a year.

Gender, education, and age are also significant independent predictors of opposition to same-sex marriage. Men are nearly twice as likely as are women to oppose same-sex marriage, and Americans with a high school education or less are about twice as likely to oppose same-sex marriage as are college graduates. Older Americans are more likely to oppose same-sex marriage than are younger Americans. For example, 40-year-olds are 1.5 times as likely to oppose same-sex marriage as are 20-year-olds, and 60-year-olds are more than twice as likely to oppose same-sex marriage as are 20-year-olds.

In a second model (not shown), we analyzed race and religious affiliation as separate independent variables.[16] The results were largely consistent with those of the first model. Political ideology had the greatest effect on views of same-sex marriage. Gender, education, age, and religious attendance had the same effect in the second model as in the first. With white evangelicals removed as an independent predictor, biblical literalism had a much greater effect, and the magnitude was increased for political ideology.

In this modified model, African Americans were nearly twice as likely as were whites to oppose same-sex marriage. Protestants were about 2.5 times as likely as were the unaffiliated to oppose same-sex marriage. These results indicate that religious affiliation is a stronger predictor of opposition to same-sex marriage than is race. Although this model separated out the effects of race and religion, it is important to note that there is a high degree of correlation between these two variables among African Americans: three-quarters of African Americans are Protestant (Pew Forum on Religion and Public Life 2007).

Conclusion

The quantitative analysis in this chapter clearly shows that African-American Protestants are more likely than is the general population to oppose not only same-sex marriage but also a number of other issues regarding gay and lesbian rights (such as civil unions and adoption). Even after controlling for demographic factors such as age, political ideology, and education, or religious factors such as views of the Bible and religious attendance, black Protestant religious affiliation remains a significant predictor. Black Protestants are more than 2.5 times as likely to oppose same-sex marriage as are the unaffiliated. When religious affiliation and race are analyzed separately, religious affiliation (being Protestant) is a stronger predictor of opposition to same-sex marriage than is race (being black).

These findings clearly suggest that, if one wants to understand the views of African Americans on same-sex marriage, one must understand what is unique about being a black Protestant. Both the qualitative and the quantitative data paint a complex portrait of black Protestant views on same-sex marriage. Significantly, our focus groups among progressive African-American clergy demonstrate that complexity in the political realm is connected to theological complexity within the context of the black church, in which two competing theological currents – a prophetic impulse emphasizing economic justice and a pietistic impulse emphasizing personal morality – exert their pull. These simultaneous impulses find expression in clergy who describe themselves as "liberal" but with "conservative vibrations."

From a politically strategic point of view, it is critically important that these insights be understood by activists at both ends of the political spectrum. For conservative political activists, it should be clear that, while black Protestants may provide some limited number of opportunistic votes against the legalization of same-sex marriage on isolated ballot initiatives (e.g., in California, the 2008 repeal of legalized same-sex marriage via Proposition 8), a growing perception of this issue as being a political wedge and not an important voting issue makes it an unlikely foundation for broader outreach. By the same token, for progressive political activists, it seems unlikely that a straightforward appeal to gay and lesbian rights as the next "civil rights" issue will be effective.

In the more uneven terrain between these options, the three strategies outlined above by the black ministers seem the likely paths that black Protestants will follow. Although the avoidance strategy, which declares that gay and lesbian issues are "not our issue," enjoyed support from a minority of ministers in our focus groups, for purely practical reasons its days seem to be numbered. Public debates about same-sex marriage and other gay and lesbian issues seem unlikely to abate any time soon. At the very least, the fact that two-thirds of African-American Protestant congregants report hearing their clergy talk about homosexuality is an indication that this strategy is not being followed.

Thus, the other two strategies outlined by African-American clergy who took part in our focus groups seem the most probable paths black Protestants will trod when it comes to the issue of same-sex marriage. Most ministers favoured a carefully calibrated appeal to human rights – one that attempts to draw a strong distinction between (1) the political issues of gay and lesbian equality, which are governed by the prophetic theological tradition, and (2) the spiritual issue of homosexuality, which is governed by the pietistic tradition. A minority of ministers, however, favoured robustly embracing the prophetic tradition by attempting to become a "whosoever church," leading congregants to rethink their negative evaluation of same-sex relationships, at least under some circumstances. This approach has the advantage of addressing the traditional tension between the prophetic and pietistic impulses in African-American theology, allowing one its due in public policy and the other its due in the church. It demands a clear dominance of the prophetic tradition. Indeed, the future of how black Protestants wrestle with same-sex marriage may hinge on which of these two theological currents – the prophetic or the pietistic – becomes more dominant.

Canadian Evangelicals and Same-Sex Marriage

JONATHAN MALLOY

In the struggle to legalize same-sex marriage in Canada, one of the most noticeable aspects was the new prominence of evangelical Christian activism. Evangelical campaigns and protests spurred media headlines like "The Rising Clout of Canada's Religious Right" (McDonald 2006) and "Gay Marriage Galvanizes Canada's Christian Right" (Mason 2006). The election of a national Conservative government in 2006 further increased speculation that evangelicals, though unsuccessful in preventing same-sex marriage, were a growing political force in Canada. The context of George W. Bush's well-known evangelicalism and the power of the American religious right led many Canadians to wonder if Canada was developing its own brand of American-style evangelical activism.

However, the evangelical presence in Canada is broader, more longstanding, and more nuanced than many realize. While Canadian evangelicals did become more prominent in the mid-2000s, this was due to the unusual political opportunities and circumstances of the same-sex marriage debate. Canadian evangelicals have been politically active since the 1980s, but much of this activism has been shaped and constrained by institutional and other factors – factors that did not necessarily apply to the special case of same-sex marriage. Thus, I suggest that, while the mobilization around same-sex marriage clearly constituted a major surge for evangelicals, it does not necessarily represent a new and permanent level of activism.

The Canadian Evangelical Presence

No one agrees how many Canadians are evangelical, especially because there is no universal definition of "evangelical." The term "fundamentalist," while sometimes used interchangeably with "evangelical," generally denotes only the most conservative evangelicals. Different categories and questions can yield very different answers (Hiemstra 2007). Grenville (2006) argues that up to 12 percent of Canadians are evangelical Protestants and that a further 7 percent are "evangelical Catholics" (Van Ginkel 2003; Rawlyk 1996). Others, like Hoover et al. (2002, 354), suggest the number is "between 10 and 12 percent." Moving beyond the category of "evangelical" makes things even more unclear. Bowen (2004) suggests that the number of "conservative Protestants" in 2001 was only 5.5 percent, falling from 7.2 percent in 1991. But a 2004 survey reported in *Maclean's* magazine found that 31 percent of Canadians declared themselves "born-again Christians" (Gatehouse 2004). In short, the "evangelical" population of Canada is hard to define or to measure precisely. It is also unclear whether it is rising – some, like Bibby (2005), argue that evangelical attendance is relatively steady and that it grows mainly through members' children rather than through newcomers.

It is also hard to discuss Canadian evangelicals without making American comparisons. Many scholars emphasize the separate roots of Canadian evangelicalism, with its own movements, figures, and doctrinal traditions that draw from Canadian (and/or UK) roots rather than from American sources (Stackhouse 1993; Rawlyk and Noll 1994). But others see evangelicalism as an American import, influenced and directed by American sources and essentially "un-Canadian." In this vein, Michael Adams (2003) argues that evangelicalism and religiosity in general are one of the most distinctive differences between Canada and the United States. Beyond that, some observations imply that evangelical political intervention is an "un-Canadian" spillover from the United States.

Comparisons between evangelicals in Canada and the United States often assume they are ideologically similar, and this is not surprising, given their shared doctrinal beliefs. Reimer finds close links between Canadian and American evangelicals in an "evangelical subculture" of churches, businesses, educational institutions, media, and other organizations that spans the Canada-US border. Hence, he argues, "evangelicals ... in both countries resemble each other far more than they resemble their fellow countrymen" (2003, 6).

But in discussing the above shared evangelical subculture, Reimer (2003, 6) finds that "the biggest and most consistent differences between evangelicals north and south of the border show up in the realm of politics." His own survey finds that, when discussing politics, "Americans are more likely to emphasize moral problems while Canadians are more likely to raise economic problems" (125). And Noll (1997) suggests that Canadian evangelicals operate in a necessarily smaller world than do American evangelicals and that this either encourages or necessitates more cooperation both among evangelicals themselves and between evangelicals and other Christian denominations and the larger society. He also finds "a different set of expectations for relations between church and state" in Canada (6). Woven into Canadian public institutions rather than officially separated, Canadian Christians (evangelical or other) do not display the same anti-state polarization that is so observable among American evangelicals. Similarly, Hoover (1997) cites survey evidence and interviews with evangelical leaders to suggest that Canadian evangelicals are less right wing than are American evangelicals, while Hoover et al. (2002) compare the political views of American and Canadian evangelicals and find that Canadians are more supportive of state intervention in the economy and attempts to alleviate economic inequalities than are Americans.

Indeed, not all evangelical groups and activists are right wing – either in Canada or in the United States (C. Smith 2000; Ballmer 2006). The Canadian social democratic left has distinctly evangelical roots, most notably in the Baptist minister Tommy Douglas and the early Co-operative Commonwealth Federation (later the New Democratic Party). And some modern denominations, such as Mennonites and Christian Reformed, which may not explicitly identify as evangelicals, combine evangelical-style conservative values on abortion and sexual orientation with social justice traditions that call for more state intervention in economic and social issues. For example, Citizens for Public Justice is a Christian Reformed organization that lobbies for improved housing and social policies, better treatment of refugees, and similar issues. And the most prominent Canadian evangelical group, the Evangelical Fellowship of Canada, combines staunch opposition to abortion and same-sex marriage with a strong commitment to anti-poverty and anti-homelessness initiatives.

The different national identities and political cultures of the two countries are also significant. In the United States, a powerful sense of national destiny and character creates a "civil religious myth" that evangelicals can easily tap into. This involves notions of American destiny, exceptionalism, and uniqueness, intricately interwoven with Christianity. Canada, without as strong a set of unifying national myths (Kim 1993), does not offer the same kind of vehicle for evangelical mobilizing. While Canadian evangelicals note the mention of God in the Constitution Act, 1982, and other Christian references in Canadian history, they do not really fit or resonate with a larger civil religious identity. Similarly, Canadian evangelicals rarely talk about God, Christianity, or the Bible in external messages directed at non-evangelicals. In the United States, even non-evangelical American politicians and groups are much more likely than are Canadian evangelicals to cite scripture and divine concepts as a matter of course.

These underlying differences suggest a Canadian evangelical population less susceptible than the American one to political mobilizing, at least as a "Christian right." It lacks the historic sense of separateness from the state and other Christian denominations, a myth of national destiny, and other social and public institutions to encourage and build an overarching sense of political separateness. Additionally, until recently, Canadian broadcast regulations prohibited single-religion radio and television stations, and they continue to discourage explicit political programming in favour of worship and "family" entertainment content (Brooks 2003) – denying a potent form of political communication and organizing.

A further Canadian-American difference involves the institutional openings for political activism. In addition to the broadcast regulations mentioned above, the Westminster parliamentary system provides fewer openings for evangelical and other political activists than does the American system (Bruce 1998; Soper 1994; Smith 2005b). Legislative affairs are dominated by the governing party, which, in turn, is dominated by its leader, and Canadian legislators have little initiative to introduce bills, ask questions without party approval, or build independent bases of power (such as in committees). Nor can they easily build local support separate from their party since the Canadian electoral system does not provide separate ballots for local candidates and national party leaders. Party power is further consolidated through concentration of financial resources and the power to manipulate or override local nominations. As well, citizen initiatives and referenda are far less common in Canada than they are in the United States, and the Canadian system also places a great deal of power in career public servants with few sub-cabinet political appointees. Overall, the Canadian and American systems differ dramatically with regard to the openings and levers available for evangelical activists.

Nevertheless, Canadian evangelicals have been politically active since at least the 1980s, but their activism has often taken different institutional and ideological routes than has American-style activism. The first such groups were the Evangelical Fellowship of Canada (EFC) and Focus on the Family Canada (FOTFCanada). The EFC, founded in 1964 as a coordinating body for evangelical ministers, launched its public policy role when Brian Stiller became executive director in 1983. FOTFCanada was also founded in 1983 as a subsidiary of James Dobson's prominent American organization. But it is important to note the multiple purposes of these groups. The EFC originated and continues to serve as a general coordinating body for evangelical churches and denominations in Canada, offering a variety of non-political services and publications. Similarly, while both the American and the Canadian branches of Focus on the Family clearly represent a particular understanding and definition of the family (Gilgoff 2007), FOTFCanada's primary focus has been books, radio shows, and other advisory services for parents. Both groups have always qualified for charitable tax status as they are only minimally involved with direct political lobbying.

Other evangelical activists were present in this period, particularly in the anti-abortion movement and often in loose alliance with Roman Catholics. Organizations like Campaign Life Canada brought evangelicals and Catholics together to focus on abortion, euthanasia, and similar issues. But evangelical-Catholic relations were and are somewhat tenuous, both over specific issues like birth control and over much larger doctrinal and theological divides. They formed "uneasy alliances" (Herman 1994). They may have shared conservative social goals, but they had a long and continuing history of profound sectarian conflict. Another organization, REAL Women, though not explicitly evangelical, was also publicly prominent in the 1980s in its opposition to abortion and other key feminist and gay rights policies. Perhaps the most notable evangelical of this era was Ken Campbell, a Baptist minister who founded Renaissance Canada in 1974 and Choose Life Canada in 1984 as vehicles for his crusades against abortion, homosexuality, and lack of parental choices in education (Csillag 2006). Campbell was highly active in the anti-abortion movement and in opposing the inclusion of sexual orientation in human rights codes (Rayside 1988). But Campbell, REAL Women, and other individual evangelical activists did not build larger organizational bases or significant political alliances. Nor did they move beyond outsider tactics like protests, letter campaigns, and publicity events.

Another form of evangelical presence involved the evangelical MPs elected in 1984 as part of the Mulroney Conservative government, forming what was thought to be a substantial "God Squad" within the caucus. But there is little evidence that these MPs had much policy influence as backbenchers, although they did develop informal caucuses and other groupings and played a role in Bill C-43 (see below). In 1993, the Reform Party arose as a major political party in Canada, led by evangelical Preston Manning. But even Manning was careful not to link his faith directly to his political positions and generally avoided references to his beliefs (Manning 2002). His successor, Stockwell Day, also an evangelical, was more open about his faith, leading to much speculation about a hidden religious agenda in the 2000 election. Day's failure to win that election and other factors not necessarily related to his faith led to his losing the leadership in 2002 and his being replaced by Stephen Harper (see below for the relationship between evangelicals and Harper).

Abortion rights was the most notable evangelical issue in the 1980s and early 1990s. But, while deeply opposed to abortion, evangelicals differed considerably regarding what political tactics to use and which policy and legal objectives to pursue. Some, like Campbell, rejected almost any compromise or exception and focused on street confrontations and blockades, at times defying legal injunctions. Other groups, such as the EFC, focused more on legal strategies, appearing as interveners in various abortion cases, while also encouraging congregations to lobby elected officials. The issue culminated in 1989-90 with Bill C-43, a compromise bill that attempted to place limits on abortion without banning it outright. Evangelical leaders such as EFC's Stiller were consulted on the bill and supported it, but many other "pro-life" activists lobbied to defeat the bill (as did many pro-choice groups). Bill C-43 was narrowly defeated, and this badly split the anti-abortion movement – a fissure that remains even today (Jalsevac 2006).

In other words, Canadian evangelicals were politically active in the 1980s and 1990s but were generally neither very high profile nor particularly effective in meeting their goals. The most prominent activists, such as Campbell, were almost entirely outside the conventional political system and relied largely on abortion clinic protests and other direct actions. A larger and more sophisticated political and organizational base did not develop, and, overall, Canada never developed anything close to the organized political clout of the American religious right in the 1980s and 1990s.

Same-Sex Marriage: An Unusual Political Opening

However, Canadian evangelical activism took major steps forward after 2000 as same-sex marriage moved towards becoming Canadian law. Why?

I argue that the key reason is not necessarily increased evangelical awareness or resources but, rather, particular institutional and ideological aspects
of the same-sex marriage debate. Many of the above-mentioned constraints
and factors did not apply. Consequently, Canadian evangelicals were able to
organize, mobilize, and lobby on a much greater scale than ever before.

Same-sex marriage arose as a significant political issue in Canada in the
late 1990s, primarily through a series of court cases involving gays and lesbians who were seeking the right to marry or the equivalent rights of married partners (Smith 2005a). By the early 2000s, gays and lesbians began
winning their marriage challenges regularly in provincial courts, and, in
2004, the Supreme Court of Canada essentially upheld earlier provincial
court rulings in favour of same-sex marriage. Meanwhile, Parliament was
split largely along party lines. While the governing Liberal Party had opposed same-sex marriage for most of the 1990s, by 2004 its leaders and
most of the parliamentary caucus supported it. In contrast, the major opposition party, the Conservatives, was generally opposed to same-sex marriage, though with a small minority in favour.[1] The smaller Bloc Québécois
and New Democratic Party both strongly favoured same-sex marriage.

The House of Commons held four key votes on same-sex marriage. In
1999, in response to growing court activism, the House of Commons overwhelmingly passed a Reform Party resolution to reaffirm the definition of
marriage as "the union of one man and one woman to the exclusion of all
others." But, in 2003, the resolution was reintroduced by same-sex marriage
opponents and narrowly defeated, with prominent Liberals, including then
prime minister Jean Chrétien and his designated successor Paul Martin,
switching their previous votes. In 2005, Parliament then passed the Civil
Marriage Act, legalizing same-sex marriage. Finally, a Conservative government was elected in 2006 and held a vote on whether to revisit the same-sex
marriage law. The motion was defeated. All these votes presented a simple,
clear choice – to support or to oppose same-sex marriage. Federal jurisdiction included only the power to define marriage (and divorce), and the
Supreme Court of Canada had made it clear that legislating a civil union
regime would not be within the federal competence.

The above parliamentary votes were all "free votes," in which most party
leaders neither directed nor disciplined their MPs. The New Democratic
Party, however, required all its members to vote in favour of same-sex marriage and expelled one dissident MP. Free votes are rare in Canadian politics
and are restricted to the most contentious issues, such as same-sex marriage
and other sexual orientation rights (Overby, Tatalovich, and Studlar 1998),

the Bill C-43 vote on abortion (1990) (Overby, Tatalovich, and Studlar 1998), and capital punishment (1987). Hence, individual MPs were unusually free and open to persuasion and pressure.

Furthermore, national elections were held in 2004 and 2006, and in both elections same-sex marriage was a prominent issue. These free votes and general elections presented multiple opportunities for conservative Christians to press candidates on their positions and to mobilize supporters and opponents. In short, many of the usual institutional obstacles and constraints did not apply, and, unusually for Canadian politics, power was placed primarily in the hands of individual legislators who had been freed from normal party discipline.

Additionally, unlike many issues, including even abortion (over which there are differences regarding what exceptions might be permissible and what political tactics and strategies should be used), same-sex marriage is an unambiguous issue for most evangelicals. It affects the heart of evangelical thinking about family structures, reproduction, and, especially, the reading of the Bible and its prohibitions against homosexual acts. Hence, the specific issue of legalizing marriage presented a clear choice – one upon which almost all evangelicals strongly agree. Whereas evangelical opinion was and is somewhat less unified regarding other issues of sexual orientation, such as anti-discrimination laws, gay/lesbian adoption, school curricula, and "civil unions," this was not and is not the case with regard to same-sex marriage. This sharp focus on legalizing same-sex marriage provided a powerful and unifying political opportunity for evangelicals.

Evangelicals took advantage of this opening in many ways. The EFC and FOTFCanada were heavily involved, sponsoring newspaper ads, letter campaigns, and other information efforts, including an FOTFCanada online guide in spring 2004 that listed every MP and his or her position on same-sex marriage. Other groups, like the Canadian Family Action Coalition (founded 1998), were more explicitly political and were not constrained by charitable tax status. Further, a flood of other groups and activists appeared on the political scene, leading to much of the new media attention on evangelicals (McDonald 2006; Dreher 2006; Mason 2006).

Some evangelical messages were highly visible to non-evangelicals, such as an FOTFCanada newspaper campaign in 2004 showing a man, woman, and child surrounded by a large multi-ethnic crowd and this message: "We Believe in Mom and Dad. We Believe in Marriage." But most evangelical messages circulated only in evangelical enclaves, through mailing lists, websites, bulletin inserts, and other media. Messages were overwhelmingly in print or online rather than on radio or television. Hence, while protests and the occasional newspaper ad received attention in the mainstream media, more important were the websites, mailings, and circulars disseminated by large and small groups to evangelicals themselves – and, of course, weekly sermons in church.

While particularly difficult to measure, anecdotal evidence suggests that many Canadian pastors spoke directly from pulpits and otherwise gave an official imprimatur to anti-same-sex marriage efforts. Many of the materials produced by evangelical groups were entitled "church action kits," "letters to pastors," and so on, and they were printed on half-sheets that were inserted into weekly bulletins. Pastors were likely convinced that this was a truly "moral" issue in which church teachings were clear and the choice was un-ambiguous – against same-sex marriage. Hence, they felt comfortable speaking out specifically against same-sex marriage, without addressing other sexual orientation rights. Additionally, pastors could avoid accusations of political involvement by not endorsing actual candidates or parties but simply urging congregants to "pray" about the issue and consider it when they voted – prayer, of course, being considered a serious and important tool in itself among evangelicals.

There is little evidence that evangelical efforts were centrally directed. While there was coordination and information exchange between individuals and groups, no truly central spokespersons or organizations developed. The closest was the Defend Marriage Coalition, which combined the Canada Family Action Coalition (CFAC), REAL Women, the Campaign Life Coalition, and the Catholic Civil Rights League in a loose organization separate from the EFC and FOTFCanada. Some individuals received mainstream media attention – most notably Charles McVety, associated with CFAC and other groups, and Tristan Emmanuel, who was associated with a new group called Equipping Christians for the Public Square. These groups worked together, particularly to organize public demonstrations on Parliament Hill and elsewhere. But, in general, activists and groups remained largely distinct from one another, with a variety of individual initiatives, events, and messages, rather than forming centralized organizations and efforts. Admittedly, there may have been more coordination in private, but there is little evidence to suggest evangelicals planned or acted in concert. Central direction was not necessarily needed since the overall message was clear – to oppose same-sex marriage. As mentioned, not all groups endorsed particular candidates. But the simplicity and centrality of the message left little ambiguity, focusing, as it did, on the need to elect and support

MPs who opposed same-sex marriage and to defeat or sway those who supported it.

New Groups and Institutionalization

Many small groups arose in the fight against same-sex marriage. But many came and went, even between the 2004 and 2006 elections, and were largely volunteer based or driven by single individuals. Often flashy websites and media attention allowed groups to appear bigger and more organized than they actually were. In fact, few new organizations became established out of the same-sex marriage fight, and the long-term survival of even these few is uncertain.

Evidence of this is found in a comparative study of Canadian evangelical political websites that were engaged in anti-same-sex marriage activism. Surveys of websites revealed that, of 25 identified sites in 2004, 10 were defunct in 2007, 11 had not been updated in a year, and only 4 were clearly up to date and maintained (including both the EFC and FOTFCanada).[2]

Existing groups, like the EFC and FOTFCanada, were all established and politically involved in other issues before same-sex marriage appeared, and, since the emergence of the latter, they have not increased significantly in size or scope. FOTFCanada has, however, established the Institute on Marriage and the Family, an Ottawa lobby office that sponsors and promotes conservative research on "family" issues. As mentioned, many of the new groups were driven largely by dynamic single individuals, like Tristan Emmanuel (Equipping Christians for the Public Square), Craig Chandler (Concerned Christians Canada, Inc)., Faytene Kryskow (4MyCanada), and Charles McVety (affiliated with several organizations, including CFAC). But the organizational base behind these charismatic individuals is often weak or unclear, with most of their focus being single high-profile actions, such as advertisements and protests. Though still active in most cases, these groups/individuals lack the characteristics of long-term institutionalization, such as a broad leadership, a stable mass membership, and a range of short- and long-term activities; rather, they resemble the earlier activism of Ken Campbell, a dynamic but marginal individual who was unable or unwilling to build a sustainable, institutionalized political organization separate from himself.

Nor did same-sex marriage lead to further consolidation or centralization of the evangelical political movement. It did inspire the Defend Marriage Coalition, a group combining evangelicals, Catholics, and the nominally non-sectarian REAL Women. Evangelical leaders were also invited to meet collectively with senior government leaders, and evangelical groups and activists continue to talk with each other formally and informally. But, significantly, no permanent structures emerged in the aftermath of the same-sex marriage fight. There is especially little evidence of coalitions or permanent relationships with conservative Catholics and other non-evangelical conservative groups (by early 2007, the Defend Marriage website was defunct and linked back to CFAC). Nor are there any examples of organized national networks bringing together autonomous local or provincial organizations under a common banner, like family policy councils in the United States (Gilgoff 2007).

In short, same-sex marriage spurred many new groups and much activism, but it led neither to major expansions of existing groups nor to significant new organizations, coalitions, or other signs of a mature political movement. Many of the new groups remain active, but none of their more charismatic activists appear to have built any immediately significant political following. Same-sex marriage may have taught these activists more about the political arena and built new contacts, mailing lists, and other valuable resources. It may also have galvanized evangelicals as a whole, raising their political awareness and priming them for further activity on other issues. This could have a long-term effect. But how and on what issues? Same-sex marriage combined an issue upon which there was unusual agreement with a clear institutional focus. Since another parliamentary vote on same-sex marriage is unlikely, evangelical groups and activists must now decide what comes next. Will groups push for restrictions on other sexual orientation issues, such as school curricula (a provincial and local issue)? Will they shift to abortion and reproductive rights? There are many choices. But that is the dilemma – many possible issues to choose, and few or no obvious ones that have clear political openings and/or reasonable chances of success. More likely is a return to the activism of an earlier era, with a continuing flow of small groups and entrepreneurial individuals but little organized effort and only marginal and sporadic influence. Even if same-sex marriage has raised the political consciousness of evangelicals generally, this does not mean that, without the right political opportunities, they will be able to mobilize in the future.

The Conservative Party

A second possible area of long-term influence and institutionalization for evangelicals involves political parties, especially the Conservative Party. As we have seen, the Conservative Party was firmly opposed to same-sex marriage (with a handful of dissenting MPs). Further, in both the 2004 and the 2006 elections, the Liberal Party argued, directly and indirectly, that the Conservatives and their leader Stephen Harper had a "hidden agenda" and were downright "scary," in part because of their alleged evangelical ties and social conservative agenda. Thus, even if evangelicals did not create major new groups of their own, they may have found a political home in the Conservative Party.

The relationship between evangelicals and political parties in Canada is unclear, partly because of the unusual circumstances of the Canadian party system in the 1990s. While the Reform Party had a number of active evangelicals, especially party founder and leader Preston Manning, it was driven more by a populist focus of economic conservatism and regional grievances (Laycock 2002) than by an overt religious agenda. After a brief name change in 2000, when it became the Canadian Alliance, the party merged with the Progressive Conservatives in 2003 to form the new Conservative Party.[3]

The few studies of Canadian evangelical voting do not always agree with each other, especially since they define and categorize evangelicals and related groups differently and hence are not comparable. Guth and Fraser (2001) found that, in the mid-1990s, evangelicals were more likely to support the Reform Party, while mainline Protestants preferred the Progressive Conservatives. Lusztig and Wilson (2005) also find strong moral conservative (i.e., not necessarily "evangelical") support for the Reform Party. But Hoover (1997, 203), who was also looking at mid-1990s data, found that over half (55 percent) of Canadian "Christian right" sympathizers favoured the Liberal Party. In Hoover's study, the Progressive Conservative Party and the Reform Party together garnered only 39 percent support. This is striking, especially given Hoover's sole focus on Christian right supporters; however, it may be explained by the complicated multi-party and regionalized Canadian political system, which sees support for conservative Liberal candidates in Ontario and Atlantic Canada, where the Reform Party was neither well established nor very competitive.

Grenville (2006) found that, in the 2006 election, two-thirds of "Protestants who attend church weekly" voted for the Conservatives – a 25 percent increase from 2004. If we assume a significant number of these Protestants are evangelical, could this suggest a possible surge driven by same-sex marriage? If so, why did it not have the same effect in 2004, when same-sex marriage was just as prominent? One possibility is increased turnout. But Grenville argues that the key determinant was "cleaning up corruption," with regular churchgoers (both Catholic and Protestant) more likely than other voters to identify this as a key election issue, ahead of social and economic policies – and same-sex marriage.

Studies of the 2008 election also yield somewhat varying results, again partly because of the incompatible definitions of "evangelical." However, both Gidengil et al. (2009) and Hutchinson and Hiemstra (2009) agree that evangelicals have become less likely to vote Liberal. Gidengil et al. (2009, 4) found that, in 2008, "Christians who believe that the bible is the literal word of God" preferred the Conservatives over the Liberals "by a margin of almost 50 points." But Hutchinson and Hiemstra, writing under the sponsorship of the EFC, argue that "evangelicals" are voting for parties other than either the Liberals or the Conservatives, with a significant NDP vote in some regions and some support for the Bloc Québécois in Quebec. They argue that, since the 1990s, evangelical support for conservative parties "was due more to Liberal Party alienation of evangelical voters than to a determined attempt on the part of evangelicals to influence politics from the 'religious right'" (Hutchinson and Hiemstra 2009, 1), and they find that by 2008 evangelical support for the Conservatives had "either reached a plateau or begun to decline" (21).

In short, while there appears to be an affinity between evangelical voters and the Conservative Party, the evidence is not overwhelmingly clear. One possible reason for this is the difference between social conservatism (anti-abortion, anti-gay rights, etc.) and economic conservatism. As we saw above, Canadian evangelicals are not by any means on the political right as a whole, and, in particular, they are not as economically conservative as are American evangelicals. Evangelicals may strongly support the social conservative agenda of the Conservative Party, but some may be less enthusiastic about its economic conservatism. This may complicate their relationship with the Conservative Party, especially under the Canadian electoral system, which allows only one vote each for provincial and federal elections – for the local legislative candidate.

Alternatively, though, evangelicals may be active within the Conservative Party itself. Prime minister and party leader Stephen Harper is an evangelical, although he says very little about his beliefs (Mackey 2005). And, while evangelicals are certainly found in the Conservative cabinet and caucus, it is difficult to establish how many. In December 2006, the *National Post* newspaper attempted to survey the religious beliefs and habits of all Canadian MPs, but nearly half did not respond to repeated queries, and another hundred specifically declined to participate (Brean and DeRosa 2006). The sixty-three participating MPs gave a wide range of answers, spanning various religious traditions, most of which were non-evangelical. The most interesting aspect of the survey is the non-participation itself, suggesting that Canadian MPs do not feel that their beliefs are a public matter or at least that they are not amenable to survey questions. In my research, I have asked self-identified evangelical Conservative MPs to estimate how many of their colleagues are evangelical. None has been able to make more than vague guesses, although this may reflect a reluctance to concede that the party has a significant evangelical wing. The most well-known evangelical grouping on Parliament Hill, the weekly prayer breakfast, attracts about fifteen to twenty attendees every week and has a total of about forty to fifty regular attendees, the majority of whom are Conservative. But not all identify as evangelical, while other evangelicals do not attend the breakfast.[4]

There are many individual connections between evangelical groups and the Conservatives (McDonald 2006). In 2007, the main Ottawa lobbyists for the EFC and FOTFCanada were both former Conservative staffers and election candidates. The former president of FOTFCanada became chief of staff to a Conservative minister in 2006, and another ministerial aide was once director of Trinity Western University's Ottawa campus institute, an outpost of evangelical education in the national capital. But these are a few individuals among hundreds of past and present Conservative staff. And, while there are identifiable evangelicals in the current cabinet, such as Chuck Strahl, former leader Stockwell Day, and Vic Toews, they are, like Harper, generally muted about their beliefs. While all are political conservatives, none has been identified as pursuing openly "evangelical" agendas (although Toews, as justice minister, followed a strong "law and order" agenda, including raising the age of heterosexual consent, a key evangelical goal). While some government policies, like cutbacks to child care and women's programs, can be interpreted as accomplishments by anti-feminist evangelicals, these also reflect an economic and anti-state agenda rather than just a socially conservative one.

Admittedly, there may be more going on behind the scenes in the relatively closed parliamentary system. As noted, the hierarchy and discipline of Canadian parties leave evangelicals with limited freedom to openly pursue their own agendas, but other meetings and influences may take place behind the scenes. As well, evangelicals have been active in local party nominations: in the summer of 2006, evangelical activist Charles McVety unsuccessfully challenged the renomination of then Conservative MP Garth Turner, largely because of Turner's support for same-sex marriage. But this effort failed, and senior party officials have criticized such efforts.

Overall, when we consider the relationship between evangelicals and the current Conservative government, the evidence can support various interpretations. One example is the December 2006 parliamentary vote on reopening same-sex marriage, as promised by the Conservatives after the Civil Marriage Act, 2005. The Conservatives were elected in January 2006 with this promise in their platform, but they did not hold the vote until December, after repeatedly promising to hold it but not scheduling a date. The vote was ultimately held with only a week's notice and failed. How can we interpret this? One perspective is that the Conservatives tried but failed to roll back same-sex marriage and may well try again, although Harper has said he will not. Another perspective is that it was a quick attempt to dispose of the obligation to hold the vote without giving evangelical groups sufficient time to mobilize and to focus their efforts, thus ultimately laying the issue to rest.

Thus, while it is clear that evangelicals have not created a major new set of political groups and coalitions as a result of same-sex marriage, they could well be pursuing more influence within the Conservative Party itself. However, even if this is the case, it may not be either an effective or an advisable option for evangelicals. A long-term Conservative-evangelical alliance would not necessarily be in evangelical interests if and when the Conservatives lose power since, in Canada's system of responsible government, governing parties control nearly all legislative and executive actions. Many evangelicals are unwilling to support a political party that pursues both social and economic conservatism. Thus, while some evangelical activists may work to mobilize their supporters to vote Conservative, others will avoid partisan entanglements, whether out of principle, for strategic reasons, or due to simple disagreement with the wider Conservative agenda.

Conclusion: Can Evangelicals Influence the Political Agenda?
In 1994, Didi Herman (276) wrote that "academics are divided over whether the Christian Right is a vibrant or a dying force in Canada." While same-sex marriage led to increased evangelical activism in Canada, Herman's statement still applies today. It is not clear whether what we are now witnessing is a new and permanent level of evangelical activism or merely a temporary surge. Same-sex marriage was an issue upon which evangelicals largely agreed and for which the political openings were clear and available. But without such political opportunities, Canadian evangelical activism is likely to return to the more low-profile and mixed patterns of the 1980s and 1990s.

A key test for any future evangelical activism is whether it can actually shape the public agenda rather than simply react to events (as was the case with same-sex-marriage). Evangelicals fought "an uphill battle" (Smith 2005a), reacting to the string of judicial rulings initiated by gay and lesbian activists against current marriage laws (in which evangelicals sought intervener status). In contrast, in the United States, gays and lesbians are the ones in a "much more defensive posture" (ibid.). Canadian evangelicals have generally been unable to seriously challenge, much less roll back, policy gains by feminists, gays and lesbians, and other groups through, for example, new abortion laws or restrictions on same-sex marriage. One possible example of pre-emptive action is the 1999 House of Commons resolution affirming the definition of marriage as "the union of one man and one woman to the exclusion of all others," which attempted to head off the same-sex marriage trend. But this had little effect on subsequent judicial rulings.

If evangelical activism becomes more prominent and influential in Canadian politics, it is likely to be in areas outside sexuality and the political right – such as social policy, the environment, international development, and human rights – areas in which groups like the EFC and the semi-evangelical Citizens for Public Justice have long been active. Here evangelicals are more likely to work in coalition with other religious and non-religious organizations and, with a more subdued profile, to focus on research and information lobbying rather than on demonstrations and choosing political candidates. Some groups, like the EFC, will continue to combine this work with activism against sexual orientation and reproductive rights. And other groups and individuals will continue to promote a true "religious right" agenda, focusing on sexuality and reproduction issues and combining them with other social and economic conservative values. But these groups will likely remain small and driven by individual activists, attracting some public notice but having minimal real influence on politics and public policy.

In conclusion, the struggle over same-sex marriage created a wave of new evangelical activism in Canada, but the evidence of a truly new level of evangelical activism, especially "religious right" activism, is at best mixed. Canadian evangelicals remain politically dispersed and disparate, without the political opportunities and institutional openings available to their American counterparts. They cannot be counted out completely as a political force, but they remain highly defensive, with little ability to shape the public agenda, especially on issues of sexuality and reproduction such as same-sex marriage.

MAINLINE PROTESTANTS

Evangelicals frame their opposition to egalitarian policies in biblical passages, but mainline Protestants have historically used a variety of theological resources to craft responses to policy issues. Although mainline denominations draw on the Bible, they also consider evolving notions of equality, family, and sexuality. That said, there are continuities in the Christian response to questions of sexuality. In Chapter 9, Pamela Dickey Young accentuates these continuities in a historical account that is relevant to all Christians but especially to the mainline churches, which are more likely than their evangelical counterparts to debate doctrine in response to social change.

Other chapters in this section emphasize the struggle over change. In both the United States and Canada, the rapid-fire emergence of political issues surrounding sexual diversity over the past forty years has led to intense deliberation within the whole range of mainline Protestant communities. In both countries, progressive voices in the mainline churches have come to support full equality, up to and including marriage. More traditional groups, in many cases, have shifted to an inclusive position on some policy fronts but stop short of full marriage or liturgical blessing of same-sex couples and the ordination of LGBT clergy. In both countries, but in the United States in particular, there have been deep divisions over these issues.

In Chapter 10, Roger Hutchinson traces the deliberations at the elite level of the United Church of Canada, the largest mainline denomination in that country. He notes that the General Council encouraged dialogue on the marriage issue. As it now stands, individual congregations can decide both whether to perform same-sex marriages and whether their minister can perform them outside of the church. This dialogue is rooted in different theological views, but the debate has been conducted in ways that suggest the possibility of a common framework and that have generally allowed for civil discussion. It is probably too soon to know if the same conclusion can be drawn about the American denomination that comes closest to this – the United Church of Christ.

In Chapter 11, Laura Olson, Paul Djupe, and Wendy Cadge trace the roots of progressivism in the US mainline denominations and their engagement with issues of equity for LGBT citizens. They show that the vast majority of mainline clergy and their congregations favour equal protections provided by the state. Using data from their own surveys, they show that adult education sessions provide an important venue for deliberation and for prophetic leadership by clergy. Like Hutchinson, they see indications that a common faith can help communities work through pronounced differences on difficult issues that have plagued Christian churches for many years.

It's All about Sex
The Roots of Opposition to Gay and Lesbian Marriages in Some Christian Churches

PAMELA DICKEY YOUNG

Gay and lesbian marriages became an important issue on the Canadian legal and social scene through a series of court and legislative decisions from the 1990s onward that granted progressively more spousal rights and responsibilities to same-sex couples.[1] By 2000, challenges to laws denying gay and lesbian couples the right to marry were under way in Ontario, Quebec, and British Columbia. Decisions in Quebec and Ontario ruled that marriage for male-female couples only was unconstitutional, though implementation of these rulings was suspended. In June 2003, the Ontario Court of Appeal upheld the trial court decision but ordered the law reversed immediately. Gay and lesbian marriages began to take place right away.

Following this, the Government of Canada drafted a bill defining civil marriage as being between two persons and sent a reference to the Supreme Court of Canada asking for advice on it. On 28 June 2005, Bill C-38 passed in the Canadian House of Commons; on 19 July 2005, it passed in the Senate. Now civil marriage is available to gay and lesbian couples in all of Canada.

The vigorous debate that surrounded these steps included many religious groups as active participants, though Christian churches were the most vocal religious participants. In this chapter I am concerned primarily with opposition to gay and lesbian marriage and with exploring its roots in Christian attitudes towards sex.

Framing the Opposition to Same-Sex Marriage

The most vocal Christian opponents of same-sex marriage were the Roman Catholic Church and the Evangelical Fellowship of Canada.[2] The United Church of Canada, the Metropolitan Community Churches, the Quakers, and the Unitarian Universalists support gay and lesbian marriage. Several churches, including the Anglican Church of Canada, the Presbyterian Church in Canada, and the Evangelical Lutheran Church in Canada did not take part in any official way in the public policy debate because they were embroiled in internal debates about same-sex relationships – debates that remain unresolved.

Most public policy arguments against gay and lesbian marriage put forward by churches that oppose it are those made on the basis of nature, procreation, child rearing, and heterosexual complementarity, which use biological, philosophical, historical, and sociological reasons to justify opposition. Often these positions assume, or argue for, a purported universality of belief or practice. To allow same-sex marriages would create a form "that would replace the institution of marriage as it has always universally been understood" (Interfaith Coalition 2003). Marriage is understood not to be variable in its essence but, rather, to be a natural state that arises inevitably from the fact that humans are male and female and need to procreate to ensure the survival of the race (CCCB 2005b).

Some church documents opposed to same-sex marriage state that procreation is *the* main purpose of marriage (La Ligue Catholique pour les Droits de l'Homme et Alliance Évangélique du Canada 2003). Many of the churches' arguments emphasize their view that heterosexual spouses are "uniquely, biologically capable of procreating children" (Interfaith Coalition 1995, 1999). The creative force of sexuality "overflows and is designed to bear fruit" (i.e., to lead to procreation) (CCCB 2003a). Marriage as traditionally defined is a matter of the "survival of humanity" (CCCB 2005f).

The Canadian Conference of Catholic Bishops (CCCB 2004a) argues, in fact, that the state's only interest in marriage should be the interest of procreation; otherwise, sex ought not to be a matter of state interest: "Central to this question [of whether gay and lesbian couples are discriminated against by not allowing them to marry] is whether the state must provide symbolic or moral approval to sexual conduct underlying these relationships by including them in marriage, hence creating a constitutional right from a sexual preference."

Sometimes the statements acknowledge that, for whatever reasons, not all heterosexual marriages are procreative. However, when such acknowledgment is made the statements quickly go on to indicate that the exception does not invalidate the point: "The inherent biological fact remains that a marriage between a man and a woman will usually produce children which no shift in thinking, social trends or technologies can alter" (CCCB 2003a).

The biological capacity to produce children is usually set alongside a view that sees male and female as two complementary parts of one human whole: "The anatomical complementarity which makes the engendering of new lives possible is fundamental to the reality of *marriage*, not to mention the psychological and affective complementarity, as well as the natural mutuality, of a man and a woman" (CCCB 2005b). Marriage, says the EFC, is "rooted in the way we are made," meaning that marriage only finds its meaning in heterosexual procreative pairing (Evangelical Fellowship of Canada 2005). Marriage is for male-female couples because biology has made men and women to "fit" together in a certain way and because the main purpose of marriage is procreation (and, by extension, child rearing).

It's All about Sex

There is very little discussion of sex per se in these debates. Churches are not, on the whole, comfortable with discussions of sexuality. I suspect, also, that discussions of sexuality are directly avoided for fear of veering off into the kind of anti-gay and lesbian discourse that permeates the churches' own internal discussions of sexual orientation.

And yet the debate about same-sex marriage in the context of the Christian church really is a debate about sex. What constitutes acceptable sex? Who can/should have sex with whom and under what circumstances?

Christians have, from about the second century on, had problems finding an appropriate place for sex. The construction of desire has been hemmed in by constraints that call it "sinful" and see it as redeemed only by childbearing. Although some Protestant churches have recently tried to claim another trajectory for sex, in line with the notion of the goodness of creation, including the goodness of sexuality, sex is, in the Christian tradition, at the very least, ambiguous. Little wonder, then, that the marriage of gay and lesbian couples is a fraught topic for Christian churches.

What happens in most discussions of same-sex marriage is that this negative view of sexuality generally gets exacerbated. The sexual relationships of same-sex couples cannot be "redeemed" by direct biological procreation. When same-sex couples do have children by use of reproductive technologies or adoption, this does not solve the problem. The problem is not lack of children: it is "illicit" sex. Often such a view is tied to a very narrow view of sex in general, which reduces all "licit" sex to placing penises in vaginas, the only truly acceptable sexual act for a tradition focused on reproduction.

Further, this negative view of sexuality is tied up with views of the proper roles of men and women. It is not an accident that the churches most opposed to same-sex marriage are also those in which women's roles are seen as vastly different from men's. In the Roman Catholic Church and in some of the evangelical Protestant churches, women cannot be ordained and can assume only limited roles of leadership. Even when women can be ordained, as in some evangelical Protestant churches, it is usually agreed that women's roles are more in the nature of helping men, especially in marriage, where it is often claimed that marriages need one clear head and that that head is the man (LaHaye and LaHaye 1976; Piper 1991). Lesbian and gay relationships do not allow for the living out of accepted sex and gender roles.

Churches have a history of being publicly concerned over matters that have to do with sex. Historically, some churches have also commented on issues like poverty, but the outcry has not been so widespread, nor have these issues grabbed media attention as have those about sex. Why sex so grabs the Christian imagination (and the attention of the media) is complex. Sex provides a high potential for scandal. Traditionally, Christians have used questions of sex to assert control over their members. Since the Enlightenment, much responsibility has devolved to the individual. Although there are exceptions (e.g., the various liberation theologies), the general attitude in Western Christianity in the modern era emphasizes the relationship of the individual to God and to the church. Because sexuality is now seen as about individual choices and individual responsibility, it has become a crucial site for determining conformity to the church's ideals.

In Christian terms (especially those influenced by Victorian attitudes), the church has seen itself as the guardian of moral purity (Valverde 1991). In Western society, the site of moral purity has primarily been sex rather than, say, money. The drive for sex is powerful. But, unlike most other drives (e.g., hunger), it can be controlled, both by the individual and by social coercion, with non-mortal consequences. The threat of sex and rules about sex can and have been used as instruments of power and control. Thus, arguments about purity can also be used to confer additional power on those who get to articulate and apply the rules. Thus, in the Christian vocabulary, the universality of sexual desire and the possibility of exerting control over it have placed sex in a particular relationship to sin. Fear of the power of sexual urges on the part of those in power (often male celibates), coupled with a fear of women, gives sex a very powerful role to play. Sex also comes to be associated with shame, and shaming is a very effective way of exerting control. Rules about sexuality offer to those who make them a power that taps deep into human emotions. Sex is bad, dirty, dangerous, shameful, chaotic, and *pleasurable*. Thus, it is to be feared and controlled.

As Foucault makes clear, the more sex is seen as a problem (in this case by the churches), the more it is emphasized, discussed, classified. In the service of prurience, sexual language is kept alive (Foucault 1978, 49). If Christian churches keep sex on the front burner by continuing to enumerate all the ways in which it is wrongly enacted, little wonder that discourse on sex continues to abound, especially discourse on the regulation of sex. The cultural power of Christianity, even in a society in which churchgoing has decreased over time, has influenced the way in which sex and, hence, same-sex marriage have been discussed.

For all that Christians have not been comfortable talking about sexuality, then, sex has dominated Christian views of sin – and no time more than in the present. Daniel Maguire (2000) speaks of our era as a time of "pelvic orthodoxy" in religious traditions. In other words, the test of right belief has to do not with theology but, rather, with what one thinks about sexuality and, further, with whether one's sexual identity and conduct are acceptable to the religious organization in question.

Early Development of Christian Dualism

Such views are deeply rooted in Christian history. As the early Christian church developed, a clear preference arose for celibacy over marriage. The earliest Christians thought that the second coming of Jesus Christ would happen very shortly and, thus, that marriage and procreation were not important. As the church endured, sexuality began to be seen as unruly, a manifestation of lack of control and an example of how the flesh could keep the spirit in bondage. Sexuality was one area of human life that presented adherents and leaders of the early church with many situations for the possibility of evil. Sexual renunciation was seen as a way to dismantle sinful society and to build up the church within a state that mirrored paradise before the fall. Celibacy was a sign of the reign of God to come (Brown 2002, 134): "When they rise from the dead, they neither marry nor are given in marriage, but are like angels in heaven" (Mark 12:25 NRSV). The perfect human state, whether before the fall or after the coming of God's kingdom, was non-sexually active. According to Peter Brown (1987, 263), "Christians tended to make their exceptional sexual discipline bear the full burden of expressing the difference between themselves and the pagan world."

By the late third century, celibacy clearly won out over sexuality as the preferable Christian choice, and the sexualized body became a locus of personal control. Virgin bodies were admirable and admired; sexually active bodies were denigrated. Several dualisms coalesce in the early centuries of Christianity to produce a negative attitude towards sexuality. The split between spirit and body, although admittedly not as pronounced in most orthodox forms of early Christianity as in forms that came to be seen as marginal, still influences the way Christians think. Most Christians may not have thought the flesh entirely evil and entirely to be overcome, yet the notion that the flesh presents opportunities for evil becomes strong even in mainstream Christianity. The spirit-body split finds a prominent form in the celibacy-marriage split. Marriage is the poor second choice to celibacy, with a second-rate spirituality attached to it. Sexuality becomes the paradigmatic case of weakness of the flesh.

We must not underestimate how strongly these two dualisms of spirit-flesh and celibacy-marriage are connected to the dualism of male-female. Early on in Christianity, femaleness began to be seen as the locus of sexual temptation, "the Devil's gateway," as expressed by early church father Tertullian (2007). According to Brown (2002, 133), "the female body came to be presented as the condensed essence of all human bondage and of all human vulnerability." The theological texts were written by men who played out their own sexual issues on the bodies of women. Thus, women were made to bear the burden of sexuality as a problem.

One indication of the heavy emphasis on sexual restraint in the early church may be found in the fourth-century Canonical Epistles of Basil of Caesarea, in which sexual offences are the subject of forty-one canons, whereas murder, for example, is the subject of only twelve (Brown 2002, 135). By the late fourth century, the effort to enforce clerical celibacy began, although it was not finally enforced until the Middle Ages. By the fifth century, the end of the present age was no longer expected, and divisions between women and men became increasingly important. Thus, the equality between virgin women and virgin men that had pertained in the early church came to an end, and even virgin women became increasingly problematic: "It was no longer a world where men and women could be safely allowed to be *one in Christ Jesus*" (Brown 2002, 137).

Augustine (354-430 CE) had a lasting influence on Christian views of sexuality, inheriting the earlier Christian view that virginity is the highest calling. He did not think marriage an evil, but it was a second-best calling – redeemable because of reproduction and the control of lust and allowing a certain bond between the two people who were married. However, with Augustine, virginity became doubly emphasized. He himself struggled with his own sexuality, and before his conversion to Christianity he had a concubine and a son. He viewed his conversion to Christianity as a release from sexual desire (Miles 1990, 121). In his autobiographical *Confessions*, he details his struggles to maintain chastity. He worries about his inability to maintain self-control over his erections – that most visible sign of male sexuality. Augustine's doctrine of original sin, which becomes central to the church's teaching, links original sin directly to sexuality. Original sin, the sin of the first couple, Adam and Eve, is passed on through lust (misplaced desire) and semen to all other future generations. Thus, all are born sinful and in need of redemption, and the vehicle of this sinfulness is sexuality. Once sexuality is linked directly with the inherited sin of all humanity, it becomes very difficult for Christians to see it as a positive part of human existence. With Augustine, Christianity's discourse about sexuality becomes firmly entrenched as being directly related to sin.

Private penance was introduced in the Fourth Lateran Council (1215). With this, emphasis was placed on the individual's confession of sins rather than on the sins of the church as a whole (Price 1996, 17-18). It comes as no surprise that sexual sins often became those sins that it was most important to confess in private penance: "Earnest Catholics had now no alternative but to impose on themselves with the help of regular private confession, the sexual restraint that the penitential system of the early Church had more proclaimed to all than imposed on each" (18). Penitential manuals from the Middle Ages provide long lists of sexual sins to guide priests in the administration of the sacrament of penance.

The Protestant Reformation is often seen as a time when sexuality was revalorized within Christianity. Certainly, celibacy was declaimed and marriage lauded: "Yet the Reformation was fought in highly sexualized language. The Protestants accused Catholic celibates, priests and nuns, of practicing secret fornication under the robes of higher holiness. Catholics, in turn, impugned the virtues of Protestant clerical marriage, implying that Luther and his confreres violated their vows of celibacy to marry because of an incapacity to contain their lustful urges" (Ruether 2000, 45). Although marriage was expected of all Protestants, views of sexuality did not change markedly. In Protestant views, marriage was primarily for the control of lust, not for the good of sexuality. In marriages, women were assumed to be under the control of their husbands, thus continuing to find themselves the devalued half of the male-female split.

The Reformation view of marriage and sexuality did not explicitly offer anything that we might now regard as framing sexuality as positive. Still, the Reformation was a turning point with regard to Protestants' views of married sexuality. Even though the Reformers were as wary of lust as were their Roman Catholic contemporaries, the fact that marriage, rather than celibacy, became the norm for all Protestant Christians and the highest calling did open the possibility of revaluing sexuality as a good in and of itself. But this would take centuries. Sex was still seen as presenting prime opportunities for sin.

Evolution of Christian Attitudes towards Homosexuality

In the early church, homosexual activity was not particularly singled out for attention. In the fourth century, John Chrysostom thought that the world was fully populated and that, therefore, no more procreation was needed. He was open to the ancient argument in favour of pederasty as the "final refinement of lovemaking" (Brown 1987, 308; Chrysostom, cited in Boswell 1980). In fact, though, Chrysostom was opposed to sex in general and saw homosexual activity as risking placing men in the inferior position of being seen like women: "For I maintain that not only are you [men] made [by it] into a woman, but you also cease to be a man" (Chrysostom, Commentary on Romans, Homily 4, translated in Boswell 1980, 361).

In the Middle Ages, Christian attitudes towards same-sex sexual activity become solidified and codified into the attitudes that are common today in churches such as the Roman Catholic Church and the evangelical Christian churches. Disapprobation of same-sex sexual activity became more specific and more catalogued than it had been in earlier Christian centuries. Christian attitudes towards same-sex sexual activity in the Middle Ages and after were shaped by the view that procreation was the only way to redeem sexual activity as a potentially licit activity. Antipathy towards homosexuality was also sharpened by the enhanced differentiation of men and women, by the attribution of specific roles according to their sex, and by the associated idea that same-sex sexual activity was against "nature."

Over the course of the Middle Ages, same-sex sexual activity was increasingly defined as a crime against nature (Wiesner-Hanks 2000, 38). During this period, there are many prohibitions in religious orders regarding particular friendships. The Third Lateran Council (1179) made clerics who could not give up homosexual activity resign their clerical status; laypeople who indulged in same-sex activity were to be excommunicated (ibid.).

In her research, Wiesner-Hanks (2000, 88) finds only a small number of sodomy cases in Protestant Europe in the sixteenth to seventeenth centuries:

> This lack of concern about sodomy in comparison with other types of sexual misconduct resulted in part because homosexual relations did not lead to a child who might require public support, and in part because most male homosexual relations seem to have occurred between a superior and inferior such as an older man and a younger, or master and servant. The dominant individual was generally married and heterosexually active, with his homosexual activities not viewed as upsetting the social order. This began to change in the late seventeenth century, when homosexual subcultures started to develop in many European cities with special styles of dress, behavior, slang terms, and meeting places; these networks brought together men of different social classes and backgrounds, and did not necessarily involve a dominant and a subordinate partner.

Female homoerotic activity was seen as masturbation and was not much worried about until the eighteenth century. In Catholic Europe, during the Aragonese Inquisition between 1570 and 1630, there were more executions for bestiality than for homosexual sodomy (Wiesner-Hanks 2000, 126).

In the nineteenth century the notion of homosexual identity as something fixed, stable, and negative became more common. Churches widely adopted the idea of a stable "homosexual" identity, providing a vehicle not only to talk about particular acts as forbidden but also to categorize the people who perform these acts as separate from those who perform normative heterosexuality. Negative attitudes towards particular acts also get translated into negative attitudes towards those who engage in those acts.

In the contemporary world these historical views of sexuality in the church continue to influence the way churches think about sexuality. Roman Catholics are still influenced by historical views that privilege celibacy and encourage fear of sexuality. Arguments about sexuality are also grounded in a view of what is assumed to be "natural" or universal (Gründel 1975). Of course, that which is assumed natural or universal does not have to be debated or discussed.

Protestants retain more than is widely recognized of earlier anxieties about sex. Since the 1970s there has been a growing body of evangelical Protestant literature on sexuality (DeRogatis 2005). This literature tends to value sex both for its procreative function and for its role in fostering a bond between couples. In all this literature, though sex is seen as a qualified good, it is good only in its God-given place. According to evangelical Christian readings of the Bible, the only acceptable sexual expression is heterosexual sex within the bounds of Christian marriage. Homosexual acts are explicitly condemned. Thus sex is still problematic, and premarital sex and gay and lesbian sex are not acceptable.

Protestant churches with a broader view of scriptural interpretation tend also to depend on contemporary sociological and scientific studies as well as on cultural trends to help them develop their views of sexuality. Since the 1960s, and even more since the 1980s, most mainline Protestant churches in Canada and elsewhere (churches like the United Church of Canada, the Anglican Church of Canada, the Presbyterian Church in Canada, and the Evangelical Lutheran Church in Canada) have published one or more reports on sex and sexuality in addition to reports on specific topics such as same-sex marriage. On the whole, these reports tend to affirm the goodness of sexuality within the bonds of heterosexual marriage as a way to promote intimacy, communication, and stable relationships. They seek to move beyond the traditional Christian ambivalence towards the body and sometimes expand the range of acceptable sexual contact beyond the bounds of heterosexual marriage by talking about permanence of commitment and the context within which sexual relationships take place.

Despite changes in the official positions of some churches, which have begun to depict sex as good rather than negative, it is still not difficult to find, lurking under the surface, the sex negativity that has so plagued Christianity. The fact that, despite these changes, many churches (e.g., the Canadian Presbyterian, Lutheran, and Anglican churches) still cannot make clear decisions about gay and lesbian relationships suggests to me that the "changed" views of sexuality have not really been internalized. As well, many Protestant churches still see marriage as the norm and cohabitation as a lesser choice, which also suggests that there are still strong views about the distinction between "licit" and "illicit" sex (see, for example, Anglican

Church of Canada 2006; Presbyterian Church in Canada 1996). In its official statements, the United Church of Canada seems unusual in having moved beyond any simple rules-based statement of licit or illicit sexuality, preferring to talk about the quality of human relationships (United Church of Canada 2005b).

Of course, it is true that no matter what a church's official position on sexuality, there are many Christian adherents who still express their own views based on the sex-negative history of Christianity. This is the reason why, even in churches like the United Church of Canada, there is no uniform support for cohabitation before marriage or for gay and lesbian marriages. Thus, even when official positions change, attitudes do not always change with them.

Conclusion

Overall, Christians do not have a promising history when it comes to dealing with sexuality. The basic Christian adage has been "don't do it," with the qualification that, "if you have to, only do it under particular and [until recently] very limited circumstances." The traditional Christian approach to sexuality has been rules based, and this is still the dominant approach in churches opposed to gay and lesbian marriage. What this means is that, predominantly, these churches have dealt with sexuality by establishing a set of seemingly invariant rules to deal with sexual issues even in the face of evidence of considerable variability (Wiesner-Hanks 2000). Sex outside marriage is seen as wrong regardless of the context.

Churches are both fascinated and repelled by sexuality. When churches are trying to downplay sexuality and to legislate repressive rules in order to avoid sexuality's dangers, they keep the subject front and centre in the ecclesiastical mind. Constant church talk about sex makes Christian adherents recognize that sex is a big problem, and this, in turn, reinforces the constant talk about it.

Churches tend to talk about sexuality as though it is a matter of rules. The moral agency and autonomy of people to make their own decisions about sexuality are not recognized. As Marvin Ellison (2004, 236) argues,

The church's lack of moral leadership on sex has in fact infantilized people, disempowering them to make responsible sexual choices. By defining a whole range of sexual experiences as sinful, the church has promoted guilt rather than sexual maturity; it has not helped people learn how to accept what they need, give and receive sexual pleasure freely, and direct their lives in order to enhance their own and other's joy and self respect. If the church is going to be helpful here, it has to be willing to undertake a major shift in its ethical sensibilities.

If those churches that are currently opposed to same-sex marriage are ever going to come to terms with same-sex relationships, they will have to modify their fundamental attitudes towards sex, moving from a view of sex as primarily dangerous and needing to be controlled to a view of sex as good or, at the very least, as neutral (although, like all other human capacities, capable of being abused). If sex is the problem and rules are the answer, then such a change seems unlikely in the near future. To put it another way, churches that espouse positive views of same-sex relationships are churches that have altered their attitudes towards sexuality, seeking to see it as being primarily good but capable of distortion. These churches have received relatively little media attention in a time when media are seeking to portray themselves as highly "secular" and, thus, as uninfluenced by religion.

To show that the genesis of Christian opposition to same-sex marriage lies in the sex-negativity of Christianity is to show how difficult it is to change points of view on gay and lesbian issues without reconceptualizing the entire history of sexuality within Christianity. I argue that churches are only able to accept gay and lesbian sexuality as potentially good when they: (1) are able to view sexuality as a genuine good, untied to procreation; (2) are able to get beyond notions of male-female complementarity and the assigning of roles on the basis of perceived sex difference; and (3) are able to give up claims to what is "natural" and "universal" and to start to see that specific views of sex, gender, and sexuality are not invariable givens but social constructions that vary over time. When gay and lesbian sexuality is seen positively, the possibility of support for same-sex marriages will arise.

10

Focusing, Framing, and Discerning
The United Church of Canada and the
Same-Sex Marriage Debate

ROGER HUTCHINSON

At the August 2003 meeting of its General Council, the United Church of Canada passed a resolution affirming its support for same-sex marriages and calling for legislation amending the legal definition of marriage. This official policy statement by the national church did not change the fact that local congregations continue to have the authority to decide whether or not same-sex marriages will be performed in a particular church and whether the congregation's minister will be permitted to officiate at the marriage of a same-sex couple at another location. As the moderator and general secretary pointed out in their commentary on the General Council's action, "the fact that General Council makes some decisions about marriage and congregations make other decisions reflects the wisdom that some decisions are best made centrally and some decisions are best made locally." An important observation is that "the United Church of Canada recognizes and honours more than one voice in this conversation of discernment" (United Church of Canada 2003b).

In making this comment, the moderator and general secretary realized that more than one voice participated in the determination of the national policy and that very different voices are striving to be heard as particular congregations attempt to decide what their practices will be. My aim in this chapter is to examine the framing and focusing of deliberations over same-sex marriage in the United Church as a case study in religious engagement with a highly politicized sexuality issue (Lakoff 2007).[1] I concentrate on the

United Church, but the larger background I am taking for granted includes the processes of dialogue and discernment involving courts, parliaments, parliamentary committees, churches, and other civil society organizations.[2]

I adopt the moderator and general secretary's language of discernment for two reasons. First, it draws attention to the importance of dialogue. It is through dialogue that we clarify the reasons used to support or criticize particular conclusions. A conversation of discernment presumes a degree of openness to the insights and critiques of others and a willingness to move beyond our initial taken for granted frameworks or "gut responses." For example, as I explain below, participants in conversations of discernment about same-sex marriage went beyond the conflict between progress and decline narratives by exchanging reasons within a shared common law tradition. A second factor involves the larger context within which dialogue takes place. Conversations of discernment both arise from and return to the need for decisions and actions regarding particular practices. On the one hand, there was a need to determine official United Church policy through the appropriate procedures of the General Council whether or not there was a church-wide consensus; on the other hand, local congregations are following appropriate procedures to determine whether or not same-sex marriages will be performed in their churches and/or by their ministers.[3]

Although the Christian churches no longer think of Canada as a Christian society, they continue to play significant roles in public conversations about society's values, policies, and practices. They take it for granted that, in a post-Christendom society, the public realm is shared space. It is *secular* in the sense that no single religion is dominant, but this understanding of secular need not be confused with the *secularist* assumption that religion is a purely private matter. In relation to the debate in the public realm about same-sex marriage, a major contribution of the United Church was the evidence it provided that all Christian churches were not opposed to the redefinition of marriage (Dickey Young 2006, 15). Its internal discussions over the issue, too, provide a window onto the ways in which the issue was framed at the local level, far away from the legislative and courtroom settings.

The United Church is Canada's largest Protestant denomination. It was formed in 1925 through the union of Canadian Methodists, Congregationalists, and 70 percent of Canadian Presbyterians. According to 2001 Statistics Canada figures, close to 3 million Canadians reported a United Church affiliation. This represented close to 10 percent of the Canadian population, about one-third of the total of 27 percent reporting a Protestant affiliation. Another one-third of Protestants are affiliated to conservative churches, so the United Church represents about one-half of mainline Protestants. Forty-three percent are Roman Catholic.

Although the United Church now has a more pluralistic understanding of its status as a "national church," through its various courts, committees, and congregations it continues to play an important role in the public realm (United Church of Canada 2005b).[4] Its governing structure consists of four courts, the General Council (national), thirteen regional conferences, and ninety presbyteries. At the end of 2007, there were 3,362 individual congregations, 3,762 ordained ministers, and 282 diaconal ministers). Even if debate over whether same-sex marriages will be performed in church or by ministers has not yet occurred in every congregation, opportunities have been or will be provided in over three thousand locations in rural, urban, and suburban settings for such conversations. This is an important fact to keep in mind when reflecting on the churches' contributions to public debate over an issue that has been deeply divisive.

Progress versus Decline as Conflicting Narratives

The United Church's positions on issues related to homosexuality have undergone considerable debate and change over the past quarter century. Prior to the 1980s, during the church's debates over gender and procreation, marriage, and divorce, the issues of homosexuality and same-sex relationships were not on the agenda. When homosexuality was mentioned in passing, it was usually in negative terms. For example, the 1960 report, *Toward a Christian Understanding of Sex, Love and Marriage*, regards homosexuality as "a deviation from normal sexual feelings." The attitude of the United Church towards such persons should be respect, sympathy, and a desire to help: "This help may include referral to a source of treatment" (United Church of Canada 1960, 14-15).

A similar tendency to take for granted the heterosexual character of marriage without a clear focus on why that should continue to be the case is apparent in the 1974 report entitled *The Permanence of Christian Marriage*. Using the term "bisexual" in a way that we would now use the term "heterosexual," as well as the exclusive language of the day, the report declares that

> Marriage is *bisexual*. Man is a bisexual animal. It is by the union of men and women that the human race – and therefore every particular human culture – is perpetuated. The existence of marriage as an institution is directly dependent on the fact that children are the result of bisexual relationships. The propagation of children has political, economic, social and cultural

consequences. Marriage is the basic institution by which these consequences are ordered in any particular society. Without the bisexuality of
human procreation there would be no reason for marriage to exist. It would
be socially redundant. (United Church of Canada 1974, 285)[5]

The above excerpts from reports from the 1960s and 1970s suggest that
there was not yet a "conversation of discernment" *between* heterosexual and
homosexual church members or a clear focus on the interests and aspirations of lesbian and gay church members.[6] However, by the time a 1969
Criminal Code amendment decriminalized homosexual acts, the changing
beliefs and attitudes of church and society had begun to inform one another.
With greater acceptance of homosexuality, the main question became what
equality for lesbians and gays required. For the United Church, the focus in
the 1980s had shifted from arguments for and against equal treatment to the
eligibility of lesbians and gays for full membership in the church. In 1988,
after a lengthy study, the United Church decided that sexual orientation was
not a barrier to full membership, including acceptance as ordained or commissioned ministers (United Church of Canada 1988). Some ministers,
church members, and congregations left the United Church over the decision to ordain and commission sexually active homosexuals. Other dissenting ministers and church members formed a group called the Community
of Concern, which included the following clause in its mission statement:

> Being convinced that the Biblical intent for sexual behaviour is loving fidel-
> ity within marriage and celibacy outside marriage, we intend to pursue a
> clear statement of policy on the part of The United Church of Canada de-
> claring the unsuitability of self-declared practicing homosexual persons for
> ordained/commissioned ministry in our church. (Community of Concern
> 2006)[7]

In the 1990s, a new focus emerged regarding the expectations of same-
sex couples when debate shifted to options for publicly celebrating same-sex
covenanted relationships. The 1992 General Council "directed that liturgical and pastoral resources for same-sex covenants be made available to congregations" (United Church of Canada, 2003c). In 1999, the United Church
expressed its "commitment to the equality of heterosexual and same-sex
relationships" by supporting Bill C-23, Modernization of Benefits and Obligations, before the Standing Committee on Justice and Human Rights

(ibid.). This legislation extended recognition of de facto same-sex relationships (in the federal jurisdiction), putting them on close to equal footing
with de facto heterosexual couples, who were already given wide recognition in Canadian public law and policy.

In August 2000, the Thirty-Seventh General Council passed resolutions
calling on the United Church "to affirm lesbian and gay partnerships and to
work for their civil recognition." In February 2003, the United Church urged
the federal government to "adopt a legislative framework that provides the
same civil recognition for heterosexual and homosexual couples" (United
Church of Canada 2003c). As an interesting illustration of the progress narrative, the authors of this submission pointed out that they did not have a
policy mandate to go beyond a recommendation of civil unions. They observed, however, that "the *trajectory of recent policy statements* of the General Council of The United Church of Canada would suggest including
same-sex couples within the definition of marriage" (United Church of
Canada 2003b, emphasis added). This identification of a trajectory leading
to support for same-sex marriages turned out to be an accurate prediction
since that position was affirmed at the August 2003 General Council.[8]

This important shift in church policy has been framed in different ways
– some of which are more helpful than others in supporting satisfying conversations of discernment. Supporters of same-sex marriage tend to take for
granted a story of progress leading from earlier policy changes regarding the
link between sex and procreation to the full acceptance of homosexuals in
church and society to the policy supporting same-sex unions and, finally, to
the United Church's current support for same-sex marriage. From this point
of view, the issue of homosexuality itself slowly made it onto the church's
agenda as the church's position evolved from exclusion of homosexuals
from full membership to inclusion and acceptance.

Critics of same-sex marriage rejected the progress narrative and took it
for granted that a transition from more restrictive to more permissive policies represented a decline from substantive convictions based upon nature
and the Bible to a subjective individualism (Anderson and Anderson 1996).
For example, in a February 2005 letter to the moderator criticizing the
church's support for legislation redefining marriage to include same-sex
couples, a group of ministers provided an illustration of the decline narrative: "The redefinition of marriage is dependent on the deconstruction of
the conjugal characteristics of marriage which are *anchored in biological and
social realities* and, for Christians, *rooted in scripture*" (emphasis added).

According to the dissenting ministers, in contrast to this respect for what nature and scripture teach, and what Canadians have always believed, the proposal to change the definition of marriage represented "a paradigm shift in which the male/female distinction is discarded in favour of a public recognition of commitment between consenting adults; the equating, if you will, of love and marriage" (United Church of Canada 2005a).

However, the dissenters also pointed out that they "uphold the sentiment that all human beings have a right to a legally constituted and recognized relationship for their protection under the law but not all of these relationships are described by the male/female covenantal term 'marriage.'" In other words, for the dissenters, the decline they experienced from convictions "anchored in biological and social realities and, for Christians, rooted in scripture" to an individualistic "commitment between consenting adults" (United Church of Canada 2005a) applied to the redefinition of marriage rather than to the question of legally recognized civil unions for same-sex couples. This shift in focus from civil unions as a human right to a debate over how marriage should be defined pointed to the possibility of a reframed conversation within a shared framework.

Competing Narratives and the Possibility of a Shared Common Law Approach

Both opponents and supporters created some room for shared understandings by implicitly or explicitly arguing that marriage could not be understood only, or at all, within the framework of human rights but that it should be seen as a characterization of a particular kind of human relationship. They shared a willingness to support civil unions or the legal recognition of de facto relationships, and they agreed that the marriage covenant represented more than simply a contract. Opponents of gay marriage, for example, sought to "uphold the sentiment that all human beings have a right to a legally constituted and recognized relationship for their protection under the law [i.e., civil unions] but not all of these relationships are described by the male/female covenantal term 'marriage'" (United Church of Canada 2005a).[9]

Supporters of the redefinition of marriage agreed that the marriage covenant represents more than a contract between two individuals and, also, that it should be framed as "an issue for conscience."[10] The Saskatchewan Conference had used the term "civil union" in its resolution prepared in the spring of 2003 for the fall General Council. When the issue came up for debate at the August General Council, Fred Braman of Montreal moved that the term "civil union" be replaced by the term "marriage." He pointed out that redefining marriage to include same-sex couples was "not just a human rights issue. This is about what we are, the church. It is an opportunity to show our faith and meet our test – to do justice, to love kindness, to walk humbly with our Lord" (Asling 2003). His amendment was adopted, and support for same-sex marriage became the United Church's official position. Opposition remained strong, but it is possible to imagine that a move beyond a human rights framework may have opened up conversational terrain that otherwise would have remained polarized around conflicting absolutes.

The recognition – clearer in hindsight than at the time – that both critics and defenders of same-sex marriage were prepared to exchange reasons to support their conclusions within a shared common law framework should not be confused with the quite different claim that they reached agreement. They could agree with Robert Leckie's (2006, 2) observation that "the tradition of civil marriage law, a 'culture of argument,' is one of pluralism and change" and continue to disagree about which changes should be resisted or endorsed.[11]

A good illustration of a common law approach to the same-sex marriage issue can be found in the way Chief Justice Roy McMurtry explained and defended the June 2003 Ontario Court of Appeal ruling that the definition of marriage ought to be changed to include same-sex couples. He pointed out that the issue at hand was a common law rule that excludes same-sex marriages. It was not a statutory definition, and the three judges on the bench felt entitled to conclude that there were no reasonable grounds for excluding same-sex couples from the civil institution of marriage. There was a form of practical reasoning, taking account not only of the Charter of Rights and Freedoms but also of social changes since the common law rule was first formally stated in the nineteenth century (*Halpern et al. v. Canada* 2003, 8, para. 37).

The Ontario Court of Appeal, and the Canadian judiciary in general, have shied away from treating the texts of the Charter or the Constitution as fixed sources of authoritative conclusions. Justice McMurtry is one of many senior judges who has invoked the metaphor of a "living tree" to describe the Constitution. He insists that "to freeze the definition of marriage to whatever meaning it had in 1867 is contrary to this country's jurisprudence of progressive constitutional interpretation" (McMurtry 2003, 9). Thus, in handing down their ruling, the judges of the Ontario Court of Appeal were not simply asserting a timeless authority: they were reporting their findings on the reasonableness of the arguments for and against the redefinition of marriage to include same-sex couples.[12]

Examples from the Appeal Court judgment illustrate the shift in focus from debate-stopping absolutes to debatable reasons for or against particular points associated with common law thinking. The attorney general of Canada had argued, as part of the case against changing the traditional definition of marriage, that "marriage, as an institution, does not produce a distinction between opposite-sex and same-sex couples. The word 'marriage' is a descriptor of a unique opposite-sex bond that is common across different times, cultures and religions as a virtually universal norm." The apparent discrimination against same-sex couples has resulted not from the definition of marriage as an opposite-sex union but, rather, from the way in which the "Canadian common law captured the definition of marriage by attaching benefits and obligations to the marriage relationship." Therefore, "the individual pieces of legislation that provide the authority for the distribution of government benefits and obligations are the source of the differential treatment" (*Halpern et al. v. Canada* 2003). These inequalities have now been addressed by the enactment of the Modernization of Benefits and Obligations Act.

McMurtry and the other Appeal Court judges did not agree that the different treatment was justifiable: "If marriage were defined as 'a union between one man and one woman of the Protestant faith,' surely the definition would be drawing a formal distinction between Protestants and all other persons." Such a definition would exclude persons with other religious identities as well as persons with no religious affiliation. "Similarly, if marriage were defined as 'a union between two white persons,' there would be a distinction between white persons and all other racial groups" (*Halpern et al. v. Canada* 2003).

Critics of same-sex marriage have not found the racial discrimination analogy convincing. From their point of view, if the marriage relationship is inherently heterosexual, then excluding same-sex couples from marriage is not an illegitimate form of discrimination. Supporters of same-sex marriage find a more compelling argument in the comparison between same-sex couples and couples who choose to remain childless. By entering into the public institution of marriage with vows of mutual love, promises of permanence, and commitments to family life, both kinds of couples fulfill the expectations of marriage as both a contract and a covenant. This, at least, is the form the argument takes within a shared common law framework.

It is not surprising to find evidence of common law thinking in judicial decisions. It is more interesting to locate examples of that approach to practical reasoning in earlier United Church reports. The 1974 United Church report entitled *The Permanence of Christian Marriage* provides a good illustration of the use of a common law framework. The document was occasioned by growing pressure on the church from couples who wanted to drop the vow of permanence from the marriage ceremony. Since the church had decided to recognize divorce and to remarry divorced persons, why not also drop the requirement to promise permanence? At the outset, the report admits that marriage is a conventional institution that could be changed if that seemed to be a theologically sound and responsible thing to do:

> To call marriage a *conventional* institution is to say that there exist conventions in any culture which must normally be satisfied by the parties in order for their relationships to be recognized as marriages. The difference between marriage and other inter-sexual relationships is conventional. The status "married" is bestowed on the couple by virtue of their observance of certain conventions which can be called "getting married." From the status gained by following the social conventions, certain political, economic and social consequences follow. What these consequences are will vary with the culture since the form of marriage reflects its whole cultural context. (United Church of Canada 1974, 284; emphasis in original)

Within the framework of common law thinking, authoritative sources receive a respectful hearing, but they do not function as debate-stopping trump cards. As *The Permanence of Christian Marriage* points out, biblical passages must be read in context and interpreted in relation to changing historical circumstances. This point was illustrated in relation to the question of divorce. For example, it had usually been taken for granted that Jesus taught that adultery is the only legitimate ground for divorce. The following passage containing this quotation from Genesis has often been cited as sufficient authority for this view:

> From the beginning of creation "God made them male and female. For this reason a man shall leave his father and mother and shall be joined to his wife, and the two shall become one." So they are not two but one. What therefore God has joined together, let no man put asunder. (Mark 10: 6-9)

As the report points out, in citing this passage Jesus was not rejecting divorce as we know it. His teaching was "directed against the right of a husband to put away his wife." As the report continues, a wife is not the husband's property: "She is a human being with rights of her own who has entered into a relationship so intimate that she cannot be disposed of as one might dispose of a piece of property or hired labour." About marriage in general, the report argues that "like all social institutions it is to be respected and observed but not absolutized." Above all, there should be a concern "that life within marriage embody a true love and mutual respect between two people" (United Church of Canada 1974, 285).

For *The Permanence of Christian Marriage* report, this emphasis on love and mutual respect is explicitly linked to a continuing emphasis on the importance of promises of permanence as a defining characteristic of marriage, without questioning the link between marriage and procreation. But the way in which it understands marriage, and this was widely accepted within the church, opened up space for continuing reflection. By the beginning of the twenty-first century, conversations about marriage included the question of the gender of the two persons exchanging vows of permanence and entering into "the metaphysical mystery in marriage which unites two people to the 'depth of their being'" (United Church of Canada 1974, 287).

These discussions, of course, came to a head in the debate over the General Council's 2003 resolution proposing the legalization of same-sex marriage and the decision facing congregations regarding whether or not to permit their ministers to perform same-sex marriages. Both critics and supporters of the redefinition of marriage argued that their positions were consistent with (and flowed from) the basic nature and structure of human life as well as from the teachings of scripture. They both then appealed to the consequences of the definition of marriage for children, society, and same-sex couples as a way to make their conclusions more convincing.

From Discernment to Decisions and Actions

When attention shifted from national policy to the question of congregational practice, two questions were posed: (1) should the authority to determine congregational practice remain at the congregational level? and (2) how could congregations determining their own practices most productively engage the intersecting issues of sex, marriage, the family, and sexual orientation?

On the governance question, and specifically on whether a congregation can set policy for a minister's conducting a same-sex marriage outside church property, the secretary of the General Council ruled in September 2003 that, "where a minister is in a pastoral relationship with a Congregation, the minister must always comply with that Congregation's policies in all marriage ceremonies conducted by that minister" (United Church of Canada, 2003a). This ruling was sustained by an appeal panel, though with an additional comment that the governing body of a congregation "must act responsibly and cannot prohibit a marriage from taking place on a capricious basis" (ibid., 4).

As a result, many congregations are in the process of deciding what they are going to do. Leaving final decisions to them may have been seen by some debaters as a dereliction of duty on the part of the national governing body of the church, but it has allowed a continuation of the conversation. The federal same-sex marriage legislation guarantees that ministers of religion and religious institutions will not be compelled to perform ceremonies that violate their consciences.[13] More broadly, then, conversations at the local level may well see same-sex marriage conceived of as "an issue for conscience," and decisions will be based on the strength of the reasons presented by different voices.

Conclusion

I use the terms "focusing" and "framing" to identify different aspects of the conversations of discernment over the legalization and sanctification of same-sex marriage. In keeping with the storytelling method outlined in "Towards a 'Pedagogy for Allies of the Oppressed'" (Hutchinson 1984), I identify the conflicting narratives of progress and decline. I extract a shared common law framework from the deeply held opposing convictions on this issue. Although particular reasons based upon claims about rights or traditional authorities appear to be presented in a non-negotiable fashion, speakers actually appealed to contrasting facts, rights claims, and consequences within a framework more shared than protagonists realized.

The Ontario Court of Appeal, in *Halpern et al. v. Canada* (2003), and the 1974 United Church report entitled *The Permanence of Christian Marriage* both agree in principle that the institution of marriage is open to debate and change if the reasons for embracing change outweigh the reasons to defend tradition. Both reject the view that the standards against which to assess claims are rigidly authoritative.

Three decades after the 1974 report, the United Church's General Council experienced the same need to take action but in the context of a recurrent consideration of what was meant by marriage. Like the judges in

Halpern, the majority of the 372 commissioners found the reasons for changing the traditional definition of marriage more compelling than the reasons for continuing to exclude same-sex couples. These reasons will be revisited by individual congregations as they face the need to decide whether or not same-sex marriages will be performed in their churches and by their ministers. Each congregation continues to have the opportunity and responsibility to determine its own practice.

One of the challenges facing courts, legislatures, and church bodies involves reaching points of decision and action in ways that leave critics and supporters of final decisions feeling satisfied with the governing procedures employed and with the character and respectfulness of the debate. The most successful conversations of discernment will reflect a careful attention to how the issues are framed and focused at each point in the conversation.

American Mainline Protestantism and Deliberation about Homosexuality

LAURA R. OLSON, PAUL A. DJUPE,
AND WENDY CADGE

In recent American history, only the debate about abortion has equalled the debate about homosexuality in terms of intensity and divisiveness.[1] Homosexuality is, of course, a centrepiece of America's "culture wars" (Hunter 1991), as is reflected in seventeen states' passing ballot measures banning same-sex marriage in 2004 and 2006. On the whole, Americans have recently become less willing to restrict the civil rights of gays and lesbians, but they continue to disagree profoundly about an entire range of related issues, such as same-sex marriage, adoption of children by same-sex couples, and whether gay and lesbian people should serve as clergy (Loftus 2001). Clearly, the debate about homosexuality in the United States is rooted in incompatible worldviews, some of which are informed by varying interpretations of Judeo-Christian teachings and traditions.

Religious beliefs and religious institutions have played powerful roles in structuring debates about homosexuality (Cadge 2002; Clark, Brown, and Hochstein 1989; Dillon 1999; Swindler 1991). Research shows that conservative religious beliefs and frequent religious practice are correlated with negative attitudes towards gay rights (Olson, Cadge, and Harrison 2006; see also Beatty and Walter 1984; Cochran and Beeghley 1991; Cotten-Huston and Waite 2000; Finlay and Walther 2003; Fisher et al. 1994; Glenn and Weaver 1979; Herek 1984; Herek and Glunt 1993; Irwin and Thompson 1977; Kirkpatrick 1993; Roof and McKinney 1987). Within religious congregations, clergy cues and friendship networks also affect opinions about homosexuality (Djupe and Gilbert 2009).

Debate within congregations over taking formal positions on homosexuality can cause strife but may result in productive dialogue and increased understanding among people who hold divergent views about homosexuality (Ammerman 1997; Cadge, Olson, and Wildeman 2008; Cadge and Wildeman 2008; Coffin 2005; Ellingson et al. 2001; Hartman 1996; Moon 2004; Zuckerman 1999). Clergy themselves often have difficulty determining how to grapple with this contentious issue within their congregations (Djupe, Olson, and Gilbert 2005; Ellingson et al. 2001; Neiheisel and Djupe 2008; Olson and Cadge 2002; Wellman 1999). Some clergy have placed themselves on the front lines of the battle over homosexuality, which, at first blush, may seem risky, but research has shown that clergy who protest often enjoy the support of their congregations (Djupe and Gilbert 2003). This support usually evolves from long internal debate and deliberation.

At the broader organizational level, religious traditions in the United States have chosen a variety of strategies for dealing with homosexuality. The Roman Catholic Church, the Church of Jesus Christ of Latter-Day Saints, and most evangelical and African-American Protestant denominations have taken official positions opposing homosexuality. Nevertheless, there are organized groups dedicated to supporting gay and lesbian people within each of these religious traditions, especially within the Roman Catholic Church. At the same time, the pastoral support gay and lesbian individuals receive varies dramatically by congregation – even within religious traditions that are more or less accepting of homosexuality. Within mainline Protestantism and Judaism, a fuller range of views on homosexuality is tolerated, but entire mainline denominations have been shaken to their foundations by debates over the appropriate treatment of gay and lesbian people (Beuttler 1999; Burgess 1999; Buzzell 2001; Cadge 2002; Ellison 2004; Koch and Curry 2000; McLain 1995; Melton 1991; Rogers 1999; Seow 1996; Siker 1994; Udis-Kessler 2002; Wellman 1999; Wood 2000; Wood and Bloch 1995).

Generally speaking, mainline Protestantism has engaged in more protracted and detailed internal dialogue about homosexuality than has any other major American religious tradition (Cadge 2002; Comstock 1996; Shallenberger 1996). In fact, Ammerman (2005, 228) reports that fully 49 percent of the mainline Protestant congregations she studied listed homosexuality as an "issue of concern," as compared to just 9 percent of Catholic and Orthodox congregations, 8 percent of conservative Protestant congregations, and 0 percent of African-American congregations. No issue other than homosexuality was a major concern of more than 11 percent of the mainline Protestant congregations she studied. These findings are not surprising as mainline denominations have taken an especially active role in grappling with homosexuality since the late 1960s. The United Church of Christ was the first major US church to take a formal stand in support of "the cause of justice and compassion for homosexual persons," but most mainline Protestant denominations have shifted towards more positive positions, even if they are still struggling over such issues as the ordination of openly lesbian and gay clergy and same-sex marriage (Cadge 2002, 267).

In this chapter, we look specifically at the ways in which mainline Protestantism has grappled with homosexuality in recent years and outline the nature of the debates that have raged in mainline circles since the 1970s. These debates have been contentious and divisive, but they have also generated a good deal of productive discourse about homosexuality through which many mainline Protestants have become better equipped to tolerate others with different opinions. We explore the ways in which the discourse about homosexuality conducted in both mainline denominations and congregations has promoted a larger-scale societal conversation about homosexuality that has served to contribute to a broader deliberative democracy in the United States.

Mainline Protestantism Confronts Homosexuality

Approximately 20 percent of all Americans are classified as mainline Protestants, belonging to one of eight historic denominations: the American Baptist Churches, USA; the Christian Church (Disciples of Christ); the Episcopal Church; the Evangelical Lutheran Church in America; the Presbyterian Church (USA); the Reformed Church in America; the United Church of Christ; and the United Methodist Church. Mainline Protestantism today is distinctive for its open approach to scriptural interpretation, its general theological liberalism, and its relatively progressive and tolerant approach to political and social issues. This outlook is exemplified by the television advertisements run by the United Methodist Church since 2003, in which it advertises its "open hearts, open minds, [and] open doors."

Generations of mainline Protestants have agreed about the value of civic engagement and tolerated ideological disagreements, especially between historically liberal clergy and moderate-to-conservative congregation members (Djupe and Gilbert 2003; Guth, Green, Smidt, Kellstedt, and Poloma 1997; Quinley 1974; Wuthnow 1988; Wuthnow and Evans 2002). Social – and even political – action is not just tolerated in mainline Protestant congregations: it is often de rigueur. In the 1920s, mainline Protestantism became associated with the Social Gospel movement, a theological and political perspective that stressed structural reform as the best means for effecting social change. Many mainline Protestants, and particularly mainline clergy, rallied to the cause of social reform, emphasizing the need to "bring the Kingdom of God to earth" by helping the poor and disadvantaged in this world rather than bringing the people of the earth to the Kingdom of God through individual sanctification and focus on the next world (Marty 1970; Niebuhr 1951; Wuthnow 1988). This imperative to reform society played out through the twentieth century as mainline Protestants worked to further the civil rights movement (Campbell and Pettigrew 1959; Findlay 1993; Friedland 1998), called for the end of the war in Vietnam (Friedland 1998; Hall 1992; Quinley 1974), and organized against the policies of President Ronald Reagan (Hertzke 1991; Smith 1996).

Consistent with its history of socio-political progressivism, mainline Protestantism has grappled with the issue of homosexuality since the early 1970s, following closely in the wake of the 1969 Stonewall riots in New York City that gave birth to the gay rights movement. Each mainline denomination has regularly engaged in formal studies and debates about homosexuality at its national meetings since the 1980s (Anderson 1997; Cadge 2002; Wood and Bloch 1995). At present, the six largest mainline denominations all formally support civil rights for gay and lesbian people, but three – the American Baptist Churches, the Presbyterian Church (USA), and the United Methodist Church – condemn homosexuality itself. "Welcoming congregation" programs exist in most mainline denominations for churches wishing to designate themselves as places that are explicitly open to gay men and lesbians.[2] Moreover, there are interest groups designed to address homosexuality and to support gay and lesbian people within every mainline denomination (Haeberle 1991). The appendix to this chapter (Table 11.A) summarizes mainline denominations' current national policies regarding welcoming congregation programs, the blessing of same-sex unions, and LGBT clergy.

The past fifteen years have witnessed a dramatic intensification in mainline Protestant debate about homosexuality, especially as some mainline denominations have adopted more tolerant attitudes and policies towards gays and lesbians. Most denominations have worked to refine formal denominational statements on their stances regarding homosexuality

(Cadge 2002; Djupe, Olson, and Gilbert 2005); the wording and content of these statements have caused many heated national-level battles within several denominations (Goodstein 2006, 2007a; Luo and Capecchi 2009; Radin 2005). Some mainline clergy preside over the blessing of same-sex unions, although this practice has created tremendous friction within some denominations (White 2000). Relatively few denominations accept openly gay clergy. For instance, the Episcopal Church made international news when it consecrated Reverend Canon V. Gene Robinson as Bishop of New Hampshire and continues to draw the ire of some of its congregations and the Worldwide Anglican Community alike (Banerjee 2004; Goodstein 2007b, 2007c). And, on 21 August 2009, the Evangelical Lutheran Church in America (ELCA) voted narrowly to allow openly gay clergy in committed relationships to serve (Luo and Capecchi 2009).

How prominent are such debates at the congregational level? A 1999 survey of Presbyterians shows that 20 percent had heard a sermon about gay and lesbian issues in the past twelve months (Presbyterian Church 1999). In a 1998-99 survey of ELCA and Episcopal congregation members, 60 percent had heard their clergy discussing gay rights and homosexuality in the past year more often than "never" (Djupe and Gilbert 2003).[3] Another national survey in 2000 found that 15 percent of all Protestants who attended church at least a few times a year recalled hearing a sermon about homosexuality in the past year (Wuthnow 2000a). One community study found that, in congregations motivated to discuss homosexuality because of denominational conflict taking place in mainline denominations, clergy advanced more arguments against the expansion of gay rights (Neiheisel and Djupe 2008). At the same time, several denominations, most notably the ELCA, have made formal study resources available to member congregations and strongly encouraged their use (see Cadge, Olson, and Wildeman 2008).

Mainline Protestantism's approach to homosexuality, therefore, has been two-pronged. The debate occurs through deliberation in denominational policy-making bodies, but it also transpires through substantial grassroots activity related to the subject in congregations. At both the denominational and the congregational levels, the issue has been addressed broadly in terms of homosexuality and more specifically in terms of the rights of gay and lesbian people.

Much of the debate about this issue would not have occurred were it not for the efforts of mainline Protestant clergy (Ellingson et al. 2001; Olson and Cadge 2002; Wellman 1999). Clergy helped found the first faith-based group designed specifically to address homosexuality, the San Francisco

Council on Religion and Homosexuality, in 1964 (D'Emilio and Freedman 1988). Clergy have also played significant roles in establishing support groups for mainline Protestant gays and lesbians (Cadge 2002). The United Church of Christ's Reverend Bill Johnson started a gay caucus within his denomination in 1972. In 1974, Reverend David Baily Sindt founded Presbyterians for Lesbian and Gay Concerns. In 1978, Reverend Robert Davidson was the catalyst behind the development of More Light, the Presbyterian Church (USA)'s grassroots network of congregations that formally welcomes gay and lesbian people. By the 1990s, programs supporting gay men and lesbians existed in all major mainline Protestant denominations, largely as a result of the work of pioneering clergy.

Despite the increase in grassroots activities and public debate during the 1990s, it is essential to recognize that the opinions of many mainline Protestants on issues related to homosexuality remain mixed. It is true that the vast majority of clergy and laity in the mainline churches strongly approve of equal rights for gays and lesbians granted by the *state* (Djupe, Olson, and Gilbert 2005). With regard to the *church*, however, recent research suggests that mainline Protestant opinion about homosexuality is divided right down to the local level (Ammerman 2000). It is within this local, and often contentious, context that mainline clergy and congregations decide whether, when, and how to express their views on homosexuality.

Building a Stronger Democracy: The Importance of Deliberation

In mainline Protestant circles, people are discussing – one might even say deliberating about – homosexuality in general terms, not just with regard to whether to ordain, marry, or welcome gays and lesbians. Such discussion is essential because it occupies a central place in the development and maintenance of democracy. If, as Chambers (2003, 308) explains, "talk-centric democratic theory [is replacing] voting-centric democratic theory," then the most important work citizens can do to strengthen democracy involves having discussions that include diverse participants, that deepen civility and tolerance, that enrich opinions with both more and new information, and that, in the end, perhaps lead to holding government accountable (see also Gutmann and Thompson 1996). The deliberations about homosexuality that continue apace in mainline Protestant contexts must, by definition, accomplish at least some of these ends.

If political processes are marked by an imbalance of resources (namely, money, expertise, and access), deliberative democracy in its most pristine form features equality and openness, the absence of elite control, and a sense of fairness that is all too infrequently associated with the rest of American politics. It is no wonder, then, that talk of deliberation is everywhere and "has become the concept du jour of political theorists and in some cases has taken on nearly religious overtones" (Hibbing and Theiss-Morse 2002, 172). Distilling from a number of accounts of a deliberative meeting, Mendelberg and Oleske outline the necessary components for "complete" deliberation (Fishkin 1995):

> (a) Meetings are public; (b) citizens reflect and decide collectively rather than individually; (c) citizens have an equal opportunity to participate; (d) decisions turn on arguments, not on coercive power; (e) citizens are fully informed; (f) all alternatives are considered; (g) deliberation is an ongoing process supported by other institutions; and (h) arguments are based on general principles and appeal to the common good, not exclusively to self-interest. (170)

For the most part, empirical research on deliberation has lagged behind the work that has been done by political theorists and has focused primarily on discussion in informal settings (Mutz 2002; Walsh 2004), experimental settings (Sulkin and Simon 2001), and formally organized meetings (Fishkin 1995; Mendelberg and Oleske 2000). Such work has found that the success of deliberation is linearly related to the degree of formality of the proceedings. Research by Mutz (2002) describes a trade-off between participation and deliberation, in which citizens are either demobilized by exposure to different views or participate mostly when surrounded by reinforcing positions, though subsequent scholarship has toned down that distinction (McClurg 2006). On the other end, Fishkin has reported great success under highly controlled conditions.

In some ways it is not surprising that little research on deliberation has taken place in organizations, including religious denominations and congregations. There is a widespread but incorrect assumption that churches are homogeneous gatherings, a characteristic that denies the possibility of deliberation. For instance, Mutz (2002) finds that disagreement is least likely among political discussants who belong to the same church, an assertion that previously had been assumed by Scheufele, Nisbet, and Brossard (2003). Much religion and politics research has done little to disabuse scholars of this invalid assumption.

When we expand our view beyond discussants who belong to the same local church, churches are often surprisingly diverse organizations (Djupe and Gilbert 2009; Gilbert 1993; Neiheisel, Djupe, and Sokhey 2009; Wald, Owen, and Hill 1988). Many clergy take prophetic stances that differ from the prevailing sentiment in their congregations on consequential matters of public policy, challenging members to re-envision their politics according to religious dictates. Congregation members might all live in the same community, but they vary in their demographic characteristics and, often, in their political stances. Small groups might gather for a purpose, such as study of a sacred text or a game of volleyball, which almost certainly would cut across political interests. Many congregations also play host to meetings explicitly designed for the discussion of politics and public policy.

The small-scale and often informal deliberative efforts undertaken in organizations like churches may not be politically consequential. As Page (1996) argues, informal discussion, however closely it may exemplify the high standards theorists set for deliberation, is connected to neither a political process nor enough voters to attract the attention of legislators. Only national institutions such as the mass media are tied closely enough to political processes and reach enough people to be consequential.

We do not disagree with Page in the broad brush of this argument. However, there are a variety of forums for discussion that may breach the threshold of consequence. In particular, the discussions that take place within particular organizational forms are worthy of note. Ideally, deliberation involves many people meeting simultaneously about a common, salient issue in a setting that has aggregating and reporting mechanisms. National federations of local groups fit this bill because they integrate vast grassroots networks vertically (Hunter 1993) and can resemble the national network of deliberative forums envisioned by scholars (Ackerman and Fishkin 2004).

Deliberation in Mainline Protestant Contexts

Religious denominations are an excellent example of just such a national network or federation, and congregations comprise the grassroots networks they integrate. At the top, national meetings of church representatives can resemble private legislatures that, at the very least, provide for society a model of how to engage contentious issues (Wood and Bloch 1995). If they live up to their greatest potential, denominations can initiate deliberation throughout their constituent congregations. And denominations, especially within mainline Protestantism, *do* accomplish this end on a regular basis. Clergy, or special committees devoted to the task of engaging a contentious issue, prepare educational materials, generate appropriate schedules, and encourage congregations to engage these issues (Cadge, Olson, and Wildeman 2008; Cadge and Wildeman 2008; Coffin 2005).

Moreover, denominations have the potential to aggregate the preferences of their constituents, although the dilemmas of democracy – especially the power acquired by minorities with intense passions – can temper their effectiveness in this regard. Mainline denominations take great pains to be representative (Wood and Bloch 1995), and Washington lobbyists for the mainline denominations are quite careful about the issues they push, preferring substantial support throughout the denomination and in the national conference before representing a position publicly (Djupe, Olson, and Gilbert 2005; Olson 2002). Furthermore, small group participation in churches has its own consequences apart from denominational influence, providing participants with politically applicable civic skills and recruitment to participate in politics (Djupe and Gilbert 2003; Verba, Schlozman, and Brady 1995). In any event, there are substantial vertical ties between local small group efforts and national representation that may better satisfy the demands of democratic theory than the observation of discourse in the mass media (Page 1996). And the engagement of issues related to homosexuality *is* happening throughout mainline Protestantism at the various levels of organization: in congregations and in regional and national governing bodies. This is especially true in denominations that provide the most concrete resources to their congregations, which seem to foster the most engaged congregational deliberation (Cadge, Olson, and Wildeman 2008).

Previous research has examined the ways in which mainline Protestant congregations have confronted homosexuality. Coffin (2005) argues that, by exercising various types of authority, clergy are often able to open up channels of dialogue between congregants and moderate deliberative exchange. Clergy's willingness to exercise moral authority may not be sufficient to generate congregational debate, however, as lay committees or other elements within their congregations often limit such authority. To overcome such barriers, clergy carefully use framing to prepare their congregations for sustained debate and minimize the chances of polarization around the issue within a given congregation. Along such lines, the frames that clergy employ in discussions of homosexuality are often quite pragmatic in nature as clergy are often occupied with concerns over splits in the congregation and membership losses that might result from their comments on the issue (Cadge and Wildeman 2008; Hadden 1969; Neiheisel and Djupe 2008; Olson and Cadge 2002).

Djupe and Neiheisel (2008) examine the role of clergy in fostering deliberation about political issues and the extent to which congregational meetings approach the deliberative gold standard. They build on Coffin's notion that deliberation might be envisioned as a discussion of competing frames (see also Knight and Johnson 1994). According to this view, clergy model the deliberative process by discussing an issue from a variety of points of view, although it is critical that they take care to present arguments with which they disagree.

To demonstrate what this looks like, Table 11.1 presents Djupe and Neiheisel's data from a survey of Columbus-area clergy who were asked two questions about each of twelve potential arguments regarding a 2004 Ohio ballot measure ("Issue 1") that proposed to ban recognition of same-sex unions by the state: (1) whether they agreed with the argument and (2) whether they discussed it publicly. The arguments were gleaned from media reports, interest group publications, and informed observers, and they represent a full range of arguments in public circulation at the time. We compare the results for *mainline* clergy in the sample to the results for all clergy in other religious traditions. The differences between mainline clergy and their counterparts in other traditions are striking and pervasive. Mainline clergy who responded were much more supportive of extending equal rights to gays and lesbians, although statistically equal proportions of other clergy also supported anti-discrimination laws. A bare majority of mainline clergy approved of same-sex marriage, and a three-fifths majority opposed Issue 1.

TABLE 11.1

Mainline Protestant clergy (versus other clergy) mention of and agreement with twelve arguments in their public deliberation over Issue 1 (on same-sex marriage), 2004

	Argument mention		Argument agreement	
Argument	Mainline	Other	Mainline	Other
Not to allow same-sex partners to marry unjustly deprives these couples of many legal benefits.	0.49	0.33	0.67	0.24
Though I oppose allowing same-sex partners to marry, I support anti-discrimination laws for gays and lesbians.	0.30	0.35 ns	0.60	0.53 ns

▶

◄ TABLE 11.1

Argument	Argument mention		Argument agreement	
	Mainline	Other	Mainline	Other
Issue 1 should be opposed because, historically, constitutional amendments in our nation extend rather than restrict rights.	0.33	0.17	0.60	0.27
We should recognize genuine love expressed between consenting adults of the same sex by allowing them to marry.	0.42	0.22	0.55	0.15
Allowing same-sex partners to marry helps to bring a once marginal group into traditional institutions and stabilizes society.	0.32	0.19 ns	0.52	0.21
Issue 1 should be opposed because only God and churches can sanctify a marriage – no constitutional amendment can do that.	0.21	0.25 ns	0.43	0.24
Though I oppose allowing same-sex partners to marry, I support granting gays and lesbians obtaining civil unions – granting secular benefits of marriage without God's blessing.	0.26	0.31 ns	0.42	0.29 ns
Issue 1 should be opposed because of potential detrimental economic effects in the state.	0.20	0.26 ns	0.37	0.20
Allowing same-sex partners to marry violates scripture.	0.47	0.74	0.35	0.81
Allowing same-sex partners to marry threatens the social fabric and traditional institutions.	0.44	0.72	0.18	0.79
Allowing same-sex partners to marry paves the way for other non-traditional forms of marriage such as polygamy.	0.17	0.47	0.16	0.63
Allowing same-sex partners to marry grants God's blessing on a sinful practice.	0.25	0.28 ns	0.15	0.44

Notes: Mainline $N \sim 58$, other $N \sim 72$. Data are derived from the proportions mentioning and agreeing with the argument. All differences are statistically significant at the $p < .05$ level except those marked "ns" (for "not significant"). A mention is coded 1 (and 0 otherwise), while agreement is coded 1 = strongly agree/agree (and 0 = otherwise).

Source: Columbus Clergy, Issue 1 Study, 2004 (see Djupe and Neiheisel 2008).

It seems clear from the results in Table 11.1 that clergy are more likely to offer public discussion of an argument if they personally agree with it. Mainline clergy reported mentioning about the same total number of arguments as other clergy; however, they were more open to discussion of arguments with which they personally *disagreed*. Among mainliners, just under one in three arguments presented were those with which they disagreed, while among other clergy the ratio is closer to one in six. Presenting such a diversity of argument frames is essential if clergy are to model the deliberative process effectively.

In further analysis of these data, Djupe and Neiheisel (2008) find that two principal forces drive the nature and diversity of clergy's public arguments about homosexuality. Clergy's "agenda" (a combination of their interest in Issue 1 and their sponsorship of adult education sessions on gay rights) drove the number of arguments they mentioned. However, it was the "political disunity" of the clergy's church that motivated the diversity of the argument presentation. Those in politically divided congregations and those serving congregations that largely disagreed with them politically (both of which are quite common in mainline Protestant churches) offered a more diverse range of arguments. While the former set of results suggests elite control over debate, the latter findings suggest that the content of a debate is also constrained by the audience. Together the findings presented here and by Djupe and Neiheisel underline not only the fact that we should consider all components of a potentially deliberative forum but also that mainline Protestants often host conditions that are especially conducive to deliberative encounters.

The involvement of elites in political discussion poses problems for some deliberative theorists since they may violate the equality principle (e.g., Dutwin 2003), but other church forums may host deliberation over significant matters of public policy that do not suffer from these theoretical dilemmas. Adult education sessions may be the most likely setting for deliberation within churches, especially mainline churches (Neiheisel, Djupe, and Sokhey 2009). As Ammerman (2005, 32) notes, "talk about the Bible is remarkably absent from [adult education classes in] most liberal Protestant churches." This suggests that mainline adult education classes might be especially likely to emphasize social issues and discourse that veers away from a strict emphasis on religious matters. Verifying this supposition, adult education covering political topics is widespread, especially in the mainline churches. While Chaves (2004, 229) reports that roughly 10 percent of American congregations sponsor groups and classes focused on politics, we feel that this estimate is remarkably low, likely because of the use of the word "politics" in his survey question. Using issue cues (such as abortion, gay rights, the environment, and the Iraq War) rather than the word "politics" in survey questions designed to generate responses about adult education provision, Neiheisel, Djupe, and Sokhey (2009) find that 45 percent of Ohio churches held at least one adult education session. The average number of sessions provided was three ("in the past year"). Just over half of mainline Protestant churches held at least one session, which equalled the rate in Catholic churches, although only one-third of evangelical Protestant churches held adult education sessions. The results for Ohio mainline Protestants compare quite closely to estimates by Djupe and Gilbert (2003), who examined a large national sample of ELCA and Episcopal clergy, suggesting a degree of reliability.

Table 11.2 is an analysis of the deliberative infrastructure of adult education sessions in mainline Protestant congregations versus non-mainline congregations. The data come from a 2004 survey of Ohio clergy in churches attended by a random sample of Ohio voting-age citizens.[4] Here we are concerned with the possibility of deliberation, which entails a very specific and highly restrictive set of ground rules, as described above, in *mainline* contexts. It appears that most congregations (regardless of denominational affiliation) uphold the rules set forth by theorists of democratic deliberation

TABLE 11.2

The deliberative infrastructure of adult education sessions in mainline and other congregations

Attitudes on deliberation	Mainline	Other	
We explicitly encourage participants to think seriously about the opinions of others.	0.88	0.79	ns
It is essential that all those present participate.	0.56	0.60	ns
It is essential that a range of views is presented.	0.94	0.67	
It is essential for participants to learn how our values relate to social/political issues.	1.00	0.68	
It is important for participants to learn how to talk through their differences in opinion.	1.00	0.85	

Notes: Mainline $N = 16$, other $N \sim 27$. Data are derived from the proportions in agreement (strongly agree and agree) with each statement versus any other response (neutral, disagree, or strongly disagree). All differences are statistically significant at the $p < .05$ level except those marked "ns" (for "not significant").

Source: Ohio Churches Survey, 2007 (see Neiheisel, Djupe, and Sokhey 2009).

(Ackerman and Fishkin 2004; Mendelberg and Oleske 2000) when hosting adult education sessions. About four in five congregational adult education sessions explicitly encourage participants to think seriously about the opinions of others, and three in five emphasize the principle that it is important for all to participate. Mainliners are not statistically different from others on these measures. They *are* distinctive, however, in that they show greater commitment to other deliberative norms: all believe it is "essential" that a range of views be presented and that the connection of values to political opinions is made tangible for participants. Moreover, *all* mainline clergy believe it is important for participants to find a way to talk through their differences in opinion. Relatively fewer clergy in other traditions are committed to these deliberative norms. Thus, the mainline Protestant denominational context appears to play a distinctive role in facilitating deliberation about contentious issues such as homosexuality. If being a member of a national body is an important spur for discussion, it is also the case that the national infrastructure charges the outcomes with political significance.

Conclusion

Throughout American history, mainline Protestants have enjoyed large measures of advantage, access, privilege, and, indeed, social hegemony. American socioeconomic elites have disproportionately been mainline Protestants, and studies show that, even today, mainline Protestants have greater educational attainments, higher incomes, and more prestigious jobs than does the average American (Park and Reimer 2002; Roof and McKinney 1987; Smith and Faris 2005; Wuthnow 1988; Wuthnow and Evans 2002). These socioeconomic advantages have meant not only that mainline Protestants have access to the channels of political power in this country but also that they often occupy those channels of power themselves. The notion that a social institution as elite-heavy as mainline Protestantism is engaging in meaningful, productive dialogue about homosexuality might suggest that a similar sort of dialogue could be spreading to the broader American society.

Critics might charge, however, that, in recent decades, mainline Protestantism's position as a cornerstone of American society has encountered significant challenges. Evangelical Protestantism has thrived in the religious market, whereas mainline Protestantism has not (Finke and Stark 1992; Hammond 1992; Iannaccone 1994; Kelley 1977; Wuthnow 1996). Roman Catholicism has maintained its market share, especially with the recent influx of new Catholic immigrants from Latin America. Increasing numbers of Americans have also turned to secularism, new religious movements, and non-Western religious traditions (Bellah et al. 1985; Cadge 2005; Gallagher 2004). Indeed, some have taken to referring to mainline Protestant denominations as "oldline" Protestantism (Hertzke 1988, 1991), and not without some cause. In the last decade of the twentieth century, for example, the United Church of Christ lost 14.8 percent of its membership, while the Presbyterian Church (USA) experienced an 11.6 percent reduction in its membership (Fowler et al. 2004).

Due to these membership losses, mainline Protestantism is now less socially central than it has been in the past. Perhaps, as a result, mainline debates about homosexuality may not be quite as relevant to political elites as would have been the case a few decades ago. Nevertheless, mainline Protestantism has not disappeared, and, as Wuthnow (2000) argues, it continues to exert a "quiet" influence on American society and politics (see also Wuthnow and Evans 2002). It does so not in the large metropolitan centres in which debates over contentious issues are usually carried out but, rather, in smaller communities and suburbs that are often below the radar screens of those who monitor American public life. The ongoing deliberation about homosexuality within and between church congregations is but one way in which mainline Protestantism exerts this quiet influence on American politics, policy, and society.

The tenets of democratic theory play an important role in how all American religious congregations are run. There is a widespread commitment to deliberative norms that can produce a cornucopia of positive outcomes for democratic citizenship: more informed opinions, tolerance for difference, and even more moderate opinions. Whether mainline Protestant (or any) churches actually produce these outcomes is perhaps less important than is the fact that they offer a deliberative process that may be exported into other realms of civic life.

TABLE 11.A

Mainline Protestant denominations' policies regarding homosexuality

Denomination	Congregational LGBT welcoming program (year established)	National policy on blessing of same-sex unions (year established/ reaffirmed)	National policy on LGBT clergy (year established/ reaffirmed)
American Baptist Churches (USA)	Association of Welcoming and Affirming Baptists (1991)	Officially banned (2005)	No national policy
Christian Church (Disciples of Christ)	None	Varies by region/ congregation	Varies by region
Episcopal Church	None	Some dioceses and bishops have policies and/or implicitly allow blessing ceremonies (2003)	"No one shall be denied access to the selection process for ordination in this Church because of ... sexual orientation" (1994)
Evangelical Lutheran Church in America	Reconciling in Christ Program (1984)	Not officially approved but unofficially tolerated in some circles (1993)	Openly gay and lesbian clergy in committed relationships are allowed to serve (2009)
Presbyterian Church (USA)	More Light Churches Network (1974)	Officially banned but unofficially tolerated in some circles (1991)	Officially banned (1997)
Reformed Church in America	None	Officially banned (2005)	Officially banned (2005)
United Church of Christ	Open and Affirming Program Congregation (1985)	Supports "equal marriage rights for couples regardless of gender" (2005)	LGBT people are ordained (1972)
United Methodist Church	Reconciling Congregation Program (1984)	Officially banned (2004)	Officially banned (1984)

Sources: Cadge (2002); denominational websites; Pew Forum (2008).

ROMAN CATHOLICISM

Of all of the religious traditions covered in this volume, the Roman Catholic Church has the most obvious capacity to act collectively in response to GLBT equality claims. With a well-defined hierarchy that can stake out authoritative theological claims and apply substantial resources in both Canada and the United States, the Church can provide a unified front to legislatures and, in theory, to its members. In both countries, the Church has officially adopted a complex position, often supportive of policies that protect individual GLBT citizens from discrimination but in opposition to those that recognize same-sex couples as families.

Despite the Church's emphasis on unity and continuity, it has a long history of adapting to different regimes and societies, and this is as evident in Canada and the United States as anywhere. In Chapter 12, Ted Jelen suggests that the Roman Catholic Church in the United States has undergone a process of "Protestantization" in which various moral teachings are taken as advisory – in part because of the strength of individualistic currents in American culture. Drawing on a survey of Catholic clergy and other survey data of Catholic laity, Jelen shows that, in the parishes, Catholics are far more accommodating to sexual minorities than elite discourse would suggest. A strong majority of priests, for example, agree that gays should have the same rights as other Americans. Even among frequently attending Catholics, there has been growing support for same-sex marriage. Infrequently attending Catholics are more supportive of marriage than are mainline Protestants.

In Chapter 13, Solange Lefebvre and Jean-François Breton focus on Catholics in Quebec – a province in which more than 83 percent of the population identifies as Catholic, a figure far higher than the overall Canadian figure of 43 percent. They show that the "quiet revolution" in Quebec ushered in a stronger state and a weaker church and, at the same time, helped to increase the indifference to church teachings on contraception, sexual relations outside of marriage, and divorce. Some elements of this dissent are evident across Canada, as they are in the United States, though they are more forcefully evident in Quebec.

These two chapters remind us of the importance of distinguishing religious leadership from the constituencies they serve. They also help us to understand the diminished political influence of the Roman Catholic hierarchy in both countries.

12

Catholicism, Homosexuality, and Same-Sex Marriage in the United States

TED G. JELEN

During the first decade of the twenty-first century, questions surrounding the legal rights of homosexuals have animated politics in the United States and have been among the most divisive in American political discourse. Indeed, a number of scholars have suggested that the issue of gay rights in general, and the more specific issue of same-sex marriage, was an important factor in George W. Bush's victory over John Kerry in the 2004 presidential election (Keeter 2007; Campbell and Monson 2007a). While gay and lesbian rights were perhaps not as salient in the 2008 election, both Barack Obama and John McCain made clear their support for civil unions for same-sex couples, while opposing same-sex marriage.

The general issue of gay rights has evolved over the past generation or so. Some observers date the contemporary gay rights movement from the Stonewall incident in 1969, in which patrons of a gay bar in New York fought back against police officers who attempted to close the establishment. Since then, debates over the rights of gays and lesbians have been intensified by court decisions that include *Bowers v. Hardwick* (1986), *Lawrence v. Texas* (2003), and *Goodridge v. Department of Public Health* (2003).

Court decisions expanding gay and lesbian rights, in *Lawrence* (over sodomy law), and *Goodridge* (over marriage), have evoked strong negative reactions not just among evangelical Protestants but also among groups not normally affiliated with the religious right, such as African Americans and Roman Catholics (Rimmerman and Wilcox 2007).

It seems likely that the reaction of the Roman Catholic Church, and of lay Catholics, will be crucial to the future of gay rights and to the question of same-sex marriage. The Roman Catholic Church in the United States has formidable organizational resources, which can render it an effective lobby and advocate for its positions. In the area of electoral politics, Catholics represent the largest single religious denomination in the United States, and they constitute an important "swing" constituency in American elections. Indeed, it has been suggested that the issue of same-sex marriage was a significant factor in Bush's narrow lead among Catholic voters in the 2004 presidential election (Mockabee 2007), and perceived support for gay and lesbian rights may have suppressed Barack Obama's standing among Catholics in 2008.

In this chapter, I make three points. First, the hierarchy of the Roman Catholic Church, both in Rome and in the United States, has been generally opposed to expanding the rights of gays and lesbians and has been particularly adamant in its opposition to same-sex marriage. Second, the Catholic hierarchy in the United States has been quite active in articulating its opposition to homosexuality and same-sex marriage. Third, while Catholic priests and laity generally share the organized Church's attitudes towards homosexuality and gay rights, such opposition is by no means universal at the level of the parish. Indeed, the pattern among lay Catholics at all levels of religious observance has been one of increasing acceptance of homosexuality, and there is a significant movement towards acceptance of same-sex marriage. Indeed, they display more accepting attitudes than do mainline Protestants.

Doctrinal Matters

Contemporary Catholic doctrine with respect to homosexuality is clear but complex. In the first instance, people of homosexual inclination are to be treated with the dignity of creatures created in the image of God. The United States Conference of Catholic Bishops (USCCB) has noted that homosexuals are often the objects of derision, prejudice, hatred, and discrimination and that the Church (at the level of the clergy and the laity) is proscribed from participating in such discrimination (USCCB 2006b; O'Reilly 2006).

Nevertheless, homosexuality is considered an objective moral disorder and is regarded as a violation of natural law. Catholic natural law doctrine with respect to sexuality defines morally acceptable sexual expression as heterosexual intercourse between married couples (USCCB 2006a). An important component of this doctrine is the procreative nature of sexuality.

Humans are created in God's image, and an essential part of God's nature, which He shares with humanity, is participation in the act of creation (Cook, Jelen, and Wilcox 1992). Marital sex, in order to be morally authentic, must be open to the possibility of the creation of new life. Homosexuality, which does not offer the possibility of procreation, is therefore a violation of natural law, and homosexual activity is considered seriously sinful.

In its most recent pronouncement on homosexuality, *Ministry to Persons with a Homosexual Inclination* (USCCB 2006b), the USCCB has sought to combine its condemnation of homosexuality with a certain level of compassion for those who are inclined towards homosexuality. The bishops have distinguished homosexual acts from homosexual inclinations and have asserted that homosexual inclinations, in and of themselves, are not sinful. Persons with homosexual inclinations are counselled to live celibate lives, if they are unable to overcome such tendencies. Catholic religious and laity are admonished to minister to homosexuals, including those who have contracted HIV/AIDS.

Applications

At both the national and the international levels, Catholic leaders have sought to act upon and implement Church doctrine towards homosexuality in a number of ways. In the first instance, the hierarchy in the United States has emphasized the authoritative nature of Catholic doctrine in this area. Indeed, the Church (specifically the USCCB) has characterized dissent from Church teaching on issues involving homosexuality as "false teaching" and "irresponsible" (Goodstein 2007a).

Second, the Vatican has reiterated its ban on gay priests. While reaffirming that the mere inclination towards homosexuality is not inherently sinful, the priesthood is to be denied to "practicing homosexual men with deep-seated 'gay' tendencies, and those who support gay culture" (CCE 2005). The Vatican requires that homosexual tendencies be "overcome" at least three years prior to ordination (Pullella 2005).

Third, the Church has reiterated its opposition to same-sex marriage at the level of the Vatican (Congregation for the Doctrine of the Faith 2003a) as well as at the level of the National Bishops' Conference (USCCB 2006b). At both levels, the Church hierarchy has reaffirmed the heterosexual, procreative nature of sexuality and of marriage and has, thereby, emphasized the illegitimacy of same-sex marriage.

Indeed, the opposition of the USCCB to same-sex marriage has been sufficiently intense to warrant cooperation with non-Catholic faith traditions and organizations that share antipathy towards same-sex unions. The Marriage Law Project, which is based at Catholic University in Washington, DC, has existed since 1996, and it began as an attempt to fight initiatives that would have legalized same-sex marriages in Alaska and Hawaii. The project represents a rather diverse coalition of theological faith tradition. The USCCB has made common cause with adherents of other religious perspectives to further the goal of preventing the legalization of same-sex marriages (Feuerherd 2004).

Finally, a number of Catholic organizations in the United States and in the United Kingdom have responded to government-sponsored anti-discrimination legislation by ceasing to provide adoption services. That is, as governments and courts have expanded the eligibility for becoming adoptive parents to gay and lesbian couples, several Catholic organizations, such as Catholic charities in certain dioceses, have decided to abandon their activities to promote the adoption of orphans rather than to comply with the anti-discrimination measures (Money 2007; Wen 2006). Absent legislative enactments of religious exemptions from anti-discrimination requirements, it seems likely that Catholic organizations in other jurisdictions will follow suit.

Thus, at the highest levels of the Roman Catholic Church in Rome and in the United States, the Church has mobilized substantially against gay and lesbian rights and has been particularly vocal in its opposition to same-sex marriage. The Church's opposition may well have contributed to the halting and uneven manner in which such rights have been recognized.

Despite the disapproval of homosexuality, same-sex marriage, and the ordination of gay priests at the level of the hierarchy, priestly dissent at the parish and community level has been far from uncommon. A number of Catholic theologians and laypeople have attempted to turn the "natural law" argument against homosexual activity on its head by suggesting that sexuality can be animative rather than simply procreative and that same-sex relationships can be quite "natural" in the sense of providing emotional and physical intimacy to couples of the same sex. Groups such as Dignity have attempted to justify the moral acceptability of homosexual activity by invoking an older, presumably more authentic and less hierarchical, Catholic tradition that predates the assertion of papal infallibility at the First Vatican Council in 1869 (Dillon 1999; Jelen 2006). In addition, theologians such as Daniel Maguire (2006) have suggested that the Catholic stance on homosexuality, and on gay marriage in particular, entails the sin of "heterosexism," which can be compared to racism or sexism (Goodstein 2007a).

Other Catholic priests, while not always challenging Church teaching on homosexuality, have nevertheless taken public positions in favour of gay and lesbian rights. In 2003, three Boston priests spoke out in opposition to an amendment to the Massachusetts Constitution that would have banned same-sex marriage. This public advocacy, which came in the wake of the *Goodridge* decision, emphasized the distinction between civil law and religious law (Zamiska 2003). Three years later, Reverend Walter Cuenin preached at the main worship service associated with Boston's Gay Pride Week. While not directly contradicting Church teaching, Father Cuenin pointed to the need to protect "the fundamental human rights of homosexual persons" (Paulson 2006).

There has not been as forceful an expression of collective dissent in the United States as in Quebec, where nineteen Catholic priests issued an open letter denouncing the opposition of the Vatican to same-sex marriage and the ordination of gays to the priesthood ("Quebec Priests Oppose" 2006). Nevertheless, signs of unease have been widespread.

Homosexuality from the Pulpit and the Pew

As the foregoing examples make clear, it is not necessarily the case that the pronouncements of the Catholic hierarchy are followed among parish priests or are considered authoritative by the laity. Indeed, the United States is often characterized as having a libertarian, individualistic political culture, in which assertions of authority, whether religious or secular, are regarded with suspicion (Jelen 2008). Moreover, some analysts have suggested that, at the level of the laity, the Roman Catholic Church in the United States has undergone a process of "Protestantization," in which individual consciences are regarded as authoritative and Church teachings are considered advisory (see McNamara 1992; D'Antonio et al. 1996; Davidson et al. 1997). This suggests the need for a close examination of attitudes towards homosexuality and same-sex marriage among Catholic priests and among lay Catholics in the United States.

Data for priests were taken from a national mail survey of Roman Catholic priests in the United States, which is part of the Combined Clergy Survey (Jelen 2005a). The mailing list came from two simple random samples of one thousand Roman Catholic parishes in the United States, drawn from the National Parish Inventory. The inventory is a database of all Catholic parishes in the United States, and it is maintained by the Center for Applied Research in the Apostolate located at Georgetown University. Two waves of the survey were sent to the first sample in January and March 2001, and a second sample received one mailing in February 2002. These mailings yielded 454 usable questionnaires, for a somewhat disappointing response rate of 22.7 percent. While this is not unusual for a mail survey, the relatively small N suggests that the results should be interpreted with caution. The priest data are further limited by the fact that the surveys were administered only at one point in time (albeit in two waves) and by the fact that data were collected prior to the *Goodridge* decision in 2003 and the sex abuse scandals that shook the Church later in the decade. Further, the survey of priests does not contain an item on gay marriage. However, it does include items measuring the frequency with which individual priests address issues of homosexuality and gay rights from the pulpit as well as attitudes towards equal rights for gays and approval of gay clergy.

Data on the attitudes of lay Catholics were taken from the General Social Survey (1972-2008). These data permit comparisons among lay Catholics over time, and recent surveys include an item concerning approval or disapproval of same-sex marriage. Thus, even if the data for Catholic clergy and laity are far from ideal, they serve to illustrate the general contours of Catholic opinion on issues surrounding homosexuality and same-sex marriage.

Table 12.1 contains the frequency distributions on the relevant questions for Catholic priests. As these data indicate, issues of homosexuality and gay rights do not seem to be a priority among US Catholic priests, with just over one-third reporting that they address such issues "very often" or "often." Moreover, the members of the clergy sample seem to make a sharp distinction between the political and the sacred. A solid majority of the members of the priest sample agree that "gays should have the same rights as other Americans." While it is true that a substantial majority of priests disapprove of gay clergy, with nearly 40 percent expressing strong disapproval, priestly opposition to gay clergy is not unanimous, with over 30 percent failing to express disapproval and 13 percent saying they would allow gays to become priests.

Not surprisingly, there is a strong correlation (424) between attitudes towards equal rights for gays and approval of gay clergy.[1] What is perhaps of greater interest is the moderately positive but statistically significant correlation between the tendency for priests to address the issues of gay rights and homosexuality from the pulpit and their support for equal rights (119) and the right of gays to be ordained as clergy (198). This somewhat counterintuitive finding suggests that, to the extent that lay Catholics receive their religious instruction from the parish priests, the doctrinal message put forth by the hierarchy is not clearly transmitted to the laity. Priests who dissent

TABLE 12.1

Gay rights responses of Catholic priests, 2001-02

	Frequency of addressing issues of homosexuality and gay rights (%)
Very often	8.5
Often	25.1
Seldom	48.3
Never	18.1
N	414.0

	Gays should have same rights as other Americans (%)	Gays should be allowed to be clergy (%)
Strongly agree	30.2	4.3
Agree	41.3	8.9
Neutral	12.3	18.4
Disagree	11.1	29.3
Strongly disagree	5.1	39.1
N	410.0	414.0

Source: Combined Clergy Survey, 2001-02.

from the Church's authoritative teaching are most likely to address the issues surrounding homosexuality in the public forum of the sermon.

Among the mass public, changes in attitudes towards gay rights seem to be largely the result of generational replacement (Wilcox and Norrander 2002). This does not appear to be the case among the Catholic clergy. While I have shown elsewhere (Jelen 2003) that there is a significant tendency for younger priests to be more doctrinally orthodox and politically conservative than their elders, there are no significant age differences among members of the priest sample with respect to attitudes towards equal rights for gays or support for gay clergy. There is a slight but statistically significant ($r = .10$) tendency for younger priests to address issues of homosexuality and gay rights more frequently than their elders. The greater orthodoxy of younger priests does not appear to extend to issues surrounding the rights of gays and lesbians.

Turning to the attitudes of the laity, Table 12.2 shows the trend among lay Catholics concerning the morality of homosexual relations. The data in Table 12.2 are clear in several respects. First, for all Catholics, in all years, the full cross-tabulations upon which Table 12.2 is based show that, across

TABLE 12.2

Disapproval of homosexual relations by church attendance, denominational tradition, and decade (percent stating that sexual relations between members of the same sex "always wrong"), 1970s-2000s.

	Catholic		Evangelical		Mainline	
	Frequent	Infrequent	Frequent	Infrequent	Frequent	Infrequent
1970s	77.3	58.5	93.0	77.4	81.7	64.5
1980s	71.6	63.1	96.2	80.4	84.6	66.0
1990s	72.3	51.2	93.4	72.1	80.7	56.9
2000s	65.8	41.7	89.7	62.7	72.3	49.1
Change	*11.5*	*16.8*	*3.3*	*14.7*	*9.4*	*15.4*

Infrequent attenders = once/twice a year or never.

Frequent attenders = once a week or more.

Source: General Social Survey (various years).

all levels of mass attendance, a plurality regard physical relationships between members of the same sex as "always wrong." Second, at all levels of church attendance, there is a strong trend in the direction of a greater acceptance of homosexuality (Wilcox and Norrander 2002; Wilcox, Merolla, and Beer 2007). In other words, despite the efforts of the Catholic hierarchy in the United States, even very observant Catholics are becoming more tolerant of homosexuality as an alternative lifestyle. Third, mass attendance has the effect of retarding the trend towards increased acceptance, though only slightly.

A comparison between lay Catholics and adherents of evangelical and mainline Protestant denominations is also revealing. At all levels of church attendance, Catholics are slightly less likely to condemn homosexuality as immoral than are their Protestant counterparts, including those belonging to mainline denominations. Although the trend towards greater acceptance of homosexuality is nearly identical among infrequent attenders of all three faith traditions, Catholics who attend Mass weekly exhibit a stronger liberalizing trend than do frequently attending Protestants.[2]

A similar pattern emerges for attitudes towards same-sex marriage. As the data in Table 12.3 show, since 1988 there has been a trend for Catholics at all levels of mass attendance to be more accepting of same-sex marriage. Same-sex marriage remains relatively unpopular among Catholics at all levels of religious activity, although, after 2003, only among weekly attenders

TABLE 12.3

Disapproval of same-sex marriage, by church attendance, denominational tradition, and year (percent disagreeing that "homosexual couples should have the right to marry one another"), 1988-2008

	Catholic		Evangelical		Mainline	
	Frequent	Infrequent	Frequent	Infrequent	Frequent	Infrequent
1988	75.7	67.0	90.3	71.4	84.9	75.4
2004	53.4	40.8	89.7	57.3	80.5	48.5
2006	62.3	36.3	82.6	58.7	71.8	45.9
2008	57.1	32.6	85.1	57.3	66.3	37.4
Change	*18.6*	*34.4*	*5.2*	*14.1*	*18.6*	*38.0*

Infrequent attenders = once/twice a year or never.

Frequent attenders = once a week or more.

Source: General Social Survey (various years).

do a majority disapprove of same-sex marriage. For both groups of Catholics, the trend is again towards greater acceptance of same-sex marriage, although, again, the rate of change is greater among less frequently attending Catholics. Disapproval of such marriage fell, remarkably, to 53.4 percent among weekly attenders in 2004 and has increased slightly since 2006 and 2008.[3]

Again, comparisons with other groups of American Christians are revealing. The pattern of increased acceptance of same-sex marriage is virtually identical for Roman Catholics and mainline Protestants, with frequent attenders in both groups increasing their support for same-sex marriage by about 13 percent, with a 30 percent increase in approval for infrequent attenders. The rate of change is much lower for evangelical Protestants.

Finally, support for the civil liberties of homosexuals has changed over time, and these changes have been uniform across levels of church attendance and denominational affiliation. Table 12.4 depicts support for the right of homosexuals to give public speeches, to teach in colleges or universities, or to be the subject of books in the public library.[4] As the data in Table 12.4 indicate, support for the First Amendment rights of homosexuals has increased by about 25 percent for Catholics, evangelical Protestants, and mainline Protestants. Again, Catholics and mainline Protestants are generally supportive of the civil liberties of gays and lesbians by the end of the time period in question, with evangelicals exhibiting less support.

TABLE 12.4

Support for civil liberties of homosexuals by church attendance, denominational tradition, and decade (percent giving most tolerant response), 1970s-2000s

	Catholic		Evangelical		Mainline	
	Frequent	Infrequent	Frequent	Infrequent	Frequent	Infrequent
1970s	43.6	50.9	19.1	34.3	35.2	47.8
1980s	40.2	59.0	24.4	44.1	36.4	58.8
1990s	62.7	68.6	36.1	53.7	51.4	68.0
2000	68.6	73.2	41.0	56.4	62.8	73.4
Change	*26.0*	*22.3*	*26.9*	*22.1*	*27.6*	*25.6*

Infrequent attenders = once/twice a year or never.

Frequent attenders = once a week or more.

Source: General Social Survey (various years).

Although the tendency to support the civil liberties of homosexuals is lower among Catholics who attend religious services frequently, lay Catholics do seem to distinguish among the morality of homosexuality, same-sex marriage, and First Amendment rights. Among lay Catholics, the product-moment correlation between support for same-sex marriage and attitudes towards the morality of homosexuality is .611, while the much lower correlations between these variables and attitudes towards basic civil liberties (.181 and .195, respectively) suggest a tendency to disconnect issue positions from morality. While all of these relationships are statistically significant, the relatively weak magnitude of the coefficients that involve the civil liberties index suggests that attitudes towards the latter are based on more than simple antipathy towards homosexuality.

Conclusion: Swimming against the Tide?

Among members of the mass public, support for the rights of gays and lesbians, and for same-sex marriage, appears to be growing. While some Catholic spokespersons have attempted to justify opposition to gay and lesbian rights in terms of long-held Catholic values, it seems clear that this has not stemmed the liberalization of American Catholic opinion. This may, in part, be a result of the individualism of the American political culture, but it also reflects a more broadly Western embrace of a "rights culture," in which autonomous individuals are to be protected with regard to making and acting on personal choices (Glendon 1991). Issue advocacy is likely to be successful to the extent that issues can be framed as applications of the principle of individual freedom (Burns 2005).

To the extent that this assertion is correct, the increasing acceptance of alternative lifestyles (including same-sex marriage) can be seen as the application of a general principle (personal liberty and autonomy) to a particular population. Unlike the issue of abortion, in which the "right" of women to bodily autonomy can be pitted against a "right to life" of the foetus, opponents of gay rights, and of same sex marriage, do not seem to have formulated an individualist counterframe to the assertions of civil and marital equality for gays and lesbians (Jelen 2005b).

The opposition of the Catholic hierarchy in the United States to the acceptance of homosexuality, and to same-sex marriage in particular, is literally countercultural. The Roman Catholic Church has a long history of conflict and accommodation with regard to liberal individualism (Burns 1994), and its opposition to gay rights is but one more chapter in that historical narrative.

The empirical data presented in this chapter suggest that the Church is fighting a losing battle in its opposition to increased equality for gays and lesbians. Parish priests have not placed a high priority on issues of homosexuality and gay rights, and there is significant opposition to the position of the hierarchy even on the issue of gay ordination. While support for gay ordination remains a minority position among Catholic priests in the United States, the existence of such support suggests that the message from the pulpit is far from unequivocal. Journalistic accounts, as well as the survey evidence presented here, suggest that the Roman Catholic Church in the United States does not speak with one voice from the parish pulpit. It seems likely that the message of the Catholic hierarchy may not be reaching the ears of many of the laity.

Lay Catholics are increasingly likely to regard homosexuality as morally acceptable and to support gay marriage. Religiously observant Catholics are less supportive of gay and lesbian rights than are Catholics who attend church less frequently, but the trend towards liberalization exists across levels of mass attendance. With respect to the morality of homosexuality and gay marriage, the rate of change is slower for Catholics who attend church at least weekly, but the direction of the change is the same for Catholics at all levels of religious observance. Moreover, comparisons between Catholics and two Protestant traditions in the United States show similar patterns for evangelical and mainline Protestants. These results suggest that Catholics are not particularly distinctive in their attitudes towards gay and lesbian rights, or towards same-sex marriage, and that the Church, as a teaching institution, has not been an effective source of resistance to the trend towards greater support for the rights of gays and lesbians.

Further, it seems unlikely that the sexual misconduct scandals that plagued a number of dioceses in the United States have affected the responses reported in this study. While these matters have had profound effects on the American hierarchy and laity, the similarity between lay Catholics and members of other Christian religious traditions suggests that Catholics in the United States make a clear distinction between homosexual activity between consenting adults and pedophilia. While support for the former is far from unanimous, the emergence of scandals involving Catholic priests does not appear to have altered the trends reported here.

Thus, the USCCB, as well as the Vatican, appear to be engaged in an effort to resist a strong trend towards the liberalization of public policies towards gays and lesbians. This effort involves both attempts at political socialization and direct action in the political realm. However, the prospects of success in the task of "defending marriage" seem limited in light of the pervasive individualism of the American political culture.

13

Roman Catholics and Same-Sex Marriage in Quebec

SOLANGE LEFEBVRE AND
JEAN-FRANÇOIS BRETON

The approach that Quebec's Roman Catholic hierarchy has taken to issues of sexuality echoes that of Roman Catholic hierarchies elsewhere, and it reflects wider changes evident in the Canadian Roman Catholic Church – but with important differences. As in the Church at large, so in the Church in Quebec, there was a relatively "liberal" approach to moral questions in the 1960s and 1970s; however, the striking difference between Quebec and the rest of Canada involves the persistence in Quebec of that relatively progressive and flexible approach to doctrine. As recently as 2000, this difference was dramatically apparent in the way Quebec bishops responded to the province's civil union legislation. Since then, particularly with regard to marriage, bishops across Canada have fallen more strictly in line with the Vatican's views, while in Quebec public dissent within priestly ranks has been voiced more boldly.

After briefly sketching French-speaking Quebec's socio-religious context and the role of the Roman Catholic Church in its development, we turn to the main subject of this chapter: a discussion of various aspects of the recent debate on same-sex marriage and civil unions in Quebec. This includes (1) a discussion of civil unions in Quebec and (2) a discussion of the Canadian Conference of Catholic Bishops' response to civil marriage.[1]

Quebec Francophone Roman Catholics

Quebec society has been greatly affected by the movement towards

secularization, which here means differentiation of the various spheres of
life (public, private, economic, scientific, political, etc.). As in other Western
societies, Christianity in Quebec is also in a state of crisis, both in terms of
the decline in numbers of adherents and the influence of its institutions.
While undeniably Canadian in many respects, Quebec also presents a few
distinguishing features. French is the first and preferred language of the majority of Quebeckers, most of whom are also at least nominally Catholic.
Statistics Canada reports that the Canadian francophone population is still
mostly composed of people of French ancestry: 80 percent of Quebec's
population aged fifteen and over have been in Canada for at least three
generations (Statistics Canada 2003, 7). In Canada as a whole, 43 percent of
the population identifies as Roman Catholic, while in Quebec 83 percent of
the population does so.[2] These factors alone make Quebec different from the
rest of Canada.[3]

The strong influence of the Roman Catholic Church on the social life of
francophones up to the 1960s has lingering effects, adding to Quebec's distinctiveness. Ever since the onset of the "Quiet Revolution" of the 1960s,
which saw a dramatic expansion of the state and a rapid decline in the role
of the Roman Catholic Church in Quebec society, the population has been
left in an often turbulent relationship with the Church. Though many of
Quebec's Catholic communities and theologians did embrace the reforms
proposed by the Second Vatican Council, a growing number of French-
speaking Quebeckers were already abandoning the practice of their traditional faith. At the same time, many "elite" or influential members of the
Catholic laity found themselves increasingly at odds with Church authorities, particularly over ideas about sexual morality, including such issues as
contraception, divorce, sexual relations before marriage, and married
priests. The focus was mainly on the traditional conception of family.
Homosexuality was not really at stake in the debates since homosexuals did
not yet have a strong voice.

As they had with regard to the sale of contraceptives in 1966, Canada's
bishops, in 1967, officially recognized a distinction between civil laws governing marriage and divorce and Canon Law, which determines conditions
for religious marriage and prohibits divorce. The following year, Pope Paul
VI's encyclical *Humanæ Vitæ* on birth control – written under the influence
of the future pope John Paul II – was published. Its strong stance against the
use of chemical birth control made it a bone of contention between so-
called progressive members of the laity and clergy and Church officials. A
few months later, Canadian bishops attempted to distance themselves

somewhat from the position on birth control presented in the encyclical, issuing a press release that called upon Catholics to be true to their own consciences when it came to matters of birth control ("Déclaration de l'épiscopat québécois" 1969, cited in Hamelin 1984).[4] In any event, some Roman Catholic laypeople in positions of public authority were tending to shy away from allowing religious edicts to influence their public actions. For instance, federal minister of justice Pierre Elliott Trudeau (though very personally attached to his Catholic faith) supported legislation to decriminalize abortion – much to the chagrin of the Catholic Episcopacy. Trudeau insisted on the fact that the decriminalization was not equivalent to public or moral approval (Lefebvre 2004). The distinction between civil laws and Canon Law or Catholic morality re-emerged as an important factor in the future debate on same-sex marriage.

In the 1970s and 1980s, Quebec's bishops appeared to adopt a much more progressive attitude than did many of their counterparts elsewhere, particularly on issues such as the role of women in the Church, priestly marriage, and access to the sacrament of communion for the divorced and re-married. While, today, Catholic bishops in Quebec generally defend the Vatican's official position on these matters in public, during the 1970s and 1980s, French-speaking Canadian bishops were well known for their progressive public positions. Monsignor Bernard Hubert, former bishop of a diocese near Montreal, once told Lefebvre, in an informal conversation, "when Canadian bishops attended an international Catholic meeting, *and were about to speak publicly*, some colleagues, smilingly, would say, 'OK! We're going to hear about improving women's condition in the Catholic Church again!'" Quebec bishops played a crucial role in this regard. While he was proud of the progressive stance taken by Franco-Catholics on questions such as women priests and contraception, Monsignor Hubert could not hide a certain resignation and battle fatigue with regard to encountering the resistance shown by the Pope and the Curia to the discussion of these matters in the Church.

Many of the ecclesiological reformist hopes of the 1970s dissipated under John Paul II's long reign. The critical questions many Catholics asked after Vatican II about matters of ecclesiology, women, and sexual ethics were simply not at the top of John Paul II's agenda. The Church's control over the public pronouncements of bishops has since grown stronger. As a result, bishops either endorse the official Church position or keep silent.[5] If one situates the most critical phase of lesbian and gay efforts to gain recognition in society in the 1980s, one must also recognize that this occurred under a strongly centralized and conservative Roman Catholic pontificate, which weakened critical progressive movements within the Church. In Quebec, as in other regions, the gay/lesbian movement took place outside of or in parallel with the Catholic Church.

During the 1990s, the climate in Quebec became such that the voices of critical and progressive French-speaking Catholics became less and less audible in the public sphere. The Church in Quebec became almost exclusively focused on such projects as preparing children for Christian initiation (first communion, confirmation) and reorganizing parishes in an attempt to cope with diminishing financial resources. It is also true that most Catholics in Quebec are mainly interested in the *rite de passage* and a basic religious education for their children. One can reflect on the mark the papacy of Benedict XVI will leave on the Church – either worldwide or, more specifically, in the context of French-speaking Quebec. Until now, he has been working mostly to improve relations with the conservative churches and groups around the world. While he is addressing very complex theological issues, it seems quite clear that we cannot expect to see any major evolution regarding sexual ethics during the coming years.

A Certain Kind of Liberalism

From the 1970s on, opinion polls gauging the values and moral attitudes of Canadians show Quebeckers to have become very liberal. Having rejected the Church's strong control and authority over their family, sexual, and social lives during the Quiet Revolution of the 1960s, most Quebeckers became fiercely resistant to any attempt to dictate morality in their private lives. In their comparative study of formal and informal volunteering and giving in Canada, Reed and Selbee (2000) also show the disaffinity of Quebeckers for formal organizations, both in their contributory behaviour and in their participation in community organizations. Aversion to organizations may be an adjunct of Québécois culture. Simply put, according to Reed and Selbee, one consequence of the traditional dominance of the Roman Catholic Church and the English economic elite in Quebec society is that Quebeckers place less trust in formal organizations than do Canadians in other parts of Canada.

In his comparative studies on religion in Canada, Reginald Bibby chronicles the magnitude of the drop-off in church attendance in Quebec from the 1970s on. In the first "severe crash," attendance dropped from 88 percent in the mid-1950s to 42 percent in 1975, and then it fell further to 28 percent by 1990 and to 20 percent in the 2000s. He observes a similar "measure of disenchantment" with the Roman Catholic Church in the other provinces, but the decline has been less dramatic, and attendance still remained at 37 percent in 1990, partly due to Catholic immigration (Bibby 2002, 17-18). The historian Ferretti (1999) agrees that Roman Catholicism has been particularly marginalized in the Province of Quebec.

In Canada's other francophone communities, the shock waves of the secularization of the 1960s were not felt so directly. A 1987 survey and comparative analysis of Catholic anglophones and francophones from Canada's four regions (the Maritimes, Quebec, Ontario, and the West) revealed that Quebec Catholics showed the lowest rate of attendance at Sunday worship (Gingras 1993, 75-92). Catholics from the West led in the importance accorded to personal prayer, books, magazines, extra-parish courses, and various ways of practising the faith. Quebeckers are to be found at the opposite end of this scale. Quebec Catholics also stand out as being the most demanding on the issue of lay involvement, which means a recognition of lay ministry and their full participation in Church leadership. In addition, they accord more importance to social justice and differ (slightly) from anglophones in claiming that the Church has not changed enough. Talin's (2006) Canadian data, part of a comparative study of religious and political values in Europe and North America, displays the considerable differences between practising Catholics in Quebec and elsewhere in Canada. Generally, to live in Quebec situates individuals less on the right than is the case in the rest of Canada (Talin 2006, 85-91). Yes, practising Catholics in Quebec are more conservative than are other Quebeckers but, on balance, no more so than is the Canadian population as a whole (see Table 13.1).

TABLE 13.1

Political orientation and religion in Canada, 2006

	Left	Centre	Right
Protestant Canada	12	56	33
Protestant Quebec	31	52	17
Catholic Canada	13	61	26
Catholic Quebec	23	56	21
Canada without religion	28	48	23
Quebec without religion	49	43	8

Source: Talin (2006).

Catholic Quebeckers are mostly "liberal" in the sense of believing in the principle of allowing people to "do whatever they want," without necessarily being willing to involve themselves in the struggle for minority rights. Catholic gays and lesbians have not had a strong collective and militant voice in Quebec. At our faculty (Faculté de théologie et de sciences des religions) at the Université de Montréal, for example, which is well known for its critical stances, we have had only a few masters and PhD students working on issues related to homosexuality. During the 1970s, two individuals worked on gay issues (Giroux 1975; Ménard 1978).[6] Since then, Réjean Bisaillon completed a PhD and published (with Guy Lapointe) the proceedings of a colloquium organized in 1996 at the Université de Montréal on the ethical dimensions of the gay and lesbian experience (Lapointe and Bisaillon 1997).[7] Manon Jourdenais, in collaboration with Jean-Guy Nadeau, looked at the spiritual experiences of homosexuals living with HIV/AIDS and developed a guide to accompanying these individuals on their spiritual journeys (Jourdenais 1997).

In Canada, one small organization – Dignity – struggles for gay rights within Roman Catholicism. Dignity has existed only since 1980, alongside an American organization of the same name. It is a movement consisting of Roman Catholics "who are concerned about [their] church's sexual theology, particularly as it pertains to gay, lesbian, bisexual, and transgendered persons."[8] On its website, most of the active members seem to be anglophones, and their so-called "local chapters" can be found in Vancouver, Edmonton, Winnipeg, Toronto, Ottawa, and Halifax. No chapter seems to exist in Montreal at the moment, though a former president of the movement lived in Montreal.

One opening for gay visibility has been created since the 1990s in an urban parish of Montreal, Saint-Pierre-Apôtre, under the direction of the Catholic Order of the Oblats de Marie Immaculée. Right at the heart of the gay village, the parish creates specific masses and forms of benediction for gay and lesbian couples and their children – a space at the frontier between the Church and the gay community (Koussens 2008). This space was created as a result of demands from the gay community, which wanted to celebrate funerals for friends who had died of AIDS. From September 1995 on, a new pastor offered a specific ministry for the gay community. In 1996, a "Chapel of Hope" dedicated to AIDS victims was created in the church.

Civil Union/Same-Sex Marriage in Quebec

As civil union and same-sex civil marriage were being debated, opinion polls indicated that Quebeckers, often much more than other Canadians, were favourably disposed towards same-sex marriage. One poll conducted by Léger Marketing between 6 and 11 April 2004 showed that 51 percent of Quebeckers agreed with extending the right to marry to same-sex couples (47 percent of British Columbians did the same, 42 percent of Maritimers, 40 percent of Ontarians, 38 percent of the residents of the Prairie provinces, and 36 percent of Albertans) (Léger 2004). Another opinion poll by Ekos Research Associates, conducted in 2002, asked this question: "The federal government is considering changing the definition of marriage – from a man and a woman to one that would include same-sex couples. If a referendum was held on this issue, how would you vote?" Fifty-four percent of Quebeckers said they would vote in favour of such a redefinition, while only 46 percent of Maritimers, 42 percent of Ontarians and British Columbians, 40 percent of Albertans, and 38 percent of the residents of the Prairie provinces said they would do the same (Ekos 2002). These figures are in line with the results of opinion polling on abortion and euthanasia. Once again, Quebeckers were at or near the forefront among those who supported these practices, along with British Columbians (Léger 2001a, 2001b).

Few figures are available to indicate the attitudes of Roman Catholics, specifically, on these issues. However, a poll on same-sex marriage conducted by Environics between 12 June and 6 July 2003 offers some insight into Catholics' views (Environics 2003). Opposition to same-sex marriage was highest among men, those over the age of sixty, Protestants, those with low incomes, and those with a high school education or less. Notably, support for allowing gay and lesbian couples to marry was actually higher than the Canadian average among those who consider themselves Catholic (58 percent). Among Quebec Catholics, 64 percent were in favour of allowing gays and lesbians to marry; among Catholics elsewhere, 51 percent were in favour.

Léger Marketing conducted a poll between 22 and 26 May 2002 (just months before Pope John Paul II's visit to Canada), asking Canadians about their perceptions of Catholic doctrine. Seventy-two percent of Canadians agreed that, on matters of abortion, contraception, and the celibacy of priests, Catholic doctrine was "outmoded" or "not in step with modern times." Surprisingly, among those polled who claimed to belong to a religious tradition, more Catholics than members of other traditions described the Roman Catholic Church's doctrine in this way – 74 percent of them (compared to 71 percent of Protestants, 70 percent of those from other traditions, and 76 percent of self-identified atheists) (Léger 2002). There cannot be any doubt that, among Quebec Catholics specifically, the numbers considering doctrine outmoded would be higher still. There is no doubt that, given Quebec's history and the role the Roman Catholic Church played in its society, francophone Quebeckers are still shaped by the backlash against the authority the Church once so powerfully wielded over their social lives.

Quebec Catholic Bishops' Position

The responses of Quebec's bishops to issues related to civil unions and marriage display elements of the progressive traditions that were relatively strong within the Church and characteristic of the broader society. They also reflect a certain caution derived from their recognition of their fragile position within the Quebec political order.

It is important to distinguish between the sphere of competence of the Assembly of Quebec Bishops (AQB) and the Canadian Conference of Catholic Bishops (CCCB). The AQB has spoken only to the issue of civil unions for same-sex couples, an area of provincial competence. The definition of civil marriage lies in federal jurisdiction and has been addressed by the CCCB. In 2001-02, faced with the federal government's reluctance to modify the definition of marriage to include same-sex couples, the Government of Quebec made the first move and proposed a civil union regime that would be equivalent to marriage (with the same rights and obligations between the partners). But there are differences between the two, notably as concerns the age of consent required for the union and the process of its dissolution. What is more, a civil marriage has legal import across Canada, whereas a civil union is governed solely by Quebec's Civil Code.

Neither the CCCB nor the AQB had much to say about the civil union proposal before the debate formally got under way. Indeed, the AQB publicly voiced no opinion about civil unions until December 2001, when a consultation document entitled *For Equal Treatment: Civil Union* was issued as an accompaniment to a draft bill (Ministère de la Justice du Québec 2001). And, at the federal level, despite the emergence of several legal challenges to the exclusion of same-sex couples from marriage, the CCCB was not publicly speaking out on the issue. In both cases, the officials of the Roman Catholic Church in Quebec and Canada seemed to have been "pulled along" by the state, reacting rather than taking any sort of initiative prior to the introduction of legislation.

When they did intervene, it seemed as though the bishops from Quebec and elsewhere in Canada had a similar approach. Both the AQB and the CCCB took the Quebec and Canadian governments to task over their haste in legalizing civil unions in Quebec and extending civil marriage to same-sex partners in Canada (AQB 2002b). The protest of the CCCB against federal legislation on same-sex marriage (Bill C-38) in June 2005 was not unlike the AQB's: "This is not the moment to rush into legislation which has such enormous social and legal consequences. Continued reflection, research, study and discussion are needed in order to ensure the best for our society and for our children, who are its future" (CCCB 2005c, n.p.; see also Veillette 2005). It seems easy to surmise that the Quebec and Canadian bishops' councils hoped to buy themselves time in which to attempt to influence public opinion and the way politicians might vote on same-sex civil union or marriage bills.

However, the Quebec bishops in fact were less intensely opposed to the civil union legislation than they may have appeared. On 9 February 2002, a telephone interview with Monsignor Luc Cyr, Bishop of Valleyfield, just after the draft bill favouring same-sex civil unions had been introduced in the National Assembly, revealed a perhaps unexpected broadmindedness on his part. Monsignor Cyr, president of the AQB at this time, called the proposal (*For Equal Treatment: Civil Union*) a "happy compromise": "This proposed form of civil union is a '*belle trouvaille*,' though it cannot be understood in the same terms as marriage between a man and a woman, and as defined by the Canadian constitution" (quoted in Cloutier 2002).[9] The monsignor's words were quoted frequently, and he did speak out to "clarify" what he had intended to say, confirming his respect for official Catholic doctrine (Cyr 2002). The bishop's initial spontaneity, though, would suggest that an in-depth, internal discussion of the position of the AQB on civil unions had not yet taken place and that there were at least some voices prepared to take an accommodating approach to laws about civic arrangements. And even after full deliberation, as far as they were concerned, the fact that civil unions were not the same as marriage meant that they had little to say about it:

> The bishops of Quebec are not opposed to extending certain benefits to same-sex couples that have, until now, been reserved for married couples. This may seem surprising to some, given that [our] position may appear out of line with Catholic morality. [However,] the fact that [we] do not object does not mean that [we offer] our approval or support. The Church has traditionally held that civil law need not conform invariably to religious moral laws. Its primary concern is to ensure the common good for all respecting freedom of conscience and religion. (AQB 2002c, n.p.)[10]

The AQB's position was similar to the position it adopted in 1967 on the matter of civil divorce. It derived from the belief in the dignity of all human beings, which, in the case of same-sex civil unions, meant respecting the "souls and consciences" of lesbians and gay men.[11] During round-table discussions on the subject of marriage organized by the AQB, Monsignor Blanchet issued this statement:

> I am well aware, as are you, of the double hurdle this question sets up, which the Church must do its best to surmount. On one hand, [we] must affirm that same-sex unions cannot be built upon the same foundations as unions between opposite-sex partners, nor can such unions be considered marriages. On the other, [we] recognise that [all people] are equally entitled to dignity and possess basic rights, in accordance with the United Nations' Universal Declaration of Human Rights which recognizes diversity within our common humanity. In this respect, I believe the Church must ask itself some serious questions about the way in which it serves the spiritual needs of homosexuals [and lesbians]." (AQB 2005a, n.p.)[12]

The AQB responded positively to changes in attitude that, as the AQB put it, favour "a welcome of and respect for their rights, and also their equal treatment in society" (2005b, n.p.).

Just as the AQB was not entirely opposed to the creation of a legal category permitting the union of same-sex couples, so it was not unequivocally opposed to the adoption of children by same-sex couples: "Obviously, the first thing to consider [in such cases] is the child's best interest. If one of the partners is the child's biological parent, it may be that adoption [by the parent's partner] is for the best" (AQB 2002b, n.p.).[13] At the same time, however, the AQB reasserted its conviction that, ideally, a child should be raised by both its mother and its father.

On the other hand, the Vatican's position is more unequivocal: "The absence of sexual complementarity in these unions creates obstacles in the normal development of children." And it goes further, claiming that "allowing children to be adopted by persons living in such unions would actually mean doing violence to these children, in the sense that their condition of dependency would be used to place them in an environment that is not conducive to their full human development" (CDF 2003a).

The AQB position did seem to change over the course of debate on the civil union measure. It had always stated that "a '*de facto*' or civil union does not hold the same significance as civil marriage, just as civil marriage is not the same as marriage in the Church" (AQB 2002c, n.p.).[14] Same-sex couples could form a legal union, therefore, on the condition that their union not be considered a marriage. Over time, the AQB became more attentive to the debate and then claimed that the bill's wording had been changed in ways that no longer drew a clear distinction between civil unions and civil marriage and that it eliminated any reference in the civil law to the sex difference required by the federal law for marriage (AQB 2002b). The bishops claimed that it was unacceptable.

Positions of the CCCB
At the beginning of the same-sex marriage debate, at the end of 2002, the AQB (Quebec is one of the four regional Episcopal assemblies in the CCCB) policies were in line with those of the CCCB. The Canadian Roman Catholic Church advocated upholding the definition of marriage as the legitimate union of a single man and a single woman, to the exclusion of all others. The Church's position was reiterated several times in more than fifty different documents and publications (official statements, letters, press releases, editorials, commentaries, and so on). These were produced and distributed by the CCCB, the Catholic Organization for Life and Family (an organization sponsored by the CCCB), and the Supreme Council of the Knights of Columbus.[15] Here is one of the CCCB's 2003 statements:

> Marriage is a unique and exclusive public commitment between a man and a woman whose love overflows in fruitfulness, and ultimately brings children into the world. We believe that the transmission of marital love from generation to generation, communicated a thousand times over from one couple to another, from one family to another, is indisputable evidence of the greatness and grace of marriage. It deserves the support and protection of society and the Church. (2003d, n.p.)

In the opinion of the CCCB, the definition of marriage could not be changed under any circumstances: "Marriage understood as the lasting union of a man and woman to the exclusion of others pre-exists the State. Because it pre-exists the State and because it is fundamental for society, the institution of marriage cannot be modified, whether by the Charter of Rights, the State or a court of law" (2003b, n.p.). This view was the same as that articulated by Chicago's cardinal archbishop Monsignor Francis George in a 2001 open letter: "Marriage predates our present government or any other and predates, as well, the founding of the Church. Marriage is not the creature of the State or Church, and neither a government nor the Church has authority to change its nature" (quoted in CCCB 2003c, n.p.).

As far as the CCCB was concerned, marriage, being the invention neither of the state nor of the Church, is a "natural institution" that serves the needs of society. Therefore, any proposed redefinition of marriage would not be "a step in evolution but a radical break with human history and with the meaning and nature of marriage" (CCCB 2005c, n.p.). Any redefinition would alter the cornerstone of society as we know it: the nuclear family.[16]

The CCCB urged a restatement of the opposite-sex meaning of marriage in the preamble of a new piece of legislation that would create an equivalent to marriage for federal purposes (either civil union or domestic partnership) for other conjugal relationships (CCCB 2003d). Like the AQB, it reminded legislators that there were other ways to recognize a variety of unions, though these could not be equivalent to marriage itself:

> We know that there are other relationships between adults that involve commitment, caring and emotional and financial interdependence. For the last 15 years, the federal and provincial governments have found ways to address their needs and requests for social benefits and three provinces have already enacted legislation allowing for domestic partnerships or civil unions. Those of us who have participated in the discussion and legislation about extension of benefits to same-sex partners have always been concerned about the impact on the definition of marriage. (CCCB 2003d, n.p.)

Throughout the debate, the CCCB encouraged Catholic laypeople to participate. A pastoral letter written in 2002 called upon Catholics, and in particular married Catholics, to make their voices heard in the growing national debate over redefining marriage (CCCB 2002; see also CCCB 2004b). At the same time, the CCCB urged Catholic politicians and others in positions of public authority "to develop their conscience through prayer, meditation, careful reading of Scripture and respectful listening to the teaching of the Church" (2003c, n.p.). The CCCB's intent was not to infringe upon politicians' freedom but to ensure that they might properly discern, "on the basis of well-formed conscience, the best way to achieve the common good." In the estimation of the CCCB, "all politicians are first and foremost accountable to their conscience, and then to their constituents" (2003c, n.p.). The CCCB's entreaties that Catholics support its position were directly in keeping with the Vatican's 2002 *Doctrinal Note on Some Questions Regarding the Participation of Catholics in Political Life* (CDF 2003b).[17]

As the debate grew heated and it seemed increasingly likely that a bill to modify the definition of civil marriage would pass, the Church's official tone became more and more strident. A review of pertinent documents produced by the CCCB at the time shows how urgent the debate was to that organization. In June 2005, shortly before Bill C-38 was passed, the general secretary of the CCCB used extremely strong language: "When a society issues arbitrary laws that reject the primacy of natural law, the result is not only the risk of social chaos and disorder but, as the twentieth century witnessed, a potential basis for state totalitarianism" (CCCB 2005c, n.p.). Not long afterwards, in July 2005, Quebec's cardinal Ouellet (newly installed as Canadian primate) asserted that same-sex marriage threatened religious freedom, referring to priests who had felt forced to remain silent on the matter, fearing accusations of homophobia (Rodrigue 2005).[18]

Monsignor Marc Ouellet's nomination in November 2002 as archbishop of Quebec and primate of Canada marked a turning point in the Quebec church – and media depictions of it. Monsignor Ouellet had been secretary of the Pontifical Council for the Promotion of Christian Unity in 2001-02 and held the Chair of Dogmatic Theology at the John Paul II Institute for the Study of Marriage and Family at the Pontifical Lateran University from 1996 to 2002. Many, particularly liberal Catholics and members of the gay community, saw Ouellet's nomination as an attempt by the Vatican to place the Quebec and Canadian Roman Catholic Church under its thumb at a time when the debate about civil union and same-sex marriage was getting under way (Côté 2003).

In Quebec: Catholic Dissent

As the Church in Quebec hewed more closely to the Vatican position, *public* dissent from that official position became more obvious. The flashpoint, however, came at least as much because of the debate over homosexuality in the priesthood as over the definition of marriage. In 2005, Benedict XVI had stated the Vatican's revised position on the priesthood in these terms: "This Dicastery, in accord with the Congregation for Divine Worship and the Discipline of the Sacraments, believes it necessary to state clearly that the Church, while profoundly respecting the persons in question, cannot admit to the seminary or to holy orders those who practise homosexuality, present deep-seated homosexual tendencies or support the so-called 'gay culture'" (CCE 2005, n.p.).

In February 2006, nineteen priests, members of the Forum André-Naud, signed and published an open letter in which they declared their disagreement with the various statements the Church had made against full, legal recognition and inclusion of homosexuals:

> [We would ask that] dialogue take place within the Church to address all questions concerning homosexuality. Unfortunately, no such dialogue is happening within our churches, particularly since diversity of opinion is being officially discouraged. Rome has already given its opinion of the subject. We would further ask that Christians pay attention to the life stories of their gay and lesbian brothers and sisters, whether in their local communities or more broadly, with their bishops. We hope that our bishops discuss these matters with one another and open up conversation about them in their various churches. We hope also that theologians contribute actively to these conversations. It is of the utmost importance that the subject be discussed freely, openly and authentically. (Forum André-Naud 2006)[19]

The Quebec bishops' response to the nineteen priests' letter was cautious. Monsignor Louis Dicaire, bishop of St-Jean-Longueil, claimed he would have appreciated the dissident priests (four of whom were from Dicaire's diocese) discussing their views with their bishops before declaring them publicly. Monsignor Marc Ouellet issued a press release indicating that he would not comment on the priests' open letter. When one of the letter's signatories, openly gay abbot Raymond Gravel, attracted media attention when he ran successfully for the Bloc Québécois in a 2006 by-election (Gravel 2003), his bishop, Monsignor Gilles Lussier of Joliette, stated that, while he regretted Gravel's tone, he would take no disciplinary action against him (Lemieux 2006). The bishop of Sherbrooke and president of the CCCB, Monsignor André Gaumont, asserted that the Vatican's directive barring homosexuals from seminary and the priesthood, mentioned in the Forum André-Naud's open letter, was intended simply to ensure that gay priests remain chaste. All these cautious reactions seem to be a very delicate public relations operation that recognizes the liberal state of public opinion in the Province of Quebec.

Conclusion

In general, we have sought to show that Quebec's population has responded with comparative liberality to issues defined by the Roman Catholic Church as moral. The Catholic hierarchy in that province has at times reflected a degree of liberal inclination but less so in the last few years. On marriage, particularly, the Quebec and Canadian bishops have been in line with the Roman Catholic authorities. There are also no visible Catholic gay militants and only a few individuals pressing for change quietly here and there. The gay community is battling outside of the Roman Catholic Church in Quebec to gain equality, not inside (at least not explicitly or publicly).

Nevertheless, dissent has been more widespread, and more public, in Quebec than elsewhere in Canada. Quebec bishops also show signs of flexibility and conciliation in their response to that dissent. They have regularly adopted a "pastoral" approach, taking into account the needs and sensibilities of the faithful, by adapting doctrine (more or less formally) to these needs and sensibilities. Monsignor Ouellet stands in some contrast to that pattern – "Roman" in his background, style, and positions. His appears to be a more "doctrinal" approach, strictly endorsing Catholic doctrine both publicly and within Christian communities.

In the wake of Vatican II, the pastoral approach to homosexuality did seem to be taking the lead in Roman Catholicism up to the pontificate of John Paul II and the interventions of Cardinal Joseph Ratzinger, which reaffirmed Church doctrine. In a debate between Cardinal Kasper and Cardinal Ratzinger, already referred to, the former mentions the enormous fault line developing between doctrine and actual practices among the faithful, especially in what concerns morality. On the level of organizational coherence, this was said to create tensions between the management of local churches and that of the universal Church. John Paul II and Benedict XVI, seeking to reaffirm the important role played by the central authority, have shown less tolerance for local differences. Since his appointment as head of the Quebec diocese, Monsignor Ouellet has been the messenger of that reaffirmation.

NON-CHRISTIAN RESPONSES

The United States and Canada are Christian majority nations, but they are not Christian nations. Neither country has an established church, and both have moved some distance in protecting the religious rights of all citizens. In both countries, non-Christians play an important and growing role in political life. In major US urban areas, there are often Christian churches, synagogues, mosques, Hindu temples, and Buddhist meditation centres in close proximity, and this is even more true of the increasingly diverse Canadian cities.

The chapters in this section focus on a couple of the most politically important non-Christian traditions in each country. In Chapter 14, Kenneth Wald begins with the question, what might we expect of American Jewish opinions on same-sex marriage? The Torah is foundational to the Christian Bible and the Quran, and it contains passages that clearly condemn homosexual behaviour, along with other passages (such as the story of Sodom and Gomorrah) that may well be more open to interpretation but that are widely read as equally condemning. However, the overall liberalism that has so strongly characterized the American Jewish community might more than counteract those factors that lean towards traditional conceptions of family. What Wald finds is that Jews are among the most supportive of lesbian/gay marriage among American faith groups – in fact, Jews who regularly attend synagogue are more supportive of same-sex marriage than are mainline Protestants who seldom attend services. These findings are reflective of what we know about the Canadian case.

In Chapter 15, Momin Rahman and Amir Hussain focus on the Muslim community in Canada and the United States. They point to the comparatively recent immigration of Muslims to North America and find, not surprisingly, that moral traditionalism persists in attitudes towards sexual diversity, though alongside relatively progressive or centrist positions on other fronts. That traditionalism may well be intensified by feelings of social or religious marginalization, especially in the post-9/11 period. At the same time, diasporic communities in major Canadian and American cities have been the source of dissenting voices on sexual diversity issues. Many younger Muslims in both countries are more centred on their religious identities and are more likely to be scriptural literalists; however, comparatively high levels of education are exposing them to more inclusive attitudes towards sexual difference.

We have seen in Europe that issues of sexual diversity can be used politically to target Muslims as difficult or impossible to integrate and, therefore, unworthy of full citizenship. Anti-immigrant sentiment has been less widely mobilized in the United States and, especially, in Canada than it has in parts of Europe. Anti-Muslim sentiment is also less widespread. But it is not impossible to imagine that prejudicial thinking about Muslim minorities, or Islam as a faith, may play on what North American Muslims purportedly believe about gender and sexuality. Yes, for now, they are more traditional on some specific issues, especially those related to homosexuality. The risk, however, is that anti-Muslim prejudice will latch onto the smattering of information about such views without the necessary understanding of the dynamics of change within Muslim communities. There may well be a similar risk in relation to other immigrant groups – Hindus from South Asia, Christian Koreans – though for now global conflicts seem to be heightening the scrutiny of Muslims, perhaps increasing the prejudice against them.

14

Paths from Emancipation
American Jews and Same-Sex Marriage

KENNETH D. WALD

The culture war model of American political life, first announced with great fanfare in the work of James D. Hunter (1991, 1994) and subsequently embraced by countless publicists and political leaders, has by now been effectively discredited by more than a decade of careful empirical research.[1] Yet, if Hunter's particular model is now widely considered overbroad and theoretically underspecified, that has not diverted attention from the persistence of cultural conflict in American public life (Leege et al. 2002; Oldmixon 2005; Layman and Green 2006). Through the mobilizing efforts of ambitious politicians, some issues on the national agenda are deeply tied to fundamental questions about "how we wish to live with other people and how we wish others to live with us" (Wildavsky 1987, 4). Such policy debates have salience precisely because they help define who we are (identity), what we do (behaviour), and what we permit (boundaries). Cultural issues tapping such diverse domains as race, nationality, gender, sexuality, and religion have the capacity to throw partisan alignments into disarray and prompt voters to depart from long-held patterns of political behaviour.

Gay marriage is one such issue, arguably the paramount issue that currently exemplifies cultural conflict in the United States. In the eyes of opponents, granting marriage rights to same-sex couples amounts to tinkering with the institution that undergirds the social order. From a religious perspective, they believe that extending marital status to gays disrupts sacred norms about sex roles.[2] To its proponents, on the other hand, enabling marriage among gay people is a powerful statement that full membership in civic society is not restricted to or based upon sexual orientation. Justice, they contend, requires extending to gay people the same rights of intimate association now currently enjoyed by heterosexuals (Kaplan 1996). Though the language is seldom used in public debate about the issue, some proponents of gay marriage also argue from a religious perspective (Wald and Glover 2007).

As a political issue, gay marriage nicely fits the cultural politics scenario outlined by Leege et al. (2002). The question of formal marriage between same-sex partners first arose due to the initiative of a small number of gay men and lesbians acting on their own volition and supported by a few sympathetic political elites (judges and elected officials). It was soon picked up by gay advocacy organizations that invested it with considerable symbolic significance as "marriage equality." The issue also attracted the attention of political leaders who constantly monitor the landscape for cultural tensions with the capacity to effect electoral change. Social conservatives framed the issue of same-sex unions – which was invariably called "gay marriage" – as a powerful symbol of cultural decay and utilized it (with uncertain effect) to aid Republicans in the 2004 elections.

Like many issues that generate cultural conflict, same-sex marriage implicates religion. Though marriage is a civil rite under law, it has long been regarded as an institution with considerable religious significance and is often performed as a religious rite even by people with otherwise limited involvement in religious life. Much of the rhetoric used in the debate by advocates and opponents of marriage equality is pregnant with religious references, symbols, and language. Proponents speak about religious freedom and the equality of all before God, while opponents often portray same-sex marriage as yet another battle in an ongoing "war against religion."

This chapter explores the nature of religiously based conflict over gay marriage through a focus on the behaviour of American Jews. With all the richness of the American religious tapestry, why concentrate on one of the smallest religious communities in the United States? From a theoretical perspective, Jews present an interesting case study. Given that much of the religious language that appears to condemn homosexuality originates in the Jewish religious tradition and that Jews have historically accorded great sanctity to the heterosexual family, they might well be expected to stand among the most determined opponents of same-sex marriage. As we shall see, however, American Jews contradict this expectation. Most of the conventional wisdom about the political behaviour of American Jews does not explain why they behave so unexpectedly on this controversial issue. However, the attitude and behaviour of the Jewish community towards same-sex marriage does make sense from another perspective – one that emphasizes the precariousness of Jewish inclusion in the American polity. The parallels between the contemporary situation of gay people and the historical experience of American Jews present an opportunity to clarify the basis of attitudes towards the contentious issue of same-sex marriage.

Why Jews Should Oppose Gay Marriage

Religious opponents of gay marriage often find ample ammunition for their position in the Hebrew Bible.[3] The starting point is usually Genesis, in which Adam and Eve, one male and one female, are taken as the archetypal model of intimate human relationships: "A man shall leave his father and his mother and cleave unto his wife, and they shall become one flesh" (Genesis 2:24). Later, in Genesis 19:1-29, the apocryphal story of Sodom and Gomorrah is often read as evidence of God's wrath against sexual transgression, particularly the lust of Sodom's male population for Lot's male guests. Elsewhere, particularly in Leviticus, more explicit language appears to condemn homosexual conduct without qualification. The most famous provision is Leviticus 18:22: "You shall not lie with a man as with a woman; it is an abomination." In defining the code of Jewish law, these injunctions have become the basis of traditional Jewish sexual ethics and thus a potent barrier to any acceptance of same-sex marriage.[4]

Although theologians have offered strong challenges to the prevailing interpretation of these verses (Bird 2000; Kahn 1989; Greenspahn 2002; Greenberg 2004), many in the Jewish community have no doubt whatsoever that the tradition is clear and straightforward on this matter. In the words of David Novak (1998, 12), a leading scholar, "there are few prohibitions that are more unambiguous than the traditional Jewish prohibition of male homosexual acts." As portrayed so poignantly in Sandi Simcha Dubowski's documentary, *Trembling before G-d*, these prohibitions have consigned Orthodox Jewish gays and lesbians to a netherworld in which they must choose between a sexual orientation they consider fixed by God and a God-saturated communal life that requires them to deny who they consider themselves to be. In the centrist world of conservative Judaism, which recognizes sexual orientation as a fixed trait rooted in nature and offers a generally sympathetic attitude towards gays and lesbians, leading rabbinic authorities nonetheless acknowledge that "heterosexual marriages alone are recognized by established Jewish law" (Dorff, Nevins, and Reisner 2006, 3).

Even the reform movement, which does not accord authoritative status to traditional Jewish sources, once acknowledged that "the biblical prohibition against homosexuality is absolutely clear" (Greenspahn 2002, 38).

Although religious doctrine is often undercut by popular religiosity, particularly when it involves sexuality (Moon 2004), the practical Judaism lived by most American Jews would seem to reinforce the exclusive legitimacy of heterosexual marriage. In Judaism, the communal domain is considered a central marker of identity and a critical venue, perhaps even more so than the synagogue, in which Jewish values are realized (Cohen et al. 2005). In the Jewish tradition, families are accorded a primary role as agents of socialization, and it is the home in which major rituals of Judaism are celebrated. Numerous accounts of Jewish life emphasize family as central to the formation and maintenance of Jewish identity (Eisen and Cohen 2000). The tradition puts a strong emphasis on marriage, treating it as "the only salutary and productive state for adult human beings" (Fishman 2000, 93). Tellingly, Judaism has no counterpart to the celibate clergy of Catholicism or to the ascetic Christian norm that lauds unmarried adults who give selflessly for others. In principle, of course, households headed by same-sex couples may (and do) perform all these functions, so an emphasis on familism does not have to lead to opposition to marriage equality.[5] Yet, in practice, the heterosexual model has defined the norm of Jewish family relationships – even as the rate of marriage and the size of families have declined among Jews.

Hence, both religious doctrines as commonly understood and social practices should act as a strong pull towards traditionalist understandings of "family values." We know from evidence relating to other socio-moral issues, however, that Jews tend to be more pro-choice on abortion, committed to feminism, tolerant of gays and lesbians, and, generally, to exhibit liberal/progressive values relating to issues of personal morality (Hertel and Hughes 1987; Cohen and Liebman 1997). Do the same tolerant attitudes that Jews have exhibited on other questions of sexuality extend to same-sex marriage? If so, how can we account for behaviour that seems so inconsistent with the inherited tradition and lived reality of contemporary Jewish communities?

Investigating Jewish Political Behaviour and Same-Sex Marriage: Study Design and Data Issues

In political science, a discipline whose practitioners largely embrace a secular worldview (Wald and Wilcox 2006), there is a strong disposition to explain the relationship between religious affiliation and political behaviour as a consequence of other factors associated both with religious commitment and political behaviour. Accordingly, the most persuasive attempt to explain why Jews are liberal on social issues denies the potency of Judaism per se by attributing those views to socio-political qualities. In the general population, support for social liberalism is most pronounced among well-educated people who live in metropolitan areas outside the South, work disproportionately in high-status and high-income professions that involve symbol manipulation, describe themselves as political liberals, identify as Democrats, and display low levels of conventional religiosity (Bruce-Briggs 1979; Mueller 1983). Demographically, social liberals are also disproportionately female, single, white, and non-Latino/a. As it happens, that description nicely captures the social reality of the majority of the American Jewish population. If the assumptions of the discipline are correct, the social liberalism of American Jews may very well be a function of these traits rather than of Judaism itself.

The immediate task before us, then, is to determine whether Jews support same-sex marriage more than do other religious traditions and whether that pattern holds with controls for traits causally unrelated to Judaism but correlated with it: education, income, occupational status, and religiosity. It is not enough to discover that such controls weaken or attenuate support for same-sex marriage among Jews, as they are expected to do so among other religious communities. The null hypothesis asserts that these correlated variables are sufficiently powerful to render Jews indistinct from other religious communities once their effects are discounted. Finding that Jews do indeed stand out from the crowd in support for gay marriage after multivariate analysis would constitute strong evidence that something in the Jewish experience promotes distinctiveness on the question of same-sex marriage.

Just 2 to 4 percent of the American population, Jews turn up in small numbers in most opinion surveys. Fortunately, one survey escapes these limitations. The National Annenberg Election Study (NAES) of 2004 (Romer et al. 2006) surveyed over eighty thousand Americans during the year before the national election in November 2004. The survey included 1,749 individuals who identified themselves as Jewish and asked respondents to report their attitudes towards same-sex marriage, providing data that enable us to compare Jews with non-Jewish religious groups.

A question about same-sex marriage was asked in five different formats over the course of the NAES (see Table 14.1). The differences among question forms should not obscure their common elements: all of the questions

TABLE 14.1

Alternate wordings of same-sex marriage question in National Annenberg Election Studies, 2003-04

Wording #1 (asked 10/7/03–12/29/03)
The federal government adopting a constitutional amendment banning gay marriage – do you favor or oppose the federal government doing this? If favor/oppose: Do you strongly (favor/oppose) or somewhat (favor/oppose) the federal government doing this?

Wording #2 (asked 12/30/03–2/4/04)
Would you favor or oppose an amendment to the U.S. Constitution that would make it illegal for two men to marry each other or for two women to marry each other? If favor/oppose: Would you strongly (favor/oppose) or somewhat (favor/oppose) the amendment?

Wording #3 (asked 12/30/03–1/4/04)
Do you favor or oppose a constitutional amendment that would allow only marriages between a man and a woman, making it illegal for two men to marry each other or for two women to marry each other? If favor/oppose: Do you strongly (favor/oppose) or somewhat (favor/oppose) the amendment?

Wording #4 (asked 1/5/04–2/4/04)
Would you favor or oppose an amendment to the U.S. Constitution that would allow marriage only between a man and a woman? If favor/oppose: Would you strongly (favor/oppose) or somewhat (favor/oppose) the amendment?

Wording #5 (asked 2/5/04–11/16/04)
Would you favor or oppose an amendment to the U.S. Constitution saying that no state can allow two men to marry each other or two women to marry each other? If favor/oppose: Would you strongly (favor/oppose) or somewhat (favor/oppose) the amendment?

asked respondents whether they favoured or opposed a constitutional amendment (in four of the five cases, a *federal* amendment) to deny marriage to same-sex couples. Because of the similarities across questions, we classify individuals' attitudes towards same-sex marriage based on the answer they gave to whatever version of the question was asked of them. The statistical model controls for differences in wording.

As suggested by previous research on social liberalism and attitudes towards gay marriage (Olson, Cadge, and Harrison 2006), the control variables include age, income, education, ideology, party identification, frequency of attendance at worship services, residence in the American South (the eleven states of the Confederacy), gender, race, ethnicity, marital status, and rural residence. I controlled for religious tradition by dividing respondents into fourteen religious categories (including Judaism) and including a separate variable for "born-again" respondents who were not identified with Protestantism.[6]

The statistical model is fairly straightforward. The goal is to determine whether Jewish attitudes towards same-sex marriage are distinctive and, if so, whether they can be explained away by factors other than Judaism itself. If the equation yields a significant, positive coefficient for Jews, it will tell us that Jews are indeed distinctive in their attitudes towards same-sex marriage and that the difference is not due to the other factors included in the model.[7]

Table 14.2 presents the basic data about religious group attitudes towards a restrictive federal marriage amendment. Overall, the American public was quite divided on same-sex marriage, with a bare majority opposed but nearly 40 percent in favour. These averages disguise enormous variation across religious traditions. At one extreme, three-fifths of white evangelical Protestants and nearly as many Mormons endorsed constitutional actions to preserve heterosexual-only marriage. By contrast, approximately three-fourths of the Jewish respondents opposed such an amendment. Of all the groups, Jews were most opposed to the restrictive amendment, outdistancing even atheists. But do such differences merely reflect social background factors – education, ideology, and so forth – or are they somehow woven into American Judaism itself? That is a question only a multivariate analysis can answer.

Table 14.3 presents the results of a complete model that incorporates question wording, religious measures, and socio-economic controls. The equation produces a great deal of information, largely confirming the conventional wisdom about the variables that affect attitudes towards gay marriage, but it is the Jewish variable that most interests us. To put it simply, once we account for all the logical sources of spurious correlation between Jews and attitudes towards same-sex marriage, there remains a powerful relationship between Jewish affiliation and attitudes towards a restrictive constitutional amendment. Jews were still significantly more likely than were most groups to oppose limiting marriage to heterosexual couples by constitutional amendment. As indicated by the final column of Table 14.3, the coefficient for being Jewish had more effect on opposition to

TABLE 14.2

Attitude towards constitutional amendment for heterosexual-only marriage by religious groups, 2003-04

	Attitude towards restrictive federal marriage amendment (%)					
Religious group	Strongly favour	Somewhat favour	Neither/ don't know	Somewhat oppose	Strongly oppose	*N* of cases
Total	33.9	7.0	9.0	11.4	38.7	79,367
White evangelical Protestant	54.1	5.7	5.8	7.6	26.8	21,185
Mormon	51.1	7.0	6.1	8.6	27.2	1,220
Latino Roman Catholic	33.3	8.7	14.8	12.2	31.1	3,470
Muslim	32.3	7.4	9.3	13.2	37.7	257
Latino/a Protestant	31.2	7.9	12.7	13.3	35.0	520
Black Protestant	32.9	5.7	10.2	10.3	41.0	5,223
White Roman Catholic	28.3	8.8	9.8	14.2	38.8	15,991
Black Roman Catholic	25.6	9.0	11.8	14.7	38.9	586
Orthodox	27.0	7.4	8.1	13.5	44.0	445
White mainline Protestant	26.1	7.8	10.4	14.2	41.5	17,438
Other	25.6	5.5	8.6	10.2	50.0	3,369
Atheist	18.5	5.3	8.8	9.9	57.6	2,097
Non-denominational Protestant	15.8	6.3	10.6	11.1	56.3	5,823
Jewish	11.6	5.1	6.2	10.8	66.3	1,743

a restrictive federal marriage amendment than did any of the denominational measures except the born-again measure, matching or exceeding all of the control variables. The distinctiveness of Jewish attitudes towards same-sex marriage, observed earlier in Table 14.2, withstood the impact of controls for social background factors that might reasonably have explained it away.

Table 14.4 uses the model to display the predicted attitudes towards same-sex marriage for "typical" respondents who are similar in all respects save their religious affiliation and rates of attendance at worship services.

TABLE 14.3

Opposition to constitutional amendment for heterosexual-only marriage, 2003-04

Variable	Regression coefficient	Effects coefficient
Mainline Protestant	.143***	.023
Roman Catholic	.116**	.029
Jewish	.429***	.067
Mormon	−.100	.016
Orthodox	.139*	.022
Muslim	−.081	.013
Other	.246***	.039
Non-denominational Protestant	.219***	.035
Atheist	.339***	.053
Black Protestant	.093*	.012
Black Catholic	.100	.016
Evangelical Protestant	−.084*	.013
Latino Protestant	.052	.008
Born-again	−.096***	.015
Liberalism	.222***	.137
Partisanship	.103***	.065
Church attendance	−.107***	.068
Female	.143*	.023
Age	.001*	.008
Married	−.086***	.010
Latino	.062*	.010
White	.088***	.014
Education	.047***	.060
South	−.014	.002
Urban	.103***	.016
Suburban	.063***	.010
N of cases	72,488	
Wald χ^2	12,183***	
Pseudo R^2	.071	

* $p \le .05$
** $p \le .01$
*** $p \le .001$

The top panel of Table 14.4 presents the predicted distribution of the dependent variable for a married forty-eight-year-old white woman who lives in the suburbs outside the American South. She is politically moderate and attends worship services once or twice a month but does not consider herself to have been born again. She was presented with version no. 4 of the

TABLE 14.4

Attitude of average respondents to constitutional amendment for heterosexual-only marriage
by religious tradition and attendance, 2003-04

	Jewish	Evangelical Protestant	Roman Catholic	Mainline Protestant	Black Protestant
Average respondent					
Favour strongly	0.28	0.47	0.40	0.39	0.44
Favour somewhat	0.08	0.09	0.09	0.09	0.09
Neither favour/oppose	0.09	0.09	0.10	0.10	0.09
Oppose somewhat	0.13	0.11	0.12	0.12	0.12
Oppose strongly	0.42	0.24	0.30	0.31	0.26
Average respondent with maximum rate of church attendance					
Favour strongly	0.36	0.56	0.48	0.47	0.53
Favour somewhat	0.08	0.09	0.09	0.09	0.09
Neither favour/oppose	0.10	0.08	0.09	0.09	0.09
Oppose somewhat	0.13	0.10	0.11	0.11	0.10
Oppose strongly	0.33	0.17	0.23	0.24	0.20
Average respondent with minimum rate of church attendance					
Favour strongly	0.22	0.39	0.32	0.31	0.36
Favour somewhat	0.07	0.09	0.08	0.08	0.08
Neither favour/oppose	0.09	0.10	0.09	0.09	0.10
Oppose somewhat	0.13	0.12	0.13	0.13	0.13
Oppose strongly	0.50	0.30	0.38	0.39	0.34

Note: The entries are predicted probabilities of respondents' attitudes towards a restrictive federal marriage amendment. For the randomly selected average Jewish respondent, there is a 55 percent probability that she will oppose the amendment either strongly or somewhat (0.13 + 0.42) versus a 36 percent probability that she will favour it to any degree (0.28 + 0.08).

question about same-sex marriage, the one that elicited the highest overall level of support for a constitutional amendment limiting marriage to heterosexuals. As the data demonstrate, it matters a great deal whether this respondent is Jewish or not. Among the four non-Jewish groups, the model predicted a probable level of support (strongly or somewhat) for a restrictive marriage amendment ranging from a low of 0.48 (white mainline Protestant) to a high of 0.56 (white evangelical Protestant).[8] The corresponding probability was only 0.36 for the Jewish respondent, and she was the only one of the five with a strong probability (0.55) of opposing a constitutional amendment that reserves marriage for heterosexuals.

The differences were equally impressive among otherwise typical respondents who attended religious services weekly or more. Even among this select group, the Jewish respondent stood out. Although the probability that she would support a restrictive marriage amendment rose from 0.36 to 0.44, that probability remains considerably below the other groups' range of 0.56 to 0.64. One way to summarize this analysis is to note that an extremely religious Jewish respondent had a lower probability of supporting a constitutional amendment limiting marriage to heterosexuals than did a much less religiously involved mainline Protestant respondent who was otherwise indistinguishable on all other variables. Equally impressive, among two average respondents who attended worship at the maximum rate, one Jewish and the other evangelical Protestant, the Jewish survey participant was one-third less likely than her Protestant counterpart to support an amendment that prohibits same-sex marriage. These differences held at the other end of the religious attendance continuum. Among those from the largest religious traditions who said they never attend worship services apart from weddings and funerals, the proportion supporting a restrictive marriage amendment averaged between roughly 0.40 and 0.50; for Jews with the same low level of religiosity, not even 30 percent supported a constitutional amendment to limit marriage to heterosexual couples.

There is only one religious group whom Jews resemble in their opposition to prohibiting gays from marriage via constitutional amendment – atheists. Even this comparison reinforces the conclusion about Jewish distinctiveness on the question of gay marriage. When the analysis was restricted to otherwise average respondents who lived in urban areas and reported the highest level of education – those whom secularization theory identifies as the least influenced by moral traditionalism – the model indicates that Jews who never attended synagogue were slightly more opposed than were comparable atheists to restrictive marriage amendments. Jews with modal rates of synagogue attendance were barely distinguishable in their attitude distribution from respondents who disclaimed religious identity altogether.

Sources of Jewish Social Liberalism

As they do on related questions about sexuality and personal morality, American Jews, then, give short shrift to moral traditionalism in considering the issue of same-sex marriage. Why?

Confronted with the general phenomenon of Jewish liberalism, scholars have emphasized such factors as the prophetic tradition in Judaism and the marginal social standing of Jews in Western history (Cohen 1983, 135-36). While it is tempting to explain support for same-sex marriage in these terms, neither approach seems wholly adequate. The Hebrew prophets of the Pentateuch certainly condemned rulers and citizens for tolerating social injustice – poor treatment of workers, penury towards the widow and orphan, and other sins. Yet such criticism was invariably coupled with ferocious denunciation of sexual immorality and licentiousness.

Jewish liberalism is sometimes attributed to identification with oppressed minority groups. Historically, Jews faced antagonism from monarchs, the church, the aristocracy, the military, and owners of large business enterprises. These historical memories are said to have left a strong residue of sympathy for groups who also suffer at the hands of the powers that be. Perhaps support for gay marriage simply reflects that historic reflex. While plausible, it should be noted that members of marginal groups do not invariably identify with others similarly oppressed. Indeed, members of marginal groups may choose to emphasize their differences with other outsiders as a means of enhancing their credentials with the arbiters of the dominant social order.[9] As I noted above, Latino/as and African Americans were less supportive of marriage equality than were white Anglos, even though Hispanics and blacks share subordinate status in the American ethnic hierarchy.

There is a variant of these traditional explanations that offers a fuller account of why American Jews might embrace same-sex marriage. Jewish interest in liberal policies grows out of their specific historical experience as a marginal population (Wald 2005, 2006, 2009).[10] The United States was the first nation to offer Jews and other groups membership in the civic community without regard to religious affiliation. This new status was conferred in the Constitution of 1787 by the obscure provision in Article VI, section 3, which states that "no religious test shall ever be required as a qualification to any office or public trust under the United States." By this provision, the United States embraced a liberal model of democracy that rendered religion formally irrelevant to civic status and thus welcomed Jews to full citizenship. This accomplished in a stroke what took decades of strife and contention to achieve in Western Europe and was never fully realized in the Eastern European Pale of Settlement where most Jews lived until the Holocaust (Birnbaum and Katznelson 1995).

This revolutionary aspect of the federal Constitution was apparent to American Jews long before 1791, when the First Amendment guarantees of religious freedom were added to the Constitution. The Jewish community of the revolutionary era understood the religious test provision of the Constitution in precisely this way. Noting that the Pennsylvania Constitution restricted public office to Christians, the Jewish community leaders of Philadelphia complained in 1783 that this action deprived Jews of "the most important and honourable part of the rights of a free citizen" and cast "a stigma upon their nation and religion" (Stokes 1950, 288). Concerned that the same restrictive language might be picked up in the national Constitution, Jonas Phillips, a Philadelphia merchant, petitioned the Constitutional Convention late in 1787 on behalf of "all the *Isrealetes* through the 13 United States of America" (Kurland and Lerner 1987). It would not be fair, he declared, to exclude from public office the Jewish residents of the colonies who "faught and bleed for liberty" just as determinedly as their Christian neighbours. He called on the delegates to avoid the kind of exclusive language that appeared in the Pennsylvania Constitution in favour of a more inclusive policy.

The religious test language that appeared in the federal document met with the enthusiastic approval of the small Jewish communities of the time, who appreciated the Constitution long before the First Amendment was adopted. A sermon preached in a New York synagogue in 1789 noted in passing "we are ... made equal partners of the benefits of government by the constitution of these states" (quoted in Kramer 2003, 17). In a memorial to George Washington, the Savannah Jewish community noted that the government he helped to create had "enfranchised us with all the privileges and immunities of free citizens" (Rabinove 1990, 136). Their co-religionists in four cities observed in 1790 that the freedom Washington won in the revolutionary war was not "perfectly secure, till [his] hand gave birth to the Federal Constitution." Rhode Island similarly thanked Washington for his part in producing a state that, by offering to all the "immunities of citizenship," made them "equal parts of the great governmental machine" (quoted in Kramer 2003, 18). The contemporary Jewish community understood the Constitution's prohibition on religious tests as their ticket to full citizenship, something no other society had offered (at least without demanding conversion as the condition of admission).

We should overlook neither the persistence of religious restrictions on office-holding at the state level (the last of which was not repealed until 1946) nor the survival of social inequality through discrimination against Jews in housing, employment, education, and other domains (finally outlawed by the Civil Rights Act, 1964). Nonetheless, Jews achieved formal and meaningful membership in the American political community long before other societies provided that option, and they capitalized on the opportunity to become active participants in civic life to a degree unmatched elsewhere (Maisel and Forman 2001).

Jews in the early twenty-first century United States may not understand the source of their commitment to liberal values in Article VI – indeed most probably have no awareness of it – but they clearly believe that their own civic equality will be threatened if public policy follows the constraints of larger and more powerful religious communities (Cohen 1992).[11] This inheritance is apparent in their ferocious commitment to maintaining the liberal character of the American state. Through organizations like the Anti-Defamation League, the American Civil Liberties Union, and the American Jewish Congress, Jews have been among the prime movers behind legal efforts to broaden the "no establishment" language of the Constitution, further removing the imprimatur of Christianity as the de facto established religion of the United States (Ivers 1995; Cohen 1992). Jewish judges have usually provided reliable votes on behalf of minority group plaintiffs in both free exercise and establishment clause cases (Sorauf 1976). In a particularly telling example of how this attitude carries over into the polling place, consider the fortunes of presidential aspirants Pat Robertson and Jesse Jackson in 1988 (Wald and Sigelman 1997). Robertson ran as a philo-Semitic presidential candidate, a friend of the Jews, while Jackson had openly embraced the cause of Palestinian nationalism and made several well-publicized anti-Semitic comments. Yet Jewish Republicans were as likely to reject Robertson as were their Democratic counterparts to oppose Jackson. Despite his overtures of friendship and respect, Robertson's known "Christian Nation" sympathies made his appeals unpersuasive to Jews in the Grand Old Party. More than one analyst has read such data to indicate that Jews are liberals because they support Jefferson's "wall of separation" between religion and state rather than the other way around.

For American Jews, the debate over same-sex marriage raises similar questions about membership in the American political community. As noted earlier, advocates of same-sex marriage see the issue in broader terms than simply economic costs and benefits or purely symbolic recognition. The ultimate stake of the marital rite is equality. Gays and lesbians believe they will be full members of the American polity only when their sexual orientation does not proscribe them from enjoying the full benefits of civic life. Marriage equality is central to emancipation.

This argument may resonate with Jews who have a history that demonstrates the danger of basing membership in civic society on the standards of any one religious tradition – even their own. The principal carriers of religious opposition to same-sex marriage, the fundamentalist evangelical Protestants who largely compose the Christian right, are disposed to believe that the United States is a Christian nation (Smith 1999) and, thus, that Christian values towards homosexuality should determine the content of family law.[12] As Jews consider such actions by fundamentalist evangelicals to be threats to their own citizenship, they are disposed to reject policies and politicians who embrace the restriction of marriage to heterosexual couples.

The distinctiveness of the American Jewish community's position on gay marriage is thrown into sharp relief when compared to the situation north of the 49th parallel. Whatever they might think about same-sex marriage, it is unlikely that Canadian Jews would perceive the issue as central to their national identity.[13] Whereas American Jews consider state neutrality towards religion of all kinds as fundamental to their inclusion in the polity, Canadian Jews understand religious equality as equal access to the public benefits available to other religious groups.

In his famous comparison of the United States and Canada, Seymour Martin Lipset (1986, 114) characterizes Canada as a more "statist, collectivity-oriented, and particularistic (group-oriented) society than the United States." He contends that these national value differences were both reflected in and reinforced by institutional differences in the religious environments of the two countries. At the founding of the republic, the American religious economy comprised mostly individualist and congregationalist traditions that distrusted links between religion and state on principle. When federation joined three of the British North American colonies in 1867, Canadian religion was dominated by hierarchically oriented religious traditions that received various forms of state support. The difference between a liberal state that privatized religion (United States) and a (Canadian) regime that conditioned public benefits on Christian affiliation shaped the political culture of the two Jewish communities.

The German Jews who dominated the American Jewish community embraced the Lockean liberal culture of the United States as a means of minimizing the differences between Judaism and Americanism (Schoenfeld 1978). Because the American system disclaimed religion as a basis for citizenship, Jews could legitimately claim the full protection of the law. The community's political priority was to ensure integration by maintaining the liberal character of the American state and its minimal engagement with religion. By contrast, Canadian Jews partook of a political system that both provided tangible benefits (funding for religious education) and symbolic

reinforcement (mandatory Sabbath observance laws) to Christianity, the religion of the vast majority of Canadians. Rather than ensure its equality by
promoting a secular state, which was the strategy of the American Jewish
community, the Canadian Jewish community initially sought to obtain a
share of the benefits, and exemption from legal obligations, that privileged
Christianity (cf. Indig 1979). This was finally accomplished in the legislative
realm in 1982 when Canada adopted its Charter of Rights and Freedoms
(Weinrib 2003). Rather than insist that the state level the playing field by
ending benefits to religion entirely, however, the Jewish community embraced the state's commitment to multiculturalism as a means of group survival, receiving, among other benefits, "heritage programs in Yiddish and
Hebrew paid for by public funds; events such as the annual Jewish book fairs
and film festivals held in a number of cities, and Toronto's Ashkenaz, a bi-
annual celebration of Eastern European Jewish culture, ... (provincial) public
funds for day schools in every province where there are day schools except
Ontario; [and] a proliferation of Jewish-studies programs in Canadian universities all of them public institutions" (Brown 2007, 6). In such an environment, the appearance of religious symbols in public spaces does not agitate
Canadian Jewry.

Conclusion
This chapter began by offering three possibilities regarding American Jewish attitudes towards same-sex marriage – that American Jews embrace a
traditionalist view that rejects gay marriage, that they accept it strongly as
part of their moral liberalism, or that there is no association between Judaism and attitudes towards same-sex marriage once external controls are
introduced. I find strong support for the second hypothesis, that American
Jews are much more favourable to extending marriage rights to gays than
are other religious groups and that the effect of Jewish affiliation is hardly
spurious. There is some evidence that those Jews who do evince strong commitment to their religious tradition through high rates of synagogue attendance are, all other things being equal, more likely than other Jews to support
enshrining traditional moral stances vis-à-vis homosexuality through a constitutional amendment. Even they, however, were much less attracted to enacting a restrictive marriage attachment than were members of other large
American religious communities. Being Jewish in the United States – even
being Jewishly involved in the most traditional way – still breeds scepticism
about the use of constitutional means to bar other minorities from the civic
membership that Jews themselves value so highly.

15

Muslims and Sexual Diversity in North America

MOMIN RAHMAN AND AMIR HUSSAIN

Muslim communities in North America have existed in significant numbers since the Muslim immigration rate increased dramatically from the late 1960s onward. Census data suggest that, in 2001, there were about 580,000 Muslims in Canada, accounting for 1.8 percent of the population. In the United States, Pew Foundation survey data estimate the number of Muslims at 1.5 million, or 0.6 percent of the population, though some scholarly estimates have been significantly higher.[1]

To talk about Muslims in Canada and the United States means referring to more than simply a religious category. Muslims increasingly identify themselves as such, and many use the term without a strong sense of faith. This is, in part, a response to the label being applied by others and by the extent to which they have been subject to heightened public attention. In fact, the visibility of these populations exceeds their numbers, in part because of the greater scrutiny they have experienced at the hands of state authorities and the media, resulting from the widespread association of "militant," or "fundamentalist," Islam with terrorism.

The populations explored here are widely varied in ethnicity, and immigrants from most of the regions of their origin include many non-Muslims. In the United States, too, a significant portion of the Muslim population is African American. Despite such diversity, explicitly Muslim organizations have emerged in recent decades, enhancing the development of a Muslim-specific identity. Among such groups are those who have been influenced by

second wave feminism and other activist movements seeking the public recognition of sexual diversity. Queer voices have faced difficult challenges but
have now emerged in both countries, challenging public perceptions of
Muslims as being inevitably conservative.

Here we explore two key themes: (1) Muslim distinctiveness from other
religiously demarcated populations in Canada and the United States with
regard to debates over sexual diversity and (2) the emergence and impact of
queer voices within Muslim communities. In addressing these themes, we
want to avoid importing a "clash-of-civilizations" framework that pits conservative theocratic Islam against a progressive secular West.[2] A discussion
of sexuality and gender can inadvertently reinstate that framework since
these issues are now regularly used to argue that a cultural and religious
chasm separates Muslims in the West from the rest of the population alongside whom they live. This all too easily translates into claims (implicit or
otherwise) of Western moral and political superiority (Howell 2005; Razack
2008; Waites 2008). We argue that this is neither a helpful frame nor a sustainable conclusion.

We explore these themes in two political and cultural contexts – the
American and the Canadian – that have important differences between
them. Contrasts in these two political systems shape the groups formed to
represent Muslim communities, and differences in media systems affect the
overall social and political climate within which they operate. The official
Canadian discourse of multiculturalism, even if it implicitly exaggerates
the acceptance of minority ethnicities, may result in lower levels of political
or social alienation among Canadian Muslims and greater opportunities to
integrate. And, finally, the more widespread shift in law and public policy
treatment of sexual minorities in Canada, compared to what is going on in
the United States, potentially makes for a difference in what are likely to be
seen as dominant values (Rayside 2008). We are interested in to what degree
such contextual differences generate contrasts in the politics of Muslim
communities and in their receptivity to recognition claims on the part of
sexual minorities.

In proceeding through such terrain, we confront serious gaps in research
on social and political change within North American Muslim communities, particularly in response to gender challenges and sexual diversity.
Writers like Amina Wadud, Yvonne Yazbeck Haddad, and Scott Kugle have
questioned conservative Islamic responses to such issues in theoretical
terms, but there has been little serious analysis of the resonance of such

debates in the everyday lives of queer Muslims, the communities in which they live, or the organizations that seek to represent them (Haddad and Smith 1994; Haddad, Smith, and Esposito 2003; Haddad 2004; Wadud 1999; Kugle 2003; Safi 2003). We readily acknowledge that some of our claims are tentative and that they are intended to provoke further research.

Immigration and Demographic Diversity

Muslims have a long history in North America: estimates claim that at least 20 percent of the slaves who came from West Africa to the United States were Muslim and that some early settlers in Canada were Muslim. The first Muslim immigrants to North America other than slaves came from the Ottoman Empire in the late nineteenth century and the first decades of the twentieth century, though in modest numbers, and they included farmers who settled permanently in the American Midwest. Numbers increased moderately after the Second World War as part of a new wave of immigration fed the North American industrial growth of the 1950s and 1960s. The US strategic interest in the Middle East and in the exploitation of oil reserves also led to the recruitment of increasing numbers of Muslim students to American universities (Haddad 2004). One 1961 estimate suggests that there were 78,000 Arab Muslims in the United States and an additional 30,000 Muslims from elsewhere (Haddad 2004). A recent writer estimates that there are 8 million Muslims in the United States and projects that by 2010 there will be over 10 million, but his sources for this claim are unclear (Farid 2008).

The 1971 Canadian census counted 34,000 Muslims due, in part, to the increasing numbers of immigrants to Canada after the removal of a quota for Asians in the 1960s. In both countries, changes in immigration rules led to dramatic increases in non-European immigration after the 1970s. The 2001 Canadian census shows that 1.9 percent of the Canadian population was Muslim, a 2.5 percent increase over the previous decade, which made it the largest non-Christian population in the country. Most are South Asian, though many are from Africa and the Middle East.

The American Islamic community has also increased in size. There is no one region of origin that dominates as much in Canada as South Asia, with the largest communities being split between one-third South Asian, one-third Middle Eastern (including both Arab and Iranian), and one-quarter African American. In the United States, there are also more native-born converts to Islam, overwhelmingly African American but also white and Latino/a.

Shi'i Muslims constitute a minority of the Muslim communities in both countries, but a larger minority (30 percent) than in the rest of the world. Among them, too, Ismai'ilis are more prominent than they are elsewhere. This is important for our purposes because they are more likely to include progressive voices on questions of family, gender, and sexuality. Such voices are also more likely to come from North American than from European Muslims due to the relatively high levels of education among the former. European Muslims tend to have a limited education and to end up economically marginalized. In Europe, too, each country's Muslim population is more ethnically or nationally homogeneous than it is in North America, with strong majorities in Britain, Germany, France, and Spain coming from South Asia, Turkey, and North Africa, respectively. The greater diversity of North American communities, coupled with their economic standing, increases the likelihood of social and political integration.

Political Organization and the Prominence of Conservative Voices on Sexuality

Even if the diversity of origins and the relative recentness of large-scale immigration caution against ascribing a monolithic religious or political identity to Muslims, they have been organizing as a religious community for decades. The first mosque in North America was built in Maine in 1915, and the second was built four years later in Connecticut. The first in Canada was built in Edmonton, Alberta, in 1938. North America's first major Muslim conference took place in 1952 (in Cedar Rapids), with four hundred attending from Canada and the United States (Hussain 2001, 2004; Ahmed 1991, 12-13). Two years later, the Federation of Islamic Associations of the United States and Canada was formed, hosting its first conference in London, Ontario, the following year.

Campus organizing was an important current in the early institutionalization of Muslim voices in North America. The Muslim Students Association (MSA) was formed in 1963 in the United States. Its local leadership was usually drawn from foreign Arab-speaking students who were seeking avenues for religious practice, and Saudi Arabian funding helped to ensure a very conservative approach to Islam (MacFarquhar 2008). In the decades to follow, chapters formed in most major universities and colleges across North America. In 1981, the Islamic Society of North America (ISNA) was established as an outgrowth of the MSA, and, for a time, it too benefited from the financial support of Saudi Arabia and other Arab countries (Haddad 2004). Like the MSA, it reflected the belief among many of the new wave of immigrants from the 1970s in that the earlier pattern of accommodating fully to American culture constituted "too high a price to pay" as it diluted Islamic traditions and cultural characteristics (Haddad 2004, 24).

The emergence of such groups reflected and reinforced a gradual shift in identities – away from association with countries of origin, in some cases with pan-Arab nationalism, and towards an identification with Muslim origins (Haddad 2004; Lo 2004). According to Haddad, this shifted the "assimmilative" balance towards more emphasis on differences from North America's dominant culture and religious patterns and less emphasis on commonality. To some extent, such a shift in identity reflected international political developments and a growing sense among Muslims, and especially Arab Muslims, of being under siege (Arat-Koc 2006). The relatively low profile of Canada on the international stage, despite its active involvement in Afghanistan, might reduce that defensive identification, though, on the other hand, the emphasis on multiculturalism in Canadian political discourse would provide an opening for a public claim to Muslim identity.[3]

ISNA, despite the collapse of financial support from Arab governments following the 1990 Gulf War, has generally retained its standing as the largest Islamic group in North America, with annual conventions attracting 35,000 participants. It retains a conservative approach to moral questions, though, like the more conservative Islamic Circle of North America, its preoccupations are more religious than political. More recently, there has been a proliferation of more politically focused groups representing Muslim perspectives in Canada and, especially, in the United States. Although conservative views on moral issues remain dominant, there has been a move towards the political mainstream, with Muslims embracing participation in the political process and moving away from isolationist rejection of Western values and politics (Khan 2003).

The institutionalization of political groups has been particularly pronounced in the United States, in part because of the pressures for groups to develop permanence and expertise within the complex American institutional framework and, in part, because of the perceived need to counteract Jewish political influence on US foreign policy. The American Muslim Alliance was established in 1989 (in California) and specifically aimed at promoting participation in elections (as voters and candidates). The Muslim Public Affairs Council (MPAC) was formed in 1988 to work for the civil rights of American Muslims. The American Muslim Council (AMC) was established in 1990; the Council on American-Islamic Relations (CAIR) in 1994; and the American Muslim Political Coordinating Council in 1998. Most of these have been small or ephemeral, though MPAC and CAIR are the most established, each of them claiming about thirty-five regional offices or chapters. CAIR, which may now be the most cited by mainstream media, focuses on challenging negative stereotypes of Muslims in the United States and discrimination against them – a mandate intensified by the post-9/11 climate in that country. As in Canada, there are progressive groups (e.g., Muslims for Progressive Values, the Progressive Muslim Union, and Muslim WakeUp!), but they are smaller and have nothing like the visibility of the more traditional groups.

Even the large Muslim-American groups have suffered from modest resources. Some received significant funding from the Gulf states, but such sources declined or dried up in the late 1990s. AMC staff, for example, declined from eighteen to seven at the end of the 1990s, and MPAC struggled to manage a large advocacy role with only two full-time directors and two part-time staff (Nimer 2002, 182).

African-American Muslim participation in political life has frequently relied more on non-Islamic organizational channels – whether they be civil rights groups or anti-poverty networks. An important exception has been the Nation of Islam (along with various splinter groups). It is not at all clear how many supporters it has even among African-American Muslims, and it is regarded with either wariness or indifference by other Islamic groups. Many Muslims do not recognize the Nation of Islam as Muslim at all, and, beyond that, tensions based on race, class, and politics persist among African American and other adherents to the faith (Leonard 2002). Still, the Nation of Islam acquires recurrent prominence in the media and clearly represents a form of nationalist militancy that draws the political energies of an important current of African-American Muslims.

The development of political groups came at the same time as a proliferation of mosques in the United States – from six hundred in 1986 to more than twice that in 2000. In 2002-03, Muqtedar Khan estimated that there were two thousand mosques and Islamic centres and twelve hundred Islamic schools – the latter representing a dramatic increase over the past few years (Khan 2003, 184). The proliferation of both mosques and schools has arisen largely from the tendency of newer immigrants, coming as most of them have from countries in which Islam was the state-sponsored religion, to seek more guidance than did their immigrant predecessors from religious leaders. Imams and the institutions they lead, then, have acquired more influence, even among those for whom religion is not necessarily central. The increased perception of American antipathy towards Islam intensified the cultural and socially defensive identification with Islam.

That said, it is also important to note that the majority of North American Muslims do not identify with a particular mosque. This may result from the lack of sufficient numbers to sustain mosques in many communities across the country, the ethnic and linguistic diversity of local Islamic populations, and a weak fit between the religious or social views dominant within religious institutions and much of the surrounding population. Estimates for the proportion of American Muslims attending a mosque at least weekly vary from 25 to 40 percent (Read 2008; Pew 2007).

A shift towards "Muslim" identity has occurred in Canada, though without quite the same institutional development as has occurred in the United States. The Canadian political system does not create nearly the same incentives for continuous institution building as does the American system, and the lack of super-power status has reduced the stakes in Muslim political engagement in Canada (even with Canada's troop presence in Afghanistan). And, while the 9/11 attacks had strong reverberations in Canada, the perception of beleaguerement and stigma appears to have been less widespread among Canadian Muslims than among their American counterparts. True, as Arat-Koc (2006) points out, there are strong similarities in the security discourse in Canada and in the United States, but in Canada it is less reinforced by scare-mongering media and by public fears about immigration.

In Canada, there are a number of organizations dedicated to providing reliable information about Muslims and Islam – both to Muslims themselves and to non-Muslims (Karim 2002; Hussain 2004). One is the Muslim Society of Canada, founded in Toronto during the 1960s (http://www.muslim-canada.org); another is the Islamic Circle of North America (http://www.icna.org), which has a presence in Canada as well as in the United States. Much local activity is based around mosques, community centres, and schools, and these, in turn, can provide the grassroots foundations of umbrella organizations. Numbers of schools are hard to come by; however, in 2001, there were nineteen Islamic schools in the Greater Toronto Area and an additional seven in the rest of Ontario – all told with about three thousand students. The modesty of state funding or tax breaks for attendance at such schools across most of Canada is one deterrent to enrolment.

For a time, the Council of Muslim Communities of Canada, founded in 1973, was recognized by provincial and federal governments as the most representative community voice. ISNA Canada, based in Mississauga, Ontario, replaced it as the largest single Muslim group in Canada in the 1980s. With ISNA seen largely as an American organization and, in any event, as being preoccupied with religious issues, there was no significant political voice for Canadian Muslims. Although in 1997 ISNA Canada formed the Canadian Muslim Council, a counterpart to the American Muslim Council, it never achieved a significant profile. More successful was the Canadian Islamic Congress, founded in Kitchener, Ontario, by Mohamed Elmasry in 1994. It was, and remains, a conservative voice and the Muslim political group most frequently cited in the media.

In 1982, the Canadian Council of Muslim Women was established, with well-educated and professional women prominent in its membership. It included a social service component to its mandate (e.g., assisting new immigrant women) but also set out to challenge some of the inequalities faced by Muslim women and to advocate a "moderate" position on a range of political issues. The Muslim Canadian Congress (MCC) was founded in 2002 by Tarek Fatah, host of the television program *The Muslim Chronicle*. In 2006, a number of MCC's board members split from it over disagreements on Middle Eastern politics and formed the Canadian Muslim Union. The MCC, however, retains higher visibility.

The Strength of Traditional Values and Openings to Challenge Them

Discussions of gender equality and sexual diversity have been largely absent from the largest of the Muslim political and religious groups in both Canada and the United States. These groups have tended to emphasize traditional interpretations of Islam and have been preoccupied with community building, immigration policy, the discriminatory treatment of Muslims, and, to some extent, foreign policy. However, as the size of their constituencies has increased, and the range of perspectives within those constituencies has also increased, there has been more pressure to respond to these gender equality and sexual diversity issues.

Diasporic communities in the large urban centres of the West have openings for those raising critical questions about traditional religious and cultural ideas, particularly after they have established roots. As contact with "host" communities intensifies, dissenting voices within immigrant or minority communities are more able than are their counterparts in the countries of origin to gather information and to form networks among those with similar views. Some such voices "exit" their communities of origin and seek full assimilation to the dominant society; however, particularly in large communities, some remain connected and mobilize a challenge to traditionalism from within. It is no coincidence, for example, that early cultural expressions of sexual diversity among South Asians appeared within migrant communities in North America before they appeared in those in

India, Pakistan, and Sri Lanka (e.g., Deepa Mehta's *Fire*, Bapsi Sidhwa's *Cracking India*, and Shyam Selvadurai's *Funny Boy*). The openings to dissent on such hitherto forbidden subjects are especially powerful in those generations born and raised in North America, particularly if the communities in which they live are not sufficiently homogeneous to be able to develop relatively segregated social structures (such as schools). The likelihood of dissent is further amplified in the Muslim communities of North America by relatively high levels of education. In general, high education increases openness to diversity and to equity claims by women and sexual minorities. The fact that Muslim minorities in Canada and the United States are less economically marginalized than are their counterparts in Europe also reduces the likelihood of strict adherence to religious belief.

On the other hand, social traditionalism may well be strengthened by the relatively recent migration of the great majority of Muslims to both Canada and the United States as well as by the starkly conservative norms relating to gender and sexuality that prevail in the countries from which they migrated. In addition, the already-established religious institutions with which new immigrants associate themselves are almost invariably conservative on moral questions. For those outside the Christian faith, and the more deeply rooted and publicly recognized Jewish religion, the importance of faith itself may well acquire an important role even among those who do not attend mosque regularly. There are indications in Ramji's work on Canada that second-generation Muslims are more likely to identify with Islam than are their parents and to do so with a stricter version of faith – a finding with echoes in the role of faith in younger Islamic cohorts in the United States (Ramji 2008; Pew 2007). This is probably less true in North America than in Europe, where religious radicalism seems frequently to be found among highly educated middle-class Muslims, but the hold of religion on young Muslims in Canada and the United States may well be firmer than it is on other young people.

Personal and family links to Islam may have been increased by global developments in the past few decades, especially after 9/11. The perception that Muslims are being targeted by Western governments, and the United States in particular, may well have more impact on American than on Canadian Muslim identity formation, but it would almost inevitably mark both communities. This could well slow the acculturation to what are perceived to be "Western" values. As Mohammed Arkoun (1994, 109) argues, "we must not lose sight of the wars of liberation and the ongoing, postcolonial battle against Western 'imperialism' if we want to understand the psychological and ideological climate in which an Islamic discourse on human rights has developed in the past ten or fifteen years."

The competing forces at work here produce a complex interaction between values brought to North America from other regions and those that dominate (or are seen to dominate) the "host" society. As Kobayashi (2008, 6) remarks, "members of the second generation have shown that they are capable of interpreting and even re-framing the dominant narrative in a variety of ways to assert their own sense of identity and Canadianness; but they do so in a social context in which the aims of multiculturalism are incomplete." That uncertainty about what to make of the social context may be more acute among North American Muslims because of perceptions from outside their communities that they are unassimilable. This adds to the unpredictability of second- and third-generation beliefs about gender and sexual equity claims.

The prominence of "diversity" in Canadian political discourse, and Canada's relatively modest role in international affairs, may well produce distinct trajectories for patterns of religious faith and moral beliefs among young and second-generation Muslims in the two countries. Comparative survey evidence shows, for example, that Canadians are more accepting of relatively high levels of immigration than are citizens of virtually every other Western country (World Values Surveys 1990 and 2000, cited in Inglehart et al. 2004). Canadian media have fewer advocates of starkly conservative views on immigration in general, and Muslims in particular, than we find in the United States.[4] This may create more inducements for Canadian Muslims to integrate and may reduce the role of religious institutions (and beliefs) in demarcating identity. Yvonne Haddad (2004, 44) may well be right when she says that, on the American side, the post-9/11 climate has forged "a new relationship between the mosqued and the un-mosqued, who had previously disagreed on issues pertaining to integration and assimilation." But it is not clear that such a claim travels across the border intact.

The dramatic shift in Canadian public policy and law towards equal treatment of lesbians and gays, in contrast to the much more uneven embrace of equity in the United States, provides more powerful cues to all immigrants and their children of what constitutes Canadian values. And it shows, in particular, that the recognition of sexual diversity is being incorporated into those values. This may produce a cross-generational shift in attitudes towards sexuality even among the faithful.

What evidence is there regarding Muslim identity in Canada and the United States and regarding the place of religion within that identity? In fact, the indicators are mixed. Even in the United States, where we might have seen greater social and cultural defensiveness, a 2007 Pew Research Center study reports that American Muslims are "highly assimilated" into American society (Pew Research Center for the People and the Press 2007b, 2). Forty-three percent favoured adopting American customs, while only 26 percent favoured trying to remain distinct. The 47 percent who thought of themselves as Muslim first rather than as American seems like a lot, but this percentage is significantly lower than what was found for British, German, and Spanish Muslims whom Pew interviewed the year before. Only in France did a comparable percentage of people identify as Muslims first.

Still, the identification as Muslim first was much higher among young American Muslims (60 percent among those 18-29) than among those over thirty (41 percent). The vast majority of American Muslims also reported religion as being very important in their lives. The United States has one of the most religious Christian populations in the West (rivalled only by Ireland), and, in this sense, the Muslim population fits right in. Pew's 2007 report showed that, for 72 percent of American Muslims, religion was "very important" in their lives, as compared to 60 percent for US Christians. Only 9 percent reported that religion is "not too important" or "not at all important." Forty percent attended mosque at least once a week, and, while that was lower than the proportion for Christians (45 percent), this likely reflects the fact that many do not live close to a mosque. The regularity of mosque attendance is higher among young Muslims (50 percent) than among those thirty or over (35 percent), a pattern not replicated among Christians. American Muslims are even more likely to be scriptural "literalists" than are Christians. Those who believe that the Quran is the word of God, to be accepted word for word, comprise 50 percent, compared to 40 percent who have similar views of the Christian Bible.[5]

We are unaware of comparable data for Canada. Environics Research conducted a survey of five hundred Muslims in 2006 but did not include questions on religious belief or practice (Canadian Broadcasting Corporation 2006). Reem Mehsal (2003), though, has observed a shift among younger generations from identification with country of origin towards closer identification with Islam, which parallels the observations of Yvonne Haddad and the data provided by Pew (2007b, 95-96).

Environics' respondents were questioned about whether they felt Canadian Muslims generally wanted to fit into Canada or remain distinct (a different question than asked by Pew, which wanted respondents to answer only for their own views). Fifty-five percent thought Muslims wanted to fit in; 23 percent thought they wanted to remain distinct. Only 17 percent said that many or most Canadians were hostile to Muslims, a much lower figure than Pew found in Britain (42 percent), Germany (51 percent), France (39 percent), or Spain (31 percent). There was no similar question in the American Muslim survey, though 53 percent agreed that being Muslim in the United States had been more difficult since 9/11, and 54 percent agreed that the government singled out Muslims for extra surveillance. One-quarter of American Muslims reported that, as Muslims, they had been the victims of discrimination.

Evidence from across the Western world, and particularly in North America, points to a strong association between religious belief and opposition to the public recognition of sexual diversity. In Christianity and Judaism, there are prominent currents of progressivism on such contentious issues as reproduction and sexuality, but those who see religion as important in their lives are more often inclined towards morally conservative views than towards progressive ones. Within Islamic religious circles, progressive interpretations are even less prominent than they are in Christianity and Judaism, so we should not be surprised to find very strong currents of moral conservatism among American Muslims, among whom there is such a strong attachment to religion and an adherence to scriptural literalism.

The 2007 Pew survey included just one question on sexuality, asking respondents whether homosexuality should be accepted or discouraged. In the general American public, 51 percent said "accepted" and 38 percent said "discouraged." The figures for Muslims were much less accepting (27 percent), with 61 percent responding "discouraged." This was not as evident in responses to a question on gay and lesbian marriage in the 2004 National Annenberg Election Study. As Kenneth Wald (in this volume) reports, the proportion of American Muslims who strongly favoured a constitutional amendment upholding the heterosexual definition of marriage (32 percent) was slightly below the national average, and the proportion strongly opposed to such a measure (38 percent) was only fractionally below that found in other groups. This could well be a function of their fear of government intervention in their lives at a time when American Muslims felt much beleaguered. It could also have reflected an antipathy to President George Bush, who was much identified with the amendment proposal.

Canadian Muslim attitudes towards homosexuality were tapped in the 2006 Environics survey, and here, too, we find evidence of strong conservatism. Only 10 percent of Canadian Muslims expressed strong agreement with the statement that "society should regard people of the same sex who live together as being the same as a married couple," compared to 22 percent of the general population. Strong disagreement was expressed by 58 percent of Canadian Muslims (compared to only 25 percent of the general population). On the basis of this admittedly very limited data, we find no significant contrast between the extent of moral conservatism among Canadian Muslims and American Muslims, despite the quite different contexts within which such opinions are shaped.

Conservative views on homosexuality do not necessarily spring from traditional views on other political issues. The Pew survey shows that 70 percent of American Muslims lean towards the provision of more rather than fewer government services. Fully 73 percent say the state should do more for the needy, in contrast to the 17 percent who say that the government cannot afford to do more. Only 19 percent describe themselves as conservative (24 percent describe themselves as liberal) as compared to 34 percent in the general public who do so (with 19 percent describing themselves as liberal). The overwhelming majority lean towards the Democratic Party (though, in part, this is in response to the Bush administration's Middle East policy).

There is no reason to believe that Canadian Muslims are any different. The Environics data reported by Amy Langstaff (this volume) show that, when asked if "taking care of home and kids is as much men's work as women's work," 70 percent strongly agreed (compared to 56 percent of the general population). When asked if they were worried about Muslim women taking on "modern" roles, only 26 percent of Muslim respondents in Canada said yes. Most Muslims have continued to vote for the centrist Liberal Party, and only 7 percent support the Conservative Party.

In light of the prominence of centrist or progressive views on other issues, the reasons for the hold of traditional beliefs on sexuality in particular are not altogether clear. One factor may well be the moral conservatism of the cues that Muslims receive from most community leaders, particularly on issues like gay rights. Another is that recent large waves of immigration have created unusually tight family bonds, which confront Muslim members of sexual minorities with real challenges with regard to being open about their differences. This could reinforce the perception that homosexuality is "Western" or, at the very least, that the set of behaviours and identities commonly linked to homosexuality in North America is foreign to Muslims. Remember, too, that the shift towards more positive views about lesbian and gay rights is a relatively recent phenomenon in North America and Western Europe and that there remains vocal opposition to the recognition of such

rights among Christians, especially in the United States. Indeed, the opposition to public acceptance of sexual diversity can easily persuade newcomers
to both Canada and the United States that religious faith of any sort naturally translates into such opposition.

There is a long documented history of homosexual eroticism and behaviour in Islamic culture, though this reflects a limited toleration of male
same-sex behaviour within boundaries that do not disturb familial and social gender norms (Schmitt and Sofer 1992; Murray and Roscoe 1997). The
political and religious regimes of countries from which the overwhelming
majority of North American Muslims trace their roots now typically deny
such histories, and that pattern of denial is undoubtedly widespread within
diasporic communities. Even if this were not the case, the notion of an identity based on homosexuality has until very recently been almost entirely absent in those countries (Waites 2008). This, of course, creates a strong
barrier to understanding and accepting claims framed in such terms.

The persistence of moral conservatism regarding sexuality issues is reflected in the public reactions of large Muslim groups on both sides of the
border. In 1994, ISNA Canada's annual report stated that it was "involved
heavily in the fight against homosexually [sic] and lesbians in Canada." In
1999, concerned Muslim parents formed the Toronto District Muslim Education Assembly to mobilize against the inclusion of sexual diversity in the
Toronto public school board's equity policy. In more recent years, the Canadian Islamic Congress has regularly intervened to oppose the public recognition of same-sex marriage, claiming that marriage has been a religiously
defined institution for ages in all religions and that the Liberal government's
introduction of a bill on the subject was suicidal.

An important exception is the Muslim Canadian Congress. The MCC
was not always supportive of inclusive positions on such issues. However,
during the debate on same-sex marriage, its board was persuaded to shift
positions, primarily by activist El-Farouk Khaki, a Toronto immigration
lawyer who was a key player in the local queer Muslim group Salaam. When
the marriage legislation was presented to Parliament in February 2005, an
MCC press release welcomed the move (MCC 2005). It reminded listeners
at a press conference that Muslim Canadians had relied on the Canadian
Charter of Rights and that it was incumbent upon the MCC "to stand up in
solidarity with Canada's gays and lesbians despite the fact that many in our
community believe our religion does not condone homosexuality." Tarek
Fatah (2005) was cited as condemning fear-mongering on the part of some

religious institutions, which camouflaged messages of hate behind claims of cultural and religious practice.

A similar pattern prevails in the United States. The major groups (religious and political) either condemn homosexuality or (more commonly) retain a telling silence on sexuality issues, even at times when mobilization over same-sex marriage has been at its height (Campbell and Robinson 2007). Even as they have become more mainstream, with, for example, MPAC's support of gender equality, there is very little sign of a significant shift towards progressive or even moderate positions on issues tied to debates over "morality" and, in particular, to those associated with lesbian/gay rights (Leonard 2002; McCloud 2003). This is as true for African-American Muslim voices as it is for others, with the prominent exception of Congressman Keith Ellison (see below). Another important exception that may indicate a shift in attitude involves MPAC's analysis of Proposition 8 (to eliminate the right of same-sex couples to marry) in the 2008 California election. While supporting the traditional Islamic definition of marriage as being between a man and a woman, MPAC writes this: "Rumors have circulated that Prop. 8 would mandate that same sex marriage would be taught in public schools and that the non-profit status of mosques who refuse to perform same-sex unions would be threatened. Regardless of how voters choose to vote, it is important to note that both of these rumors are false" (2008). While supporting the traditional position, MPAC did ask Muslims to vote out of religious convictions rather than out of unfounded fears.

The Emergence of Queer Muslim Voices
The morally conservative ideas that remain so dominant among Muslim Canadians and Muslim Americans are being challenged, now more vocally than ever. Queer Muslim networks and groups have formed in both countries and have received considerable media attention. The Lavender Crescent Society appeared briefly in 1977-78, formed by pre-revolutionary Iranian students in the San Francisco area. In Toronto, the queer Muslim group Salaam was first established in 1991-92, possibly the first such organization in North America. It quickly expanded its contacts across North America but, in the face of intense hostility from the Muslim community, lasted only a couple of years. In 1997, the website Queer Jihad was launched in the United States, alongside an e-mail discussion list established by young Muslim-American Faisal Alam. A year later, Alam spearheaded the formation of Al-Fatiha (The Opening) after a successful retreat in Boston (http://

www.al-fatiha.org). One year later, the first North American conference sponsored by the group was held, with sixty people attending. Also in 1999, a chapter was formed in Toronto, which then restored the name "Salaam" in 2001. In its early years, it had a membership of up to seventy-five, with roots in a variety of ethnicities and regions (Africa, the Middle East, and, especially, South Asia) and events that typically attracted around sixty people.[6] In 2003, it organized a conference in Toronto, alongside the US group Al-Fatiha, which attracted over 150 people. Most of the headline speakers were American, but the MCC's Tarek Fatah and openly gay MP Svend Robinson were among them. Concerns about safety and security were still prominent, even in such a remarkably successful gathering, with the location revealed only with great care to conference registrants (Salaam Toronto 2003).

One ambition of the 2003 conference was to stimulate the formation of queer Muslim groups in other Canadian cities. There are queer networks in two other cities with significant English-speaking Muslim populations – Ottawa and Montreal – but no sign of stable group formation. The now substantial Muslim community in Montreal is populated mostly by relatively recent immigrants from countries in North Africa and the Middle East who have a French-language history, are less likely to be well educated, and are even more likely than Muslim communities elsewhere in Canada to have conservative views on gender and sexuality issues. This would make the formation of a queer Muslim group even more challenging here than in other cities.

The American group Al-Fatiha was first based on Faisal Alam's experiences in leading an on-line discussion group. Alam, who led Al-Fatiha energetically for eight years, described its mission as empowering LGBT Muslims who were "seeking ways to integrate their faith and their sexual orientation or gender identity" (2008). One set of interviews with a cluster of activists in the group pointed to the challenges they faced in pressing for the reinterpretation of religious texts and beliefs so as to emphasize more tolerant aspects of Islam; managing cultural differences over family responsibility and marriage; and countering racial stereotypes in their everyday lives (Minwalla et al. 2005). They were also negotiating cultural differences regarding how same-sex desire was understood and regarding the formation of an identity publicly identified with sexuality.

Al-Fatiha's strongest base has been in Los Angeles, the site of an extraordinarily ambitious North American conference in 2004, though there are also groups in New York and Atlanta. There are other cities in which queer Muslims have access to LGBT South Asian groups (e.g., Boston; New York;

Philadelphia; Washington, DC; San Francisco; Los Angeles) or Arab groups (e.g., New York). Media coverage of the 2003 Toronto conference, and a presentation by Alam himself, indicated that there were nine to ten Al-Fatiha chapters in the United States (alongside three in Canada, two in the United Kingdom, and two in South Africa), though some of these are not firmly based groups (Giese 2003; Levitz 2003). The impressive growth of profile and membership was partly due to Alam's extraordinary energy as well as to the group's access to the resources required for his travels to other countries and to many cities in the United States. Moreover, when comparisons are made to Europe, it does not seem that queer Muslims in North America are any less visible or any more fragile in their institutional existence.[7]

At the time of the group's formation and early growth, Muslim-American academics and lawyers were challenging the traditional constructions of gender and sexuality and dominating the main Muslim-American groups. Most progressive academic work focuses on gender, and successful challenges to traditional attitudes towards women have often helped pave the way for claims based on sexual diversity. Amina Wadud (at Virginia Commonwealth University) first published *Quran and Woman* in 1992, now translated into six other languages. The 2003 publication of *Progressive Muslims*, edited by Omid Safi (at the University of North Carolina-Chapel Hill), was an important stimulus to debate. This book includes an article by Scott Kugle that offers a reinterpretation of the Quranic story of Lot – widely used to justify condemnation of homosexuality.

Muslim women activists have also acquired a more prominent voice within at least some of the mainstream organizations. They have challenged ISNA's leadership, for example, to develop more inclusive language and policies to encourage women's participation. They are also becoming more vocal in their engagement with Western feminism over such issues as head covering. They will often adopt views of equality that diverge from the dominant views in Western feminism, but controversies over such issues as veils have created significant openings for Muslim women to engage in political debate within Muslim communities. Even if most women activists are still reluctant to engage in questions of sexual difference, the discussion of gender equity (however embodied) will create space for queer claims.

One dramatic illustration of the newly created openings through which prominent Muslim Americans may ally themselves with such challenging views is Keith Ellison's July 2008 agreement to join the Bipartisan Congressional LGBT Equality Caucus as vice-chair and to do so uttering words like these: "I believe when my gay, lesbian, bisexual or transgender neighbor suffers from discrimination, then I suffer, and so does our whole community" (Ellison 2008). Ellison is the first Muslim to be elected to Congress (in 2006) as well as the first African American to be elected from Minnesota to the federal House of Representatives. He is respected by virtually all major Muslim organizations in the United States.

That said, queer Muslim groups in the United States continue to have a fragile existence, with members still confronting either conservative condemnation of homosexuality or silence within their families, among religious leaders, and in mainstream Muslim groups. Not long after the end of Faisal Alam's term as Al-Fatiha leader, there seemed to be a decline in the group's activity, which, after all, depended entirely on volunteers.[8] The post-9/11 climate in the United States has pushed other political issues to the fore among Muslim Americans and may well have reinforced a certain defensiveness about community values and religion.

Conclusion

The debate over queer inclusiveness has been slow to start among Muslim communities in Canada and the United States, and it has been challenging to sustain. However, there are encouraging signs in the openings created by feminists and the emergence of queer activist networks. Until now, it has been too easy to see Muslims in these two countries, as in other Western countries, as illustrating a "clash of civilizations." Without diminishing the challenge facing LGBT activists, we try to complicate that picture.

While gender equality features regularly and prominently in public discussions of Canadian and/or American values, we should remember that women in North America continue to suffer from inequalities (Howell 2005; Thobani 2007). It is all too easy to juxtapose a construct of the "West," in which gender equity has been secured, and a "Third World" other, often Islamic, in which women's agency and resistance are ignored or rendered invisible (Thobani 2007; Vakulenko 2007). As for the public recognition of sexual diversity, there is still considerable opposition to full recognition across North America and Europe, much of it marshalled in the name of religious belief. In most countries in which public policy and popular attitudes have shifted towards greater inclusiveness, most such change has occurred only in the past two decades. And, in some areas (e.g., parenting and schooling), the issues at stake remain hotly contested. The question of whether sexual diversity is actually an embedded part of the social and political landscape in the West remains an open one.

There are also complex unresolved questions in both Canada and the United States regarding how to incorporate the full recognition of sexual diversity and, at the same time, respect religious freedom. Some of the advocacy around sexual minority rights aims to enshrine a conception of religious rights that restricts them to the private realm – a framework antithetical to many Muslims (and adherents of other faiths). This remains a key question that is much wider in scope than is the question of how Muslims in North America react to issues of sexuality.

Muslims in North America usually value many of the "liberal" aspects of the country in which they have roots as well as those values they see around them in Canada and the United States. In those social and political areas (like sexuality) in which change has been most rapid, the messages can easily be mixed and the responses complex, especially among those who are negotiating their lives and identities between many political and cultural reference points.

We also suggest that there needs to be much more research on queer Muslims themselves. There is a limited body of published research on the emergence of such queer visibility. Minwalla et al. (2005) have reported on a small study of Muslim men in North America who were part of Al-Fatiha. Beyond North America, Yip's (2005, 2007, 2008a, 2008b, 2009) work remains the most significant research contribution, focusing on the challenges LGBT Muslims in the United Kingdom face within their ethnic communities and the identities that emerge from that social location. Siraj (2009) focuses on Muslim heterosexual response to homosexuality in Scotland, and Rahman's (2008) autobiographical work is drawn from both English and Scottish experience, while Abraham (2009) focuses on Australia. However, these studies are based on small groups of respondents and tend to look at the position of LGBT Muslims as individuals who are attempting to reconcile their religiously based and cultural identities with their queerness. There is no systematic work either on the emergence of social and political groups centred on sexual diversity or on the response of the surrounding Muslim communities and the groups representing them.

Yvonne Haddad (2004) concludes her assessment of Arab and Muslim identity in the United States by highlighting intergenerational change. Younger activists are more likely to cooperate with non-Muslim groups to work towards equity and justice, and they take American values seriously. They wish to retain their religion, or, at the very least, the right of co-religionists to practise their faith without discrimination, but not necessarily the cultural norms that their parents defended. Much of what she says could be said of Canadian Muslims. In both settings, we join in not being able to predict with any certainty how this new generation will adapt to the heightened fears of prejudice associated with the post-9/11 world. Equally uncertain is the path they will take on issues related to sexual diversity – how they will decide between the conservative values still reflected in the religious leaders with whom they worship and the much more progressive views of their non-Muslim friends and work associates.

POLITICAL PARTIES

Religious communities have a long history of deploying their organizational resources to influence policy and opinion, and these resources can be attractive to political parties. Parties are regularly on the lookout for new constituencies as well as being interested in cementing support among established constituencies. The American and Canadian party systems are similar in some respects. The national systems have been historically dominated by two parties; they stand astride significant regional identities and partisan variations across state and provincial borders; and they have experienced major faith-based realignments within the past thirty years.

But the differences between the two party systems are far more important than are the similarities, and they help explain the different patterns of religious mobilization in each country. The United States has had the same two political parties since the 1860s, though with major shifts in outlook. They are institutionally weak and lack an authoritative central leadership, relying on state parties and interest groups to mobilize political support. Canadian parties are built on less enduring coalitions, with more forceful regionalist demands and less powerful faith community pressure. They also have stronger central leadership, with more control over the party organization and, when in power, more leverage over the policy agenda.

In Chapter 16, David Rayside's account of the relationship between Canada's Conservative Party and its Christian right constituency spotlights the contrasts between it and the Republican Party across the border, even in a period when the Conservative leadership has so obviously followed some Republican Party leads. As Canadian opinion has rapidly trended towards more support for sexual minorities, Conservative leaders have engaged in a delicate dance with religious conservatives – sending out signals that they share broad sympathies but are unwilling to use these issues in political campaigns. The contradictory pressures on party strategists are amplified by the fact that recent Conservative governments have not won a legislative majority. Even if they do win most seats in Parliament, it is not clear that they would be interested in foregrounding issues related to sexual diversity.

In Chapter 17, John Green describes differences in the attitudes of delegates to the 2004 Republican and Democratic party conventions. He shows that the interest group configuration of the porous

American parties allows the Republican Party to take a more unified position on the key LGBT issue of our time – same-sex marriage – than the Democratic Party. This is because Christian right groups and their allies constitute such a sizable portion of Republican Party activists. Yet the party has been less united over other LGBT issues, and there are signs that its strategists have been reluctant to be on the "wrong" side of a rapidly changing set of issues. Meanwhile, Democratic elites have strongly endorsed a variety of egalitarian policies but are reluctant to embrace marriage equality, in part because their coalition is more heterogeneous than is that of the Republicans, and their constituencies include many voters who are uneasy about or opposed to gay/lesbian marriage rights.

Although these chapters highlight party system differences, there are some similarities in the way in which parties on the right have taken up sexual diversity issues. In 2008, the Republican Party in the United States engaged in a delicate "dance" over LGBT rights that had some resemblance to that engaged in by the Canadian Conservative leadership and that was exemplified in the vice-presidential debate by Sarah Palin's defence of Alaska's protections for same-sex couples and her claims of personal friendships with lesbians. The steady shift of public attitudes towards more acceptance (even regarding marriage) will increase the difficulties they will face in grappling with the issue.

And yet both parties have to retain the votes and, just as important, the energies of religious conservatives. There is also no doubt that the Republicans have been more willing to play on public anxieties about or opposition to a full recognition of LGBT rights than have the Conservatives.

16

The Conservative Party of Canada and Its Religious Constituencies

DAVID RAYSIDE

The high profile acquired by debates over the public recognition of sexual diversity in Canada, up to the mid-2000s, exposed tension between and within parties on the right that will not easily disappear. The present-day Conservative Party of Canada emerged from a combination of two parties: a populist party with important similarities to many new-right formations in Europe, and a mainstream Progressive Conservative party with a long history of "brokerage" politics (Nevitte et al. 1998). The Conservatives garnered enough votes to win office in 2006, and, while that provided the party leadership with powerful disciplinary tools, it did not eliminate the longer-term challenges in managing the ambitions of the many activists who have retained strong views on such issues as gay rights.

Some internal tension derives from inherent contradictions between policy claims by moral traditionalists and those prioritized by neoliberals. Calls for a reduction in the scale and scope of state authority in the name of enhanced individual liberty do not, after all, easily travel alongside calls for state intervention to enforce a moral authority over individual choice. Traditionally, conservative advocates of strict enforcement of moral codes would retain their consistency if they were also wary of excessive individualism, but that is not the kind of message we get from the US Republicans since Ronald Reagan or from Conservative Party leadership since the 1990s re-alignment of the Canadian party system.

In the American case, the incentive to combine these two rightist currents is enhanced by the sheer size of the religious right and the organizational resources of evangelical Protestants (in particular). It is also facilitated
by the distinctive individualism of American Protestant faith, which creates
a large constituency of believers in both traditional moral regulation and
neoliberal deregulation.

However, as Chris Cochrane (2008) and Neil Nevitte (2006) argue, using
data from Canada and Europe, popular adherence to policy positions we
associate with economic neoliberalism does not correlate either to moral
conservatism or to what are generally construed as right-wing policies on
immigration. This builds on other writing that points to the diversity of constituencies supporting new and sometimes radically xenophobic European
parties on the right and to the overall fragmentation of the political right in
Europe (Kitschelt and McGann 1995; Schain, Zolberg, and Hossay 2002).
What makes the Canadian case interesting is that we see a Conservative
Party attempting a Republican-style coalition but without the conditions
that allow it to easily flourish. Yet we also see within that coalition a religious
right constituency better organized and self-conscious than ever, having
demonstrated in the recent past its willingness to exit an established party
after perceiving that its voice was insufficiently heard.

This is not an unfamiliar challenge for those parties that have been largely or partially founded on social movement activism and that move towards
mainstream institutionalization – an evolution explored by such writers as
Robert Michels (1966), Maurice Duverger (1969), and Angelo Panebianco
(1988). In fact, almost any party will combine supporters who are primarily
office-seekers and those who are true believers. For the Canadian Conservative Party, the shift that many of its most committed supporters have witnessed – from a party primarily driven by believers to one with strong signs
of preoccupation with office-seeking – has been a rapid one. So the potential for exit-inducing discontent is substantial among those for whom such
change has been too sudden.

Canadian Party Realignment
Canada's party system at the federal level has undergone radical change
since the 1980s (Carty, Cross, and Young 2000; Leduc 2007). For much of
Canada's post-Confederation history, two dominant parties "brokered"
regional and other interests. The Liberals and Progressive Conservatives
were centrist, each of them centre-right on some policy fronts and centre-
left on others. At various times, other "third" parties have successfully

contested parliamentary seats, the New Democratic Party taking up this position on the left for most of the post-Second World War period.

There were strains inside the Progressive Conservatives' coalition of regional forces in the 1980s, and they spawned two new parties late in that decade. One was the Bloc Québécois, a federal counterpart to the sovereigntist Parti Québécois; the other was the western-based Reform Party, founded by Preston Manning, the evangelical son of a former premier of Alberta. Reform sought major cuts in taxes, a much reduced federal government, and an end to what it saw as special treatment for Quebec, for ethnic minorities, and for Aboriginals. A significant part of its base also opposed abortion and favoured "traditional" family values.

The Reform Party scored a breakthrough in 1993, contributing to the decimation of Progressive Conservative parliamentary ranks in the west. This, combined with the staggering Progressive Conservative losses in Quebec, propelled the Liberal Party into government. Reform improved on its record slightly in 1997, taking sixty seats, though still confined entirely to the west.

During this period of Liberal government, lesbian and gay rights issues were recurrently debated in Parliament, creating opportunities for morally conservative Reformers to stake out unequivocally anti-gay positions. Preston Manning was disturbed at the intemperate remarks from some members of his caucus when gay rights issues were up for debate. Faron Ellis (2005, chap. 6) points appropriately to a pragmatic side of Preston Manning's leadership during this period, saying that he sought "to position the party within what he perceived to be the contemporary currents of public opinion." But there were limits to this pragmatism, and, in any event, Manning had to motivate an ideologically driven activist base, particularly on moral issues.

A divided right was destined for the legislative margins, and the first attempt at unity, in 2000, was to create the Canadian Alliance in place of Reform, ostensibly as a broader tent. But the most conservative of the veteran Reform activists spearheaded the successful leadership campaign of Stockwell Day – a former Alberta treasurer and Pentecostal preacher with unequivocal views on such issues as abortion and gay rights. The new party then won only 25 percent of the national vote in the 2000 election and remained based overwhelmingly in western Canada. The governing Liberals were more than ready to use the abortion issue to target the new leader as outside the political mainstream (Greenspon 2001; Marzolini 2001).

Flagging popular support helped fuel a revolt against Day, and Stephen Harper replaced him as leader in 2002 (Flanagan 2007, chap. 1). While not as close to evangelicals as either Manning or Day, Harper soon attracted the support of many moral conservatives who believed him more able to expand the party's base. He then spearheaded a second attempt at uniting the right in 2003. In March 2004, he was elected leader of the new Conservative Party, which brought together supporters of the Canadian Alliance and the Progressive Conservative Party.

At the outset, the Conservative leadership was dominated by Reform/Alliance supporters, but Harper knew that too much emphasis on the moral conservatism that was so strongly associated with them would doom attempts to gain votes and to secure office. Tight discipline was imposed on the party's legislators and prospective candidates to ensure that the voices of the moral right were subdued. However, the issue of same-sex marriage was in the public limelight precisely at the time of the new party's birth and during its first two elections.

Conservative Missteps While Marriage Rights Were Being Won

Through the 1990s, most of the rights and obligations associated with marriage were extended to de facto same-sex couples (Rayside 2008; Appendix A, this volume). By the early 2000s, all but a few of the legal consequences of marriage applied to lesbian and gay couples, including most of those associated with parenting.

In June 2003, an appeal court in Ontario ruled that the exclusion of same-sex couples from civil marriage contravened section 15 of Canada's Charter of Rights and Freedoms (not the first court in Canada to do so) and then surprised most observers by declaring that its judgment was to take immediate effect.[1] Knowing it would lose, the federal government chose not to appeal the ruling to the Supreme Court of Canada, and courts in other provinces quickly opened up civil marriage to same-sex couples.

Liberal prime minister Martin announced a federal election for the end of June 2004, and there seemed little doubt that same-sex marriage would be prominent in the campaign. By this time, Liberals were being hurt in the polls by a scandal over misspending in Quebec during the leadership of former prime minister Jean Chrétien. This gave the Conservatives a powerful weapon for attacking the government and for avoiding issues that would alienate precisely the centrist voters whom the party most needed to win over.

The Conservatives' national campaign was closely scripted to avoid fuelling fears of a "hidden agenda" of moral conservatism, with telling silence on issues like abortion, multiculturalism, and capital punishment. Even on the inescapable issue of same-sex marriage, the campaign focused less on substance than on the need for Parliament, rather than unelected judges, to make decisions (Flanagan 2007, 156). But the Liberals knew that public opinion was slowly shifting towards majority support for same-sex marriage and that a policy of upholding the Charter of Rights would play well in the media and in public opinion. A tactic of highlighting the Conservative opposition to a Charter-based equity right would also amplify fears of a hidden agenda.

In the end, Stephen Harper did express his opposition to same-sex marriage in the campaign, and some of his party's candidates took advantage of the opening to express what were easily characterized as extreme positions. The prominence of the issue was enhanced by religious right groups mobilizing over marriage.

Even with the spending scandal so continuously in the air, the Liberals won the election. Their seat count slipped below a clear majority in Parliament, but the fact that they remained in government was widely attributed to public fears of the Conservatives' moral agenda. Even if analyses of national election study data indicated that the marriage issue had not been prominent, there were party strategists who agreed that campaigning on it had hurt the Conservatives (Gidengil et al. 2006; Segal 2007).

The Conservatives held their first national policy convention in early 2005, and the Harper team made sure that the public face of the party sidestepped as many moral hot buttons as possible (Flanagan 2007, 203-05). However, a resolution on gay and lesbian marriage was allowed, in part because of its immediacy and also because public opinion seemed more evenly divided on the issue than others that had preoccupied Reform/Alliance veterans. Also, Harper himself had been using the marriage issue since the turn of the year in order to draw support from "ethnic" communities that traditionally voted Liberal – especially Chinese, South Asian, and Italian (Flanagan 2007, 200-01; Leblanc 2007; Laghi et al. 2005).

In June 2005, the precarious Liberal minority government secured passage of legislation that explicitly did what the courts had already effected: it eliminated the heterosexual restrictiveness of marriage. Soon after, that fall, the government was defeated in a parliamentary vote, precipitating a January 2006 election. Once again, the religious right re-energized its supporters for what it thought would be a rematch on the marriage question.

The Harper team was more determined than ever to downplay moral conservatism, but it judged the marriage question to be unavoidable. So very early in the campaign Stephen Harper promised to allow a free (unwhipped) vote on a resolution to reopen the marriage question. He did not raise the question again, and the party's website was silent on it (Flanagan 2007, 232). In a campaign that was as tightly disciplined as any within recent memory, candidates with particularly strong conservative views on issues like abortion and homosexuality were kept away from the media.

At the same time, the party could not ignore its morally traditional base. Conservative campaigners were undoubtedly promoting the party's moral agenda within evangelical religious congregations and encouraging sympathetic clergy to deliver positive messages to their flocks. And the party, after all, did have a number of candidates known to have close ties to pro-life and family values groups, and such links were highlighted by both religious right groups and Liberal campaigners (Flanagan 2007, 264).

The election gave the Conservatives fewer parliamentary seats than expected, but they still received more than any other party, therefore giving them a chance to form the government. Prime Minister Harper then faced a dilemma over what to do with the marriage issue, which may well have cost his party votes and had certainly not won him many. At first, Harper indicated that a vote on the marriage resolution would occur early in the mandate. But then he procrastinated, perhaps recognizing a rise in popular support for same-sex marriage and an even greater public antipathy to revisiting the issue.[2]

Delaying as much as possible, the government scheduled a truncated parliamentary debate shortly before the 2006 Christmas recess and heavily scripted caucus members' speeches in order to avoid inflammatory remarks. The party leadership knew that its resolution would lose and worked behind the scenes with other parties to ensure as short and uneventful a debate as possible. The House of Commons, as expected, then voted down the motion on 7 December 2006, with a convincing 175-123 majority. Among the "no's" were thirteen Conservatives, including six cabinet ministers. When meeting reporters afterwards, Harper announced, "I don't see reopening this question in the future" (Galloway 2006). And then, just to make sure that no one missed the message, he repeated himself in French! During the election of fall 2008, the Conservatives ensured that nothing was said about moral issues from their camp, except to deny that any measures would be taken to roll back access to abortion.

Two quite distinct propositions emerge out of this story. One is that the Harper team remains determined to secure radical change on both moral conservative and neoliberal fronts and that this will become much more evident if the party wins a parliamentary majority (a view forcibly articulated by Marci McDonald [2010] and Tom Warner [2010] and implied by some of Tom Flanagan's [2007] writing). The other is that Harper has successfully steered his party towards the familiar brokerage model of Canadian parties and that, even with a majority in Parliament, the party leadership would take particular care to avoid associating the party with religious conservatism (Segal 2007).

Moderating Pressures

There are strong points to be made for the brokerage argument on moral issues. First, the party's leadership is driven by other priorities and engages moral conservatism only insofar as doing so is useful in winning votes. Another is that popular beliefs in Canada increasingly limit the appeal of the kind of policies that moral conservatives seek. A related argument is that court interpretations of the Charter have permanently hemmed the party in on the major issues associated with homosexuality, and to some extent abortion, and the Charter's popularity makes it difficult for any government to confront so-called judicial activism frontally. And, finally, the religious right is too small and fragmented a political force to provide enough rewards to balance the risks of a close association with its aims.

Stephen Harper's Preoccupations

We do not have to adhere to the neo-Machiavellianism of Robert Michels and, more recently, of Angelo Panebianco to observe that most political parties in liberal democratic systems have become leader-centred and that understanding the policy priorities of a party must begin with deciphering the priorities of its leader. That is truer in Canada, and has been so for a longer period, than in most systems. Steve Patten and Reg Whitaker both argue that Canadian parties have long been virtually "hollow shells" providing policy vehicles for party leaders and their inner circles (Patten 2007; Whitaker 1977). Party leadership in Canada also comes with very powerful leverage over the party's legislators and, when holding the reins of government, with especially strong mechanisms to discipline dissenters.

The control exercised by Stephen Harper over Conservative MPs and cabinet ministers is as tight as is that exercised by any federal party leader within living memory. Harper keeps his own counsel on many issues and structures his office to minimize the likelihood that his key advisers will develop a collective view independently of him.[3] The leader's own policy preoccupations, then, count for a great deal in any calculation of future policy directions.

Assessments of those preoccupations by current or past insiders reflect widely divergent interpretations (Flanagan 2007; Segal 2007). Most of them agree that Harper is the most partisan leader in recent Canadian history, determined to destroy the Liberal Party.[4] Others, like Segal and Flanagan, suggest that he will mould the party's policies and strategies around the single-minded goal of winning votes. On the other hand, all observers point to a strong commitment to smaller government and lower taxes – in other words, to neoliberalism (Laycock 2002).

How does religious belief and moral traditionalism fit in? Hugh Segal's (2007, 141-44) view is that Harper does have strong religious views, and that they tend towards morally conservative positions, but that he separates those views from his party's or his government's policy priorities. Another view, articulated by highly perceptive journalist Chantal Hébert, downplays Harper's moral beliefs even further, arguing that, with his selection as Canadian Alliance leader, the party's membership had "signalled its willingness to ditch the party's social conservative credo" (quoted without comment in Flanagan 2007, 62). One anonymous insider has argued that Harper's references to conservative stances on moral issues are entirely strategic and designed only to secure the loyalty of religious traditionalists (interview, July 2008).

There were strong indications from Harper's earliest days as leader of the Conservatives that he was prepared to take a strategic distance from moral traditionalism, and, as we have seen, he was certainly told after the 2004 election that overplaying same-sex marriage cost him votes.[5] For the 2006 election, Harper chose as heads of the campaign team Hugh Segal and Marjorie LeBreton – both from the Progressive Conservative side of the party and averse to prioritizing moral issues (Segal 2007). In fact, LeBreton belonged to "Tories for Choice" when abortion was up for debate during the Brian Mulroney prime ministership of the 1980s.[6]

Jim Farney also points out that the denomination of the church he attends in Ottawa is moderate by comparison to those attended by most evangelicals.[7] The Christian and Missionary Alliance was formed to bring a variety of evangelical communities together, so it is not as doctrinaire as are churches in other conservative currents. According to one close observer of Christian intervention in politics, Harper also came to his evangelical faith in his twenties, after many of his core political principles were formed.[8] His wife does not share his particular faith and may well have been alienated from some versions of Protestant conservatism.

FIGURE 16.1

Cross-national comparison of attitudes towards homosexuality (percent viewing it as "never justified"), 1981-2000

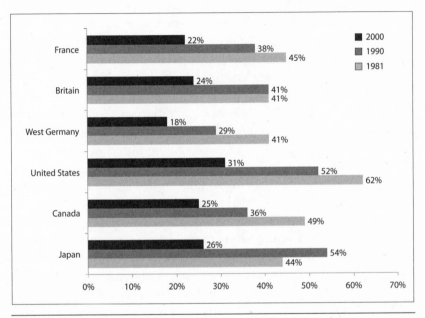

Source: World Values Surveys (various years). Data provided by Chris Cochrane.

Public Attitudes and the Charter

Canadian public opinion on the crucial issue of lesbian and gay marriage shifted significantly towards majority acceptance over the period when it was in the limelight. During the height of debate between 2003 and 2005, there was some slippage, but polls since then have shown 55 percent support for same-sex marriage or more, about 20 percent higher than in the United States.[9] By 2006, over 60 percent of Canadians did not want to revive the same-sex marriage issue. Even among Conservative supporters, close to 50 percent were now approving of gay marriage.[10] As Cochrane points out, there is no issue where the shift towards more "liberal" views on moral questions was more pronounced than on issues related to homosexuality (see Figure 16.1).[11] On the World Values Survey question about the "acceptability" of homosexuality, with 10 indicating "never justified" and 1 "always justified," the average Canadian score dropped from a very hostile 7.9 in 1982 to a middling 5.6 in 2000 and to 5.3 in 2006. Reform-Alliance supporters moved from 7.8 in 1990 to 6.2 in 2000. Conservatives averaged 6.2 in 2006 – significantly more negative than the Liberals (at 5.3, the Canadian average), the NDP (4.5), and the Bloc (4.1) – but a good deal less hostile than either Reform or PC supporters a decade earlier.

Public support for equity has been strengthened by the inclusion of sexual orientation within the ambit of the Charter of Rights and Freedoms, in turn a widely respected institution (Fletcher and Howe 2000). One 2007 Strategic Counsel poll showed that 53 percent of Canadians thought the Charter had a positive impact on Canada, and only 12 percent thought it had a negative impact (Makin 2007). The fact that court rulings have had a prominent role in securing rights for lesbians and gays has provided many centrist politicians and their supporters with the "cover" of acquiescing to the Charter's equality provisions. Such rulings have also placed the onus on opponents to reverse the course of events – in other words, to take Charter rights away.

Canadian religious conservatives themselves may well be more willing than their American counterparts to move on from their opposition to the public recognition of sexual diversity. Sam Reimer (2003, 118-51) has shown the commonalities in patterns of religious faith among evangelicals across the border. However, he also points out that, even if Canadian believers still treat moral issues as politically important, their concerns are less tied than are those of Americans to apocalyptic visions of societal disintegration. He has also pointed out, using large national samples, less personal animosity towards sexual minorities among Canadians than among Americans (Reimer, this volume).

Religious Right Weakness

As Table 16.1 indicates, the proportion of the population that could be counted as religiously conservative, or what some writers refer to as "evangelical," is between one-third and one-half of what it is in the United States. Even among Conservative Party supporters, only 31 percent of respondents to the 2006 World Values Survey said that they attended church once a week or more, only slightly more than the 28 percent of church-attending Liberal supporters and 25 percent of Canadians overall (Cochrane 2009).

Canada's religious conservatives are also more fragmented than are their American counterparts, in ways that weaken their political voice in all but exceptional times. The higher proportion of Catholics in Canada than in the United States might be construed as bolstering moral traditionalism. After all, the Roman Catholic Church hierarchy in Canada was as active in

TABLE 16.1

Religiosity in Canada and the US, 2002-05

	US (%)	Canada (%)
Weekly church attendance or more*	42	22
Religion is very important in my life†	55	28
Bible is actual word of God, to be taken literally‡	34	17

Sources: * Reported in Adams (2004, 50).
        † Gallup, 2004 survey, http://www.gallup.org/.
        ‡ Canadian Election Study (2000); American National Election Study (2000).

opposing same-sex marriage as it had been on any political issue in recent times, issuing public declarations and requiring priests to read letters to parishioners urging them to contact politicians.[12] But the influence of the hierarchy on Catholics seems modest at most, polls regularly showing them to be no more conservative than other Canadians on issues related to homosexuality (Bowen 2004). Sam Reimer (2003) has shown that only a small minority of evangelicals in Canada (as in the United States) feel close to Roman Catholics (see also Appleby 1997). Jonathan Malloy (this volume) argues that the unspoken alliance between Catholic and evangelical Protestant leaders on the issue of marriage may have represented a high-water mark of religious right influence on Canadian politics and will not likely translate into a sustained link.

This fragmentation, and the relatively small size of the religious right's electoral constituency, mean that the Conservative Party has to be careful about forming too close an association with representatives of either evangelical Protestantism or the Catholic hierarchy. The political interventions of the former are regularly viewed by the Canadian media as extreme and as reflecting an Americanizing influence on political life. Being seen to pay close attention to the Catholic hierarchy may well win few friends among Protestant believers and would certainly win few votes in highly secularized Quebec.

Polarizing Pressures

And yet there remains a strong current of conservative moral values in the leadership of the Conservative Party, among voters, activists, and political leaders. The legislators who now represent the party and whose parliamentary careers go back to the Reform and Alliance periods, with few exceptions, opposed every bill introduced to Parliament implying public recognition of sexual diversity. Many of the party's activists come with extremely strong views that are antithetical to the recognition of sexual diversity. To what extent do such moral conservatives have the strategic standing and determination to counter the moderating forces pushing such concerns to the margins of the policy agenda?

Strength of Moral Conservatism in the Parliamentary Party
Whatever disciplining clamps were placed on Conservative politicians after the merger, there was never any doubt about where most of its members stood. When faced with a vote on redefining marriage, in June 2005, only a paltry three of the party's MPs supported the Liberal government's bill. And this was after an election that dramatically increased the party's parliamentary contingent beyond the Reform/Alliance western base. The even further enlarged Conservative caucus that arrived in Ottawa after the 2006 election retained an unusually traditional outlook. Marci McDonald (2006) estimates that 70 of the Conservatives' 124 MPs were evangelical Christians. Beyond them are others who are intimidated by the number or prominence of religious conservatives in their constituencies and who are inclined to support policy concessions to retain their loyalty.

When Harper formed his first government, two of the most prominent representatives of religious conservatism in that caucus were appointed to cabinet. Vic Toews was named to the crucial justice portfolio, and, even if he is a "lapsed" evangelical, he has been one of the party's extreme voices in opposing gay rights. Stockwell Day was appointed to the public safety portfolio. Jason Kenney, a conservative pro-life Catholic with a record of fiercely anti-gay rhetoric, was made parliamentary secretary to the prime minister and designated a contact point with religious right groups (McDonald 2006; 2010, 39). In the cabinet installed after the 2006 election, there were about six evangelical Protestant members (including the prime minister), plus four morally conservative Catholics, making for a total of about one-third of the cabinet.[13] There have been key advisers in the Prime Minister's Office who are Christian conservatives. Guy Giorno, the prime minister's chief of staff from mid-2008 to September 2010, is very strongly committed to a pro-life position on abortion.[14] Darrel Reid, formerly with Focus on the Family Canada, was appointed to the Prime Minister's Office and then for a time served as deputy chief of staff (McDonald 2010, 92).

Stephen Harper himself never once dissented from the Reform and Alliance rejection of lesbian/gay rights measures, and there cannot be serious doubt that he would like to defend traditional heterosexual family forms against what he would see as corrosive influences. In a 2003 speech to a conservative audience, Harper railed against "moral relativism" and urged attending to "family" issues, including the age of sexual consent and other measures designed to strengthen the institution of marriage (McDonald 2006; 2010, 34-35).

Priority Attached to Moral Issues by a Major Conservative Party Constituency

The Conservative leadership knows that religious conservatives are an important electoral constituency, that they fuel much electoral activism, and that they provide an important component of the party's fundraising success.[15] In 2006, one post-election poll showed that 64 percent of weekly church-attending Protestants voted Conservative, 24 percent more than two years earlier.[16] And even if moral issues did not feature prominently among the priorities of most voters, 40 percent of these churchgoers reported that issues like abortion and same-sex marriage mattered most in deciding which party to support. In 2006 and 2008, the party was also successful, for the first time, in securing the votes of more devout Catholics than the Liberals, their long-standing electoral preference (McDonald 2010, 19, 45). Environics data reported by Amy Langstaff (this volume) show that a strikingly high 56 percent of Conservative respondents "disapproved" of homosexuality in 2004, compared to 36 percent of Liberals and 18 percent of New Democrats.

The more "believers" there are among such respondents, as distinct from "office-seeking" pragmatists, the more important it is for the party's leadership to keep them motivated. Western supporters of the former Progressive Conservative Party, including many religious conservatives, demonstrated their willingness to abandon their traditional party home in favour of Reform in the late 1980s, as had their counterparts in BC provincial politics (McKenzie 2005). When the Canadian Alliance was formed, they elected Stockwell Day as their standard bearer, ignoring warnings that this would prevent electoral growth (Carty, Cross, and Young 2000, chap. 3).

There is no question that the Conservatives pay very close attention to the role that "values" play in voter minds. After the 2004 election, the party commissioned a huge poll (sample of about ten thousand) to explore popular beliefs, and they have updated it since.[17] They recognize the critical role of moral conservatives among the electorates they need to court or retain, and they have armoured themselves with nuanced information in order to do so strategically.

Religious Right Strength

Even if Canada's religious right is a far weaker force than its American counterpart, the battles over lesbian/gay rights over the past twenty years energized the political voices of conservative Christianity – and in a period when they have been able to benefit from intense mobilizing by the American religious right on the marriage issue. In 2003, only the Evangelical Fellowship of Canada had a staffed office in Ottawa. By 2006, so did the Institute of Marriage and Family Canada (formed by the Canadian branch of the US-based Focus on the Family), the Canada Family Action Coalition, and the Institute for Canadian Values (Dreher 2006).[18] The EFC and FOTF-Canada had at least twenty staff each, creating the capacity for more professionalized lobbying. There are now seven evangelical groups with permanent offices in Ottawa, and graduates of Canada's fifteen evangelical Christian universities are now more visible on Parliament Hill than at any time in the past. Though newer on the political scene, the youth-oriented evangelical group 4MyCanada has shown its capacity to mobilize large numbers and to marshal that enthusiasm to communicate messages to politicians.[19]

These organizations have grown significantly not only in the resources they can marshal for applying political pressure but also in the sophistication of their approach. In a parliamentary system, they recognize the huge significance of having a government in power that is open to their concerns. In its absence, after all, they would have no useful access and almost no capacity for exercising political influence. Most Christian right groups, then, acknowledge that the Conservative leadership will not help them on all issues that matter, but they are prepared to give the party some slack, recognizing the complexity of pressures on the prime minister and the constraints operating on a minority government. They still expect significant policy payoffs but are prepared to bide their time.[20]

Despite concerns about too close an association with the religious right, the Conservative leadership has strong links to it (McDonald 2006). Dave Quist, the executive director of the Institute of Marriage and Family Canada, ran for the Conservatives in 2004 and was a Harper aide after that. Charles McVety, head of a Christian college and two Christian right lobby groups – Canada Family Action Coalition and Defend Marriage Coalition – was close enough to the Harper government that he was called upon to help sell the new child care plan. Other key players in the Prime Minister's Office, like Giorno and Reid, had easy access to pro-life and family values groups, both Catholic and Protestant, while they served in Ottawa.[21]

Evidence from the Conservatives in Office

The Stephen Harper government has clearly sidelined any talk of major policy initiatives in the areas of abortion and homosexuality – the centre-pieces of the religious right agenda until now. However, it has taken steps in these areas that signal its commitment to "traditional values," particularly since the 2008 election. These steps are presumably calculated to convince its morally conservative supporters that it has done what it can.

Child care legislation presented and passed during its first year in office was one area in which it chose a policy direction with strong support among religious conservatives. The Harper government opted for a monthly allowance paid directly to parents with children and steered sharply away from supporting accessible child care facilities. In international affairs, it tilted Middle East foreign policy more assertively towards the Israeli side. In terms of law and order, it staked out a tough stance – one heavily favoured by moral conservatives. It also modified the advisory process through which federally appointed judges would be selected, enhancing the influence of the government and of police representatives. In late 2006, the government also made clear that it would seek out judges who were not only tough on crime but who also held relatively restrictive interpretations of the Charter.

Several other policy moves were more explicitly tied to sexual diversity. Justice Minister Vic Toews lost little time in announcing that the age of consent for sexual activity would be raised from fourteen to sixteen.[22] The relatively low age of consent had become a contentious issue, particularly among religious conservatives, when the threshold for heterosexual and homosexual sex was harmonized in the 1980s, so this represented a not-so-subtle response to concerns about youthful exposure to homosexuality.[23]

Another signal was sent by the prime minister's refusal to appear at the major international AIDS conference held in Toronto during August 2006. Despite almost universal condemnation in the mainstream media, that decision is still thought to have been a legitimate and effective one by Conservative insiders.[24] Yet another signal was sent in late 2007, when new regulations were issued on organ donation that increased the impediments for gay men. On the face of it this was a technical change, and it may even have been viewed as a mistake by some Conservatives after it was attacked by senior public health spokespeople. But it was likely approved by Conservative policy makers who were fully prepared to reinforce the health stigma, which, among conservative evangelical Christians, is so widely associated with homosexuality.

Soon after that, the government included a provision in a tax bill (C-10) that allowed for the denial of tax credits for films deemed incompatible with public policy. If it were not already obvious that this was designed to appeal to moral traditionalists, it became so when evangelist Charles McVety (probably exaggerating) eagerly took credit for having lobbied Stockwell Day and the Prime Minister's Office on the measure. Among the reasons he cited for supporting such censorship was that tax credits had been given to films promoting homosexuality and graphic sex (Curry and MacDonald 2008). In the summer of 2008, the government cut budgets for programs where it was deemed that "inappropriate" funding decisions had been made (Posner 2008).

Bill C-10 soon became a liability for the government, provoking widespread protest from the mainstream media and from many prominent Canadians who worked in the film industry in Canada's three biggest cities (including Montreal). Before long, the Prime Minister's Office realized that the film tax credit measures were a "huge mistake."[25] On the other hand, the government knew that dropping the measure would alienate an important constituency that had now attached itself to the proposal. The indecision during 2008 on how to handle the matter was strong evidence of the importance the party leadership attaches to just that constituency.

Bill C-484 was another indicator of the same dilemma. This was a private member's bill, introduced in November 2007 by Conservative Edmonton MP Ken Epp. It sought to add extra criminal sanctions in the event of the death of a foetus during an assault on or murder of the mother (Arthur 2008). This would have been the first legislative measure to recognize the full human status of the foetus, and it was thereby treated as highly significant by evangelical Protestants and pro-life Catholics. The government was probably hoping that the bill would either be defeated or not come to a final vote, but its (uneven) commitment to allowing its MPs to introduce policy initiatives through private members' bills reduced the room for manoeuvre.[26]

The government called an election for October 2008, with polls showing a strong likelihood of a renewed government mandate for the Conservatives. Both of these bills were recognized as endangering that outcome. Harper went further than ever in promising not only that his government would not introduce legislation on abortion but also that government ministers would be obliged to vote against any private member's bill on the subject (an obvious, though implicit, reference to Bill C-484). When anger at cuts to the arts was mobilized during the October 2008 campaign, especially in Quebec, Harper felt impelled to promise that the tax credit measure contained in Bill C-10 would be rescinded.

Since that election, perhaps even more since the government's survival of an attempt by opposition parties to form a coalition in late 2008, the party's leadership appears to have become bolder in its pursuit of socially conservative policies.

According to McDonald (2010, 45-46), the party's religiously conservative MPs were given more room than before to express their views publicly. The prime minister himself accepted an invitation to convey Easter greetings on the evangelical television show *Listen Up!* – something he had refused to do during the campaign (McDonald 2010, 47).

In July 2009, morally conservative MPs expressed substantial anger at a $400,000 grant given to Toronto's Pride organization under the rubric of the federal government's economic stimulus program aimed at premier tourist events. So intense was the pressure that the responsibility for the program was transferred out of the Ministry of Tourism, leading one colleague to charge that veteran Conservative Diane Ablonczy had been "hung out to dry" (Chase 2009). In 2010, to the surprise of no one, Pride Toronto's application for funds was turned down. Also in 2010 the government was reported to be ready to preclude funding for contraceptives and abortion in a foreign aid initiative focusing on maternal health (Ibbitson 2010a, 2010b; Galloway 2010; and for background see McDonald 2010, 257). As host of the G8 and G20 summits, the government was marshalling international support for the plan with the funding exclusions. This sparked a media flurry, and there were clear indications of opposition from other G8 partners. Uncertainty remained for some weeks over whether the government would try to impose abortion-related exclusions in the proposal. In the end, the prime minister succeeded in convincing other leaders that each country would set the terms for its own contribution to the initiative, and it was clear that the Canadian contributions would include at least some reproduction-related conditions, including abortion.[27]

Also in 2010, Stockwell Day, now president of the Treasury Board, indicated that the government would review the federal government's employment equity law, targeted at historically disadvantaged segments of the population. This was in the midst of an even more controversial move to change the Canadian census in response to what the government claimed were popular complaints about intrusiveness. The latter was driven more by anti-state libertarianism than social conservatism, but it demonstrated an apparent drive to play to the government's core supporters (Ibbitson 2010c, 2010d; Valpy 2010).

In some sense, the extent of the government's pitch to social conservatives in recent years is a surprise and does not accord with a brokerage portrayal of the new Conservative Party. Indeed, the single-minded aggressiveness on the controversial initiatives it has taken in the 2009-10 period does not conform to the image of tightrope walker that might have otherwise applied to Harper's balancing of competing interests within his own party.

A partial explanation for this apparent puzzle is provided by Tom Flanagan, who frames the Conservative Party's strategy not in brokerage terms but as "coalition building." The party solidifies its various core constituencies and then aims to get particular categories of "soft" voters to swing to the party so as to enlarge the electoral coalition.[28] He acknowledges that the party tried a targeted appeal on same-sex marriage to attract a variety of religious constituencies but that this was "not particularly successful." It was still important to show respect for evangelical supporters of the Conservative Party but also to "find things that they would like that others would also like."

Until 2008, the government focused on avoiding high-profile issues explicitly tied to sexual diversity or reproduction, choosing issues that it calculated had low profile or broad appeal. In the years following 2008, it still avoided a frontal attack on domestic policies that voters would identify with moral conservatism. But at the same time it accelerated moves pitched to core conservative constituencies. To some extent this reflected a willingness to forsake votes in those areas of the country most likely to be opposed (large central cities, for example) and an acknowledgment of the likelihood of continuing minority governments.

The government's moves reflecting core ideological beliefs also came from the weakness of the opposition parties and their reluctance to trigger an election. This weakness was further exacerbated by Liberal Party divisions and by the public thrashing Harper successfully administered to supporters of a proposed coalition among the three opposition parties (in late 2008 and early 2009).[29]

Even with the confidence that these circumstances bolstered, the Conservatives seemed for a time more ideologically than strategically driven. Lawrence Martin (2010) attributed this in part to staffing changes in Harper's inner circle and particularly the appointment of Guy Giorno as chief of staff from 2008 to 2010. There may also have been some strategic miscalculations. Some of the policy fronts on which the government moved may have been thought destined for the back pages of the newspapers. The government was likely surprised at the attention attracted to and the opposition mobilized by something as complex as the census.

Taken as a whole, the government's moves in recent years reinforce arguments that the coalitional approach taken by the Conservatives coincides with an ideologically coherent drive to shift Canadian politics toward neoliberalism. Do they also suggest an enhanced preparedness to shift public policy comprehensively in directions favoured by social conservatives? Maybe yes, but only insofar as it does not jeopardize the party's chances of remaining in power.

Conclusion

Across Canada, unequivocally right-wing politicians have focused on tax cuts and deregulation, and have avoided a close association with moral traditionalism. When former Ontario premier Mike Harris was forced to enact legislation widely recognizing same-sex relationships in the wake of the Supreme Court's 1999 decision in *M. v. H.*, he did so grudgingly but in a lightning-quick fashion that all but eliminated the room for morally conservative voices within his own party. Alberta's former premier Ralph Klein was not above playing to the strong current of evangelical Christianity in his electorate, but he knew better than to steer his policy agenda too strongly in that direction. His message to national convention delegates contemplating a united right in 1999 was basically that a deregulative approach to the economy would be inconsistent with a "nanny-state" view of moral regulation: "To be consistent, those who promote individual choice in the market should at least permit individual choice in the setting of moral compasses" (Laycock 2002, 170).

Outside the United States, parties that successfully effect an ideological merger between neoliberalism and moral conservatism are rare. Christian democratic parties in Europe have echoed Roman Catholic positions on such issues as divorce, abortion, and homosexuality, though they often campaign on them less than the Church hierarchy would prefer, hoping that a lower-key approach will allow them to retain centrist voters.[30] The wisdom of doing so is especially obvious in Western Europe, where even Catholic faithful have been shifting away from moral traditionalism (Nevitte and Cochrane 2006). And, while Christian Democratic parties have certainly been supporters of private ownership, and uneasy about what they may regard as excessive state regulation, they provided crucial support for expansive welfare state regimes in the period following the Second World War and have not shifted nearly as far to the neoliberal right as have US Republicans, and British Conservatives under Margaret Thatcher.

Newer parties of the right, some of them on the extreme, are also unlikely to combine full-fledged moral conservatism with neoliberalism. Western European parties on the extreme right are typically backed by anti-immigrant supporters whose views tend to the right on economic issues as well but range widely on moral ones (Cochrane 2008; Benoit and Laver 2006). Among electors generally in Europe, there are few strong correlations between rightist positions on economic, immigration, and such "moral" issues as gay rights.[31] The same is true in Canada (Cochrane 2010).

However, the challenge for the Conservatives, not unknown to rightist parties elsewhere, is that an important part of its morally traditional electoral constituency, and of its activist base, is ideologically committed enough to eschew electoral success. The Conservative Party of Canada is now a major party, often pragmatically aspiring to government office, but it retains a large and persistent current of "believers" (Carty and Young 2000; Panebianco 1988). And as Jim Farney (2008) so properly points out, the Conservative Party's social conservatives have been "much slower to move from being policy-motivated to office-motivated actors than their populist or fiscal conservative co-partisans."

The Conservatives, then, combine some characteristics of populist parties of the right in Europe and the more established parties of the centre-right (Betz 1998). They depend, as do the newer parties of the hard right, not only on mobilizing resentment but also on attracting voters closer to the pragmatic centre. In some ways, as Neil Nevitte and his colleagues point out, the Reform and Alliance parties in Canada had less extremism in their supporters than did most of their counterparts in the populist parties of Western Europe (Nevitte et al. 1998). Still, these were constituencies that opposed the brokerage politics that had so long dominated the federal party system, and they held to views on some issues (including gay rights) that were distinctly to the right of those of the other parties.

It is tempting to regard the Conservative Party's religious constituency as a continuing "cheap date." It can easily be seen as having nowhere else to go and needing little in the way of care or concession. But, as Clyde Wilcox has argued about the US Republican Party, discontent with President George W. Bush was widespread among Christian conservatives, who saw him as having done much less for the religious right than the administration's rhetoric would suggest (Wilcox 2007a). The exit option is at least as sobering a possibility for Canadian evangelicals as it is for their American counterparts.

Yes, there are undoubtedly indications that the Harper Conservatives are moving towards pragmatism in their approach to issues that have been important to core constituencies of the Reform and Alliance parties – among them populist democratic reform, the treatment of Quebec, and levels of government spending (Flanagan 2010). On the other hand, there can be little doubt about the determination of the Harper leadership to pursue a radical neoliberal agenda where there are opportunities to do so, however much its minority government status and the financial crisis of 2009-10 have compromised its ability to act for the time being. There is also no doubt that the Conservatives are paying attention to their religious constituency, and its allies, on moral issues, even if the book has been firmly and publicly closed on same-sex marriage. Sexual diversity may not be the named target of initiatives related to sexual offences, assisted reproduction, and polygamy, but LGBT visibility will be read as one of the problems being addressed by more restrictive policy on such fronts.

The Conservative Party, like parties of the right in several European countries, is faced with a continuing dilemma, and we are likely to see oscillation between brokerage styles on the one hand and appeals to core religious supporters on the other. The party will continue its pattern of communicating electoral messages to religious conservatives as much as possible under the radar, relying on the pragmatism of Christian right political groups to convince supporters that keeping even a constrained Conservative Party in power is infinitely preferable to the alternatives.

17

The Politics of Marriage and American Party Politics
Evidence from the 2004 US Election

JOHN C. GREEN

The legal status of marriage suddenly burst more dramatically than ever onto the American political agenda during the 2004 presidential election (Wilcox, Merolla, and Beer 2007). The proximate cause was a 2003 ruling of the Massachusetts state Supreme Court legalizing same-sex marriage. This decision and the controversies that followed added a new element to an already hard-fought election. At the federal level, Republicans proposed an amendment to the US Constitution prohibiting same-sex marriage (eventually failing to obtain a large enough majority to pass in the US Congress). At the state level, eleven measures appeared on ballots amending state constitutions to prohibited same-sex marriage (all of which passed). At least some of the state ballot initiatives appeared to have had an effect on the outcome of the 2004 presidential campaign (Campbell and Monson 2007a). This controversy continued after 2004, with, on the one hand, Connecticut (2008), Iowa (2009), Vermont (2009), the District of Columbia (2009), and New Hampshire (2010) joining Massachusetts in legalizing same-sex marriage, and, on the other, additional state ballot measures rejecting same-sex marriage, including Florida (2006), California (2008), and Maine (2009).

The visibility given to the marriage issue during 2004 revealed how the major American political parties responded to what was still a relatively new issue. Historically, such responses have been of two varieties. One approach has been to adopt a clear position on the new issue, incorporating it into the party's existing agenda as much as possible. Such "issue adoption" can extend conflict to new areas, recruiting new supporters but also losing old ones. This "conflict extension" appears not to have been common in American history, but there is good evidence that it occurred in the 1990s and 2000s (Layman and Carsey 2002). The other approach has been to avoid taking clear stands in new issues for as long as possible, sticking with the existing party agenda. Such "issue avoidance" can prevent the disruption of a party's coalition in the short run; however, in the long run, it can cause some issues to be displaced by the new one. This "conflict displacement" has been common in American history (Sundquist 1983).

Whether a party chooses issue adoption or issue avoidance depends on many factors, among them, especially, the relative balance of opinion among the parties' interest group allies and followers in the public. In 2004, the major parties had asymmetric responses to the marriage issue. The Republican Party had already practised issue adoption on gay-related issues and now intensified its opposition to same-sex marriage in its party platform and campaign repertoire. Meanwhile, the Democrats largely practised issue avoidance, with many party leaders and candidates voicing opposition to same-sex marriage but, at the same time, shifting attention to issues on which they felt able to declare themselves positively – civil unions and the broader issue of gay rights.

This chapter offers a brief description of attitudes towards marriage in 2004, using special surveys of major party elites, of delegates to the Republican and Democratic national conventions, and of the American public.[1] These surveys reveal some of the details of the politics of marriage in 2004, including the views of major religious communities, interest groups allied with the major parties, and advocates on both sides of the marriage issue.

Views on Marriage in 2004

The first section of Table 17.1 reports basic opinion on the legal status of marriage in 2004 for both the party delegates and the public. Here the survey respondents were asked to choose from three mutually exclusive options:

1   The law should define marriage as a union between one man and one woman OR
2   The law should define marriage as a union between one man and one woman but recognize legal agreements between same-sex couples OR
3   The law should define marriage as a union between two people, regardless of their gender.

TABLE 17.1

Views of marriage: Party delegates and the public, 2004

| | Delegates (%) | | | Public (%) | | | |
Law should allow	All	Rep	Dem	All	Rep	Ind	Dem
Opposite-sex marriage	42.9	72.4	12.1	55.1	70.5	49.2	49.0
Civil unions	31.7	23.8	39.9	17.6	17.1	18.6	16.7
Same-sex marriage	25.4	3.9	48.0	27.3	12.4	32.3	34.3
Total	100.0	100.0	100.0	100.0	100.0	100.0	100.0

Sources: Party Elite Survey, 2004 (*N* = 960); National Survey of Religion and Politics, 2004 (*N* = 4,000).

This question produced similar results to other survey questions on the subject, which used different wording and were conducted in 2004.[2] For ease of discussion, the first option can be labelled "opposite-sex" marriage, the second "civil unions," and the third "same-sex" marriage.

Overall, a two-fifths plurality of the party delegates (combining representatives of the two parties) favoured restricting marriage to opposite-sex couples, about one-third supported civil unions for same-sex couples, and only one-quarter supported same-sex marriage rights. However, party differences here are extremely important. On the one hand, seven in ten Republican delegates favoured the most restrictive option, fewer than one-quarter chose even the civil union option, and fewer than one-twentieth backed same-sex marriage; on the other hand, two-fifths of Democratic delegates favoured the civil union option, and almost one-half backed same-sex marriage, meaning that only 12 percent opposed all recognition of same-sex relationships.

A comparison to public opinion shows that convention delegates were significantly more polarized, though most of the difference results from Democratic electoral supporters being more traditional than the party's convention delegates. Overall, a solid majority of the public (Democrats, Republicans, Independents) supported the opposite-sex restriction, and only one-quarter backed same-sex marriage. Seven in ten Republican citizens chose the most restrictive option, compared to just under one-half of independents and Democrats. Only one-eighth of Republicans backed same-sex marriage, compared to one-third of Independents and Democrats.

Hence the views of the Republican delegates largely mirrored those of Republican citizens but with the citizens being somewhat more favourable towards same-sex marriage than the delegates. This pattern helps explain why the Republican Party engaged in issue adoption when marriage suddenly appeared on the national agenda. In contrast, the views of the Democratic delegates did not match the views of Democratic citizens, with almost a majority of the delegates favouring same-sex marriage rights and almost a majority of rank-and-file Democrats favouring the most restrictive option. Democrats in the electorate were more divided on this new issue, a pattern that helps explain why the party chose issue avoidance.

Religion and Marriage

One of the strongest predictors of opinion on marriage is religion (Wilcox, Brewer, Shames, and Lake 2007), so Table 17.2 and Table 17.3 provide breakdowns of party delegate and partisan supporters in the general public by religious affiliation and practice. Both tables include adherents of the three largest denominational groupings, dividing them into the "observant" (reported attendance of once a week or more often) and "less observant" (reported attendance of less than once a week). Most of the remaining religious categories are composites of small religious communities: other Christians (Mormons, Eastern Orthodox); minority Protestants (blacks, Latino/as); minority Catholics (Latino/as, blacks, and Asians); other faiths (Jews, Muslims). The final category is respondents unaffiliated with organized religion.[3]

Table 17.2 shows striking differences on marriage views among the religious groups. Observant white evangelicals were most likely to support the opposite-sex option (93 percent), and this group was also the most heavily Republican. A majority of observant mainline Protestants (55 percent) did the same, as did a noticeably smaller portion (42 percent) of observant Catholics. Less observant evangelicals, mainline Protestants, and Catholics, of course, were much less likely to opt for an exclusively heterosexual conception of marriage than were their observant co-religionists. The contrast between the observant and less observant is especially stark among white evangelicals, with better than a 25 percentage point gap between these groups on support for opposite-sex marriage. In fact, the less observant resemble the observant among white mainline Protestants and Catholics. Among the composite religious groups, more than one-half of minority Protestants (largely due to African-American Protestants), other Christians, and minority Catholics favoured restricting relationship recognition to opposite-sex couples, while the "other faiths" and the unaffiliated were the most likely to support same-sex marriage.

TABLE 17.2

Religious groups and marriage: Party delegates, 2004

	% support			
Religious affiliation	Opposite-sex marriage	Civil unions	Same-sex marriage	Net partisanship
White evangelical Protestants				
Observant	93.1	3.1	3.8	77.0
Less observant	42.3	36.5	21.2	7.6
White mainline Protestants				
Observant	55.3	25.0	19.7	42.8
Less observant	34.3	40.2	25.4	15.6
White Catholics				
Observant	41.6	44.9	13.5	3.2
Less observant	22.9	45.0	32.1	−20.8
Other Christians	35.6	33.9	30.5	−19.4
Minority Protestant	50.5	31.7	17.8	−47.0
Minority Catholic	48.3	27.6	24.1	−5.0
Other faiths	17.6	41.2	41.2	−49.0
Unaffiliated	10.5	19.7	69.7	−59.0
All	42.9	31.7	25.4	0.0

Source: Party Elite Survey, 2004 (N = 960).

Table 17.2 also shows the net partisan leanings of each religious group – calculated by subtracting the percentage of each religious group that identified as Democrats from the percentage that identified as Republican (a positive number means a net Republican advantage, and a negative number means a net Democratic advantage). Observant white evangelical Protestants show up as the most overwhelmingly Republican in 2004 (with a 77 percent net Republican advantage), with observant white mainline Protestants the second most heavily Republican (with a 43 percent net advantage to that party). For the most part, we can see a close relationship between Republican leaning and traditional views of marriage, with minority Protestants a dramatic exception. This largely reflects the combination of strong Democratic leanings and moral traditionalism among African Americans.

Table 17.3 presents analogous information for religious groups in the public. Here, too, observant white evangelical Protestants were most likely

TABLE 17.3

Religious groups and marriage: The public, 2004

| Religious affiliation | % support | | | |
	Opposite-sex marriage	Civil unions	Same-sex marriage	Net partisanship
White evangelical Protestants				
Observant	85.6	8.1	6.2	37.8
Less observant	59.7	19.5	20.8	9.0
White mainline Protestants				
Observant	64.2	20.0	15.8	7.3
Less observant	40.0	31.5	28.5	0.4
White Catholics				
Observant	56.6	24.7	18.8	5.2
Less observant	34.8	21.4	43.8	−11.1
Other Christians	60.8	12.7	26.6	5.7
Minority Protestants	72.7	8.8	18.4	−44.2
Minority Catholics	56.9	12.6	30.5	−35.6
Other faiths	23.1	23.8	53.1	−30.3
Unaffiliated	31.7	18.6	49.7	−12.9
All	55.1	17.6	27.3	−3.7

Source: National Survey of Religion and Politics, 2004 (N = 4,000).

to support the opposite-sex restriction, at levels not much lower than those found among party delegates. Differences in attitudes towards same-sex relationships between religious groups are broadly similar to the patterns found among party delegates, though opposition to gay marriage and civil unions was noticeably higher in several groups, including white Catholics (observant and non-observant), minority Protestants, and "other Christians." By and large the support for the opposite-sex marriage option came at the expense of the civil union option.

The partisan breakdown of most religious groups in the public was more balanced than it was among party delegates. Strongly pro-Republican leanings were evident only among observant white evangelicals, though much less strongly so than among delegates. As with the delegates, the less observant groups were more Democratic in net partisanship, though Democrats fared significantly better among observant white evangelicals and

TABLE 17.4

Religious practice and homosexuality: The public, 2004

	% opposed	
Religious affiliation	Conducting · same-sex marriages	Ordaining homosexuals
White evangelical Protestants		
Observant	91.8	92.5
Less observant	70.2	74.4
White mainline Protestants		
Observant	72.2	73.0
Less observant	52.5	55.2
White Catholics		
Observant	73.4	76.3
Less observant	50.9	53.9
Other Christians	68.2	65.6
Minority Protestants	80.6	84.4
Minority Catholics	70.5	75.4
Other faiths	39.1	39.4
All	70.2	72.5

Source: National Survey of Religion and Politics, 2004 (N = 4,000).

mainline Protestants in the general public than among party delegates. This pattern has contributed to the difficulties for Democratic campaigners in adoption positions supportive of gay marriage.

Table 17.4 provides further illustration of the role of religious faith in shaping attitudes towards gay/lesbian rights claims – specifically on issues related to religious institutions themselves. Respondents in the general public with a minimum of participation in religious activities were asked about two issues that have been the focus of debate within a number of religious denominations: conducting same-sex marriage ceremonies and ordaining homosexual clergy.

Large majorities of observant white Christians opposed both conducting same-sex marriages and ordaining homosexuals within their churches, with observant evangelical Protestants being the most opposed, but strong majorities of less observant white Christians and the observant among both mainline Protestant and Catholic churches also opposed these practices.

Less observant white mainline Protestants and Catholics were more evenly divided.

In sum, among delegates and the public, evangelical Protestants and observant white Christians were a primary source for the Republican opposition to same-sex marriage in 2004. Meanwhile, the unaffiliated, other faiths, and less observant white Christians were a primary source of Democratic support for same-sex marriage. Minority Protestants and minority Catholics were mixed cases: groups opposed to same-sex marriage but with Democratic net partisanship.

Interest Group Allies and Marriage

The contrasting pressures on the Democratic and Republican parties can also be explored by clustering delegates by interest group association and contrasting their views on marriage and their partisanship. As Table 17.5 shows, the net partisanship scores indicate just how strongly Republican the members of Christian right groups are – not surprising in light of the party delegate data already displayed. Among party delegates, the other group members most clearly siding with the Republicans are pro-life, business, and farm groups.

The members of these most Republican of interest groups, and particularly Christian right and pro-life groups, strongly supported the opposite-sex restriction to the other options. Of the four, business groups have the largest portion of delegates supporting same-sex marriage (16 percent) and civil unions (30 percent), indicating that their leanings towards laissez-faire politics and lower taxes do not necessarily predict moral conservatism.

The group members most strongly leaning towards the Democrats were linked to environmentalism, civil rights, pro-choice work, and organized labour, though none could match the virtual partisan unanimity among Christian right group members. In contrast to the pattern among Republican-leaning groups, in only two of these sectors (pro-choice groups and, of course, gay rights groups) was there majority support for same-sex marriage. About one-half of environmental group members were in favour, and just under two-fifths of civil rights group members and union members were supportive. Preferences for an exclusively heterosexual conception of marriage were voiced by one-quarter of union members and a little less than one-third of civil rights group members. So overall, while marriage views were closely linked to key interest groups allied to each of the major parties, Republican allies were more strongly in favour of the most traditional option than Democratic allies were in favour of same-sex marriage.

TABLE 17.5

Interest group members and marriage: Party delegates, 2004

| | % support | | | |
Religious affiliation	Opposite-sex marriage	Civil unions	Same-sex marriage	Net partisanship
Republican-leaning groups				
Conservative Christian groups	90.2	8.7	1.1	97.8
Pro-life groups	73.2	17.0	9.8	56.4
Business groups	54.1	30.4	15.5	35.0
Farm groups	59.5	27.6	12.9	33.4
Veterans groups	54.7	29.2	16.0	8.2
Community service groups	48.3	33.5	18.2	7.4
Democratic-leaning groups				
Professional associations	38.0	34.6	27.4	−5.2
Environmental groups	22.8	28.6	48.7	−54.8
Civil rights groups	30.4	30.9	38.7	−59.6
Pro-choice groups	12.6	31.6	55.8	−63.6
Gay rights groups	18.0	13.1	68.9	−73.8
Labour unions	25.0	35.5	39.5	−76.2

Source: Party Elite Survey, 2004 (*N* = 960).

The asymmetry apparent here is amplified by the numerical strength of Christian right group members, constituting almost two-fifths of the Republican delegates. Members of gay rights groups, those with the strongest interest in and support for same-sex marriage, made up only one-tenth of Democratic delegates (and less than 2 percent of Republican delegates). Overall, delegates formally linked to groups with strongly negative responses to the recognition of same-sex relationships had a much stronger presence in the Republican convention than the few groups with a strong commitment to same-sex marriage had in the Democratic convention.

Conservative Christian and Gay Rights Groups

The profiles and activities of conservative Christian groups most certainly contributed to the Republican's decision to adopt the marriage issue in 2004 (Campbell and Robinson 2007). By tabulating results of questions asking delegates if they felt close to such groups, Table 17.6 provides additional evidence of their influence. These responses indicate not only that over four-fifths of observant white evangelical Christians felt close to them but

TABLE 17.6

Conservative Christian groups, religion, and marriage: Party delegates, 2004

Religious affiliation	% close to conservative Christians	% support for opposite-sex marriage			Net partisanship
		Close	Far	Difference	
White evangelical Protestants					
Observant	86.5	100.0	41.7	58.3	77.0
Less observant	45.1	78.3	9.1	69.2	7.6
White Mainline Protestants					
Observant	52.7	79.5	28.0	51.5	42.8
Less observant	27.1	72.7	12.4	60.3	15.6
White Catholics					
Observant	37.6	65.6	20.0	45.6	3.2
Less observant	26.2	66.7	2.9	63.8	−20.8
Other Christians	33.3	90.0	0.0	90.0	−19.4
Minority Protestant	25.0	83.3	30.8	52.5	−47.0
Minority Catholic	22.2	66.7	46.7	20.0	−5.0
Other faiths	18.0	70.0	2.9	67.1	−49.0
Unaffiliated	9.5	100.0	1.7	98.3	−59.0
All	37.2	83.2	13.3	69.9	0.0

Source: Party Elite Survey, 2004 ($N = 960$).

also that about half of non-observant evangelicals and observant white mainline Protestants did as well. Between one-quarter and two-fifths of several other groups also felt close to conservative Christian groups, including less observant white mainline Protestants, all white Catholics, minority Protestants, and other Christians. This table also shows that traditionalist views on marriage are very closely associated with respondents' closeness to conservative Christian groups, though somewhat less so among Catholics (white and minority). The fourth column in this table displays the difference between the figures, where a positive number indicates that those who felt close to conservative Christian groups were more in favour of opposite-sex marriage than were those who felt far from them.[4]

Table 17.7 is organized the same way as is Table 17.6, but it is for the public. The overall pattern of feelings of closeness to conservative religious groups is similar to that among party delegates, though close feelings were

TABLE 17.7

Conservative Christian groups, religion, and marriage: The public, 2004

Religious affiliation	% close to conservative Christians	% support for opposite-sex marriage			Net partisanship
		Close	Far	Difference	
White evangelical Protestants					
Observant	53.2	91.6	68.6	23.0	37.8
Less observant	28.2	67.2	51.0	16.2	9.0
White mainline Protestants					
Observant	25.5	89.7	41.2	48.5	7.3
Less observant	9.1	70.4	28.0	33.7	0.4
White Catholics					
Observant	16.8	73.7	36.7	37.0	5.2
Less observant	9.3	47.6	29.6	18.0	−11.1
Other Christians	10.1	81.8	47.5	34.3	5.7
Minority Protestants	42.9	82.7	53.5	29.2	−44.2
Minority Catholics	20.1	53.1	56.5	-3.4	−35.6
Other faiths	2.2	100.0	22.2	77.8	−30.3
Unaffiliated	8.2	53.8	22.4	31.4	−12.9
All	23.8	79.5	36.5	43.0	−3.7

Source: National Survey of Religion and Politics, 2004 (N = 4,000).

registered at significantly lower levels. For example, only 53 percent of observant white evangelical Protestants and 26 percent of observant white mainline Protestants in the general public felt close to conservative religious groups, as compared to 87 percent and 53 percent, respectively, of their party delegate counterparts. Two exceptions stand out. Among black Protestants, fully 43 percent reported closeness to conservative Christian groups in the general public, compared to one-quarter of their delegate counterparts. Affinity to conservative Christian groups among minority Catholics was about as strong in the general public (20 percent) as among delegates (22 percent). The substantial number of minority Protestants who feel close to such groups translates into strong support for traditional marriage (83 percent among those who feel close). This pattern is markedly less true among minority Catholics (among whom only 53 percent who feel close also support retaining the traditional view of marriage). As we have seen in other data, the strong African-American tilt to the Democratic Party translates into a strong moral traditionalist constituency within that party's electoral ranks, complicating substantially the approach to issues like same-sex marriage.

Adding to the leverage of the Christian right is the fact that, as Table 17.7 shows, support for the traditional definition of marriage is strong within many religious circles whose members are not close to conservative Christian groups. Among white evangelicals, observant or not, and among minority Protestants and Catholics, more than half of those who do not feel themselves close to conservative groups support only the opposite-sex definition of marriage. Among white observant mainline Protestants and Catholics who are not close to Christian right groups, more than 35 percent support the position on marriage adopted by those groups. This pattern is less widely true among party delegates, but support for a conservative position on marriage still extends significantly beyond that population that feels close to conservative groups, and this is particularly so among minority Protestants and Catholics and among the small number of observant white evangelicals who do not feel close to those groups.

There is also evidence of some slippage from traditional views among some of those who profess closeness to Christian right organizations. Among non-observant white Catholics and minority Catholics in general, support for traditional marriage is only in the 50 percent range. This is less dramatically in evidence among party delegates, though once again Catholics stand out for their preparedness to declare their support for some form of recognition of same-sex relationships while at the same time expressing support for the Christian right.

What about gay/lesbian/bisexual/transgender groups and the extent to which they find support among both delegates and the general public? There is no doubt that such groups have influenced the Democratic Party in the past by mobilizing its supporters on their issues, and they have certainly pressed hard on the marriage issue (Campbell and Robinson 2007). Table 17.8, however, shows the challenges facing such activists. It displays information about party delegates analogous to that in Table 17.6, though using responses to questions asking them to rate gays and lesbians (not groups) on a thermometer scale ranging from warm to frigid.[5] Note first how low the rate of reporting closeness to such groups is among most religious denominational clusterings. There is majority "warmth" among the unaffiliated, among other faiths, and, strikingly, among minority Catholics. About

TABLE 17.8

Gay rights groups, religion, and marriage: Party delegates, 2004

Religious affiliation	% close to gay rights groups	% support for opposite-sex marriage			Net partisanship
		Close	Far	Difference	
White evangelical Protestants					
Observant	6.1	71.4	97.8	−26.4	77.0
Less observant	16.1	12.5	70.0	−57.5	7.6
White mainline Protestants					
Observant	29.9	0.0	47.4	−47.4	42.8
Less observant	33.1	0.0	45.7	−45.7	15.6
White Catholics					
Observant	21.5	6.3	50.8	−44.5	3.2
Less observant	34.0	0.0	68.1	−68.1	−20.8
Other Christians	13.6	0.0	84.6	−84.6	−19.4
Minority Protestant	23.7	7.1	75.0	−67.9	−47.0
Minority Catholic	53.6	14.0	44.4	−30.4	−5.0
Other faiths	66.0	2.2	55.6	−53.4	−49.0
Unaffiliated	70.4	0.0	40.0	−40.0	−59.0
All	35.8	4.4	67.5	−63.1	0.0

Source: Convention Delegate Survey, 2004 ($N = 972$).

one-third of all white mainline Protestants and less observant Catholics report warm feelings. Less than one-quarter of other groupings, including observant Catholics, minority Protestants, and, of course, white evangelicals, are warm. There are strong and predictable relationships between reports of such affective positiveness and attitudes towards same-sex marriage.

Table 17.9 looks at affect towards gay rights groups in the public.[5] The level of positive affect is significantly lower than it is among delegates, though this is difficult to directly compare because different objects are being measured. The level of positive feeling towards gay rights groups is often only about half as widespread among public respondents as it is among the delegates who express positive feelings about gays and lesbians. The gap between public and delegate responses is especially large among minority Protestants and minority Catholics. Gay rights groups have no very strong

TABLE 17.9

Gay rights groups, religion, and marriage: The public, 2004

Religious affiliation	% close to gay rights groups	% support for opposite-sex marriage			Net partisanship
		Close	Far	Difference	
White Evangelical Protestants					
Observant	4.0	52.9	91.4	−38.5	37.8
Less observant	8.8	19.0	70.8	−51.8	9.0
White mainline Protestants					
Observant	12.5	5.6	75.3	−69.7	7.3
Less observant	12.9	0.0	58.5	−58.5	0.4
White Catholics					
Observant	5.5	25.0	66.4	−41.4	5.2
Less observant	15.9	8.3	47.1	−38.8	−11.1
Other Christians	18.3	4.8	85.5	−80.7	5.7
Minority Protestants	6.2	70.0	78.1	−8.1	−44.2
Minority Catholics	11.7	11.1	68.3	−57.2	−35.6
Other faiths	31.5	6.9	40.5	−33.6	−30.3
Unaffiliated	26.0	3.3	48.7	−45.4	−12.9
All	12.9	12.2	70.6	−58.4	−3.7

Source: National Survey of Religion and Politics, 2004 (*N* = 4,000).

pool of support within any of the religious groupings tabulated, except for the one-quarter to one-third of respondents within the other faiths and unaffiliated categories. Even among the less observant of the major denominations, the highest proportion of the population expressing affinity was 16 percent (among white Catholics). True without exception, those who reported being close to gay rights groups were less likely to prefer opposite-sex marriage, and those who felt far from these groups were more likely to favour opposite-sex marriage; however, the numbers among the former were relatively modest. Here, too, there was a close match between these patterns and net partisanship.

What about the kind of "slippage" shown in Table 17.7? There is less here, but, among the very small numbers of observant white Catholics, observant evangelicals, and, especially, minority Protestants who profess closeness to gay rights groups, there remain significant levels of support for exclusively heterosexual marriage – 25 percent, 53 percent, and 70 percent, respectively. On the other hand, there is support for some form of same-sex relationship recognition among many of those who do not feel close to gay rights groups, particularly so among less observant white mainline Protestants and less observant Catholics. This kind of "peripheral" support for gay rights, however, is less widespread than is that which benefits the Christian right.

Taken together, these data suggest that views on marriage and attitudes towards gay rights groups are closely linked across the major religious communities at the elite and mass levels. However, the lower levels of affect towards gay rights groups, especially among the public, suggest that gay rights advocates had limited political purchase in 2004, even within the Democratic Party. While these patterns did not necessarily cause the Democratic Party to avoid stating a clear position on the marriage issue, they do suggest that gay rights advocates had fewer opportunities to effectively mobilize support for their perspective on the marriage issue.

Politics of Marriage in 2004 – and Beyond

What can we conclude about the politics of marriage in 2004? First, Republicans were strongly in favour of opposite-sex marriage at the elite and mass levels, and the Democrats were more divided at both levels, with the balance of preferences quite different between the party elites and followers. Religion was an important factor in shaping opinion on marriage among party delegates and partisans in the public – this being evident not only regarding attitudes towards relationship recognition but also regarding opinion on recognizing homosexuality in religious practice. In addition, interest groups allied with the Republican Party were more favourable towards restricting relationship recognition to opposite-sex couples, while interest groups allied with the Democratic Party were more favourable towards same-sex marriage. Those forming part of the Republican coalition were more numerous, however, had more support from other allies, and, therefore, had more opportunities to mobilize supporters.

Taken together, these patterns help explain the Republican Party's choice of issue adoption and the Democratic Party's choice of issue avoidance. The confluence of political forces in 2004 moved the issue of marriage to a prominent place on the Republican agenda but kept it less prominent on the Democratic agenda. These patterns appear to have largely persisted in the

2008 election, albeit in a campaign dominated by economic issues. The Democrats worked at increasing their electoral appeal to practising Christians during that campaign, and they did increase their vote levels among Protestant evangelicals, aided to some extent by the publicity given to Barack Obama's own faith. This amplified the pressures to keep same-sex marriage off the platform and to repeat the presidential candidate's opposition to same-sex marriage, replaying the asymmetry in the two parties' engagement with the issue that was so evident in 2004.

Eventually, both political parties may adopt opposite and symmetrical positions on marriage, extending partisan conflict to this issue. Because views on marriage are deeply rooted in religious communities, sharply conflicting views will likely persist both in the general public and among party elites.[6] It seems unlikely that, in the future, the issue of marriage will occupy as prominent a place as it did in 2004. And it could well be that, in coming campaigns, the growing support for the public recognition of same-sex relationships among younger people of all religious groupings will help push the issue to the back burner.

RIGHTS CLAIMING

The struggles for rights based on sexual diversity and religion do not necessarily collide, but they often do. The political and legal recognition of rights related to sexual orientation and gender identity has often been opposed by religious conservatives. Religious groups making claims for the recognition of religiously based rights are often moved to do so by the expanding recognition of LGBT rights. As Washington, DC, moved to allow same-sex marriage in late 2009, the Catholic archdiocese warned that it might suspend its many social service programs for the homeless as well as in the areas of adoption and health care if the law did not grant it the right to discriminate on grounds of religious freedom. Other Catholic institutions did not feel the same conflict: Georgetown University avoids acknowledging same-sex arrangements by allowing any employee to designate any other adult who lives with her or him as part of her or his family and thereby entitled to benefits.

In the United States and Canada, as in most countries, rights claims occupy central stage in political life. There are, however, few countries where the courts have played a prominent role as settings for making claims about equity and recognition. The United States has a longer history of using litigation as a core political strategy for advocacy groups, but Canada "caught up" significantly with the constitutional entrenchment of the expansive Charter of Rights and Freedoms in 1982. The Charter has provided wide coverage for claims opposing discrimination based on sexual orientation, including marriage. No such sweeping coverage is provided by the US Constitution.

As Richard Moon argues in Chapter 18, conflict over diverging rights claims has been evident in Canada, with schooling often at the centre of opposing claims. The court has attempted Solomonic compromises in balancing these claims, but Moon finds them wanting, and we can imagine that the ambiguities and ambivalences inherent in those judgments will leave room for a good deal of additional litigation. We also anticipate a continuation of conflict over the meaning of hate speech provisions in criminal and civil statutes. An Alberta human rights tribunal ruling that a letter by a pastor to a local newspaper attacking homosexuality violated the province's human rights laws reinforced the fearful claims of Christian right groups in both Canada and the United States, who warn that the Bible will be declared "hate speech." That ruling was overturned by an Alberta court in November 2009, but the original conviction amplifies concerns that we are dealing with a collision of rights claims.

Despite the absence of comprehensive prohibitions on LGBT-related discrimination in the United States, as Jason Pierceson points out in Chapter 19, LGBT groups have successfully advanced claims based on the implicit privacy right in the national Constitution and on the explicit privacy and equity rights provisions in many state constitutions. These gains have been slowed, and in some cases reversed, by the use of the initiative and referenda in state constitution making, though gains gradually secured by LGBT people have continued to spread.

More recently, Christian conservative groups have made arguments in the public sphere, presenting religious freedom claims to discriminate against gays and lesbians and free speech claims to denounce homosexuality. Rights claims by people of faith have somewhat different constitutional foundations in Canada than they do in the United States, but there remain large areas of uncertainty regarding how much room religious institutions have to discriminate.

What we see in these chapters is the persistence of just such uncertainty regarding how to combine a public respect for sexual diversity with religious faith. Although faith has been increasingly seen in North America as private and individualized, it inevitably has a role in public life and in the participation of people of faith in all corners of the public square. As faith communities proliferate, both inside and outside the Christian tradition, the recognition of religious differences is becoming a more public, rather than less public, concern. By the same token, sexual diversity is inevitably a public issue – the increased visibility of queer families makes that obvious. This creates much room for conflict, as well as opportunity for creative accommodation.

18

The Supreme Court of Canada's Attempt to Reconcile Freedom of Religion and Sexual Orientation Equality in the Public Schools

RICHARD MOON

In recent years, the Canadian courts have been confronted with a number of cases in which freedom of religion and sexual orientation equality appeared to clash. Specifically, the courts have had to decide whether religiously motivated anti-gay expression violated a provincial human rights code restriction on hateful expression (*Owens v. Saskatchewan* 2006). They have also had to rule on whether a human rights code ban on discrimination in the provision of services to the public was breached when a business owner refused to provide services to a gay advocacy group (*Ontario v. Brillinger* 2002).[1] And, in two judgments, *Trinity Western University v. British Columbia College of Teachers* (2001) and *Chamberlain v. Surrey School District No. 36* (2002), the Supreme Court of Canada dealt with the competing claims of sexual orientation equality and religious freedom in the public schools.

These last two cases are the focus of the discussion that follows. I argue that the court's reconciliation of the claims of sexual orientation equality and religious freedom in these cases depends on a narrow conception of sexual orientation equality – narrower than that advanced by the court in other sexual orientation cases – and on an understanding of the role and authority of teachers that is more limited than that adopted by the court in other freedom of religion cases. I argue that the court's awkward attempt to reconcile religious freedom and sexual orientation equality points to deeper problems with its conception of religious freedom and, more particularly, with its commitment to the principle of religious neutrality – the view that the state should neither favour nor disfavour a particular religious belief system. This principle, I argue, is unworkable when applied to religious beliefs that address the rights and interests of others in the community.

The Canadian Charter of Rights and Freedoms guarantees a variety of rights, including "freedom of conscience and religion" (s.2a)[2] and "the right to the equal protection and equal benefit of the law without discrimination, and, in particular, without discrimination based on ... religion" (s.15). The Canadian courts have held that section 15 prohibits discrimination based not only on the grounds listed in section 15 but also on "analogous" grounds such as sexual orientation (*Egan v. Canada* 1995 and *M. v. H.* 1999)

In *TWU v. BCCT* the issue was whether the British Columbia College of Teachers had acted outside its powers when it refused to accredit the teacher training program of a private evangelical Christian university because the program affirmed the view that homosexuality is immoral. The court in *TWU* held that the decision not to accredit the program was an unnecessary interference with the religious freedom of Trinity Western University and its graduates since there was no evidence that the program's graduates had engaged in discriminatory acts against gays and lesbians in the public schools.

In *Chamberlain*, the issue was whether a local school board acted outside its powers when it refused to approve as teaching materials for the primary grades three books depicting same-sex-parent families. The court held that the decision to exclude the books was *ultra vires* the board because it was based on the belief, of parents and board members, that same-sex relationships are immoral and should not be affirmed, or even represented, to younger students. In the court's view, the requirement in the BC School Act that the public schools operate according to secular principles precluded the school board from supporting or enforcing a religious/moral view that denies respect or recognition to another group or perspective in the community.

When confronted with the competing claims of sexual orientation equality and religious freedom/equality in the public schools, the Supreme Court of Canada, in *TWU* and *Chamberlain*, tried to square the circle and held that the schools should affirm sexual orientation equality without repudiating the religious view that homosexuality is immoral or unnatural. The inconsistency in the demands the court makes on the schools – to both affirm central public values and to remain agnostic on issues of religious value – is blurred by two ambiguities in the court's reasoning: its account of sexual orientation equality and its understanding of the authority of teachers and schools.

In *TWU* and *Chamberlain*, selective reliance on an artificially narrow view of sexual orientation equality, and an unrealistically broad view of the autonomy of students, enabled the court to affirm sexual orientation equality without repudiating the religious view that homosexuality is sinful. In both cases the court sometimes seemed to rely on a narrower conception of the equality right, which required that the schools *tolerate* sexual diversity, and refrain from interfering with the lifestyle choices of gays and lesbians, but not that they *affirm* the equal value of gay/lesbian relationships or identities. And, in both cases, the court seemed to assume that teachers play no special role, and have no particular authority, in the lives of their students – that teachers simply "expose" students to different values and ideas in the classroom.[3]

The court was reluctant to repudiate the religious view that homosexuality is sinful, but it could only avoid doing so by relying on a narrow reading of sexual orientation – narrower than that relied on by the court in other contexts. The courts were understandably reluctant to explicitly repudiate a religious view that is still widely held in the community. While the state has an interest in ensuring that children are taught important public values, such as equality, democratic participation, and religious tolerance, the primary responsibility for the moral and spiritual development of children is generally thought to lie with their parents. Indeed, the courts have previously held that freedom of religion encompasses the right of parents to oversee the spiritual lives of their children (*B(R) v. Children's AID Society of Toronto* 1995).

However, I want to suggest that the court's reluctance to repudiate anti-gay religious views may also (or at a deeper level) reflect the court's (and the general public's) uncertainty or ambivalence about the nature and value of religious commitment – an ambivalence that is not unfamiliar to those interested in issues of sexual diversity. While the formal defence of religious freedom, in modern liberal democracies such as Canada, emphasizes the value of individual autonomy or choice, the protection of religious freedom sometimes seems to rest, also, or instead, on the idea that religion is a matter of identity. According to this view, religious belief is not simply a choice or judgment the individual makes; rather, it is a deeply rooted part of her/his identity or character that should be treated with equal respect. It orients the individual in the world, shapes her/his perception of the social realm and the natural order, and provides a moral framework for her/his actions.

If religious beliefs are valuable because they have been chosen, or because they are the product of autonomous judgment, then the *adoption* or *rejection* of an individual's religious values and practices, in the democratic law-making process, will not affect her/his sense of belonging or worth, any more than will the adoption or rejection of her/his political views about capital punishment or public medicare (which, for some citizens, are grounded in religion). But if religious belief is instead a matter of identity (and outside the scope of reasonable or accessible political contest), then the state should neither affirm nor repudiate the values or practices of a particular religious group. To base public action on religious grounds is to impose on some individuals the religious values and practices of others; and to give legal support to the values and practices of one religious group over those of another is to engage in religious discrimination. It is also objectionable – a failure to show equal respect – for the state to base its actions on grounds that a particular religious group rejects as immoral or wrongful. When the state treats an individual's religious practices/beliefs as less important or less true than the practices of others, or when her/his religious community is marginalized by the state in some way, the individual adherent may experience this not simply as a rejection of her/his views and values but as a denial of her/his equal worth or desert – as unequal treatment that affects her/his dignity.

However, the difficulty with the requirement that the state treat different religions in an even-handed way, or remain neutral on religious matters, is that most religions have something to say about how we should act towards others and about the kind of community we should work to create. Religion is the source of values for many community members and the ground upon which they engage with others in the community on questions of justice and the collective good. Because most religions have public implications, they cannot be excluded entirely from the public sphere, and they cannot be completely insulated from public debate and judgment. While the state may seek to avoid direct involvement in debates about spiritual truth, it must sometimes prefer or advance some values over others. If it is permissible for governments to rely on, or advance, particular (religious) values when determining public policy, then it must also be permissible for them to reject or repudiate other (religious) values.

TWU v. BCCT

In *Trinity Western University v. British Columbia College of Teachers*, the issue is whether the British Columbia College of Teachers (BCCT) had acted outside its powers when it refused to accredit the teacher training program of a private evangelical Christian university on the grounds that the program taught or affirmed the view that homosexuality is sinful. In deciding not to accredit the Trinity Western University (TWU) program, the BCCT referred specifically to the contract of "Responsibilities of Membership in the Community of Trinity Western University," which teachers and students were expected to sign (*TWU v. BCCT* 2001, para. 6). Of particular concern to the BCCT was the obligation, assumed by teachers and students, to "refrain from practices that are biblically condemned such as premarital sex, adultery and homosexual behaviour" (para. 10). According to the BCCT, an institution that wishes to train teachers for the public school system must "provide an institutional setting that appropriately prepares future teachers for the public school environment, and in particular the diversity of public school students" (para. 11). A teacher in the public system must be able "to support all children regardless of race, colour, religion or sexual orientation with a respectful and nonjudgmental relationship" (*TWU v. BCCT* 1997, 181).

The majority of the Supreme Court of Canada, in a judgment written by Justice Iacobucci and Justice Bastarache ("the court"), held that the decision of the BCCT to deny accreditation to TWU's teaching program should be overturned.[4] For the court, "the issue at the heart of this appeal was how to reconcile the religious freedoms of individuals wishing to attend TWU with the equality concerns of students in BC's public school system" (*TWU v. BCCT* 2001, para. 28). The court found that, while the BCCT acted properly in considering whether the TWU program might contribute to discrimination against gays and lesbians in the public schools, it should also have taken account of the religious freedom rights of TWU and its graduates. The court observed that the BCCT accreditation decision "places a burden on members of a particular religious group ... preventing them from expressing freely beliefs and associating to put them into practice" (para. 32). The BCCT decision means that TWU must abandon its religiously based "Community Standards" if it is to run a program that trains teachers for the public school system. Graduates of TWU "are likewise affected because the affirmation of their religious beliefs and attendance at TWU will not lead to certification as public school teachers" (para. 32).

The court accepted that freedom of religion is limited by the rights and freedoms of others and does not protect religious practices that are harmful, including explicit acts of discrimination against gays and lesbians. However, it found that the limitation in this case on the religious freedom of the staff and graduates of TWU (the denial of accreditation) was imposed in the absence of any evidence that the program had a detrimental impact on the school system. According to the court, the TWU Community Standards simply proscribed the conduct of members while attending TWU and so gave no reason to anticipate intolerant behaviour by TWU-trained teachers in the public schools. The signatory simply undertakes not to participate in this form of activity while she/he is a student at TWU. Moreover, noted the court, even if some or all of the graduates of TWU believe that homosexuality is sinful, they are, as Christians, bound to treat others, even sinners, with respect. The court concluded that, in the absence of any concrete evidence that training teachers at TWU fosters discrimination in the public schools of BC, the BCCT had no grounds to deny accreditation to TWU and to interfere with the religious freedom of TWU instructors and students to hold certain beliefs.

According to the court, had there been evidence of clear and direct acts of discrimination on the part of TWU graduates, the BCCT would have been justified in refusing to accredit the TWU teacher-training program. Yet it is not clear why this should be so. Once the court distinguished between anti-gay/lesbian belief and action, and accepted that a teacher may hold such beliefs provided she/he does not act on them, why was it relevant whether any TWU graduates had engaged in acts of discrimination? If belief and action are separable in this way (public action as wrongful and personal belief as not), then TWU, even though it supported anti-gay/lesbian views, should not be responsible for any discriminatory actions taken by its graduates. Similarly, the improper actions of some graduates should not affect the accreditation of other graduates, who may believe that homosexuality is immoral but who refrain from engaging in acts of discrimination.

The court found no conflict in this case between religious freedom and sexual orientation equality. Once the proper scope of each right is understood, the "potential conflict" between them dissolves (*TWU v. BCCT* 2001, para. 29). According to the court, "the freedom to hold beliefs is broader than the freedom to act on them" (para. 36). If a teacher engages in discriminatory conduct, she/he "can be subject to disciplinary proceedings before the BCCT" (para. 37). But, said the court, the right of gays and lesbians to be free from discrimination is not violated simply because a teacher holds discriminatory views. A teacher may believe that homosexuality is sinful or wrongful, and even that gays and lesbians are less worthy or deserving than others, but as long as she/he does not act on those views, denying benefits to, or imposing burdens on, particular individuals because of their sexual orientation she/he will not be found to have breached their right to equality.

While the distinction between belief and action is central in human rights codes (which prohibit acts of discrimination in the market but do not otherwise regulate an individual's beliefs or the decisions she/he makes concerning "private" matters), it may not be applicable to the role of a teacher in a public school. An important part of a teacher's role is to *teach* her/his students basic values, including tolerance for different religious belief systems and respect for the equal worth of all people. As the court observed, "schools are meant to develop civic virtue and responsible citizenship, to educate in an environment free of bias, prejudice and intolerance" (*TWU v. BCCT* 2001, para. 13). But teachers do not simply instruct students in these values. They are role models and counsellors.[5] If sexual orientation equality is to be affirmed in the public schools, teachers must do more than simply refrain from direct acts of discrimination against gay and lesbian students. A teacher, when confronted with bigoted words from students about gays and lesbians, should contradict those words, or when approached by an individual who is struggling with her/his sexual identity, should provide support and reassurance or direct the student to an individual or group that can offer support.

Because the public values of the school curriculum (broadly understood) are taught by example, and because they must be affirmed in different ways, it may be that a teacher who is not personally committed to these values cannot perform her/his role effectively. More significantly, a teacher training program that affirms values that are incompatible with the civic curriculum will not adequately prepare its students to teach in the public schools.

There may be good reasons not to examine individual teachers on their views about sexual orientation equality (or racial and gender equality). A serious probe into the individual's thoughts or unconscious attitudes about sexual orientation might involve too great an invasion of her/his personal life. Moreover, no person is entirely free of the taint of prejudice, and so there is no simple or easy test for determining when someone is or is not homophobic (or racist or sexist). We should not preclude an individual from teaching in the public schools simply because we suspect she/he is racist or homophobic – because, for example, she/he belongs to a particular church or because she/he attended a particular religious school. But this is not the same as saying that it is all right to employ an anti-gay/lesbian teacher, provided she/he refrains from explicit acts of discrimination in the classroom. A teacher should be excluded from the schools if she/he has indicated by her/his public statements or actions that she/he regards homosexuality as sinful or objectionable, even though there is no evidence that she/he has directly discriminated against gays and lesbians in the classroom. She/he should be excluded not only because discrimination is sometimes subtle and difficult to prove but also because a teacher should do more than simply tolerate gays and lesbians. She/he should affirm their equal value.

In *Ross v. New Brunswick School District No. 15* (1996), the Supreme Court of Canada held that an individual who holds racist views, evidenced by her/his words or actions inside or outside the classroom, may be disqualified from serving as a classroom teacher in the public schools. Laforest J, for the court, upheld the decision of an adjudicator, appointed under the New Brunswick Human Rights Code, that ordered the school board to remove from the classroom a teacher who had expressed racist views in public settings outside the school.[6] In *Ross*, there was no evidence that the teacher had treated any minority students in his class unfairly, or differently from other students, or that he had deviated from the curriculum and taught racist views. However, because Mr. Ross had expressed racist opinions at public meetings, and in the local media, students in his school (and the general community) had come to know of his views. The court found that Mr. Ross's public racist statements had "poisoned" the learning environment in the school.

The court in *Ross* recognized that a teacher is a role model, an authority figure, and a conduit for public values.[7] Public knowledge of Mr. Ross's racist views mattered because his support for such views might have legitimized them in the minds of some students and undermined the school's affirmation of racial equality. If all that is expected of a teacher is that she/he refrain from teaching racist views, then it might be possible to separate what she/he says and does in the classroom from what she/he says and does outside on her/his own time. There are very few jobs from which an individual would be dismissed because she/he (publicly) expressed racist views after work hours (unless contrary to the Criminal Code).[8] Moreover, there are views that a teacher is *not* permitted to express inside the classroom but is free to express outside. For example, a teacher should not expressly support the Liberal Party, or the Communist Party, inside the classroom, but she/he is permitted to do so outside. We expect the teacher in the classroom to remain neutral on issues of partisan politics. But, in the case of racial equality, we expect more than formal neutrality in the classroom: we expect the teacher to positively support the value of equality. A teacher who publicly affirms racist views cannot perform this role. It would seem to be even more obvious that a teacher training program that affirms such views does not adequately prepare its students to teach in the public school system.

The court found no evidence that any TWU graduate had acted in a discriminatory way in the classroom or even that any graduate held anti-gay/lesbian views. But the issue in the *TWU* case was not whether a particular graduate/prospective teacher might be anti-gay/lesbian because she/he attended an educational institute that affirmed anti-gay/lesbian views; rather, it was whether a teacher training program that affirmed such views should be denied accreditation because it did not adequately prepare its students to teach in the public school system – a system in which gays and lesbians should be treated with equal respect and not simply tolerated.[9]

The existence of TWU and, more specifically, its teacher training program rests on a belief that the values of those who teach are important in the education process. TWU recognizes that its students will become better Christians or Christian school teachers if they are taught in an environment that is fully Christian in its values and practices. This is why TWU requires that all instructors adhere to the code of conduct, which, among other things, forbids "homosexual behaviour." Even if anti-gay views are not an explicit part of the teacher training program, they form part of the ethos of TWU. Moreover, TWU has applied for accreditation so that it can train teachers who will support or model evangelical Christian virtues in the public system.

Had the BCCT denied accreditation to a teacher training program that had a racist element in its curriculum, it seems unlikely that its decision would have been overturned by the court, even though not every graduate of the racist program would carry the lesson of racism with her/him (see MacDougall 2002; Wintemute 2002). A program that teaches or affirms values so fundamentally at odds with the basic civic values of the public school system would not be accredited. Yet TWU sought accreditation for a program that supported values that the BCCT thought were incompatible with the civic mission of the public schools – based on the public commitment to sexual orientation equality expressed in both provincial and federal human rights codes.

In *TWU*, the court seemed unwilling to confront the anti-gay/lesbian content of the TWU program. The most obvious explanation for this is that the court wanted to avoid repudiating, directly, the religious view that homosexuality is sinful or, at least, to avoid excluding from the schools teachers who believed that homosexuality was sinful. In the court's view, the public schools are a secular or common space that must be open to individuals from diverse religious communities or belief systems.[10]

The requirement that public schools be inclusive, and respect diversity in the community, may be understood to mean that they must be "agnostic" or neutral on questions of religious truth or on issues that are the subject of religious or moral disagreement in the community. Or it may mean that the schools must tolerate all moral/religious values or perspectives – that they must not exclude or marginalize any particular view.[11] Yet the difficulty with this position is that a school is not simply a public forum. Students should be educated in an environment in which everyone is treated with equal respect, regardless of their race or gender or sexual orientation. The public schools cannot include or tolerate those views that oppose diversity and that deny respect to certain individuals or groups on racial or other grounds. Moreover, the schools have a civic purpose that is incompatible with certain religious/moral perspectives. If the public schools are to prepare students for life in a culturally and religiously diverse society, and a democratic political community, they must foster civic virtues such as religious tolerance, racial equality, and democratic engagement. While the schools should endeavour to respect deeply held religious commitments, they cannot be neutral towards, or even tolerate, all values. The affirmation of any value or set of values will involve the exclusion or rejection of other values, perspectives, or commitments in the community, including the deeply held religious beliefs of some teachers, parents, and students.

More often, the court in *TWU* seemed to accept that "secular" or "public" inclusion did not require that the schools remain neutral on the "issue" of homosexuality but, rather, that the schools include – be open to – all individuals, regardless of their religious views. According to the court, the schools should affirm the value of different sexualities (sexual orientation equality) but should not exclude teachers and students who hold a different view. In the court's view, a substantial part of the community's population should not be excluded from this "neutral" space because of their religious beliefs. Because the public school system is meant to encompass all members of the community, whatever their religious beliefs, the court was unwilling to accept either that the adherents of widely held religious views could not serve as teachers or that a teacher training program that affirms such views did not adequately prepare teachers to work in the public school system. Instead, the court strikes an awkward balance: the individuals are included (may serve as teachers) but their beliefs are not (must not be manifested in the classroom). The individual must leave her/his religious beliefs about homosexuality at the entry to the school and must act in accordance with the tolerance/respect values of the civic curriculum. She/he must separate her/his private beliefs from her/his public actions and conform to, and even teach, civic values that are at odds with her/his personal religious beliefs. This approach fits with the contemporary understanding of public secularism as the exclusion of religion from public life or the "privatization" of religious commitment.[12]

Yet, if an individual's religious beliefs should be respected because they are deeply rooted, is it realistic to expect her/him to put them aside when she/he serves as a teacher? The court in *TWU* accepted that religious beliefs are a central part of the individual's identity and should therefore be respected and even accommodated; yet, at the same time, the court also accepted that the individual can and should separate her/himself from her/his religious beliefs when participating in public life – or at least should do so if her/his beliefs are inconsistent with public values. In the *Chamberlain* case, which is the focus of the next section, McLachlin CJ observed that "religion is an integral part of people's lives" and, thus, that it is unrealistic to ask the members of a school board to leave their religious values and concerns "at the boardroom door" and to take no account of them when making decisions (*Chamberlain v. Surrey School District #36* 2002, para. 19). If it is unrealistic to expect a religious adherent to shed her/his spiritual beliefs or values when she/he participates in public life, then a teacher who is opposed on religious grounds to the values of the public school curriculum (particularly if she/he has declared her/his views publicly) will not be able to effectively perform her/his public role, and, even more obviously, a teacher training program that affirms values that are inconsistent with the curriculum will not properly prepare teachers for the public schools.

Even if the general community must tolerate the expression of a wide range of views, including some that are sexist or racist or anti-gay, it does not follow that the schools should remain neutral on these issues or that all individuals, regardless of their religious beliefs, can effectively perform the role of teacher. The court downplays the teacher's role, and describes sexual orientation equality in narrow terms, in order to avoid the conclusion that a particular religious teaching program does not adequately prepare its graduates to serve as teachers in the public school system. They do this, I suggest, because they think that the state fails to treat religious believers with equal respect when it repudiates their beliefs.

Chamberlain v. Surrey School District

In *Chamberlain v. Surrey School District #36*, a local school board rejected a proposal to include three books depicting same-sex parent families – *Belinda's Bouquet; Asha's Mum;* and *One Dad, Two Dads, Brown Dad, Blue Dads* – on the list of approved teaching resources for the primary grades.[13]

The appellants challenged the board's decision (the resolution) on two grounds, arguing (1) that the board had acted outside its mandate under the School Act of British Columbia,[14] which provided that "all schools ... must be conducted on strictly secular and non-sectarian principles," and (2) that the resolution violated the Charter of Rights. A majority of the Supreme Court of Canada, in a judgment written by Chief Justice McLachlin, held that the school board "acted outside the mandate of the *School Act* ... and [its] own regulation for approval of supplementary material" when it refused to include these three books on the list of approved teaching resources (*Chamberlain* 2002, para. 2).[15] Having reached this conclusion, it was unnecessary for the majority to consider the appellant's second argument that the resolution was contrary to the Charter of Rights.

McLachlin CJ accepted that religious considerations or concerns cannot be excluded from public decision making or, more particularly in this case, from the school board's deliberations concerning the curriculum. In her view, "because religion plays an important role in the life of many communities, the ... views [of parents and communities] will often be motivated by religious concerns. Religion is an integral aspect of people's lives, and cannot be left at the boardroom door" (*Chamberlain* 2002, para. 19). What the "secularism" requirement means, said McLachlin CJ, is that "the Board must conduct its deliberations on all matters, including approval of supplementary resources, in a manner that respects the views of all members of the school community" (para. 25). The board cannot "prefer the religious views of some people in its district to the views of other segments of the community," and it cannot "appeal to views that deny the equal validity of the lawful lifestyles of some in the school community" (para. 25).

The principal reason offered by the board for its refusal to approve the three books was that their use in the classroom "might teach values to children divergent to those taught at home, confusing the children with inconsistent values" (*Chamberlain* 2002, para. 52). The board argued that children at the kindergarten level did not yet have "the ability to resolve divergent moral lessons" (para. 53). McLachlin CJ acknowledged that parental views are important but held that they "cannot override the imperative placed on British Columbia public schools to mirror the diversity of the community and teach tolerance and understanding of difference."[16] She found that the board, in acting on the concerns of some parents about the morality of same-sex relationships, had failed to take seriously the right of same-sex parents, and the children of such relationships, to be equally respected within the public school system. The board in this case had "failed to proceed as required by the secular mandate of the *School Act* by letting the religious views of a certain part of the community trump the need to show equal respect for the values of other members of the community" (para. 71).

While McLachlin CJ insisted that the commitment in the School Act to a secular and non-sectarian education did not preclude the board from relying on religious considerations when making curriculum and other policy decisions, she also said that board support for one moral view over another, or for a moral view that denies the worth or value of another group or perspective, is contrary to the secularism requirement. She recognized that religious values cannot be wholly excluded from public life and, in particular, from the public schools. Yet, at the same time, she was uncomfortable with the imposition of religious/moral values, which she saw as inconsistent with the inclusive or pluralistic character of the public schools. In setting the curriculum, the board must act in a way that respects all individuals and perspectives: "[The secularism requirement] simply signals the need for educational decisions and policies, whatever their motivation, to respect the multiplicity of religious and moral views that are held by families in the school community" (*Chamberlain* 2002, para. 59). If by this McLachlin CJ meant that the schools should not favour one moral perspective over another in their teaching (that they should remain neutral on moral/religious issues), then religion (and indeed any value system) will have a role in board (and public) decision making only when it has no bite, only when it does not involve the repudiation of other values or viewpoints.

According to McLachlin CJ, public authorities committed to "values of accommodation, tolerance and respect for diversity" (*Chamberlain* 2002, para. 21) must ensure "that each group is given as much recognition as it can consistently demand while giving the same recognition to others" (para. 19). But if the exclusion (based on anti-gay/lesbian religious views) of the three books from primary classrooms amounts to the exclusion or rejection of gay and lesbian views or lifestyles, would not the inclusion of the books, by the same token, amount to the exclusion or rejection of the religious views of those parents who regard homosexuality as sinful?[17] Can the schools affirm the equal value of same-sex relationships without, in effect, repudiating the religious belief that homosexuality is immoral or unnatural?

McLachlin CJ thought that the inclusion of these books as teaching materials did not amount to the affirmation of same-sex relationships and the repudiation of contrary views. In her view, the books would simply "expose" children to non-traditional family forms and encourage them to tolerate these forms. According to the chief justice, what the School Act demanded was tolerance:

> The demand for tolerance cannot be interpreted as the demand to approve another person's beliefs or practices. When we ask people to be tolerant of others, we don't ask them to abandon their personal convictions. We merely ask them to respect the rights, values and ways of being of those who may not share those convictions. The belief that others are entitled to equal respect depends, not on the belief that their values are right, but only on the belief that they have a claim to equal respect regardless of whether they are right. (Chamberlain 2002, para. 66)

Tolerance requires only that we respect the right of each individual to make her/his own judgments – and, in this case, her/his choice of intimate partners or family arrangements. Teaching tolerance does not require that public actors, such as the schools, affirm a particular value or viewpoint. More specifically, it does not require that the schools teach or affirm that same-sex and opposite-sex relationships are equally valuable.

According to McLachlin CJ, the use of the three books in the kindergarten classes would encourage "discussion and understanding of all family groups." Quoting LaForest J in *Ross* (1996), she described the school as an "arena for the exchange of ideas" that "must, therefore, be premised upon principles of tolerance and impartiality so that all persons within the school environment feel equally free to participate" (*Chamberlain* 2002, para. 23). However, at the kindergarten level, there is no way simply to expose children to same-sex relationships as a social reality or to engage them in an open discussion about such relationships. Including these stories in the kindergarten curriculum will normalize same-sex relationships and, in effect, affirm their value.[18] To claim otherwise is to fail to recognize the authority of the school in the lives of students, particularly those in the primary grades.

Sometimes McLachlin CJ seemed to say that the reason for including these stories was to affirm the value of same-sex-parent families, not to all children (some of whose parents are deeply opposed to same-sex relationships) but only to the children from such families. She stressed the importance of providing "a nurturing and validating learning experience for all children, regardless of the types of families they come from" (*Chamberlain* 2002, para. 49). In her view, the school board should seek to affirm the personal circumstances of students from non-traditional families, without imposing any views or values on other students in the school community.

Yet it is not clear that affirmation can be segregated in this way, either practically or normatively. If the three books were used as teaching resources, then every student in the class would be exposed to them, regardless of her/his family situation or perspective. McLachlin CJ recognized this but was not troubled by it:

> The number of different family models in the community means that some children will inevitably come from families of which certain parents disapprove. Giving these children an opportunity to discuss their family models may expose other children to some cognitive dissonance. But such dissonance is neither avoidable nor noxious. Children encounter it every day in the public school system as members of a diverse student body. They see their classmates, and perhaps also their teachers, eating foods at lunch that they themselves are not permitted to eat, whether because of their parents' religious strictures or because of other moral beliefs. They see their classmates wearing clothes with features or brand labels which their parents have forbidden them to wear. And they see their classmates engaging in behaviour on the playground that their parents have told them not to engage in. The cognitive dissonance that results from such encounters is simply part of living in a diverse society. It is also part of growing up. Through such experiences, children come to realize that not all their values are shared by others. (para. 65)

Once again, McLachlin CJ's answer to concerns about "cognitive dissonance" is that the books will do no more than "expose" students to other perspectives or ways of life.[19] But the impact on a primary student of being exposed to these books in the classroom is not the same as discovering that some of her/his classmates have same-sex parents. The books would be used by teachers, and, as the court in *TWU* recognized, teachers are authority figures and role models.

More significantly, affirmation is not an individualized process. It is not particularly affirming to a child from a same-sex-parent family when a teacher says to her/his class that same-sex-parent families are fine for those who happen to be in them but may not be fine for anyone else or if a teacher informs the class that, while some in the community feel this is an acceptable or valuable form of family, others regard it as immoral and that both views are entitled to respect. If what children need is affirmation of the equal value of their family arrangements, then the school must do more than indicate that there are such families and that this may or may not be a good thing. We have increasingly come to recognize that our sense of self, of our value, is tied up with the recognition we receive from others. To be meaningful, the acceptance or affirmation of same-sex relationships must involve a public statement or indication that such relationships are normal and valuable.

McLachlin CJ seems to accept that the schools should affirm the equal value of same-sex-parent families. Yet, at the same time, she seems to believe that the schools should remain neutral on religious or moral matters – that the state should neither affirm nor deny the value or truth of a particular religious belief, including the belief that homosexuality is immoral.

If equality, including sexual orientation equality, is an important public value, it should be affirmed in the schools and should underpin classroom learning, even in the face of religiously based opposition from some parents. Indeed, the failure of the public schools to affirm clearly the equal value of same-sex relationships, when opposite-sex relationships are constantly represented and affirmed in books and lessons, will be experienced as exclusion, as discrimination. We cannot include or exclude all values in/ from the schools. If a school board or provincial government decides to advance or affirm a particular set of values, they must also reject other values – values that may be part of the religious commitment of some community members. Parents may have to live with the democratic consequence that their values are not included in the civic curriculum and perhaps even that their children are exposed to, or taught, views to which they are opposed.[20] Of course, when affirming certain values, the schools should be sensitive to the dissonance younger students may experience when they are taught something very different at home: but this is not the same thing as remaining neutral on questions of value.

Conclusion: Identity and Public Decision Making

In both *TWU* and *Chamberlain* the court sought to protect or affirm sexual orientation equality in the schools, without repudiating the religious view that homosexuality is immoral. In *TWU* the court held that the accreditation of the TWU program (and the inclusion of its graduates as public school teachers) would not compromise the affirmation or protection of sexual orientation equality in the schools. In *Chamberlain* the court assumed that the inclusion in the schools of three books depicting same-sex family relationships did not amount to the repudiation of the religious view that homosexuality is immoral. By selectively invoking a narrow conception of sexual orientation equality and a limited view of the role and authority of teachers, the court was able to "reconcile" the protection of sexual orientation equality with a commitment to religious neutrality or inclusion. While the court sometimes seemed to assume that sexual orientation equality required the affirmation by the schools of same-sex relationships, at other times it seemed to rely on a narrower conception of the right that emphasized tolerance rather than equal respect, non-interference rather than affirmation. And while sometimes the court seemed to recognize that the schools have a significant role in advancing public values, at other times it seemed to assume that the schools should remain neutral on issues of value and simply expose students to different views.

The court's reluctance to repudiate the religious belief that homosexuality is sinful rests, in part, on the view that religion is a deeply rooted part of the individual's identity that should be treated with equal respect.[21] Yet religious beliefs often have public implications. They cannot, therefore, be confined entirely to the private sphere and insulated from public debate and judgment. Moreover, the individual's commitment to these beliefs or values rests on her/his acceptance or assumption that they are true or right and that other views are false. If the state is to take meaningful action, it must prefer some values or moral judgments over others. While the schools may endeavour to respect "all cultures and family backgrounds," as McLachlin CJ proposes in *Chamberlain* (2002, para. 23), it cannot treat them all equally – as equally true or right.

The challenge for the courts is to articulate a richer or more complex conception of religious adherence. Religious belief is not simply a personal choice or preference, nor is it simply a fixed attribute. Indeed, the significance or value of religion, from the broader public perspective, may depend on its dual character as both a personal commitment to certain truths or values and as a deeply rooted part of the individual's cultural identity. Given the depth of the religious commitment of many citizens and the apparent difficulty in debating matters of religious belief, it makes sense for the state sometimes to treat religion as a matter of identity. It may be appropriate for the state, even when advancing an otherwise legitimate public policy, to make some accommodation for different religious practices by creating exceptions to rules concerning, for example, hard hats, police uniforms, and drug use, provided the accommodation has no direct or significant impact on others. However, religious beliefs that directly address the rights or interests of others, or the ordering of public institutions, cannot be insulated from public debate and action and must be treated as contestable and as open to public repudiation.

The public commitment to sexual orientation equality, expressed in federal and provincial human rights laws, and recognized under the Canadian Charter of Rights and Freedoms, should be affirmed in the public schools. This affirmation will involve nothing less than a repudiation of the religious view that homosexuality is sinful.

19

Law, Sexuality, and Morality in the United States

JASON PIERCESON

The legal and constitutional framework for gay and lesbian rights in the United States has only recently begun to develop in a positive direction and still leaves much of the lives of gay and lesbian citizens unprotected by the Constitution and unsupported by the law. While many factors have contributed to the creation of this situation, including institutional and social mobilization factors, this chapter focuses on the role of political and religious norms on legal developments. In particular, I focus on the potency of libertarian moralism in US political culture.

The positive change that has occurred can be linked to a judicial defence of libertarian notions of freedom, evident in the decriminalization of same-sex sexual behaviour, especially through state courts. However, when calls for gay and lesbian rights and equality reflect less libertarian and more positive notions of freedom, such as the demand for state recognition of same-sex relationships, courts have been more, though not completely, limited in their ability to expand rights. Intertwined with this dynamic is the conservative morality in US political culture, which is particularly harmful to gay rights claims the more these claims are removed from the protection of libertarianism.

Religious and Moral Roots of Anti-Gay Politics and Litigation

Religion affects the legal status of sexuality in the United States primarily in two, often mutually reinforcing, ways. First, religiously derived anti-gay rhetoric and policy preferences have resonated and continue to resonate in policy discussions. Whenever rights for sexual minorities are on the public agenda, legally or politically, conservative religious activists and church leaders make public statements condemning homosexuality as a sin and lobby courts and public officials against legal protections for sexual minorities, dismissing protective laws and policies as "special rights" and the perverted demands of the "gay agenda." For instance, from the start of the national political discussion on same-sex marriage, organized religious groups have been at the forefront of political and legal lobbying against same-sex marriage recognition, even if some denominations are beginning to rethink their position on homosexuality (see Cahill 1997; Kirkpatrick 1993).

A second factor inhibiting rights gains for sexual minorities is that opponents are moving away from a morality argument and more widely embracing arguments that point to the negative effects of pro-gay rights policies and legal protections on religious freedom. Particularly in a polity that privileges free speech and "religious exercise" rhetoric over equality demands, this is an effective tool. It risks neutralizing the rights claims of sexual minorities with the rights claims of religious individuals and groups, who are routinely portrayed as at risk of political and cultural marginalization. The constraint of anti-gay religious perspectives can be seen in recent attempts to enact federal anti-discrimination legislation. President Bush, threatening a veto of the Employment Non-Discrimination Act (ENDA), emphasized the fear that this type of statute, if enacted, would interfere with the free exercise of religion by criminalizing religiously based anti-gay perspectives.[1]

Religion is not the sole source of anti-gay politics: religious claims are reinforced by neoconservative arguments about family decline and moral crisis. These arguments play a role in judicial deference to legislative positions in same-sex marriage litigation. As will be shown, state governments defend themselves against same-sex marriage lawsuits by claiming they have an important interest in anchoring the family and by drawing from neoconservative policy assumptions that the heterosexual nuclear family is an essential building block of society (see Himmelfarb 1996).

Despite this tactical shift, anti-same-sex marriage politics is still anti-gay politics, as it has been from the start. From Hawaii to Vermont and beyond, conservative religious and cultural advocates have grounded their primary opposition to relationship equality in terms of the sinfulness and "unnaturalness" of homosexuality, and this has been linked to explicit notions of majoritarian Christian power. As stated by Jonathan Goldberg-Hiller (2002, 45-46), "when these [same-sex] 'perversions' are said to be protected by 'special rights' ... a fusion of voters into an outraged majority has been driven to the polls in the quest for political purification and the restoration of political sovereignty." This is particularly powerful in a polity such as the United States, with its easy access to majoritarian institutions like the popular referendum process. This impulse overrides traditional theological divisions, like those between (and among) conservative Protestants, Roman Catholics, and Mormons. And this helps to explain why many amendments prevent any legal recognition of same-sex couples. At the heart of the campaigns for their approval have been religiously rooted arguments that state policy must not condone same-sex relationships in any form because of their intrinsic sinfulness or social and moral disruptiveness.

In the legal arena, these arguments are either toned down or not presented at all; instead, advocates focus on doctrinal arguments opposing relationship equality and neoconservative arguments about the family as an essential institution. "Religious freedom" arguments are being offered to courts more frequently now, though so far they have not been picked up by judges ruling against relationship equality claims.[2] There is still enough jurisprudence to deny these claims without utilizing this new argument. In fact, in 2007, the Maryland Court of Appeals was presented with this argument through friend of the court briefs, but it avoided invoking the religious freedom argument in ruling against same-sex marriage claimants (*Conaway v. Deane* 2007).

The dynamic that Goldberg-Hiller describes is more evident in the political arena. In 2006, voters in Wisconsin approved a state constitutional amendment banning all forms of same-sex relationship recognition. Supporters of the amendment toned town the anti-gay rhetoric in the public campaign, but they waged a Christian "purification" campaign through church networks. In particular, the Roman Catholic Church was highly active in supporting the amendment, leveraging the power of the state's 1.7 million Catholics. In one recorded homily played in every parish, Bishop Robert Morlino of Madison stated that same-sex marriage would result in the collapse of "society in due time." This was not simply an argument about religious freedom but, rather, a clear message identifying a threat to society itself. This is consistent with the Roman Catholic Church's position on homosexuality as being a "moral disorder" (Davidoff 2006; Imrie 2006; USCCB 2006b).

James Morone (2003) has extensively documented the role that religion and religious fervour has played in American political development, particularly in the framing of political insiders and outsiders. Because of the openness and relative mobility of American society, and in the absence of a distinct ethnically based American identity, "Americans measure one another by a vaguely delineated, highly moralistic code of conduct." This creates a dynamic in which "there's always a group who seems a dubious us, who endanger our special status as a city on a hill" (12). Even though Morone does not focus on sexual minorities, sexual outsiders clearly have been the recipients of this outsider ostracism. Sexual minorities have long been painted as a threat to the moral fabric and social stability and cohesion in the United States.

In the US congressional debate over the Defense of Marriage Act in 1996, supporters of the law painted sexual minorities as a threat to society and its institutions. Republican representative (now senator) Tom Coburn of Oklahoma cited his constituents' belief that "homosexuality is immoral, that it is based on perversion."[3] Republican representative David Funderburk of North Carolina linked the issue of immorality to social destruction: "As the Family Research Council points out: Homosexuality has been discouraged in all cultures because it is inherently wrong and harmful to individuals, families and societies."[4] Republican representative Robert Barr took this line of reasoning further, arguing that demands for same-sex marriage were part of a plot by gays and lesbians to destroy the country. "[Same-sex marriage] is an issue that is being used to divide America. It is part of a deliberate, coldly calculated power move to confront the basic social institutions on which our country not only was founded but has prospered and will continue to prosper."[5]

In addition to this moralistic constraint, a powerful strain of libertarianism mitigates against progress on sexuality-based equality in the law. American political discourse and jurisprudence have been strongly influenced by negative notions of freedom. Even though versions of liberalism that emphasize more positive notions of freedom are present in American political discourse, rights tend to be defined negatively, in terms of freedom from government. The problem for sexual minorities is that strong notions of negative freedom tend to privatize gay politics, preventing discussion of full citizenship for sexual minorities by divorcing sex from full personhood and dismissing calls for positive state and societal intervention. Arguments for a fuller and more affirming liberalism can certainly be found among rights advocates and legal interveners, but these arguments are overshadowed by the more dominant negative liberalism. When state courts moved against sodomy laws, there was little negative backlash from the political arena because these decisions usually relied on libertarian notions of privacy. However, the intense backlash to same-sex marriage litigation partially derives from the fact that same-sex marriage requires affirmative recognition of same-sex relationships.[6]

Even supporters of gay rights feel the need to frame the political discussion in terms of negative rights. During the DOMA debate in Congress, progressive Democrat Ron Wyden revealed the limits of the frame that he himself adopted or at least felt obliged to articulate: "Not once has a gay or lesbian Oregonian come to me and asked that the Federal Government endorse their lifestyle. They simply ask to be left alone. In this regard, they are very similar to what I hear from ranchers and small business owners and fisherman and scores of other citizens."[7] American libertarian liberalism is a sticking point for full inclusion and citizenship for sexual minorities, and it powerfully combines with moralism to create legal and political stagnation.

Dominant Legal Frameworks Interpreting Gay Existence

Until quite recently, sexual minorities were far outside of the law's protection. As homosexuality became visible and was associated with a distinct group around the turn into the twentieth century, legal regulation intensified. Through the early decades of that century, sodomy laws moved from targeting a range of deviant sexual behaviour to regulation of the same-sex variety (Eskridge 1999). These laws were a powerful tool in countering political and social organizing by sexual minorities, supporting intensified police attacks on gay bars, sting operations on cruise areas, and official hostility towards sexual minorities at all levels, and in all branches, of government. There was simply no positive space in the law for visible sexual minorities.

This hostile climate reached its peak in the 1950s, during what has been described as the "Lavender Scare." Sexual minorities were seen as dire threats to the nation, along with communists. The two groups were often linked in public discourse, and the powers of the national security state were applied to an increasingly visible gay and lesbian population energized by the publication of the Kinsey Report in 1948 and by the community-creating effects of the Second World War (Johnson 2004). In the words of a 1950 Senate report, "sex perverts, like all other persons who by their overt acts violate moral codes and laws and the accepted standards of conduct, must be treated as *transgressors and dealt with accordingly*" (United States Senate 1950, para. 8; emphasis added).

At the same time, courts and legal elites provided a fractional opening for the emerging social and political movements of sexual minorities in the gradual decoupling of morality and the law. In 1957, the American Law Institute (ALI) called for the decriminalization of private, consensual sexual behaviour between persons of the same gender.[8] To be sure, sodomy laws remained on the books for decades after this, but legal thinking was evolving.

The US Supreme Court was not the same ally for sexual minorities that it was for racial minorities in the mid-twentieth century, but it indirectly assisted the nascent gay rights movement through its relatively new obscenity and First Amendment jurisprudence of the 1950s. The early movement's main form of communication was through magazines such as *ONE*, a mix of culture and politics. In 1958, the Supreme Court ruled as unconstitutional a postal seizure of copies of the magazine on grounds of obscenity simply on the basis of its discussion of homosexuality. Relying on the landmark obscenity decision of the court in *Roth v. U.S.* (1957), this one-sentence ruling repudiated the postmaster's actions and carved out space for a wide range of controversial material under the First Amendment, and it removed a potentially devastating barrier to political organizing (*One v. Oleson* 1958).

Additionally, a few lower court decisions placed restrictions on police harassment of gay bars and cruise areas – often the only social outlet in an era of intense social stigma.[9] This allowed for a greater degree of social organization, which sometimes led to political organizing. In the 1960s, two decisions from the DC Court of Appeals weakened the federal ban on gay employees, a policy that was a staple of the official hostility towards sexual minorities (*Scott v. Macy* 1965; *Norton v. Macy* 1969).

However, the Supreme Court's hostility towards gay existence remained throughout this period. Its 1967 ruling in *Boutilier v. INS* (1967) affirmed the power of the federal government to deport sexual minorities as "psychopathic personalities." The decision was not unanimous; indeed, Justice Douglas saw the government policy as irrational and in violation of individual liberty. But this notion of gay personhood as being worthy of constitutional protection was not close to prevailing on the high court. Indeed, Joyce Murdoch and Deb Price describe this case as the point at which "the US Supreme Court joined the government war against homosexuals" (2001, 134). Indeed, the Supreme Court did not begin to accept the notion of full legal and citizenship status for sexual minorities until 1996. Even then, as will be seen, the court refused to place sexuality within its most robust jurisprudential frame.

By the 1970s, the statutes at the centre of the legal marginalization of sexual minorities – sodomy laws – were being challenged as unconstitutional and unsound. About half of the states repealed their sodomy laws by the early 1980s, in part because of the ALI recommendations years before, in part because of activist lobbying. Litigation was pursued in Virginia, but the court turned away the case and let a pro-sodomy law decision stand in *Doe v. Commonwealth's Attorney* (1976) (Shilts 1993, 283-84). The debate behind the scenes of the court over the case indicates that judicial sentiment for overturning these laws was emerging, but when the court next addressed the same issue a decade later in a Georgia case the argument for gay personhood was again defeated. In upholding the constitutionality of sodomy laws in *Bowers v. Hardwick* in 1986, the court refused to apply its rich privacy jurisprudence to sexual minorities and held that morality alone was enough to keep the laws, and their accompanying limits on a wide range of gay and lesbian existence, on the books.

Not surprisingly, the focus of sodomy law challenges shifted to state courts in the period following the *Bowers* defeat. This was a period in which a number of state judiciaries were taking up the 1950s and '60s liberal Warren court's agenda in the face of an increasingly conservative federal judiciary, a shift referred to as the "new judicial federalism." By the time that sodomy laws were finally declared unconstitutional in the 2003 *Lawrence v. Texas* ruling by the US Supreme Court, numerous state high courts had already done so using privacy arguments under state constitutions. This was most likely in states where privacy and equality jurisprudence were robust, but it was also possible where progressive judges were willing to apply a more inclusive privacy jurisprudence. The most ironic example was the invalidation of the Georgia statute upheld in *Bowers* by the state's high court in *Powell v. Georgia* (1998).[10]

The US Supreme Court's *Lawrence* decision was not, in that sense, breaking radically new ground, but it did mark a new era in the legal framework of lesbian and gay existence in the United States. Justice Anthony Kennedy's plurality opinion in the case was remarkable for several reasons. It repudiated the tone of the *Bowers* opinion and concurrences. It disassociated moral judgments from the law and used language to describe gay and lesbian individuals and their relationships in affirming terms. So striking was this tone that Justice Antonin Scalia claimed in a dissent that the opinion appeared to open the door for court recognition of same-sex marriage.

Although the language of *Lawrence* marked a significant shift in the court's acceptance of gay personhood, US federal law and policy was still denying status and personhood to sexual minorities. The ban on federal employment was lifted in the early 1970s, the ban on military service is still in effect, and immigration law continues to be largely exclusionary. Valid same-sex marriages performed in other countries, such as Canada, Spain, Belgium, South Africa, and the Netherlands, are not recognized under US law, and non-American same-sex partners of citizens do not have the same legal path to citizenship through marriage as do similarly situated opposite-sex couples. Sexual minorities are also not fully covered in a range of federal laws, the opposition to their inclusion being reinforced by religious conservatives, both inside and outside the legislative arena, who frame their resistance, in part, by speaking of the supposed threat these people pose to religious freedom.[11]

Equality and Anti-Discrimination Law and Jurisprudence

In the mid-twentieth century, the Supreme Court began to readdress the issue of the meaning of the Constitution's equal protection clause. By the 1940s, a relatively liberal court began to see this clause in the Fourteenth Amendment as a more stringent requirement on states, at times placing the court in an adversarial relationship with policy makers. As Evan Gerstmann (1999, 37) has claimed, the equal protection clause was the "constitutional equivalent of the atomic bomb."

The court developed a three-tiered framework for analyzing equal protection claims. Race (and a few other categories) was placed in the most protected category, gender was placed in a middle category, and most other dimensions, including sexuality, were placed in the lowest tier. These tiers are mostly indicators of the amount of deference that the court will show towards a discriminatory legislative enactment. For example, racial classifications trigger a highly non-deferential "compelling interest" test that seldom allows for discrimination. Discrimination on the basis of sexuality, however, triggers a very deferential "rational basis" test, which essentially means that a wide range of policy rationales is seen as legitimate and as justifying discrimination.[12]

The equal protection clause has been used to favourable effect on some sexuality cases. In *Romer v. Evans* (1996), the Supreme Court invalidated Colorado's Amendment 2, which forbad local jurisdictions from including sexual orientation in statutes and ordinances outlawing discrimination in the workplace and in public accommodations. Justice Kennedy applied only the rational basis test but found that "animus" or dislike of a group alone is not a rational basis. Justice Scalia, in dissent, argued that it was perfectly appropriate to express dislike of a group through statutes and constitutional provisions and that majoritarian morality was a rational basis. Still, the fact that a majority sided with him did not portend a systematic shift in scrutiny.

Though First Amendment freedoms of speech and association have been successful bases of gay and lesbian rights litigation, strongly libertarian interpretations have undercut them in notable cases. In *Hurley v. Irish-American Gay, Lesbian, and Bisexual Group of Boston* (1995), the Supreme Court overturned a decision by the Massachusetts high court, which held that the organizers of South Boston's St. Patrick's Day parade violated the state's sexual orientation-inclusive public accommodation anti-discrimination law. The Massachusetts court emphasized the public nature of the parade, with the use of public streets and police, as a way to bring the anti-discrimination law to bear, while the Supreme Court ruled unanimously that the right of parade organizers to control the content of the parade was nearly absolute and certainly not restricted by the anti-discrimination law. As Justice Souter stated for the court, the issue "boils down to the choice of a speaker not to propound a particular point of view, and that choice is presumed to lie beyond the government's power to control" (574-75). This decision was followed by the Supreme Court's pronouncement in *Boy Scouts of America v. Dale* (2000), in which it upheld James Dale's dismissal from the Scouts for being openly gay. While the New Jersey courts condemned the actions of the Boy Scouts, the Supreme Court narrowly upheld their actions as constitutionally protected, despite court precedents on race and gender questions allowing the application of state anti-discrimination laws to private associations. In their own defence, the Boy Scouts asserted their right to insist on adherence to what amounted to a morally driven portrayal of the heterosexual family, and the court found this sufficient rationale for exclusion.

Marriage Litigation and Backlash

Apart from the federal domain, US law has, in recent decades, reflected an increasing recognition of the status of lesbian and gay families through the recognition of same-sex relationships and parenting responsibilities. Relationship recognition has not proliferated as extensively in US law as it has in Canadian law. In Canada, same-sex marriage was legalized nationally in 2005 after extensive legalization by appeal courts in most provinces. Nevertheless, the United States has seen an often quiet, court-driven legal revolution spreading across jurisdictions.

As of early 2010, same-sex relationships are legally recognized in more than fourteen of the fifty states. Same-sex marriage is legal in Massachusetts, Iowa, Connecticut, Vermont, New Hampshire (the last three all "upgrades" from civil unions), plus the District of Columbia. Civil unions, or domestic partnerships equivalent to marriage arrangements, exist in New Jersey, California, Oregon, Washington, and Nevada. Partial domestic partnership regimes exist in Colorado, Hawaii, Maine, Wisconsin, Maryland, and Rhode Island. Two states (New York and Maryland) recognize marriages performed elsewhere. Partnership recognition has thus proliferated in the Northeast and on the West Coast, with a foothold in the Midwest, and much of this is connected to litigation.

Several factors have contributed to widening recognition of couples and families. The lesbian baby boom, the family and care considerations that stemmed from the AIDS crisis, and continuing discrimination faced by same-sex couples, particularly in the context of a welfare state that ties benefits to marital status, brought the issue of same-sex marriage to the front of the activist movement in the late 1980s and early 1990s. Many of these issues were brought to public attention, especially in the LGBT community, by the Sharon Kowalski case from the 1980s and early 1990s, in which legal guardianship for lesbian partners was challenged by the family of the partner who was incapacitated by injury. Even though the case ended favourably for the lesbian couple, it illustrated the legally tenuous nature of same-sex relationships. Profound changes in the cultural meaning of marriage, particularly the move towards companionate marriage away from more traditional economic and procreative notions, allowed gay couples to view themselves as appropriately asking for the same love-affirming institution that heterosexuals had created. Changes in divorce law in the 1960s helped to define marriage as a legal contract, open to negotiation between two individuals, rather than as a permanent, fixed, morally and religiously framed institution essential for social stability (*Re Guardianship of Kowalski* 1991).

Same-sex marriage became the focus of litigation, and backlash was generated from 1993 on, when, in *Baehr v. Lewin*, the Supreme Court of Hawaii ruled that the state's ban on same-sex marriage was likely a violation of the state Constitution. The litigation illustrated the opportunities created in a federalized court system, and the backlash of course demonstrated the force of religious conservatism even in a state not widely seen as a bastion for the religious right.

The first major victory for same-sex relationship claimants that stuck oc-curred in Vermont. This litigation was carefully orchestrated and planned, unlike the Hawaii litigation, and it included a grassroots political effort to support the expected positive outcome in the courts. The decision by the Vermont Supreme Court was the clearest statement by judges in any state to that point about the unconstitutionality of excluding same-sex couples from protection and recognition, though the court was divided about a remedy, reflecting a concern over judicial power and democratic accountability. De-spite vocal moralistic opposition, the legislature took the legal mandate of equality seriously and enacted the more politically palatable civil union law (Pierceson 2005, chaps. 7-9).

The decision of the Massachusetts Supreme Judicial Court in 2003 in favour of same-sex marriage was both a tremendous advance for advocates of relationship equality and a further spur to the conservative backlash. It was an unqualified judicial declaration of the equal rights of same-sex couples, and it coincided with a high-profile same-sex marriage victory in Canada. *Lawrence v. Texas* had also been decided earlier in the year and was cited by the Massachusetts court.[13]

A powerful political backlash now gained momentum. The spread of defence-of-marriage statutes continued across most states and was now ac-companied by a new formidable weapon in the form of amendments to state constitutions approved by popular referendum. By 2009, twenty-nine states had such amendments, including nineteen sweeping bans on marriage, civil unions, and domestic partnerships. The year 2004 was the high point of the backlash, with voters in eleven states approving constitutional bans on same-sex marriage by wide margins. Media coverage of these ballot initia-tives connected them with higher turnout among religious voters in key states such as Ohio, and many commentators made the case that this con-tributed to the re-election of George W. Bush. This has been disputed in subsequent studies, but the perceptions remained unchecked and were an important lever for Christian conservatives. In 2006, the tide ebbed some-what, with seven constitutional bans enacted and with some approved by much narrower margins, in addition to the failure of a ballot initiative in Arizona. It is clear, however, that religious views on sexuality and marriage are the driving force behind these ballot initiatives.[14]

For grassroots social movement organizations such as those that form the core of the religious right, these initiatives are relatively easy to place on the ballot and are a vehicle for responding to or anticipating judicial developments. Rights claims by sexual minorities fare poorly when the "scope of the conflict" is expanded, and popular referenda have usually disadvantaged advocates of minority protective policies (Haider-Markel and Meier 1996, 332-49; Haider-Markel, Querze, and Lindaman 2007, 304-14). The referendum process can empower opponents of same-sex marriage in progressive states, as demonstrated by the enactment of Proposition 8 in 2008, where a relatively close vote (52 to 48 percent) led to the revocation of a right to same-sex marriage declared by the state high court earlier that year. As developments in Maine in 2009 reflect, referenda are used not only to overturn judicial pronouncements of same-sex marriage rights but also to nullify legislative enactments.

Nevertheless, the backlash has not yet slowed the gradual increase of statewide recognition of same-sex relationships, in part on the basis of marriage-focused challenges. The New Jersey Supreme Court handed down a Vermont-style decision in 2006, and the legislature subsequently enacted a civil union law. In 2008, the Connecticut high court mandated same-sex marriage beyond the state's already-existing civil union law. In 2009, Vermont and New Hampshire also enacted marriage statutes when civil union laws were in place not through courts but through legislative enactment. A same-sex marriage law was passed by the Maine legislature and signed by the governor, but, as mentioned above, it was soon nullified in a relatively narrow vote (53 to 47 percent) by voters in this mostly rural state. It should be noted that this was a citizen "veto" rather than a constitutional amendment, thus leaving open the possibility of future legislation. In 2010, Maryland's attorney general issued an advisory opinion indicating that marriages performed would be recognized, and, in the same year, the District of Columbia enacted marriage legislation. This has secured the standing of the Northeastern region of the United States as the law and policy leader on same-sex relationship recognition.

This state of affairs is perhaps why the decision of the Iowa Supreme Court in 2009 mandating same-sex marriage in that state was such a surprise for so many. Same-sex marriage soon became legal in the state, and the policy appears to be secure, given Democratic control of the state and a constitution that is not easily amended. Arguably, this decision spurred the developments in Vermont, New Hampshire, and Maine already discussed. Thus, litigation has the power to shape policy development both inside and outside the borders of a state where litigation is initiated.

Indeed, judges in progressive states are increasingly convinced that same-sex couples are entitled to recognition and legal protection. The decisions in

Vermont, New Jersey, and Iowa were unanimous. Even high court losses on marriage challenges in New York, Washington State, and Maryland were close votes. In all the state high court rulings over marriage since the 1993 *Baehr* judgment in Hawaii, judges wishing to challenge the prohibition on same-sex marriage in their states outnumber those who would uphold the bans by a forty-to-twenty-one margin.

Success or failure for same-sex marriage advocates often hinges on judges' views of whether a state's interest in procreation is a legitimate reason to continue discrimination against same-sex couples under the deferential rational basis test. This "procreation justification" was first questioned by the courts in Hawaii, and it has been challenged by judges when mandating equal treatment for same-sex couples.

There is not a strong and sustained trend in the direction of state court recognition of same-sex marriage claims, and public support has only recently broken through the 40 percent threshold that has been substantially breached in Canada and several European countries.[15] However, even on this most contentious of issues, jurisprudence is in flux. Despite the formidable backlash, litigation for same-sex marriage in the United States has had positive consequences. Indeed, it is difficult to imagine the domestic partnership, civil union, and marriage policies without the leverage and discursive effects of litigation in marriage cases.

Evolution of Family Law

Much less public and even more judicially driven change has taken place in family law beyond the question of marriage, and nowhere more strikingly than in custody and adoption cases. Generally following the legal doctrine of resolving child custody issues in "the best interest of the child," more and more state judges have facilitated same-sex parenting and adoption by allowing gay or lesbian parents to retain custody of children after a heterosexual divorce or by sanctioning second-parent adoption. The hostility that sexual minorities have faced, and still face, has prevented statutory frameworks for gay and lesbian parenting from developing. Only four states, for example, authorize second-parent adoption by statute. The absence of favourable policy has, of course, forced gay fathers and especially lesbians to go to court to protect or establish and maintain their legal ties to their children, particularly in response to the rapid increase in lesbian and gay parenting in the past thirty years. Indeed, a highly coordinated litigation strategy developed in the late 1970s and 1980s to assist individual litigants not only by offering legal services but also by providing a framework for

policy coordination through centralized documentation of favourable decisions and through the publicizing of evolving research proving the validity
of lesbian and gay parenting. This was done largely to educate judges and to
create the possibility of cross-citation (Polikoff 2000, 318-19). One marker
of change is that courts have allowed second-parent adoptions in seventeen
states, and many states have moved away from withdrawing custody of children only on the basis of the sexuality of a parent. Judicial discrimination
against lesbian and gay parents continues in many places, and conservatives
have been mobilizing as strongly as ever around the spectre of lesbian and
gay parents. Since 1995, three states (Nebraska, Utah, and Mississippi) have
enacted statutes barring gays and lesbians from adopting, joining Florida's
ban, which was enacted in 1977 during an early backlash to gay visibility (see
Polikoff 2000; NGLTF 2010a, 2010b, 2010c; Turner 2002). Nevertheless, the
steady spread of favourable court rulings has remained undiminished.

Conclusion

On the issues of sodomy law elimination, same-sex marriage, and lesbian
and gay parenting, state courts have played a vital role in expanding the
legal protections for sexual minorities. In fact, except for *Romer* and *Lawrence*, most positive judicial change has come from state courts. This point
is often lost in debates about the role of the courts in achieving social
change, which often focus solely on the US Supreme Court. While courts
have not achieved change on their own, or in isolation from rights-seeking
advocacy on other fronts, they have been vitally useful in their capacity to
fuel policy innovation. Sexual minorities in the United States have been
able to frame new arguments in the legal setting that have spilled over into
the political arena, and they have used courts as protectors of their rights
in the face of legislative inaction and hostility. Courts have proven to be
imperfect vehicles, but they have proven to be the institutions most amenable to the legal claims of sexual minorities. They have often done so in the
face of majoritarian, moralistic opposition. As Susan Mezey (2007, 238)
states, "the portrayal of federal and state court judges as judicial activists
has often been deserved and, in such cases, has been essential to advancing
the interests of the gay community."[16]

Some state courts have been willing not only to favour egalitarianism
over libertarianism in gay rights cases but also to push back against the
construction of sexual minorities as immoral outsiders. The federal judiciary has continued to hew more closely to a libertarian approach, but even
within that frame it has privileged anti-gay religious perspectives over equal

protection and other constitutional values. Current justices seem concerned that their predecessors have stifled religious expression through their strict notions of the separation of church and state and wish to bring religion back more robustly to the public square.

For the conservative majority in the 1995 case, *Rosenberger v. The University of Virginia*, Justice Kennedy saw the university's decision to deny funding to a Christian magazine as illegitimate "viewpoint discrimination," arguing that the "government must abstain from regulating speech when the specific motivating ideology or the opinion or perspective of the speaker is the rationale of the restriction" (829). This went even further than the court majority in *Hurley*. Not only did freedom of expression trump egalitarian values, but in *Rosenberger* the court set aside concerns about the constitutional prohibition on religious establishment. Justice David Souter's dissent pointed out that "using public funds for the direct subsidization of preaching of the word is categorically forbidden under the Establishment Clause" (868), but the majority was unmoved. It is not hard to imagine that the legal status of sexual minorities risks harm from a court more robustly bringing religion back into the public sphere, as long as most Christian American faithful adhere to churches that condemn homosexuality.

The relationship between law, sexuality, and heavily religiously based morality has thus created a complicated and challenging situation for the expansion of rights and equality for sexual minorities that continues to this day. State courts have been effective tools for challenging libertarian moralism, but litigation alone cannot create change in a polity in which sexual minorities face such entrenched legal, political, religious, and cultural nonrecognition and are still seen as outsiders and threats. There is no question that the status of sexual minorities has improved, but entrenched cultural factors that are reflected in law and policy continue to impede progress.

CONCLUSION

20

Cross-Border Parallels at the Political Intersection of Sexuality and Religion

DAVID RAYSIDE

The space in which religion and sexuality intersect seems so different on the two sides of the 49th parallel. In Canada, many claims for the public recognition of sexual diversity have been formally settled, and the intensity of religiously based opposition has subsided. For decades, American activists have secured pioneering victories on individual rights and relationship recognition, but what we find today remains a patchwork of gains and losses on terrain fiercely fought over. The organizational strength of the American religious right, and the sheer size of religiously faithful constituencies in the United States, mean that the struggle over sexuality remains a recurrent – if not constant – feature of political life. This seems even more likely to be the American destiny because issues related to homosexuality and gender nonconformity are so regularly in the foreground during struggles over the separation of church and state – struggles that seem so interminable.

This portrayal seems to dovetail easily with arguments by Seymour Martin Lipset and, more recently, Michael Adams, which hold that social, cultural, and political contrasts between Canada and the United States run deep (Lipset 1990; Adams 2003). Policy changes recognizing sexual diversity, in fact, seem to position Canada more and more in the same camp as the most progressive of Western European states and further away than ever from the United States.

This view has important elements of truth. Clyde Wilcox and I opened this volume by recognizing that some arguments about Canadian-American contrasts ring true. As several authors in this collection point out, the power of religion in US politics has slowed the pace of policy change on sexuality issues, as have the limits on constitutional guarantees and the complexity of the political process. Social anxiety and fears about moral decay are more widespread among Americans than Canadians, reinforcing unease about changes in family structure even among the secular. Despite mixed policy records that frustrate Christian conservatives, the Republican Party retains a large number of legislators prepared to exploit such unease, while its Canadian counterpart (the federal Conservative Party) can now do little more than nibble at the edges of such issues. American Christian conservatives regularly insist on the place of faith in the public square and pursue such claims in legislatures and courtrooms across the country. In doing so, they routinely use homosexuality and gender non-conformity to mobilize their constituency. They continue to do so in terms that are sometimes starkly hateful, and lessons from the 2008 election in California and the 2009 marriage referendum in Maine suggest that they continue to have clout. That can hardly be said of the Canadian equivalent of the American religious right, despite its organizational development and political skill.

This, however, is far from the whole story. First off, activist challenges to policy discrimination against sexual minorities in Canada would not have been as successful as they have been were it not for the Charter of Rights and Freedoms and the readiness of courts to include sexual orientation within its equality provisions. This does not mean that "activist" judges have ruled in isolation from other social and political changes. In the vast majority of their equity-related cases, their rulings have coincided with shifts in public opinion. In matters of sexual diversity, and to some extent faith, elected politicians have been content enough to leave issues for the courts to resolve. This has cleared the path for courts to act, a path that they have embarked upon cautiously. It took about a decade after the key equality provision of the Charter (section 15) came into effect for the Supreme Court of Canada to declare that sexual orientation was indeed covered by it (*Egan v. Canada*); it took another four to declare that this coverage extended to the rights and obligations of gay and lesbian couples. At each of those junctures, the court's ruling was backed by a clear majority of the general population (by the time of the Ontario Appeal Court's ruling on same-sex marriage in 2003, over 50 percent of Canadians supported it). In these and other sexual orientation cases, activist claims have been boosted by the fact that they have typically confronted cases of explicit and direct discrimination, not the kind of indirect discrimination so often at stake in equity cases.

I urge caution in setting up Canada and the United States as starkly con-trasted also because there are important areas in which Canadian public policy and institutional practice have moved only slowly. Schooling is one area that is marked by complacent inaction at all levels or, at best, patchy implementation of ostensibly inclusive policies. Discriminatory censorship of erotic material is another area in which Canada can stake out no higher ground than the United States. On the US side, schools may well be no more inclusive overall than they are in Canada, but they are no worse, and there has been a noticeably longer history of widespread activism aimed at mak-ing them better. With regard to some aspects of parenting, same-sex couples on the American side have more choices than do those on the Canadian side. Legal and policy responses to transgender activism are also no more advanced in Canada than in the United States, though within each there are a few states or provinces that have begun to act.

Canadian policy and law have moved further than their American counterparts in requiring accommodation to faith practices in the public square (e.g., allowing kirpans to be worn by Sikhs in school), but constitu-tional prohibitions on discrimination based on sexual orientation would act as a barrier to some faith-based claims of a right to discriminate on that ground. No such country-wide barrier exists in the United States since there the Constitution is still being interpreted in ways that allow discrimination based on sexual orientation. However, the judicial treatment of the "free exercise" clause has been more restrained in creating protections for faith practices than have court rulings in Canada. The end result may not be much different in cases where religious rights and sexual diversity claims conflict, though much uncertainty remains.

In both Canada and the United States, there are similar questions that are not yet resolved, some of them perhaps incapable of permanent resolution. Schooling again is an example, where debates persist over how much recog-nition should be given to, on the one hand, homosexuality and gender vari-ance and, on the other hand, Christian traditions and practices associated with other religions. Neither country is free of unsettling questions about the role of faith in the public square. Is faith to be construed as an entirely private matter? Under what circumstances and to what degree should state authority support faith-based institutions? Do hate speech codes risk infrin-ging dangerously on free speech and, in particular, on the rights of faith communities? To what extent do religious authorities have rights to dis-criminate on the basis of sexual diversity? Does the historical role and con-tinuing demographic dominance of Christianity give it special standing in the public arena? Does a thoroughgoing commitment to multiculturalism require full accommodation to the religious practice of minorities, whether Christian, Jewish, Islamic, Sikh, Hindu, or Buddhist, even when such practice supports discrimination based on sexual diversity? All such issues become more complex as waves of immigration to North America diversify the religious complexion of each country.

Shifts in Common

Public Attitudes
When I first wrote about public attitudes towards homosexuality in Canada, the United States, and Britain in 1988, shifts towards more inclusive attitudes on questions related to gay rights coexisted with tenacious moral disapproval (Rayside and Bowler 1988). What has happened in the intervening two decades is a continuing movement towards more positive views, this time accompanied by a very substantial reduction in the proportion of both Americans and Canadians who express disapproval of homosexuality. It is hard to find any issue area on which the shift in opinion has been as radical. It is also hard to find any other area in which generational differences are as dramatic, which naturally leads to the prediction that liberalization will continue.

These changes have occurred in both countries and across all religious traditions. Roman Catholics in both Canada and the United States have long demonstrated a willingness in their everyday lives to sidestep Vatican strictures on reproduction, and opinion surveys indicate a similar tendency in their attitudes towards lesbian and gay rights. Lefebvre and Breton's contribution to this volume indicates that this is most spectacularly evident in Quebec, but there are subtler indications of more widespread dissent among Catholics across the continent. In both Canada and the United States, Catholics are rarely more conservative on rights questions than is the rest of the population, and, usually, they are more inclusive.

More remarkable, in some respects, are the shifts in view among evangelical Protestants. As Clyde Wilcox and Rentaro Iida have pointed out, they have started from a more critical or oppositional stance but have changed at the same rate as has the rest of the population. Commentators in both Canada and the United States have pointed to significant gaps between younger evangelicals and their elders. In a book tellingly titled *UnChristian*, Kinnaman and Lyons (2007, 53) point to a huge generational gap in judging the moral acceptability of homosexuality and in treating this as a major issue. Kinnaman, himself an evangelical Christian, further points out that, "while most young churchgoers believe the Bible does not condone homosexuality, their conviction about this is waning, and they are embarrassed by the church's treatment of gays and lesbians" (101).

The groups that intervene politically on behalf of Christian conservatives, particularly in the United States, do not yet reflect much of this change, but we do see glimmers of recognition in surprising places. Even Sarah Palin, chosen as vice-presidential candidate in large part because of her support among conservative evangelical Protestants, was moved to declare that she supported anti-discrimination protections for gays and lesbians, even while reiterating her opposition to same-sex marriage. Once chosen to speak at Barack Obama's inauguration, Rick Warren pulled back from, and to some extent apologized for, earlier comments about homosexuality and California's Proposition 8. Late in 2009, he condemned a Ugandan colleague who was supporting a notoriously anti-gay bill before that country's parliament.

The intensity of the fight over same-sex marriage has certainly led to important setbacks, but it may well have opened up space for more Americans to support civil unions and other forms of recognition for lesbian/gay relationships. Attitudes in Canada and the United States towards marriage remain strikingly different from one another – more so than do views about any other rights questions associated with sexuality – but even here we see a slow but steady shift towards more positive views among Americans.

LGBT Visibility within Communities of Faith

Another development with stronger similarities than differences across the international border is the increased visibility of sexual minorities within religious communities. This has long been true of Quakers, Unitarians, and the most progressive of mainline Protestant churches and Jewish congregations. Now, with each passing year, there is a wider range of religious communities that has either welcomed LGBT members or begun the process of wrestling with the issues arising from their very presence. Pentecostal and fundamentalist church members increasingly know of friends, relatives, and workplace colleagues who are lesbian, gay, bisexual, or transgendered, and increasingly they realize that their church's membership includes them.

This is beginning to happen in African-American and black Canadian evangelical communities, long dominated by a rejection of sexual diversity.

In early 2008, Barack Obama pointed to anti-gay sentiment in African-American communities as an injustice. And he did this during an address to the congregation in Martin Luther King's church on the day honouring King's memory – a sign that such debate was emerging within a community much shaped by evangelical Christianity and marked by persistent disapproval of homosexuality.

In all mainline Protestant church policy-making bodies, on both sides of the border, there have been debates over such issues as the blessing of same-sex unions and the ordination of openly lesbian or gay ministers. What this has produced in a few cases, most notably in the United Church of Canada and the United Church of Christ (in the United States), is substantial policy change. In particular dioceses of the Anglican communion, there has also been considerable movement. At the local level, across a wide range of faiths, individual churches have made their own shifts towards more welcoming stances, sometimes beyond what is encouraged or permitted in official policy.

Jewish communities have faced much the same internal discussion over issues of sexuality. In both countries, reform and reconstructionist congregations took these issues up first, followed by conservative and eventually even orthodox congregations. As in analogous Christian denominations, change has come slowly and unevenly across particular communities but with strong parallels across the international border. Such debate is also facilitated by the relative inclusiveness of Jewish public opinion regarding sexuality issues.

Islamic religious communities have contained fewer progressive voices on these questions, so there have been far fewer settings in which inclusive theological stances have been debated, let alone adopted. Still, the formation of explicitly LGBT Muslim groups in both Canada and the United States in the 1990s and early 2000s was an important first step, supported by progressive allies within Muslim communities (mostly secular or from the small Ismaili religious community).

These developments are critical for challenging the view that religious faith and queer-related advocacy are inevitably at odds. Until now, opposition to LGBT rights claims has been dominated by members of conservative faith communities, and the strength of their voices has led many in the public to equate faith with opposition to the public recognition of sexual diversity. More inclusive voices of faith have long been there but will likely speak more loudly as religious communities engage in their own struggles and deliberations over difference.

Continuing Challenges

Persistent Prejudice

For all the encouraging developments that work towards a tempering of conflict between people of faith and advocates of sexual equality, there are elements of what might still be referred to as a culture war. And while this is more obviously true in the United States, there are chasmic divides in Canada that require thoughtful reflection.

Prejudice directed at sexual minorities remains a powerful force, and anxiety about sexual diversity and gender non-conformity is more widespread than is commonly admitted. In both Canada and the United States, there remains a strong relationship between religious faith and antipathy towards homosexuality – a relationship increasingly weak in much of Europe (Nevitte and Cochrane 2006).

The very important shifts towards more acceptance of homosexuality, and tolerance of it among those still disapproving, continue to leave us with a minority of about one-third with deep antipathy towards both homosexuality and lesbians and gays – slightly more than that in the United States, slightly less in Canada. Levels of discomfort and disapproval are undoubtedly higher with regard to bisexuality and transgenderism. More so in the United States than in Canada, the hatred of the "sins" of sexual "deviance" coexists with a hatred of the sinners.

Scores on thermometer scales in Canada and the United States show a significant rise in warmth over the years, but they still position gays and lesbians as colder than almost all other groups. The average American score is about 45 degrees, and about 35 percent of the population places homosexuals dead last (Egan and Sherrill 2005). In Canada, the average of the thermometer ratings scored by respondents to 2004 and 2006 national election studies was around 59, warmer than in the United States but still low compared to other groups, and with about 10 percent scoring zero.[1]

Surveys also reveal a continuing opposition to or anxiety about gays and lesbians' being parents. Here, too, we see important positive shifts, but Canadians and Americans are about evenly divided between those who favour and those who oppose extending adoption rights to gays and lesbians. This is despite a steady widening of parental rights in the United States and extensive country-wide rights in Canada. The doubts about parenting are rooted in adult anxieties over children's "fitting" in, most obviously in gender terms, but some of the opposition comes from fears about their being turned gay as well as from prejudicial thinking regarding the very idea of lesbians and gay men as parents. Unease about bisexuals and the transgendered serving as parents is probably even more acute.

Such fears and doubts are reinforced by the continued willingness of conservative religious groups to campaign against LGBT rights on the basis of the most fearsome stereotypes – especially in the United States. Media campaigns favouring prohibitions on same-sex marriage in California and Florida during the 2008 election featured images of children and were obviously intended to stoke the fires of prejudice.

Canada has had fewer such campaigns in recent years aimed explicitly at LGBT rights and, therefore, fewer openings to such vitriol. On the other hand, Christian evangelical advocate Charles McVety was able to provoke significant media attention and government anxiety in 2010 when he attacked new provincial guidelines on sex education that allowed for discussion of sexual diversity in elementary schools (Rayside 2010). There is no evidence that school harassment and bullying directed at sexual minorities are less widespread in Canada than in the United States (see GLSEN 2008; Cianciotto and Cahill 2003; Egale Canada 2009).

In the political work of countering anti-gay prejudice, evidence of dramatic intergenerational shifts in attitudes towards sexual diversity among Christian evangelicals means that no community should be written off. No faith group, in other words, is immune to calls for justice and equity. In some, the most that can be achieved is "tolerance" – widely understood among minority advocates to be an insufficient goal. But tolerance and civility, as Sam Reimer argues, are an improvement over their opposite.

Risk of Racializing the Condemnation of Homosexuality and Gender Non-Conformity

In both countries, there are indications of relatively strong antipathy towards homosexuality among some minority groups who are strongly identified with faith. African Americans couple a tendency to support protections for LGBT people against job and housing discrimination with moral condemnation of homosexuality and stronger-than-average opposition to same-sex marriage. There is no comparable evidence on Canadian blacks, but there are strong anecdotal indications of a similar pattern. Muslims on both sides of the border are also relatively conservative in their responses to questions of sexual diversity. Among Asians, there is evidence that Korean Americans stand out for their moral conservatism on issues related to homosexuality, and the same is found in Canada (Asian Pacific Legal Center

2009). In these cases, adherence to faith communities in which condemnation of homosexuality is unequivocal is a key factor, potentially explaining most of the difference between these communities and national averages.

For Muslims and, to some extent, Koreans, the relative recentness of immigration is obviously another contributing factor. For blacks in both countries, social and economic marginalization has created anxieties about family structure and resistance to sexualized stereotypes – all working against accommodation to homosexuality and gender non-conformity.

What may further "racialize" this divide is the widespread portrayal of sexual minorities as white, both in the mainstream media and in ethno-racial communities. This is no less true in Canada than it is in the United States, and in both places it reinforces perceptions within minority communities that to be gay or lesbian or bisexual or transgender is to be outside those communities.

The flip side of that coin is that growing acceptance of some forms of sexual diversity – the safe and respectable forms – will reinforce the "otherness" of those communities already marginalized in racial terms and further denigrate them for seeming to be out of synch with mainstream shifts in tolerance or acceptance. The risk, then, is that indications of anti-gay prejudice among minorities, even if mirrored in a significant white majority, will be used as a cudgel. This has been a growing phenomenon in such places as the Netherlands and Denmark, where ethnic minorities are targeted as unassimilably non-Western because of their attitudes towards sexual diversity. This falsely associates acceptance of such diversity with "Western" culture and ignores the potential for major generational change within such communities. Still, the conservative attitudes towards sexual diversity within these communities need frank and honest discussion.

Risks of Expansive Definitions of Hate Speech

We find strong impulses within communities of faith and of sexual minorities to "regulate" or "police" opponents, and much of the heated debate over the regulation of "hate speech" has been at the intersection of faith and sexual diversity. The language used by conservative clerics, and by the political organizations claiming to represent them, often contains levels of vitriol and stereotype unmatched by their opponents. On the other hand, this does not mean it needs to be, or should be, policed as unlawful. Most equity advocates agree on this, but there are some who have attempted to shut down anti-gay campaigning through the use of speech codes or hate crimes law.

In the United States, the First Amendment to the Constitution enshrines robust protection for free expression, and Supreme Court rulings have leaned strongly towards allowing speech widely understood to be abhorrent. They have allowed a pro-Nazi march in Skoke, Illinois, a suburb with many concentration camp survivors.

In Canada, section 2 of the Charter of Rights and Freedoms is written even more expansively than are its comparable American provisions. Among the "fundamental freedoms" is the "freedom of thought, belief, opinion and expression, including freedom of the press and other media of communication." The same section also guarantees freedom of conscience and religion.

Canadian criminal law also includes sexual orientation under the rubric of hate crimes (since 2003). The courts have applied quite rigorous tests in order to assess whether speech itself is hateful enough to draw criminal sanctions, and few convictions have resulted. Human rights codes at the federal and provincial and territorial levels also have analogous provisions, and here the record is less clear cut. What it shows is an unsettling tendency for a few critics of anti-gay campaigning to respond with calls for policing – in other words, for the use of law to prohibit the airing of reprehensible views.

What is more unsettling is that, in at least two cases, such attempts have been successful at one stage or another. In an Alberta case, a Red Deer newspaper published a letter from Stephen Boissoin, which condemned homosexuality in very strong terms. A human rights tribunal ruled that this contravened a provision of the Human Rights, Citizenship, and Multiculturalism Act, which prohibited the publishing of discriminatory statements (using very broad language), even though the act also makes a clear commitment to free expression. This verdict was eventually reversed by a 2009 court ruling, but it is the initial conviction that is troubling.

Without entering into the specifics of the case, I want to question the impulse to prohibit the distasteful and abhorrent, in part because it portrays the listener as too vulnerable to manage such language and, in part, because the prohibitive impulse was once so widely used to silence sexual minorities. Indeed, there are still American Christian right groups that are trying to shut down positive talk about sexual diversity in schools by aiming to prevent the establishment of gay-straight alliances. It is more than ironic to marshall such tools of regulatory policing in response to anti-gay speech.

This does not mean that free expression does, or should, allow absolutely everything. There is a place for prohibitions on speech so hateful that it directly incites violence, for example. But most of what we might agree to call "hateful" in the everyday sense of the word does not qualify as "hate" in the legally prohibitable sense of the word. Those who oppose such expressions must do what John Stuart Mill imagined and combat them with whatever argumentation and criticism are possible. At the same time, those who end up the butt of such criticism cannot claim that their faith immunizes them from attack.

Unresolved Debates over Schooling

In both Canada and the United States, anxieties persist about gender learning on the part of young people and about what they are taught. Many Christian conservatives still fear that public school recognition of homosexuality will result in their own children becoming gay or experimenting with it. Others fear an absence of clear messages about masculinity and femininity; still others fear that if their own children were to be sexually different they would experience intolerable harassment from other students. This produces disturbing cross-border similarities in the extent to which public schools avoid positive or inclusive discussion of sexual diversity. Addressing this pattern of avoidance, however, requires a recognition of just how complex and fraught schooling debates are.

On the American side, in particular, debates over education easily get polarized. From the 1980s on, evangelical Christian organizing was intensified at the state and local levels and became increasingly vigilant over any accommodation to "the gay agenda." This was part of a broader concern to ensure that schools instilled traditional family values and reflected a curriculum that did not challenge scriptures – for example, by privileging evolutionary theory. The very breadth of the religious right's schooling agenda expanded the alliances available to advocates for LGBT inclusiveness, though persistent opposition to even modest equity steps has made the development of systematically inclusive practices difficult in most school districts and impossible in many.

In Canada, there is far less concerted campaigning by religious conservatives directed at public schools. One reason, of course, is the smaller number of such conservatives, but another reason is the state-funded Catholic school systems that exist across important parts of the country. They draw away from the public system an important constituency of conservative devout Catholics whose aim is to ensure that schools continue transmitting traditional family values.

Still, the 2010 furor over sex education in Ontario schools illustrates the persistent reluctance to discuss sexuality issues of any sort in public schools – particularly with respect to non-traditional sexuality. Unease about inclusive discussion of sexual diversity, too, extends far beyond the ranks of religious conservatives. Even where inclusive policies have been developed, such as in Toronto, implementation remains highly uneven, and across Canada provincial ministries have taken few steps to produce serious change on the ground.

The high proportion of immigrants in Canada's largest cities fuels opposition to school initiatives on this front since most come from countries without strong challenges to traditional gender and sexual norms. In many minority communities, too, religious institutions play major community-building and cultural-transmission roles, and this often gives morally traditional voices great prominence. Chinese-Canadian Christians in Vancouver and Muslim Canadians in Toronto have been prominent in protests against school recognition of sexual diversity. It is wrong to overgeneralize here and to discount the dramatic changes that occur from one generation to another. But moral traditionalism retains a significant hold in some minority communities. Educators, already fearful of parental backlash against discussions of sexuality, may overgeneralize or exaggerate the prospect of negative reaction, especially if their classrooms have significant numbers of immigrant or minority students.

In both Canada and the United States, schools also have an uneasy relationship to religious diversification. They are widely committed, at least officially, to the recognition of ethnic or cultural differences, and, to some extent, this has produced an accommodation to religious differences, particularly where the number of non-Christians has increased. This inevitably muddies the waters around "separation" even in those circles most dominated by "strict separationist" views of public education. In the United States, where battle lines on this front are so hardened, there are growing zones of pragmatic fuzziness in responding to diversity, alongside growing uncertainty about how far to go.

In both countries, the recognition of sexual and religious diversity raises unresolved questions about the fundamental role of schooling. These are more explicitly debated and fought over in the United States, but they create uncertainty and debate in Canada too. Among the points of debate over what values schools should articulate and transmit are these:

- Are the moral or ethical principles conveyed by schools based on a single religious faith, multiple faiths, or secular reasoning?
- Should schools emphasize values that have traditionally prevailed in society, or do they encourage the questioning of dominant ideas?

- Should educators emphasize that which is common to students and the rest of the population, or should they emphasize diversity?
- Should schools protect students from certain aspects of the world around them, or should they fully expose them to even the harsh elements of that world?
- Should educators defer to and privilege parental authority and leave discussions of such issues as sex and morality to the family?
- In deliberating school policy, what is the proper balance between the views of parents and the views of educational professionals?

These questions are not simple to resolve and are not prone to categorical resolution by simple rules. I have no doubt that schools should take up questions of sexual diversity in an inclusive way from elementary school onward. I also believe that they should take faith more seriously and help students understand a range of faith traditions. Equipping students for living in communities and countries more culturally and religiously pluralized than ever requires that we no longer request that questions of faith be left at the school's front door. Travelling down both of these roads simultaneously will inevitably raise complex and sometimes uncomfortable questions.

Broad Uncertainties over Accommodating Religious Differences
On a range of fronts extending beyond schooling, Canadian and American policy makers and jurists are torn between quite different tendencies. Perhaps more than ever, there are areas of legal and policy muddle, without any indication of final resolution. This is, in part, because long-standing disagreements about the kind of role that faith has in the public square are now compounded by the diversification of religious traditions that comes with immigration from non-Christian countries.

In the United States there have been decades of debate and litigation over the meaning of the "establishment" and "free exercise" clauses of the Constitution. Behind the courtroom battle, there have also been long-lasting debates over whether governments could support any religious function, whether religion was to be legally construed as strictly private, and whether equitable recognition had to be extended to all faiths. All of these issues have been posed in Canada, and, even if there is less acrimony in most of the legal and policy debates here, the difficulty of finding clear solutions to conflicting demands is just as evident.

These debates have serious consequences for the extent to which sexual diversity is publicly recognized and for the terms in which such recognition is debated. The important place of religion in many minority communities, and among many immigrants, has quite properly pushed many governments, courts, and private institutions to accommodate religious practices. This is true to some extent in the United States, where "strict separationism" has such a large following and where the pressures on minorities to assimilate are so strong. The tendency for policy makers and courts to accommodate religious minorities is usually stronger in Canada, built, in part, on multicultural policy developed in the 1970s and 1980s and a policy legacy of accommodating religious difference.

There are widely agreed-upon limits to religious accommodation, however. Yes, religious communities can choose their clerics according to rules that discriminate on the basis of gender and sexuality. Women can be barred from the Catholic priesthood, and they can face almost insurmountable odds in securing mosque leadership. Gays, lesbians, bisexuals, and the transgendered can be officially barred from religious positions by official policy or established practice. Houses of worship can refuse to perform marriage ceremonies for same-sex couples where the civil right to such marriage has been made available. Many people have reason to dislike those barriers, but protections for religious practice do impose serious barriers to state infringement on faith community rights to make those determinations.

Beyond that lies much that has been the subject of ambiguity, disagreement, and litigation. Can religiously based schools discriminate on the basis of sexual orientation or gender identity when determining who becomes and stays a teacher? Is the same true for non-teaching positions? Does the provision of state funding affect the answer to that question? Can such schools prevent students from forming a gay-straight alliance, or can they bar LGBT groups from using school property after hours? Can religiously based social agencies refuse to provide services to lesbian and gay couples, for example in the placement of children for adoption or fostering, in jurisdictions that formally prohibit discrimination based on sexual orientation? Is a Christian or Islamic bookstore able to refuse employment to a gay, lesbian, or trans job applicant – again, in those jurisdictions with generic prohibitions on such discrimination?

Decades of litigation in the United States over religious rights have not prevented waves of new cases on such points, and much remains unclear. In Canada, as Richard Moon indicates, there has been considerable jurisprudence on these questions but little in the way of sustained clarity. Cases arise with only a fraction of the frequency that they do in the United States, but there are similar zones of uncertainty, and ambivalence, about where the boundaries around religious liberty should be drawn.

Among the hardest issues to wrestle with here are the sometimes-conflicting claims of individual and community. Some theorists argue that a fully respectful recognition of the social and cultural integrity of a minority group may suggest accommodation to some practices inimical to full individual equality (Carens and Williams 1996). Even if we draw the line at "undue harm," we are still left with the very real possibility of reinforcing gender and sexual hierarchies within the community. It is not hard to find communities in which such forms of "recognition" would result in a reinforced marginalization for sexual minorities.

Here the potential is very real for rights claims based on religious and sexual diversity to come into conflict. And here the debating lines are ambiguous and the positions taken by many thoughtful contributors ambivalent. These are multidimensional issues and necessarily require tentative and nuanced responses.

Conclusion

The Christian right claims that people of faith are now as widely reviled as is any group in the United States. I would argue that they are not treated with nearly the prejudice, harassment, and violence that are directed at sexual minorities, but there is no doubt that many of them accurately report instances in which their religious beliefs are belittled or attacked. This is especially true for evangelical Christians and Muslims who adhere to conservative interpretations of scripture.[2]

Some claims about anti-faith prejudice seem aimed at erecting a rhetorical protective shield around anti-gay advocates, portraying any criticism of religious actions or beliefs as constituting an attack on religion itself. And yes, there are critics of the religious right in both countries who state or imply that the expression of faith-based views in the public square is inappropriate in itself. In Canada, particularly, politicians who have a strong religious faith that they believe has a role in public debate have often commented on the risks of talking faith in political arenas. Anti-clericalism has long had a firmer foothold in Continental Europe than in either Canada or the United States, though it is now a strong force in Quebec. And there is a widespread readiness to criticize all religious belief as irrational and as dangerous to serious debate over public issues. This, of course, puts those who take their Christianity as an important guide to political action on the defensive. It also may contribute to the marginalization of communities with non-Christian beliefs.

Widespread scepticism about the political role of faith, combined with equally widespread indifference to religion, leaves most Canadians and Americans vulnerable to claims by Christian right political groups that serious adherence to scripture precludes any room for positive views of sexual diversity. So when such groups, or when individual clerics, claim to oppose gay rights in the name of all faithful, much of the population is ill armed to disagree. And when there are indications of a shift of priorities away from homosexuality among younger evangelicals (and some preachers), there are few outsiders who are ready to pay attention.

The conflict, ambivalence, and anxiety that are occasioned by debates over sexuality within religious communities speak about the power of the issues at stake. Political claims based on sexual orientation and gender identity inevitably raise questions about family, sexual desire, gender, and tradition. The difficulties that we find in so much deliberation about these issues speak to much larger questions about how to understand the modern or postmodern world and how to ensure human justice and social solidarity within such a world. The fact that there is any deliberation at all is evidence of remarkable openings to change created by queer visibility and activism, but the painfulness of the discussions we so often see within communities of faith teaches us more than do public opinion surveys about how slow the shift is towards deeply felt acceptance.

Within a wide array of institutions and political settings – on both sides of the border – debates over the public recognition of sexual diversity have taken place alongside struggles over the place of faith in the public square and the appropriateness of using state authority to support religious institutions. We have seen innumerable illustrations of the complex connections between these issues and the number of policy issues that remain unresolved. We have also seen that the growing multiculturalism of these two countries, shall we say, embellishes the questions being posed and perhaps complicates the spaces in which religion and sexuality intersect.

Shifts towards public support of rights based on sexual orientation, and even gender identity, have been more pronounced in the United States than anti-gay ballot measure success on marriage would suggest. Legal and policy gains reflective of that shift have also been widespread, even on such issues as parenting – where change has been painfully slow in most countries otherwise seen as progressive. In Canada, on the other hand, shifts in public acceptance have not been as radically distinct from those in the United

States, as is generally believed, particularly when issues related to children are involved. Changes in school policy have come more slowly than most Canadians appreciate, with dramatic unevenness in implementation.

On the many questions associated with the role of faith in the public arena, the contrasts between Canada and the United States are less sharp than they seem. There are similar zones of public policy inconsistency and legal ambivalence, likely to become more difficult as non-Christian populations become larger. The struggle over church-state issues has been more continuously high profile in the United States, and the battle lines have been more entrenched. In Canada, there are more issues that have been settled, or at least acquiesced to, but there is plenty of public disagreement as to what degree public institutions should privilege Christianity and even more about how much recognition should be extended to other religions.

Sexuality issues can all too easily become a weapon for protagonists in these debates. Lesbians, gay men, bisexuals, and the transgendered are the rhetorical symbols of moral decay in the campaigns of moral traditionalists. Religious faith itself too easily gets castigated as irretrievably exclusionary and as inevitably a carrier of prejudice against sexual minorities, thus reinforcing a readiness to engage in political mobilization that makes all people of faith, from minority or majority religions, feel denigrated. Deliberations that bring people of faith and members of sexual minorities together will long pose complex challenges and will need all the fair-mindedness, the capacity to understand "the other," and the willingness to build bridges that we can muster.

Appendix A
Canadian Legal and Institutional Context

The Charter of Rights and Freedoms, constitutionally embedded in 1982, applies to all acts of government at all levels. It contains the following provisions relevant to sexual diversity and religion:

Sec. 2. Everyone has the following fundamental freedoms: (a) freedom of conscience and religion; (b) freedom of thought, belief, opinion and expression, including freedom of the press and other media of communication; (c) freedom of peaceful assembly; and (d) freedom of association.

Sec. 15. (1) Every individual is equal before and under the law and has the right to the equal protection and equal benefit of the law without discrimination and, in particular, without discrimination based on race, national or ethnic origin, colour, religion, sex, age or mental or physical disability. (2) Subsection (1) does not preclude any law, program or activity that has as its object the amelioration of conditions of disadvantaged individuals or groups including those that are disadvantaged because of race, national or ethnic origin, colour, religion, sex, age or mental or physical disability. (84)

Sec. 27. This Charter shall be interpreted in a manner consistent with the preservation and enhancement of the multicultural heritage of Canadians.

Sec. 29. Nothing in this Charter abrogates or derogates from any rights or privileges guaranteed by or under the Constitution of Canada in respect of denominational, separate or dissentient schools.

During the 1990s, the Charter's section 15 (which came into effect in 1985, after a three-year delay) was interpreted by courts to include sexual orientation. There has been a tendency for courts and tribunals to treat discrimination based on gender identity as covered by "sex," though no definitive ruling has yet appeared. The judicial interpretation of provisions on religion has reflected the view that public institutions should not privilege any one religion, but it gives somewhat more weight to religious claims than do US courts (e.g., in claims directed at employers). Courts have also ruled in favour of claimants wishing to wear signs of religious faith in schools (e.g., kirpans for Sikhs) and in other official settings (e.g., turbans in the RCMP). Many issues related to the "accommodation" of religious belief, including minority faith, have yet to be definitively resolved.

Canadian federalism places an unusually expansive set of public policies under provincial jurisdiction, and, in practice, the federal government has been reducing its interventions in social policy areas formally controlled by the provinces and territories. Schooling, social welfare, family law, health – all belong exclusively to the provinces. Among the areas of relevance to both sexual difference and religion that belong to the federal domain are criminal law, immigration (with some provincial role, especially in Quebec), the definition of marriage (as distinct from its administration, which is under provincial control), and the regulation of companies with a national mandate (e.g., airlines, transportation, communications, etc.). Although provinces have substantial tax powers, outside Quebec the federal government is the tax collector and, therefore, sets rules about what counts as "family" for tax purposes.

Canadian Statutory and Constitutional Milestones on Sexual Diversity

1969   Federal Criminal Code amendments partially decriminalize homosexuality and abortion and ease access to divorce.

1982   Charter of Rights and Freedoms becomes part of the Canadian Constitution. Sexual orientation is not explicitly included, but section 15 (on discrimination), which comes into effect after a three-year delay, includes open-ended wording that will eventually be interpreted to include grounds not explicitly named, including sexual orientation.

1990   *Correctional Services of Canada v. Veysey* (Federal Appeal Court) grants prison conjugal visiting rights to same-sex partner.

1993   *Canada (A.G). v. Mossop* (Supreme Court of Canada) turns down relationship claim based on marital status but indicates that a claim based on sexual orientation may well have succeeded, implicitly indicating that the Charter's section 15 could be read as prohibiting discrimination on that ground.

1995 *Egan v. Canada* (Supreme Court of Canada) narrowly turns down relationship claim but rules explicitly that discrimination based on sexual orientation is prohibited by section 15 of the Charter.

– *Miron v. Trudel* (Supreme Court of Canada) rules that discrimination based on marital status is implicitly prohibited by section 15 and that exclusion of cohabiting couples from an insurance benefit given married couples is discriminatory, though allowing some differential treatment.

– BC legislature includes same-sex couples in new adoption law.

– *Re K.* (Ontario Court, provincial division) rules in favour of same-sex couples who are seeking second-parent adoption of children; soon interpreted as covering joint adoption.

1999 *M. v. H.* (Supreme Court of Canada) strikes down exclusionary provisions of Ontario family law, effectively ruling that same-sex couples cannot be discriminated against by comparison to cohabiting opposite-sex couples, by now given most of the rights and obligations accorded married couples. This was soon followed by sweeping changes in provincial and federal statutes.

2000 *Little Sisters v. Canada* (Supreme Court of Canada) ruling agrees with Vancouver LGBT bookstore that Canada Customs discriminated in screening erotic material but does not strike down the statutory provisions enabling that discrimination.

2003 *Halpern v. Canada (A.G.).* (Ontario Court of Appeal) rules against heterosexual exclusion in civil marriage and orders ruling to take effect immediately. Federal government chooses not to appeal, and courts in several other provinces soon follow suit.

2005 Federal Parliament passes legislation extending civil marriage to same-sex couples.

Canadian Statutory and Constitutional Milestones on Religion

1969 Federal Criminal Code amendments partially decriminalize homosexuality and abortion and ease access to divorce.

1971 Canadian Parliament enacts Multicultural Act, which declares Canada as multicultural within a bilingual framework.

1982   Charter of Rights and Freedoms incorporated into Canadian Consti-
       tution and includes prohibitions on discrimination based on religion
       as well as affirmation of multicultural character of Canada.

1984   *Caldwell v. St. Thomas Aquinas High School* (Supreme Court of Can-
       ada) upholds right of Roman Catholic school to not rehire a teacher
       who had married a divorced person outside the Church.

1985   *O'Malley v. Simpsons-Sears* (Supreme Court of Canada) supports
       Seventh Day Adventist claim that obligation to work on her sabbath
       (Friday evening and Saturday morning) violates duty to reasonably
       accommodate, especially with no evidence that this constituted
       undue hardship for the employer.

–   *R. v. Big M Drug Mart* (Supreme Court of Canada) rules against fed-
       eral Lord's Day Act, prohibiting Sunday business operation, on the
       grounds that it constitutes religious compulsion, arguing that the
       guarantee of religious equality may be violated by effects or practices
       and that remedies may call for differential treatment of religions.

1986   *R. v. Edwards Books and Art* (Supreme Court of Canada) rules
       against a provincial (Ontario) Sunday closing law, even if its motive
       was not religious but, rather, to create a common pause day.

1988   *Zylberberg v. Sudbury Board of Education* (Ontario Court of Appeal)
       rules against recitation of the Lord's Prayer in opening school exer-
       cises on grounds that even with opt-out provision it, in effect, com-
       pelled religious practice.

–   *Canadian Civil Liberties Association v. Minister of Education and
       Elgin County* (Ontario Court of Appeal) rules against provincial
       ministry requiring religious education classes in schools.

1989   *Russow v. British Columbia Attorney General* (British Columbia Su-
       preme Court) rules against religious opening exercises in school.

1991   *Pandori v. Peel Board of Education* (Ontario Court of Appeal) rules
       in favour of Sikh student's wearing kirpan in school.

1993   *Smart v. T. Eaton* (Quebec Human Rights Tribunal) confirms that
       Catholic employee could refuse to work on Sunday.

1994   *Commission scolaire regionale de Chambly v. Bergevin* (Supreme
       Court of Canada) rules that school board had to reimburse Jewish
       teachers for Yom Kippur leave.

1995   *B(R) v. Children's Aid Society of Metropolitan Toronto* (Supreme
       Court of Canada) rules that forced blood transfusion for one-year-

old child of Jehovah's Witness parents was a legitimate infringement on religious freedom.

– *Grant v. Canada* (Federal Court of Canada) rules in favour of RCMP regulation allowing turban-wearing for Sikhs and against challenge to the 1990 change in uniform policy.

1996 *Adler v. Ontario* (Supreme Court of Canada) rules that Charter creates no constitutional obligation to fund religious schools (in this case private non-Catholic), apart from the constitutional guarantees extended to denominational schools (largely affecting Roman Catholic education). Provinces were able to extend such funding but were not obliged to do so.

2001 *Trinity Western University v. BC College of Teachers* (Supreme Court of Canada) rules against requirement for extra year of teacher training for graduates of TWU, a Christian university, despite explicit bar to homosexual activity, though the court affirms the secular nature of BC schools. It argues, therefore, that for legal purposes religious belief and practice can be distinguished.

2002 *Chamberlain v. Surrey School District No. 36* (Supreme Court of Canada) rules against elementary school prohibition on gay-themed books, saying that religious grounds could not be the basis for exclusion in the public school system of British Columbia.

2004 *Syndicat Northcrest v. Amselem* (Supreme Court of Canada) rules in favour of allowing Jewish residents to build a sukkah, despite residential building's prohibitions.

2005 Government of Ontario abolishes all enforceable family-related religious arbitration, following controversy over Boyd Report of 2004, recommending allowance of such arbitration based on Sharia law (alongside controls to protect vulnerable individuals).

2006 *Payette v. Ville de Laval* (Quebec Human Rights Tribunal) orders city to stop recital of Lord's Prayer at public meetings of council.

– *Multani v. Commission scolaire Marguerite Bourgeoys* (Supreme Court of Canada) rules in favour of Sikh students wearing a kirpan at school, based on his sincere belief that his faith requires it, allowing authorities to add conditions to secure the ceremonial dagger.

2008 *R. v. Badesha* (Ontario Court of Justice) rules against helmet exemption for Sikh motorcycle owner, despite claims that religious convictions obliged wearing a turban.

Appendix B
US Legal and Institutional Context

The US Constitution includes the following articles and amendments, with relevant sections highlighted:

Article VI (part). The Senators and Representatives before mentioned, and the members of the several state legislatures, and all executive and judicial officers, both of the United States and of the several states, shall be bound by oath or affirmation, to support this Constitution; but *no religious test shall ever be required as a qualification to any office* or public trust under the United States.

Amendment I. *Congress shall make no law respecting an establishment of religion, or prohibiting the free exercise thereof;* or abridging the freedom of speech, or of the press; or the right of the people peaceably to assemble, and to petition the government for a redress of grievances.

Amendment XIV, Section 1. All persons born or naturalized in the United States, and subject to the jurisdiction thereof, are citizens of the United States and of the state wherein they reside. No state shall make or enforce any law which shall abridge the privileges or immunities of citizens of the United States; nor shall any state deprive any person of life, liberty, or property, without due process of law; *nor deny to any person within its jurisdiction the equal protection of the laws.*

The US Supreme Court has yet to rule that the "equal protection" clause of the Fourteenth Amendment extends fully to sexual orientation, while it has done so for race and gender. Some cases related to sexual diversity have resulted in victory for lesbian and gay claimants but on grounds other than the Fourteenth Amendment (e.g., privacy rights). The courts in general, and, by implication, the US Supreme Court, have been viewing discrimination against transgender employees as prohibited under the "sex" provisions of Title VII in the Civil Rights Act, 1964.

The absence of clear direction on sexual orientation from the Supreme Court has left room for state courts to rule in widely divergent ways, depending on provisions in state constitutions and statutes, and previous court decisions. As of mid-2010, twenty-one states (plus the District of Columbia) explicitly ban discrimination based on sexual orientation; thirteen (plus the District of Columbia) also include gender identity. At the same time, many states (thirty-one) have amended their constitutions to prohibit the recognition of same-sex marriage, the language in most of those amendments extending beyond marriage to other forms of relationship recognition. Most other states have defence of marriage acts (DOMAs) in statute form. The impact of "super-DOMA" constitutional amendments on non-material recognition of same-sex couples is still unclear.

The relationship between church and state has been the subject of intense litigation over many decades, centred on the interpretation of the "establishment" and "free exercise" clauses in the Constitution's First Amendment. Until now, most disputes have focused on the place of Christian symbols and practices in public institutions, though some claims have been advanced on behalf of religious minorities. The Supreme Court moved towards a "strict separationist" view in the three decades after the Second World War but since the 1980s has moved unevenly away from that categorical position.

The US Congress has been an important player in creating religious exemptions from various laws that are, in effect, "free exercise" claims. This has been evident in legislation on abortion, allowing health practitioners to exempt themselves from the duty to perform operations that offend their religious beliefs. There are legislators at the federal and state levels who have been pushing for such measures with regard to marital and relationship regimes for same-sex couples.

American federalism accords less policy leverage and tax room to the states than provinces have in Canada, but state jurisdiction includes matters relevant to sexuality that, in Canada, are under federal control. This includes criminal law (a shared jurisdiction) and the power to define marriage. These are in addition to the primacy of state jurisdiction in education, family law, and so on. Federal policy makers have regularly used their spending power to enact laws in areas primarily governed by states, schooling being an important example.

US Supreme Court Decisions on Sexual Diversity and on Other Major Law and Policy Landmarks

1958   *One, Inc. v. Oleson* (US Supreme Court) reverses lower court ruling that supported Postal Service refusal to deliver gay magazine.

1961   Illinois is the first state to decriminalize homosexual activity.

1967   *Boutilier v. Immigration and Naturalization Services* (US Supreme Court) sustains a deportation order based on his being homosexual.

1971-80 Twenty-three additional states decriminalize homosexuality.

1986   *Bowers v. Hardwick* (US Supreme Court) upholds Georgia law criminalizing homosexual activity.

1989   *Price Waterhouse v. Hopkins* (US Supreme Court) rules against employer for discriminating against a female employee thought to look too masculine, under the "sex" provision of Title VII of the 1964 Civil Rights Act.

1993   *Baehr v. Lewin* (Hawai'i Supreme Court) rules in favour of same-sex marriage claimants, though impact undone by state referendum.

1995   *Hurley v. Irish-American Gay, Lesbian and Bisexual Group of Boston* (US Supreme Court) upholds right of St. Patrick's Day parade to exclude group.

1996   *Romer v. Evans* (US Supreme Court) overturns Colorado ballot measure that precluded state and local authorities from passing laws prohibiting discrimination based on sexual orientation.

1999   *Baker v. Vermont* (Vermont Supreme Court) supports same-sex marriage claimants, leaving state legislature the option of using marriage or civil union remedy.

2000   *Boy Scouts of America v. Dale* (US Supreme Court) supports Boy Scout exclusion of gay man.

2003   *Lawrence v. Texas* (US Supreme Court) overturns Texas sodomy statute criminalizing homosexual activity.

–   *Goodridge v. Department of Public Health* (Massachusetts Supreme Judicial Council) rules in favour of same-sex marriage claimants, leading to first marriages in the United States (though without effect on rights and obligations in federal jurisdiction).

2004   *Smith v. City of Salem* (6th Circuit Court) rules that Title VII of the Civil Rights Act extended workplace protection to transgender employees.

–   Thirteen state referenda add same-sex marriage prohibitions to state constitutions; by late 2009, thirty-one states have such constitutional prohibitions.

2009   Same-sex marriage recognition in Iowa, Vermont, New Hampshire, DC, and Maine (the last reversed in a November referendum).

Selected US Supreme Court Rulings on Religious Rights, 1945+

1945   *Everson v. Board of Education* upholds provision of state funding for school busing to religious and public schools alike.

1952   *Zorach v. Clauson* upholds public schools' granting release time to attend religious functions.

1962   *Engel v. Vitale* rules against required daily prayers in school, one of a few such rulings on prayer in publicly funded institutions.

1963   *Sherbert v. Verner* rules against denial of unemployment insurance payments after employee was dismissed from a job when he refused to work on his sabbath, the court imposing the burden on state authorities to establish that a law's purpose had to be sufficiently compelling to warrant hindering religious observance.

1968   *Epperson v. Arkansas* rules against a state law prohibiting teaching of evolution in public educational institutions, on the basis of the "establishment" clause.

1970   *Walz v. Tax Commission* upholds property tax exemption for church property.

1971   *Lemon v. Kurtzman* rules that state funds cannot cover part of teacher salaries and instructional materials in religious schools, even if for non-religious activity. Court creates test for "establishment" clause interpretation, stipulating that legislative act had to have primarily a secular purpose, primarily a secular consequence, and avoid "excessive entanglement" between church and state.

1972   *Wisconsin v. Yoder* upholds Amish exemption for public school attendance on religious grounds.

1980   *Stone v. Graham* strikes down state law requiring that Ten Commandments be displayed in schools.

1984   *Lynch v. Donnelly* upholds right of city to display nativity scene in its Christmas display, on the grounds that the overall effect of the display did not emphasize religion and had the legitimate secular purpose of pointing to the historical origins of the holiday season.

1987   *Edwards v. Aguillard* rules against law requiring teaching of both creationism and evolution if there were to be any teaching of origins.

1990   *Employment Division v. Smith* upholds firing of state workers for using peyote, despite claim based on Aboriginal religious ritual, reducing "Sherbert" test from "compelling purpose" of state action to "rational basis."

1992   *Lee v. International Society for Krishna Consciousness* strikes down ban on distributing religious materials in airports.

1993   *Lamb's Chapel v. Center Moriches Union Free School District* rules in favour of equal access for groups using school facilities after school and against excluding those that are religiously based.

1995   *Rosenberger v. University of Virginia* rules against the university for withholding funding from a religious student publication that it provided to other student publications, on grounds that it discriminated with respect to viewpoint.

2000   *Mitchell et al. v. Helms et al.* rules that federal funds may be used in religious schools, for example to purchase computers and library books, if these were not central to the school's religious purposes.

2002   *Zelman v. Simmons-Harris* upholds a school voucher program that allows choice that could include private religious schools.

2010   *Christian Legal Society v. Martinez et al.* upholds Hastings College of Law (University of California) policy denying recognition and funding to student group that proposed barring homosexual members.

Notes

CHAPTER 2: CULTURE WAR?

The authors would like to thank Clyde Wilcox, David Rayside, Carin Robinson, Celinda Lake, Micah Jensen, Jennifer Howk, and anonymous reviewers for their help and comments. We would also like to thank the Association of Religion Data Archives at Pennsylvania State University.

1 The voters of California overturned this judicial extension of marriage rights to same-sex couples with Proposition 8, passed in November 2008. In New Jersey, state Supreme Court justices mandated the extension of all the rights of marriage to same-sex couples but left it up to the legislature to determine whether to call such unions "marriage." In 2006, the legislature voted for the term "civil unions" instead.

2 The differences between the ANES, Gallup, and *Los Angeles Times* poll numbers may be due to differences in question wording. It is conceivable that phrasing this question in the negative rather than in the positive changes the response; it is also possible that Gallup's more stringent requirement that the gay or lesbian person(s) had "personally" come out to the respondent and the ANES use of "immediate" may be the reasons for the lower Gallup and ANES numbers. Regardless, even the lowest number (50 percent) suggests that a large number of people are close to people whom they know to be homosexual.

3 We use Layman's (2001) categorization of religions and denominations to classify respondents as mainline, evangelical, or black Protestant (see Appendix A, 345-47).

4 Regression results available by request from the authors, significant at the $p < .05$ level.

5 We also checked for demographic differences on gay rights issues and religiosity (see, for example, LaMar and Kite 1998, finding differences based on respondent gender). Results were not significant in 2004; women were slightly more likely to

attend church, but men were more likely to take the Bible literally. As of 2008, women are slightly more likely than men both to attend church and to take the Bible literally. However, gender is not significantly correlated with religious indicators when controlling for evangelicism.

6 It is important to note that many scholars believe that the "religious restructuring" thesis has been overstated. For example, Holben's (1999) presentation of six Christian viewpoints on homosexuality suggests a continuum of opinions rather than the extreme polarization indicated by restructuring.

7 Although we include transgenderism and transsexualism in our discussion because of their growing social and political importance, we do not mean to imply that they are sexual orientations in the same sense as are heterosexuality, homosexuality, or bisexuality. Instead, they should be properly understood as gender identities, with no necessary connection to individuals' sexual orientations. Yet, because transgenderism and transsexualism both challenge traditional gender and sex binaries, they function similarly to minority sexual orientations in inciting fear and backlash.

CHAPTER 3: SURVEY OF CANADIAN ATTITUDES

1 In 1987, the question asked about approval or disapproval of "homosexuals." Unless otherwise noted, all figures are drawn from Environics Focus Canada data for the year indicated. Focus Canada is a quarterly omnibus survey of a random sample of approximately two thousand Canadians.

2 Question wording: "In fact, the Canadian Bill of Rights does not extend these guarantees to homosexuals. In your opinion, should the constitution prohibit discrimination against homosexuals?"

3 In the 1990, 1993, and 1996 surveys, question wording was changed to the following: "The Canadian Charter of Rights and Freedoms in the constitution prohibits discrimination against women, ethnic and religious minorities, and other groups when it comes to housing, jobs, and education. The Charter does not extend these rights to gays and lesbians. In your opinion, should the constitution prohibit discrimination against gays and lesbians?"

4 "Do you think that gay and lesbian couples should or should not be included in employee benefit plans which provide things like health and dental benefits to spouses of employees?"

5 Question wording in 1999: "The federal government is considering changing federal laws so that gay and lesbian couples can have the same treatment as heterosexual couples. Do you strongly support, somewhat support, somewhat oppose, or strongly oppose this?"

6 "Currently, gay and lesbian couples have the same treatment under Canadian law as common-law heterosexual couples. Would you strongly support, somewhat support, somewhat oppose, or strongly oppose allowing gay and lesbian couples to marry?"

7 I am indebted to some helpful compilations of US polling data on homosexuality and gay rights, including Yang (1999); Bowman (2006); and Egan and Sherrill (2005).

8 Question wording: "We have heard a lot these days about the changing of the family. I'd like to know your opinion on what a family is. For each of the following types of

living arrangements, please tell me whether you would definitely call it a family or definitely would not call it a family."

9 There was a minor variance in the preamble, which, in the Gallup item, refers to the "changing American family" and, in the Environics version, refers simply to the changing family. The American version of the question also included a number of family model examples not included in the Canadian survey.

10 Environics Social Values Survey data.

11 Sample sizes are too small to enable the analysis of immigrant subpopulations, such as recent arrivals or those arriving from particular regions.

12 "Do you think homosexual marriages should or should not be recognized as valid, with the same rights as traditional marriages?" Should: 40 percent; should not: 56 percent; unsure: 3 percent ($N = 1,200$).

13 "Do you think the federal government should, or should not, do each of the following ... bring back the issue of same-sex marriage to Parliament for another vote?"

14 According to the 2006 census, 19 percent of Canadians are foreign born.

15 See Citizenship and Immigration Canada (2006).

CHAPTER 4: "CIVILITY WITHOUT COMPROMISE"

1 In fact, neither Haggard nor the leaders of New Life Church referred to the homosexual nature of the allegations: they only referred to the fact that Haggard admitted to immorality.

2 However, more than a few evangelicals, most notably Peggy Campolo (wife of Tony Campolo) and Mel White (former ghost writer for Jerry Falwell), support monogamous same-sex unions.

3 Since certain Christian right organizations (e.g., Focus on the Family) have used stronger anti-gay rhetoric in internal communications (mass mailings, etc.) and more civil language in external communications (publicized media statements, etc.; see Green 2000), it is not clear if this change in rhetoric reflects actual attitudinal change. From the standpoint of pro-gay groups, the "conversionist" tactics of groups like Focus on the Family cannot be compassionate because they reject the legitimacy of non-heterosexual orientations. For many evangelicals, proselytizing for conversion is seen as a compassionate response since failure to do so condemns the unrepentant individual to hell for eternity. Regardless, it is not necessary to determine whether Focus on the Family has become more compassionate; rather, the point is that many evangelicals hold similar views to this group and evince increasingly positive regard towards homosexuals over time.

4 Many evangelicals wish to distance themselves from fundamentalism. This is true in both countries, but especially in Canada, where fundamentalists are less common (Reimer 2003; Smith 2000). Some scholars consider fundamentalists and evangelicals to be distinct groups (Smith et al. 1998). For this study, however, I have placed all conservative Protestants, including fundamentalists, within the larger evangelical camp.

5 ProCan data are generated every five years (from 1975 to 2005) through mail surveys sent out to Canadian adults (18 and over) who, through the use of telephone directories, are randomly selected within certain communities. These data are weighted

to match the Canadian census, resulting in a sample size of roughly 1,200 Canadians and between 70 and 100 evangelicals (and 40 to 60 regularly attending evangelicals) per survey (2005 has 1,600 Canadians and about 140 evangelicals). The response rate is roughly 60 percent across the history of the surveys (for more information, see Bibby 2002). The GSS data represent face-to-face interviews with a random sample of non-institutionalized Americans aged 18 and up. The surveys are conducted every one to two years (for more information, see Davis, Smith, and Marsden 2005). The total sample includes 46,510 Americans, of which about 11,417 are evangelicals (5,161 attending evangelicals). The NES data are also from face-to-face interviews with American adults with pre-election and post-election day samples (for more information, see http://www.electionstudies.org/).

6 Factor analysis revealed the following groupings: (1) the dis-ease/deviant group (alcoholic, mental patient, drug user, drug addict, ex-convict); (2) the at-ease/ethnic group (Native, Oriental/Asian, black, East Indian, Jew); (3) and the sexual orientation group (gay, lesbian). The groupings were fairly consistent across years and cross-rotation methods (varimax, equamax, oblimin). To test for change over time, I computed slope coefficient, which gives the average change in the mean per year (for more information on this technique, see Firebaugh 1997).

7 The degree to which these influences penetrate evangelical ideological boundaries is an open question since many evangelicals maintain tension with the world and reject "worldly" influences. There is no lack of antipathy among evangelicals towards media producers, for example. However, national differences clearly suggest that some external factors influence evangelical attitudes (Reimer 2003).

8 The survey questions are worded differently in the two countries. The ProCan survey asks respondents if they "approve and accept," "disapprove and accept," or "disapprove and don't accept" same-sex marriage. Bibby (2006, 21-22) reasons that the majority would tolerate or "accept" these behaviours, even among their own children, because of the enshrinement of pluralism in Canada. By dividing between approval and acceptance, he seeks to test the proposition that Canadians are willing to tolerate diversity in sexual issues, even if they do not approve. In Canada, 1.2 percent of CPs both "approve and accept" same-sex marriage. Percentages would likely be higher if they were asked if they "approve" only.

9 GSS item wording:

> There's been a lot of discussion about the way morals and attitudes about sex are changing in this country. If a man and woman have sex relations before marriage, do you think it is always wrong, almost always wrong, wrong only sometimes, or not wrong at all?
> What about sexual relations between two adults of the same sex?

ProCan item wording:

> What is your opinion of the following?
> A man and woman having sexual relations before marriage.
> Two adults of the same sex having sexual relations.

10 To measure abortion attributes, I created a "pro-life" scale ranging from 7 to 14 of the following items (alpha = .892).
GSS wording:

> Please tell me whether or not you think it should be possible for a pregnant woman to obtain a legal abortion:
> If she is married and does not want any more children?
> If there is a strong chance of serious defect in the baby?
> If the family has a very low income and cannot afford any more children?
> If she became pregnant as a result of rape?
> If the woman's own health is seriously endangered by the pregnancy?
> If she is not married and does not want to marry the man?
> The woman wants it for any reason?

Pro-Can wording:

> Do you think it should be possible for a pregnant woman to obtain a legal abortion if:
> There is a strong chance of a serious defect in the baby.
> She is married and does not want to have any more children.
> Her own health is seriously endangered by the pregnancy.
> The family has a very low income and cannot afford more children.
> She became pregnant as a result of rape.
> She is not married and does not want to marry the man.
> She wants an abortion for any reason.

This scale shows that evangelicals are becoming significantly more conservative across all items (CN slope = .029; US slope = 0.24) while non-CP Canadians are becoming less conservative (−.017) and non-CP Americans are holding steady (−.003).

11 It is important to note that both feelings towards homosexuals and sexual ethics influence attitudes towards same-sex marriage and gay rights. This is true of both Americans (Wilcox and Wolpert 2000) and Canadians and Canadian evangelicals. Ordinal regression analysis was used to analyze the effects of various predictor variables on attitudes towards same-sex marriage from ProCan (2005). The results reveal that sexual morals (homosexual sex, premarital sex, and extramarital sex) and comfort meeting a homosexual are the strongest predictors of support for same-sex marriage, trumping the effects of church attendance, education, age, gender, and even whether or not one is an evangelical. In other words, once one accounts for sexual morals and comfort meeting a homosexual, the evangelical difference is not significant. The two issues are also powerful when analyzing a sample of evangelicals. Results are similar for attitudes towards equal rights for homosexuals and same-sex adoptions.

12 Regression results from the GSS show that whether or not the respondent views homosexuality as inherent or as a choice is the strongest predictor of attitudes towards homosexual sex (beta −.276**). It is stronger than gender (−.098), education (−.146), age (.104), and church attendance (.209*) among evangelicals (N = 110). I know of no similar question in Canada.

CHAPTER 6: EVANGELICALS, THE CHRISTIAN RIGHT

1 In Florida and Arizona the propositions would have been defeated if white evangelicals had constituted only 8 percent of the population. California's Proposition 8 would have narrowly passed, but this calculation does not include African-American and Latino(a) evangelicals or evangelically leaning mainline Protestants.

2 Emphasis added.

3 The survey is of Republican presidential donors, and Christian right members were identified by several of its questions. The questions on tolerance in teaching did not specify any particular grade, but they did begin with an assumption of professional conduct.

4 See http://ag.org/.

5 Of course, these passages are socially constructed within religious communities. The men of Sodom sought to rape the angels of God, and the gender of the angels would seem irrelevant to the magnitude of that offence. Fundamentalists often also cite a story of the attempted rape of a Levite man in Judges, conveniently ignoring the part of the story in which the Levite offers his concubine, who is raped to death.

6 Some point out that there are no job protections for those who engage in adultery or fornication and that, therefore, protection for gays and lesbians is a "special protection."

7 In the ANES, regular attendees were those who went to services almost every week or more often. In the GSS, they are those who went at least once a week.

8 The former is from the ANES, the latter is from the GSS.

9 Lisa Miller, "Belief Watch: Joining the 'Out' Club," *Newsweek*, 16 June 2008, available at http://www.newsweek.com/.

10 States that refuse the money frequently discuss abstinence but not in the way that the national program demands.

11 For a different view, see "Massachusetts Supreme Court Orders All Citizens to Gay Marry," *The Onion*, 25 February 2004, available at http://www.theonion.com/.

12 One other example of symbolic appeals to the Christian right concerns the case of Terry Schiavo, a brain-dead woman whose husband wished to withdraw artificial life support. Congressional Republicans voted to allow Terry Schiavo's parents to sue in federal courts to prevent the withdrawal of life support. But they did not create any legal justification for the case to succeed, with the result that the case was dismissed by federal judges. Meanwhile, in a more substantive move, the Republican Congress also voted to reduce the amount of federal funds that states use to keep badly injured Americans such as Schiavo alive.

CHAPTER 7: LIBERAL, WITH CONSERVATIVE "VIBRATIONS"

1 Part of a focus group discussion at the African-American Leadership Council meeting of 2005.

2 In fact, of all the issues relevant to voting asked by the Pew Research Center, no issue has ever ranked as less important to the American public than same-sex marriage. Moreover, since 2004, the number of Americans who claimed the issue was "very important" has fallen six points, from 34 percent to 28 percent (Pew Research Center 2004-08).

3 These are (1) three two-hour focus groups conducted from 18 to 20 October 2005, with thirty-three African-American ministers (four women, twenty-nine men) from seventeen states, all of whom were members of the African American Ministers Leadership Council (AAMLC); and (2) an extended two-day focus group conducted from 6 to 7 April 2006, with eight prominent progressive African-American ministers and five prominent progressive African-American community leaders. All focus groups were conducted by Robert P. Jones and Daniel Cox at the Center for American Values in Public Life at the People for the American Way Foundation in Washington, DC. The 2005 focus groups were recorded and transcribed for analysis; the 2006 focus group was documented using extensive field notes from two observers.

4 Lincoln and Mamiya identify six pairs of dialectical tensions that all black churches navigate in constituting their own culture and theology: (1) priestly versus prophetic – the tension between activities concerned with worship and spiritual life versus those concerned with political concerns; (2) other-worldly versus this-worldly – the tension between an orientation towards heaven versus an orientation towards politics and social life in the here and now; (3) universalism versus particularism – the tension between a universal Christian message of salvation for all and a particular awareness of black consciousness; (4) communal versus privatistic – the tension between the historic tradition of the black church's involvement in all spheres of members' lives versus a focus on private individual needs; (5) charismatic versus bureaucratic – the tension between an emphasis on the charismatic authority of a leader versus an emphasis on institutional authority; (6) resistance versus accommodation – the tension between affirming a distinct cultural heritage versus adopting the norms of a wider society.

5 Using multivariate analysis of three different surveys and controlling for variables commonly associated with religiosity (e.g., living in rural area, south, denominational affiliation), Taylor et al. (1996) found that race was a statistically significant predictor of religiosity.

6 This focus on ethnic group solidarity as a governing social orientation has been supported in Gurin, Hatchett, and Jackson (1989), Tate (1994), and Dawson (1994). Dawson notably advances the argument that black political unity is the result of a "black utility heuristic," where the shared black history of slavery and discrimination creates a propensity for evaluating policies according to impact on the racial group rather than on the individual.

7 The AAMLC clearly sees itself as emphasizing the prophetic tradition of African-American theology. The AAMLC mission statement, for example, "celebrates the historical role of the Black Church as a place of refuge and a source of strength in the midst of oppression." Available at http://www.aamlc.net/.

8 This link between believing that homosexuality is a choice and a rejection of a civil rights frame was also evident in political scientist Nancy Wadsworth's work. She argues that the belief that homosexuality is a choice makes African Americans open to arguments from political conservatives that homosexuals are seeking "special rights" and that true civil rights ought to be restricted to legitimate minorities (Wadsworth 1997).

9 As this quotation indicates, the ban on using the term "civil rights" was not universally followed, even in these discussions.

10 The First National Black Religious Summit on Sexuality was held in 1997 and was organized by Reverend Carlton Veazey under the auspices of the Religious Coalition for Reproductive Choice. It is a testimony to how difficult the issues of same-sex marriage and homosexuality in general are within the African-American community that this summit, whose theme was "Breaking the Silence," hardly addressed issues of homophobia (Douglas 1999).

11 Notably, many of the ministers who spoke out for full marriage equality for gay and lesbian people also told stories of considerable backlash within their own communities.

12 This theme, in fact, was the title of the only existing book of interviews among African-American ministers who are supportive of gay and lesbian rights: *A Whosoever Church: Welcoming Lesbians and Gay Men into African American Congregations* (Comstock 2001).

13 Although ballot initiatives did not receive as much national media attention in 2006, seven states had propositions on the ballot that sought to ban same-sex marriage (Arizona, Idaho, South Carolina, South Dakota, Tennessee, Virginia, and Wisconsin).

14 The religious engagement scale we use here includes two religious practices (frequency of worship attendance and prayer) and religious salience. Using these three measures, we created a composite scale ranging from 0 to 3, and an average score was then computed for each religious tradition.

15 For a more complete discussion of categorizing religious traditions in the United States, see Steensland et al. (2000) and Olson, Cadge, and Harrison (2006).

16 In this model, race was coded into four categories: white, black, Hispanic, and other. Religious affiliation was divided into five categories: Protestant, Catholic, other Christian, non-Christian, and unaffiliated.

CHAPTER 8: CANADIAN EVANGELICALS AND SAME-SEX MARRIAGE

This research has been supported by a Standard Research Grant from the Social Sciences and Humanities Research Council of Canada and by the Canada-US Fulbright Foundation through the Visiting Chair in Canadian Studies at Duke University.

1 As explained in more detail below, the Conservative Party was formed in 2003 by merging the Progressive Conservative Party and the Canadian Alliance (formerly known as the Reform Party).

2 Findings drawn from research commissioned by author.

3 Additionally, for some years evangelicals have had a political party of their own – the Christian Heritage Party (CHP). Active since 1988, the CHP has always been very marginal, even in evangelical circles. The party's best showing was its first, in 1988, when it ran sixty-three candidates and received about 100,000 votes. The CHP is a mix of evangelicals, Catholics, and Christian (Dutch) Reformed groups that, through most of the 1990s, disagreed over strategies (although, more recently, it has settled into a generally conservative approach to all issues, with abortion and same-sex marriage the natural priorities). In 2004, it ran sixty-two candidates (out of 301 electoral districts in Canada) and received 40,283 votes; in 2006, it had forty-five candidates (out of 308 districts) and received 28,163 votes, a very marginal effort in which

no candidate won even 10 percent of the district vote. The CHP remains very much a fringe party in Canadian politics, with little evidence that it even has an impact in local races by dividing the "Christian" vote.

4 Information based on interviews with past and present participants.

CHAPTER 9: IT'S ALL ABOUT SEX

1 For a full chronicle of legislation and court cases around same-sex marriage, see Leahy and Alderson (2004) or the Equal Marriage website (http://www.same sexmarriage.ca/).

2 The Evangelical Fellowship of Canada is an umbrella organization for a wide variety of evangelical Christian churches in Canada. For a list of its members, see http://www.evangelicalfellowship.ca/. The EFC was also the major force behind the several interfaith groups that made presentations and interventions to legislatures and courts on the extension of rights and responsibilities (and, ultimately, the right to marry) to lesbian and gay couples.

CHAPTER 10: FOCUSING, FRAMING, AND DISCERNING

1 According to Lakoff (2007), "when a frame is applied to an issue, it leads people to think and reason about the issue in a specific way. Suddenly, certain conclusions seem to become inevitable and others become nearly impossible. This is what framing is about." For background on my use of the notion of focusing, see Gendlin (1981).

2 For a compelling defence of dialogical relationships among courts, parliaments, parliamentary committees, civil society organizations, and individuals, see Roach (2001). For a useful description and analysis of the arguments presented by the churches supporting and rejecting same-sex marriage, see Dickey Young (2006).

3 For introductions to the comparative ethics approach informing this study, see Hutchinson (1984, 1992).

4 According to the Basis of Union signed by the founding denominations in 1925, "it shall be the policy of the United Church to foster the spirit of unity in the hope that this sentiment of unity may in due time, so far as Canada is concerned, take shape in a Church which may fittingly be described as national."

5 The term "bisexual" is now used to refer to persons attracted to both sexes rather than, as in *The Permanence of Christian Marriage* report, to a heterosexual relationship.

6 As Tracy Trothen (2003) points out, it wasn't until women themselves gained a greater voice on church committees and in staff positions that euphemistic references to male-female relations were replaced by tougher language, such as sexism and violence against women. The fact that issues of homosexuality and same-sex relationships made it onto the church's agenda was also related to the growing visibility and participation of lesbians and gays in both church and community.

7 During the late 1980s, as a response to conflicting claims about what the Bible taught, the Theology and Faith Committee of General Council had engaged the church in a study of the authority and interpretation of scripture. Its final report, *The Authority and Interpretation of Scripture: A Statement of the United Church of Canada,* was published in 1992. It reaffirmed earlier church teachings, which held that reading the Bible required interpretation and attention to changing historical circumstances.

8 One of the continuing signs of a progress narrative in church documents is the assumption that it is up to the supporters of same-sex marriage to "bring along" the dissenters.

9 For a convincing treatment of the limitations of the rights framework for the same-sex marriage debate, see Jennifer Nedelsky's comments in our jointly authored chapter, "Dialogue amidst a Plurality of Principles (and a Principle of Pluralism)," in Moon (2008). As Dickey Young (2006, 5) points out, church documents opposing same-sex marriage "usually make a statement that they wish to uphold the civil rights of 'homosexuals' but that marriage is not a right."

10 There is a large literature on the difference between defining marriage as a contract and as a covenant, and the importance of a covenantal understanding of marriage is a constant theme in United Church marriage documents. See also Witte (1998).

11 For the term "culture of argument," see White (1985, 35).

12 "The task of expounding a constitution is crucially different from that of construing a statute. A statute defines present rights and obligations. It is easily enacted and as easily repealed. A constitution, by contrast, is drafted with an eye to the future. Its function is to provide a continuing framework for the legitimate exercise of governmental power and, when joined by a *Bill* or a *Charter of Rights*, for the unremitting protection of individual rights and liberties ... It must ... be capable of growth and development over time to meet new social, political and historical realities often unimagined by its framers" (*Halpern et al. v. Canada* 2003, 9, para. 42).

13 Whether or not municipal and provincial officials will have the same right to refuse to perform same-sex marriages is a contested question beyond the scope of this chapter.

CHAPTER 11: AMERICAN MAINLINE PROTESTANTISM

1 We frequently use the blanket term "homosexuality" throughout this chapter to refer to homosexuality, homosexual people, and gay and lesbian concerns. We do not address the concerns of bisexual and transgender people, largely because such concerns have rarely been addressed in mainline churches.

2 Some denominations also sponsor programs for "ex-gays" or people who no longer understand themselves to be homosexual.

3 Only one-third reported hearing some discussion more often than "rarely." Moreover, very few (2-3 percent) reported clergy discussion of these issues "very often."

4 The Ohio State University Political Science department sponsored a survey of Ohio voters in the fall of 2004 and included a question asking what church the respondent attended. We took these data and subsequently surveyed the clergy of these churches. Details about the sample and other methodological matters may be found in Neiheisel, Djupe, and Sokhey (2009).

CHAPTER 12: CATHOLICISM, HOMOSEXUALITY, AND SAME-SEX MARRIAGE

1 The gamma coefficient for this relationship is .501, indicating that the product-moment correlation between the two items is not suppressed by the skewed marginal distributions of these two items.

2 This liberalizing trend among Catholics is perhaps exacerbated by the declining percentage of Catholics who attend religious services at least weekly. In the 1970s, the

percentage of Catholics who reported weekly attendance was 43.7 percent; in the 1980s, it was 38.3 percent; in the 1990s, 31.2 percent; and, during the first decade of the twenty-first century, 27.7 percent, for an overall decrease of 16 percent. Conversely, the percentage of infrequently attending Catholics increased by 7.9 percent during the same period (from 25.1 percent to 33.0 percent). By contrast, trends in church attendance for both groups of Protestants are much more stable.

3 I am at a loss to account for this finding. Two possibilities suggest themselves. First, this result may simply represent a sampling anomaly; second, it may be a reaction to the *Goodridge* decision of the previous year. Other studies have suggested that Catholics may experience short-term attitude change in response to public events (Wald 1992).

4 These items are combined to form an index, with a reliability (Cronbach's alpha) of .792.

CHAPTER 13: ROMAN CATHOLICS AND SAME-SEX MARRIAGE IN QUEBEC

1 The Assemblée des évêques du Québec (AQB) is one of the four regional Episcopal assemblies of the CCCB. These regional assemblies are autonomous with regard to the specific pastoral needs of their areas.

2 In Quebec, Protestants count for a mere 6 percent of all inhabitants. Among the Pentecostals, however, we find a noticeable two-thirds increase in population; this group presently boasts some thirty thousand members in Quebec. Meanwhile, 93 percent of Quebeckers see themselves as rooted in one of the great religious traditions. One must note here the specific character of the Montreal region in relation to the rest of Quebec: Montreal's religious and ethnic pluralism is much greater than is that found in the rest of the province. This discrepancy could already be noted, though to a lesser degree, in 1961 (the beginning of the Quiet Revolution).

3 Debating the positive or negative effects of pluralism on religious institutions, Daniel V.A. Olson and Kirk Hadaway have analyzed the general Canadian statistics from 1991. On the basis of these statistics, they have concluded that the degree of religious affiliation in Canada is lower in cities and in counties in which religious pluralism is greater (affiliation here does not mean regular practice). They have also noted that Canada comprises more regions with a low rate of religious pluralism than does the United States (several of these being in Quebec). In less pluralistic counties, where 5 million people are living, the rate of religious affiliation is 98 percent, about 11 percent above the national average (Olson and Hadaway 1999).

4 Compare with Hamelin (1984, 333).

5 One could refer to a recent fundamental theological debate between the progressive German cardinal Walter Kasper and the conservative cardinal Joseph Ratzinger, who became Pope Benedict XVI. Kasper upholds a better balance between the local churches and their bishops on the one hand and the universal Church and the Pope's primacy on the other: "In ethical, sacramental or ecumenical matters many Catholics, priests as much as lay people, 'tend to ignore' the norms promulgated by Rome" (Lefebvre 2006). Here he is speaking within the limits of a heterosexual vision of human love, never mentioning the homosexuality issue. In response, Ratzinger very much strengthens the central authority of the pope. See Lefebvre (2006).

6 One of them, Guy Ménard, also recently published a collection of documents that served as a sort of inventory of the key players involved in the debate and their various opinions on the same-sex marriage (Ménard 2003).

7 See also Bisaillon (1999).

8 See http://www.dignitycanada.org/. "Dignity is an international lay movement of lesbian, gay, bisexual, and transgender Catholics, their families, and their friends. Begun in 1969 in Los Angeles under the leadership of Fr. Patrick Nidorf, O.S.A. in 1973, Dignity became a North American organization with chapters in the United States and Canada. In 1980 Dignity Canada Dignité formed its own organization to address the ecclesiastical issues unique to Canada."

9 Our translation.

10 Ibid.

11 "It is deplorable that homosexual persons have been and are the object of violent malice in speech or in action. Such treatment deserves condemnation from the Church's pastors wherever it occurs. It reveals a kind of disregard for others which endangers the most fundamental principles of a healthy society. The intrinsic dignity of each person must always be respected in word, in action and in law. But the proper reaction to crimes committed against homosexual persons should not be to claim that the homosexual condition is not disordered" (CDF 1986, 10).

12 Our translation.

13 Ibid. See also AQB (2002a, 2005a).

14 Our translation.

15 From the CCCB's collection of documents about marriage, published online at http://www.cccb.ca/.

16 In 2006, when the federal Parliament voted to reopen the debate on the redefinition of civil marriage (the motion was defeated), the CCCB reaffirmed all its positions.

17 This document also sought to instruct Catholics, especially Catholic politicians, on the positions they should adopt when participating in public debates in Western, democratic societies.

18 Quebec's gay and lesbian magazine *Fugues* published this comment on the CCCB's testimonial before the Standing Senate Committee on Legal and Constitutional Affairs (CCCB 2005f, n.p.):

> The recent installation of the Roman Catholic Church's Canadian Primate and his declaration that the Church is threatened by the bill to legalise same-sex marriage [are] deeply troubling. If the Church is so terribly threatened, the threat comes from within its own ranks, from those who deny the foundations of [the Church's] essential purpose: to teach love. Moreover, in its opposition to the institution of a model of domestic life that might finally do something positive for the many young people who despair when they discover their homosexuality, the Church itself represents a threat to our society – much wiser than the Church – striving as we are to eliminate exclusion of [gays and lesbians]. Is Monsignor Ouellet prepared to assume responsibility for the consequences of [our] exclusion which can be as dire, in some cases, as suicide? ("Quand l'église" 2005 [our translation])

19 Our translation. Guy Ménard argues that Quebec Catholic circles had not seen any similar dissent since the intense disagreements within the Church over *Humanae Vitae*, the papal encyclical on chemical contraception (Leclerc 2006).

CHAPTER 14: PATHS FROM EMANCIPATION

My thanks to Clyde Wilcox, Laura Olson, Graham Glover, and David Rayside for helpful comments on this chapter.

1 Some of the best sources are Williams (1998); Layman and Green (2006); Fiorina (2005); Olson and Carroll (1992); Smith (2000); and Wolfe (1998). In his analysis of survey data, Hunter uses a forced-choice question-wording technique that presents respondents with only two fairly extreme response options. This in itself tends to inflate disagreement and creates a much higher level of polarization than do other techniques. In systematic surveys with graded response options and in-depth interviews, distributions of attitudes on "hot button" issues usually take on a normal distribution, suggesting moderation. Hunter's model is also underspecified because it adopts a teleological model such that culture → religion → politics (Leege et al. 2002).

2 Purely for stylistic reasons, I use "gay" as an all-encompassing term to refer to male and female homosexuals.

3 Called the Old Testament in the Christian tradition, the Hebrew Bible comprises the five books of Moses: Exodus, Genesis, Numbers, Deuteronomy, and Leviticus.

4 Of course, there is a gap between considering homosexuality as an intrinsically sinful act and urging the state to deny legal status to gay unions. In practice, however, opposition to homosexuality as illicit sex promotes hostility to any state recognition or protection of gays and lesbians (Wilcox and Wolpert 2000).

5 The case of Israel presents an interesting example of this disjuncture. It is commonly argued that the strong emphasis on maintaining family ties in Jewish culture has overridden homophobia by encouraging close ties between parents and their gay children. The Israeli Supreme Court has also created gay partner benefits without raising much of a stir.

6 Religious affiliation was initially based on a screening question asked of respondents who reported that they attended religious services at least a few times a year: "Do you mostly attend a place of worship that is Protestant, Roman Catholic, Jewish, Mormon, an Orthodox Church, Muslim, or some other religion?" Respondents who had indicated that they never attended were asked this question instead: "Regardless of whether you now attend any religious services do you ever think of yourself as part of a particular church or denomination? If yes: Do you consider yourself as Protestant, Roman Catholic, Jewish, Mormon, as Orthodox Church, Muslim, or some other religion?" Protestants who reported a born-again experience were separated out as evangelicals, and the other categories were based on respondent race and ethnicity. The category for mainline Protestant and evangelical Protestant includes only white respondents.

7 Specialists should note that the model was estimated with an ordered probit routine using robust standard errors. The omitted comparison group, Latino Roman Catholics, represents the sample mean on the dependent variable. For more specifics, please contact the author directly.

8 The evangelical respondents were defined by both their Protestant affiliation and their self-description as born-again Christians. So they differ in two respects from the other groups in the table who were assigned a 0 on the born-again variable.

9 For example, the tendency of Roman Catholics to embrace anti-communism during the Cold War was often explained as an effort to dispel the Protestant calumny against their Americanism. Similarly, among Israeli Jews, Sephardim who originate from Arab countries are usually the most determined opponents of Arabs both inside and outside the borders of the state.

10 As further evidence that attitudes towards minorities reflect Jewish status in the polity, consider that Jews in Israel, the one society with a dominant Jewish majority, are notably less tolerant of and concerned with protecting the rights of religious minorities (Liebman and Cohen 1990).

11 As with any statement about American Jews, this one must be qualified by recognizing the existence of movements within Judaism – such as Toward Tradition or the National Association of Christians and Jews – that have joined forces with the Christian right on the assumption that Jews are safer in a country that openly venerates religion than in one committed to secularism. These movements are clearly deviant when compared to the entire community.

12 Experts on the subject usually define evangelical Protestantism as a religious tradition that houses many subgroups, including fundamentalists. While fundamentalists share with evangelicals a belief in the primacy of a personal relationship with God, the necessity of evangelism, and the high status of scripture, they frequently draw sharp boundaries between the saved/unsaved and embrace biblical literalism. This study cannot distinguish between the two empirically – nor, for that matter, can most Jews!

13 I was unable to locate any empirical data on the topic. However, the Canadian Jewish Congress intervened on behalf of homosexuals when they sought protection under Canada's human rights laws (Weinrib 2003, 60).

CHAPTER 15: MUSLIMS AND SEXUAL DIVERSITY IN NORTH AMERICA

1 Information from the Statistics Canada 2001 census, available at http://www.statcan.gc.ca, identifies 579,640 Muslims from a total population of 29,639,035, making them the largest non-Christian group (Jews are the next largest at 329,995). US figures are difficult to come by from official government sources. Until the Pew survey, estimates varied widely, up to four times its finding of 0.6 percent of the population (see http://religions.pewforum.org/). For example, Carol Stone (1991, 27-29) estimated an American Muslim population of 3.3 million in 1980, increasing to 4 million by 1986 and perhaps reaching 6.6 million by 2000 (again, hard to pinpoint because of the difficulty of estimating accurately).

2 As Turner (2002, 109) argues, "with the collapse of organised communism in 1989-92, western politics lost its 'Other.' During the last decade, Islam, and in particular fundamentalist Islam, has been constructed as the unambiguous enemy of western civilisation." For Samuel Huntington (1993, 1996), the clash is inevitable and deeply embedded in two different cultural systems, one that separates God and Caesar, and one that pulls them together." Turner argues that such commentaries fail to consider

the heterogeneity of contemporary Islamic belief and treat it as a foreign religion without recognizing its role in Western history. Razack (2008, 5) adds to this critique "Three allegorical figures have come to dominate the social landscape of the 'war on terror' and its ideological underpinning of a clash of civilizations: the dangerous Muslim man, the imperilled Muslim woman, and the civilized European." Rizzo, Abdel-Latif, and Meyer (2007, 1165) point out that "complexities in Arab Muslim majority countries over women's rights and democracy abound and, in fact, may dwarf the importance of divisions between the West and Muslim populations over gender."

3 In 2007, the Canadian government promoted Islamic History Month to "motivate and inspire Canadian Muslims to annually share their history, heritage and culture with fellow Canadians" (http://www.islamichistorymonth.com).

4 Which is not to say that this media conservatism is absent in Canada. One need only to look at Muslim concerns over *Maclean's*, the country's leading news magazine, and the coverage of Muslims by Margaret Wente in the *Globe and Mail*, the country's leading national newspaper.

5 Of course, belief in the Quran as being the literal word of God is one of the articles of faith for Muslims. By contrast, Christians have a variety of views on the Bible, ranging from those of fundamentalists (who believe that every word of the Bible is from God and is true), to those who think of the text as written by humans who were divinely inspired, to those who think of the book as a purely human text.

6 Interview with Mohammed Khan, conducted by David Rayside, May 2008.

7 The NAZ project in London, UK, has been providing some support to British queer Muslims in the context of sexual health services for black and minority ethnic groups (http://www.naz.org.uk). The Safra project, also in the United Kingdom, provides online information resources (http://www.safraproject.org). The recent launch of an Arab initiative by the Swedish Federation for LGBT rights is moving in a similar direction (personal interviews, Copenhagen, 2009). Human rights groups that work around the world and include LGBT rights in their agendas – such as Amnesty International and Human Rights Watch – publicize information on conditions and support networks for LGBT Muslims but mostly focus on non-Western societies (Long 2009; Waites 2008, 2009; Kollman and Waites 2009).

8 Al-Fatiha's website (http://www.al-fatiha.org) cites seven chapters but provides only one PO box for contact in Washington, DC, and no current contact details. The large American lobbying organization, Human Rights Campaign, has a discussion of issues relating to Muslims and sexuality at http://www.hrc.org/ and includes a link to Al-Fatiha. In Canada, Egale Canada includes a news report saying that the MCC supported same-sex marriage legislation in 2005, and, for those in search of support groups, it also contains a link to Al-Fatiha in the United States and to Salaam in Toronto (http://www.egale.ca).

CHAPTER 16: THE CONSERVATIVE PARTY OF CANADA

I owe a special thanks to Chris Cochrane, who provided me with data and advice on attitudes towards homosexuality in Canada and other countries. I also benefited substantially from the advice of Jim Farney, when he was in the PhD program in Political Science at the University of Toronto. They, Scott Matthews, and Clyde Wilcox commented incisively on an earlier version. I also benefited immeasurably from three confidential interviews undertaken for this chapter in particular. I am also grateful to a significant number of legislators, reporters, academics, and activists in Alberta whom I interviewed confidentially some years ago and who helped shape my views about the complex position in which Canadian politicians can place themselves when they try to appeal simultaneously to neoliberal and morally conservative constituencies. That research was undertaken with funding from the Social Sciences and Humanities Research Council of Canada.

 1 The marriages that then took place were the first in the world to have no explicit restrictions on parenting rights, as was the case with Dutch marriage (enacted before this) and Belgian marriage (also enacted in 2003).
 2 An Environics poll in the spring of 2006 showed that 66 percent did not want the issue re-raised. See "Environics/CBC 2006 Federal Election Survey," available at http://erg.environics.net/. On the substantive question, 59 percent supported lesbian/gay marriage, and only 24 percent strongly opposed. See Environics Research Group, "Canadians for Equal Marriage," available at http://erg.environics.net/.
 3 Confidential interview, conducted by author, April 2004. Federal leaders invariably exercise great leverage over their legislative colleagues, but journalistic accounts out of the Ottawa press gallery are virtually unanimous in characterizing Harper's control as without equal.
 4 Confidential interview, conducted by author, July 2008.
 5 This is a view obviously shared by Hugh Segal (2007), but it also comes from a Conservative insider (confidential interview, conducted by author, August 2007).
 6 This point comes from Farney, interviewed by author, 3 August 2007.
 7 Confidential interview, conducted by author, 3 August 2007.
 8 Ibid., May 2008.
 9 This is not true of all issues related to sexual diversity. On protecting gays and lesbians against discrimination in work and housing, Americans and Canadians are not much different. They are also not very distinct from one another in being evenly divided on the question of same-sex adoption, even though adoption rights are (in law) almost entirely extended to same-sex couples in Canada and only spottily so in the United States.
10 An Environics poll in the spring of 2006 showed that 47 percent of Conservative supporters supported gay marriage. Among all Canadians, 59 percent favoured gay marriage, and 62 percent did not want the issue re-raised.
11 In 2000 World Values Surveys, the proportion of the population responding that homosexuality was "never justified" dropped to half of what it had been in 1980 in Canada, the United States, Western Germany, and France. Data sent to author in August 2007 and August 2009.
12 There was, of course, reticence or avoidance among many priests, though the ferocity of the Vatican's attack on gay marriage narrowed the room for dissidence.
13 Confidential interview, conducted by author, May 2008.

14 Giorno came from the Progressive Conservative side of the party, having been chief of staff to Ontario premier Mike Harris, whose government prioritized neoliberal policies. Still, his pro-life views are well known and would be a source of some satisfaction to religious conservatives.

15 Since the merger, the Conservatives have revolutionized their donor base by bringing in many small contributors, and it is highly likely that religious conservatives constitute a high proportion of those donors. Confidential interview, conducted by author, April 2008.

16 Ipsos-Reid poll, 2006.

17 Confidential interview, conducted by author, April 2008.

18 Focus on the Family already had a foundation in Canada before the creation of its branch plant and Ottawa-based family institute. James Dobson's radio program is heard on 130 Canadian radio stations.

19 From a presentation by Lorna Dueck at the University of Toronto, November 2009.

20 Confidential interview, conducted by author, July 2007.

21 Reid left the Prime Minister's Office in 2010, though McDonald (2010) argues that the office still has a strong contingent of religious conservatives.

22 For many conservatives, this had only become an issue when homosexual activity was decriminalized (1969) and when courts in the 1980s and 1990s made clear that discrimination based on sexual orientation was unconstitutional. There was a remaining discriminatory provision on the statute books criminalizing anal sex for those under eighteen. Even though it had been ruled unconstitutional in two provinces, the Conservative government resisted any amendment to their bill to remove that anomalous provision.

23 It was not harmonized for anal sex, for which the age of consent was set at eighteen. Even though that discriminatory provision has been ruled unconstitutional by courts in two provinces, the anomalous wording remains in the statute books. Although the issue was raised during debate over the Conservative bill to raise the overall age of consent to sixteen, there is no chance that the Conservatives would accept such an amendment.

24 Confidential interview, conducted by author, April 2008.

25 Ibid., July 2008.

26 Ibid.

27 During the previous fall, a petition initiated by Conservative MP Brad Trost, and signed by thirty of his colleagues, had called for an end to government funding for Planned Parenthood (Diebel 2010).

28 Remarks to a panel discussion on religion and Canadian politics, at the annual meeting of the American Political Science Association, Toronto, September 2009.

29 In December 2008, the Liberals, the NDP, and the Bloc Québécois signed an agreement on forming a coalition to defeat the Conservatives in Parliament. The prime minister convinced the governor general to allow a prorogation of Parliament to avoid that immediate prospect. And even if a coalition was an entirely legitimate alternative to his minority government, he effectively won the public relations war in attacking the proposal as illegitimate.

30 Spain's Popular Party has certainly opposed same-sex marriage but with a voice noticeably more muted than those of Catholic bishops, its leadership recognizing that 60 percent or more of the electorate supports such marriage.

31 The only positive correlation (a modest .2) is found between opposition to immigration and animosity towards gays and lesbians.

CHAPTER 17: THE POLITICS OF MARRIAGE AND AMERICAN PARTY POLITICS

1   Data for the American public came from the fourth National Survey of Religion and Politics (NSRP), conducted at the University of Akron in 2004 (N = 4,000). The data on party delegates come from two sources, the 2004 Party Elite Survey (PES), conducted jointly by Southern Illinois University and the University of Akron in 2004 (N = 960), and the 2004 Convention Delegate Study (CDS), conducted at Arizona State University and the University of Akron in 2005 (N = 972). For the delegate studies, Republicans and Democrats were weighted equally. More details available from the author upon request.

2   See "Gay Marriage" at http://pewforum.org/.

3   For more details on the definition of these categories in the public, see Green et al. (2007); for the delegates, see Green and Jackson (2007).

4   Affect towards the conservative Christian groups was measured with a five-point Likert-scale in the PES (Table 17.6) and NSRP (Table 17.7). Each item was worded differently, but both assessed how close to or far from the conservative Christian groups the respondent felt. The "very close" and "close" responses were combined.

5   Because the PES did not have a measure of closeness to gay rights groups, data from the 2004 CDS were used. This involved using a recoded thermometer rating of gays and lesbians into five parts to match the five-point Likert-scale item in the NSRP. Evidence from the 2000 CDS suggests that this measure is highly correlated with affect towards gay rights groups. The 2004 CDS had the same item on marriage as did the PES.

6   Affect towards gay rights groups was measured by a five-point Likert-scale in the NSRP (Table 17.9).

CHAPTER 18: THE SUPREME COURT OF CANADA

The author's research is supported by a general grant from the Social Sciences and Humanities Research Council. Amy Ohler, David Rayside, Don Laing, and Bruce Ryder provided valuable comments on an earlier draft.

1   See also *Smith and Chymyshyn v. Knights of Columbus* (2005), in which a religious organization refused to rent its hall to a same-sex couple for a wedding reception.

2   The Canadian Charter does not include an equivalent to the Establishment Clause of the First Amendment to the US Constitution. However, the Canadian courts have interpreted section 2(a) as precluding government support for the practices of one religion over another. For a discussion, see Moon (2003).

3   In previous cases, the courts have held that any support in the schools for the practices of a particular religion amounts to religious compulsion by the state contrary to section 2(a) of the Charter, freedom of conscience and religion. The courts recognized that affirmation of, and even exposure to, particular values in the schools may

amount to value indoctrination because children, particularly those in the primary grades, are not yet independent agents and because the school represents a significant authority in their lives (*Zylberberg v. Sudbury School Bd.* 1988).

4 A dissenting judgment was written by Madame Justice L'Heureux-Dube.

5 L'Heureux-Dube J, dissenting in *TWU v. BCCT* (2001) at 80, observed that "the modern role of the teacher has developed into a multi-faceted one, including counselling as well as educative functions."

6 The Supreme Court of Canada held that the adjudicator's order removing the teacher from the classroom constituted a restriction on the teacher's freedom of expression and freedom of religion rights but that it was justified under section 1.

7 *Ross* (1996, para. 44): "By their conduct, teachers as 'medium' must be perceived to uphold the values, beliefs and knowledge sought to be transmitted by the school system. The conduct of a teacher is evaluated on the basis of his or her position, rather than whether the conduct occurs within the classroom or beyond. Teachers are seen by the community to be the medium for the educational message and because of the community position they occupy, they are not able to choose which hat they will wear on which occasion."

8 It is worth noting that, while the court in *Ross* thought that the public expression of racist views by Mr. Ross required his removal from the classroom, it did not accept that the expression of these views justified his dismissal from a non-teaching position with the school board.

9 In the case of religious schools, the courts have accepted that a teacher's personal practices are relevant to her/his role in the classroom. Publicly funded Roman Catholic school boards, for example, may dismiss, or refuse to hire, teachers who are not members of the Church or who do not adhere to Church doctrine. See, for example, *Caldwell v. St. Thomas Aquinas High School* (1984). Presumably, the public system has the same right to dismiss a teacher who has repudiated the basic values of the school system.

10 While it is true that racist views, including those of Mr. Ross, are sometimes part of a religious belief system, the courts (and the community in general) seem unwilling to regard such views as part of a serious system that should be treated with respect.

11 According to the court, "tolerance of divergent beliefs is a hallmark of a democratic society" (*TWU v. BCCT* 2001, para. 36).

12 In the case of *Kempling v. BCCT* (2005), the BC Court of Appeal upheld the decision of the BCCT to suspend the licence of a teacher who had written discriminatory letters about gays and lesbians to a local newspaper. The court noted that Mr. Kempling had stated clearly in his letters that he was writing as a teacher and that his views about homosexuality would govern his actions as a teacher.

13 McLachlin CJ, *Chamberlain* (2002, para. 35), noted that inclusion of these books on the list of approved teaching resources only meant that a teacher could choose to use these books in the classroom. It did not mean "that all teachers were obliged to use them or even that they were strongly encouraged to use them."

14 The board had also adopted a resolution that resources from gay and lesbian groups were not approved for use in the Surrey School District. This resolution was quashed by the Supreme Court of British Columbia and was not under appeal. But, according

to McLachlin CJ, *Chamberlain* (2002 para. 45), "it provides the context of what occurred later."

15 Section 76 of the School Act, R.S.B.C. 1996 c. 412, s. 76. The act also stated that "the
highest morality must be inculcated, but no religious dogma or creed is to be taught
in a school."

16 *Chamberlain* (2002, para. 33). McLachlin CJ: "The curriculum requires that all children be made aware of the array of family models that exist in our society, and that
all be able to discuss their particular family model in the classroom" (para. 64).

17 According to Shariff, Case, and Manley-Casimir (2000, 103), "one way or another,
one group's wishes must be compromised."

18 The dissenting judgment of Gonthier J made this point and argued that the "issue" of
same-sex relationships should be left to the upper grades, where it can be presented
as a legitimate but debatable perspective.

19 *Chamberlain* (2002, para. 69): "Tolerance is always age-appropriate."

20 McLachlin CJ, *Chamberlain* (2002, para. 33): "Parental views, however important,
cannot override the imperative placed upon the British Columbia public schools to
mirror the diversity of the community and teach tolerance and understanding of
difference."

21 This reluctance is apparent in most of the other cases referred to in the introductory
paragraph. In *Owens v. Sask. Human Rights Comm.* (2006), for example, the Saskatchewan Court of Appeal held that a particular instance of anti-gay and lesbian
expression should be seen as a contribution to the political debate about same-sex
marriage rather than as the expression of hatred against gays and lesbians.

CHAPTER 19: LAW, SEXUALITY, AND MORALITY IN THE US

1 For an excellent discussion of the tactics and arguments of conservative religious
activists, see Snyder (2006, chap. 4).

2 See the amicus brief filed by the Beckett Fund for Religious Liberty in the Maryland
same-sex marriage litigation at http://www.becketfund.org/files/. The fund has also
filed briefs in Connecticut, Iowa, and Rhode Island.

3 *Journal of the House of Representatives of the United States,* 11 July 1996, H7444.

4 Ibid., H7487.

5 Ibid., H7444.

6 This argument about the power of political culture has also been made by Barry
Adam (2003), who notes the lack of a social welfare tradition in the United States
that is supportive of "claims for entitlements, benefits, or simply comparable treatment," which are vulnerable to stigmatizing demands for "special rights" or to dis-
crediting as "victim talk." In the United States, "the public space for communication
about 'the good' remains more strongly occupied by religion and competitive individualism" (266).

7 *Journal of the Senate of the United States,* 10 September 1996, S10124.

8 This can be viewed as the legal response to the Kinsey Report as the new matter-of-
fact approach to sexuality in that report was reflected in ALI staff reports. See, for
example, "Article 201 – Sexual Offenses," submitted to the Criminal Law Advisory
Group of the American Law Institute for discussion at the meeting on 13-15 January

1955, 7 January 1955. For more discussion of the ALI and the larger issues involving the law and morality, see Pierceson (2005, chap. 4). These legal developments were important because medical elites were still mostly hostile towards sexual minorities.

9   For an example, see *Kelly v. US*, 194 F.2d 150 (D.C. Cir. 1952). See also Johnson (2004).

10 278 Ga. 327 (1998). For more discussion of the legislative and judicial repeal of sodomy laws, see Pierceson (2005, chaps. 4 and 5).

11 For a recent example, see "House Passes Gay Hate Bill, White House Threatens Veto" (2007). No federal civil rights statutes cover sexuality (the fate of such a measure is uncertain even with Democrats in control of Congress and the White House), and fewer than half of the states outlaw sexual orientation discrimination.

12 For a fuller discussion of the jurisprudence, see *City of Cleburne v. Cleburne Living Center*, 473 US 432 (1985).

13 Momentum continued early in 2004, when San Francisco mayor Gavin Newsom began granting marriage licences to same-sex couples, with other municipal leaders in New York, Oregon, and New Mexico following suit. While these efforts were halted by courts, they reflected an increasing desire on the part of same-sex marriage advocates located in more progressive jurisdictions to take action through "official" civil disobedience. See Pierceson (2005, 153-58).

14 On the 2004 election dynamics, see Sherrill and Egan (2008). For the influence of religious perspectives on anti-gay politics, see Eskridge (2000, 1327-411) and Wilson (2007, 561-679).

15 However, those opposed do not necessarily favour no legal recognition for same-sex couples; sometimes they favour civil unions. Only about one-third of the public opposes any legal recognition. This also varies state by state, with some more progressive states approaching majority support for same-sex marriage. For the state bans, see "Anti-Gay Marriage Measures in the US" (NGLTF 2010b). For public opinion dynamics, see http://pollingreport.com/.

16 Mezey (2007, 238). For the most prominent argument against using courts for social change in the United States, see Rosenberg (1991). I offer a counter-argument and more fully explore the ways that courts have achieved change for sexual minorities in Pierceson (2005).

CONCLUSION

1   Thanks to Steve White, PhD candidate at the University of Toronto, for supplying those numbers.

2   Anti-Semitism is at least as widespread but is less based on religious stereotypes than on race-like conceptions of Jewish ethnicity.

References

Abraham, Ibrahim. 2009. "'Out to Get Us': Queer Muslims and the Clash of Sexual Civilization in Australia." *Contemporary Islam* 3 (1): 79-97.

Ackerman, Bruce, and James S. Fishkin. 2004. *Deliberation Day.* New Haven: Yale University Press.

Adam, Barry. 1995. *The Rise of a Gay and Lesbian Movement.* Rev. ed. Boston: Twayne.

–. 2003. "The Defense of Marriage Act and American Exceptionalism: The 'Gay Marriage' Panic in the United States." *Journal of the History of Sexuality* 12 (2): 259-76.

Adams, Michael. 2003. *Fire and Ice: The United States, Canada, and the Myth of Converging Values.* Toronto: Penguin.

Adams, Michael, and Amy Langstaff. 2005. "New Canadians, Old Values?" *Globe and Mail*, 2 March.

Ahmed, Gutbi Mahdi. 1991. "Muslim Organizations in the United States." In *The Muslims of America*, ed. Yvonne Yazbeck Haddad, 11-24. New York: Oxford University Press.

Ahmed, Leila. 1992. *Women and Gender in Islam: Historical Roots of a Modern Debate.* New Haven: Yale University Press.

Airhart, Phyllis. 1990. "Ordering a New Nation and Reordering a Protestantism." In *The Canadian Protestant Experience, 1760-1990*, ed. George A. Rawlyk, 98-138. Burlington, ON: Welch Publishing Company.

Alam, Faisal. "Welcome to Hidden Voices: The Lives of LGBT Muslims." http://www.hiddenvoices.info/.

American National Election Studies (ANES). 2002, 2004, 2008. "ANES 2004 Data-Set and ANES Complete Data File." Ann Arbor: University of Michigan, Center for Political Studies. http://www.electionstudies.org/.

Ammerman, Nancy T. 1997. *Congregation and Community*. New Brunswick, NJ: Rutgers University Press.

–. 2000. "A Quick Question: What Is the Most Volatile Issue Facing Mainline Denominations?" http://www.hirr.hartsem.edu/.

–. 2005. *Pillars of Faith: American Congregations and Their Partners*. Berkeley: University of California Press.

Anderson, Daphne J., and Terence R. Anderson. 1996. "United Church of Canada: Kingdom Symbol or Lifestyle Choice." In *Faith Traditions and the Family*, ed. Phyllis D. Airhart and Margaret Lamberts Bendroth, 126-42. Louisville, KY: Westminster John Knox Press.

Anderson, Ellen Ann. 2005. *Out of the Closets and into the Courts: Legal Opportunity Structure and Gay Rights Litigation*. Ann Arbor: University of Michigan Press.

Anderson, James. 1997. "The Lesbian and Gay Liberation Movement in the Presbyterian Church (USA), 1974-1996." *Journal of Homosexuality* 34: 37-65.

Anglican Church of Canada. 2006. *Marriage: An Exploration of Marriage in Church and Society*. http://www.anglican.ca/.

Apostolidis, Paul. 2000. *Stations of the Cross: Adorno and Christian Right Radio*. Durham, NC: Duke University Press.

Appleby, R. Scott. 1997. "Catholics and the Christian Right: An Uneasy Alliance." In *Sojourners in the Wilderness: The Christian Right in Comparative Perspective*, ed. Corwin E. Smidt and James M. Penning, 93-113. Lanham, MD: Rowman and Littlefield.

Arat-Koc, Sedef. 2006. "Whose Transnationalism? Canada, 'Clash of Civilisations Discourse,' and Arab and Muslim Canadians." In *Transnational Identities and Practices in Canada*, ed. V. Satzewich and L. Wong, 216-40. Vancouver: UBC Press.

Arkoun, Mohammed. 1994. *Rethinking Islam: Common Questions, Uncommon Answers*. Boulder: Westview Press.

Arthur, Joyce. 2008. "Bill C-484 Isn't about Protecting Pregnant Women, It's about Recriminalizing Abortion." *National Post*, 31 March.

Asian Pacific American Legal Center of South California. 2009. "Asian Americans at the Ballot Box: The 2008 General Election in Los Angeles County." http://www.apalc.org/.

Asling, John. 2003. "Past General Councils: Council Tells Federal Government to Legalize Same-Sex Marriages." General Council 38. http://www.united-church.ca/.

Assembly of Quebec Bishops/Assemblée des évêques du Québec (AQB). 2002a. "Deux sujets à portée éthique: L'union civile et les biotechnologies." Déclaration, 6 mars. http://www.eveques.qc.ca/.

–. 2002b. "Réactions de l'Assemblée des évêques catholiques du Québec au Projet de loi sur l'union civile." 15 mai. http://www.eveques.qc.ca/.

–. 2002c. "L'union civile et le mariage." Lettre ouverte de Mgr Bertrand Blanchet, évêque de Rimouski, 15 mars. http://www.eveques.qc.ca/.

–. 2005a. "La définition du mariage et les enjeux d'une définition." (Sous la signature de Mgr Bertrand Blanchet). Table ronde sur le mariage. Université du Québec a Rimouski, 16 janvier.

−. 2005b. "Mariage et société: Pour un vote libre et éclairé à la chambre des communes/Marriage and Society: For a Free and Enlightened Vote in Parliament." Déclaration de Mgr Marc Ouellet, 22 janvier. http://www.eveques.qc.ca/.

Association of Religion Data Archives. 2008. "Association of Religion Database." Philadelphia: Pennsylvania State University. http://www.thearda.com/.

Baer, Douglas, Edward Grabb, and William Johnston. 1990. "The Values of Canadians and Americans: A Critical Analysis and Reassessment." *Social Forces* 68: 693-713.

−. 1993. "National Character, Regional Culture, and the Values of Canadians and Americans." *Canadian Review of Sociology and Anthropology* 30: 13-36.

Ballmer, Randall. 2006. *Thy Kingdom Come: An Evangelical's Lament.* New York: BasicBooks.

Banerjee, Neela. 2004. "American Ruptures Shaking the Episcopal Church." *New York Times*, 3 October.

Barr, John J. 1974. *The Dynasty: The Rise and Fall of Social Credit in Alberta.* Toronto: McClelland and Stewart.

Bartkowski, John P. 2001. *Remaking the Godly Marriage: Gender Negotiation in Evangelical Families.* New Brunswick, NJ: Rutgers University Press.

Bashevkin, Sylvia. 1998. *Women on the Defensive: Living through Conservative Times.* Toronto: University of Toronto Press.

Beatty, Kathleen M., and Oliver Walter. 1984. "Religious Preference and Practice: Reevaluating Their Impact on Political Tolerance." *Public Opinion Quarterly* 48: 318-29.

Bellah, Robert N., Richard Madsen, William M. Sullivan, Ann Swidler, and Steven M. Tipton. 1985. *Habits of the Heart: Individualism and Commitment in American Life.* San Francisco: Harper.

Benoit, Kenneth, and Michael Laver. 2006. *Party Policy in Modern Democracies.* New York: Routledge.

Berlant, Lauren, and Michael Warner. 2002. "Sex in Public." In *Publics and Counterpublics,* ed. Michael Warner, 187-208. New York: Zone.

Betz, Hans-George. 1998. "Introduction." In *The New Politics of the Right: Neo-Populist Parties and Movements in Established Democracies,* ed. Hans-Georg Betz and Stefan Immerfall, 1-10. New York: St. Martin's Press.

Beuttler, Fred. 1999. "Making Theology Matter: Power, Polity and the Theological Debate over Homosexual Ordination in the Presbyterian Church (USA)." *Review of Religious Research* 41: 239-61.

Bibby, Reginald. 1975-2005. Project Canada Survey Series. http://www.reginaldbibby.com/.

−. 1987. *Fragmented Gods: The Poverty and Potential of Religion in Canada.* Toronto: Irwin.

−. 2002. *Restless Gods: The Renaissance of Religion in Canada.* Toronto: Stoddart.

−. 2004. *The Future Families Project: A Survey of Canadian Hopes and Dreams.* Ottawa: The Vanier Institute of the Family.

−. 2005. *Restless Churches: How Canada's Churches Can Contribute to the Emerging Religious Renaissance.* Toronto: Novalis.

–. 2006. *The Boomer Factor: What Canada's Most Famous Generation Is Leaving Behind.* Toronto: Bastian Books.

Bird, Phyllis. 2000. "The Bible in Christian Ethical Deliberation Concerning Homosexuality: Old Testament Contributions." In *Homosexuality, Science, and the "Plain Sense" of Scripture,* ed. David L. Balch, 142-76. Grand Rapids, MI: W.B. Eerdmans.

Birnbaum, Pierre, and Ira Katznelson. 1995. *Paths of Emancipation: Jews, States and Citizenship.* Princeton, NJ: Princeton University Press.

Bisaillon, Réjean. 1999. "La problématisation de l'homosexualité en théologie morale: Vers une éthique gaie et chrétienne." PhD diss., Faculté de théologie et de sciences des religions, Université de Montréal.

Blumstock, Robert. 1993. "Canadian Civil Religion." In *The Sociology of Religion: A Canadian Focus,* ed. W.E. Hewitt, 173-94. Toronto: Butterworths.

Boorstein, Michelle, and Jacqueline L. Salmon. 2007. "Episcopal Church: Diocese Sues 11 Seceding Congregations over Property Ownership." *Washington Post,* 1 February.

Boswell, John. 1980. *Christianity, Social Tolerance and Homosexuality: Gay People in Western Europe from the Beginning of the Christian Era to the Fourteenth Century.* Chicago: University of Chicago Press.

Bowen, Kurt. 2004. *Christians in a Secular World: The Canadian Experience.* Montreal and Kingston: McGill-Queen's University Press.

Bowman, Karlyn. 2006. "Attitudes about Homosexuality and Gay Marriage." American Enterprise Institute. http://www.aei.org/.

Boykin, Keith. 2005. *Beyond the Down Low: Sex, Lies, and Denial in Black America.* New York: Carroll and Graf.

Brean, Joseph, and Katie DeRosa. 2006. "Empowered by Prayer." *National Post,* 30 December.

Brewer, Paul. 2003. "The Shifting Foundations of Public Opinion about Gay Rights." *Journal of Politics* 65: 1208-20.

Brodie, Janine. 2003. *Reinventing Canada: Politics of the 21st Century.* Toronto: Prentice-Hall.

Brooks, R.T. 2003. "The Canadian 'Electronic Church': The Development of Single-Faith Broadcasting in Canada." MA thesis, McMaster University.

Brown, Michael. 2007. "Canadian Jews and Multiculturalism: Myths and Realities." *Jewish Political Studies Review* 19: 1-15. http://www.secured4.catom.com/.

Brown, Peter. 1987. "Late Antiquity." In *A History of Private Life.* Vol. 1: *From Pagan Rome to Byzantium,* ed. Paul Veyne, 235-312. Cambridge: Belknap Press of Harvard University.

–. 2002. "Bodies and Minds: Sexuality and Renunciation in Early Christianity." In *Sexualities in History: A Reader,* ed. Kim M. Phillips and Barry Reay, 129-40. New York: Routledge.

Bruce, Steve. 1998. *Conservative Protestant Politics.* London: Oxford University Press.

Bruce-Briggs, B. 1979. *The New Class?* New Brunswick, NJ: Transaction.

Bull, Chris, and John Gallagher. 1996. *Perfect Enemies: The Religious Right, the Gay Movement, and the Politics of the 1990s.* New York: Crown Books.

Burgess, John. 1999. "Framing the Homosexuality Debate Theologically: Lessons from the Presbyterian Church (USA)." *Review of Religious Research* 41: 262-74.

Burkinshaw, Robert K. 1994. "Conservative Evangelicalism in the Twentieth-Century 'West.'" In *Amazing Grace: Evangelicalism in Australia, Britain, Canada, and the United States,* ed. George A. Rawlyk and Mark Noll, 317-48. Montreal: McGill-Queen's University Press.

–. 1995. *Pilgrims in Lotus Land: Conservative Protestantism in British Columbia, 1917-1981.* Montreal: McGill-Queen's University Press.

Burns, Gene. 1994. *The Frontiers of Catholicism: The Politics of Ideology in a Liberal World.* Berkeley: University of California Press.

–. 2005. *The Moral Veto: Framing Contraception, Abortion, and Cultural Pluralism in the United States.* New York: Cambridge University Press.

Buzzell, Timothy. 2001. "Gay and Lesbian Activism in American Protestant Churches: Religion, Homosexuality, and the Politics of Inclusion." *Politics of Social Inequality* 9: 83-114.

Cadge, Wendy. 2002. "Vital Conflicts: The Mainline Denominations Debate Homosexuality." In *The Quiet Hand of God: Faith-Based Activism and the Public Role of Mainline Protestantism,* ed. Robert Wuthnow and John H. Evans, 265-86. Berkeley: University of California Press.

–. 2005. *Heartwood: The First Generation of Theravada Buddhism in America.* Chicago: University of Chicago Press.

Cadge, Wendy, Laura R. Olson, and Christopher Wildeman. 2008. "How Denominational Resources Influence Debates about Homosexuality in Mainline Protestant Congregations." *Sociology of Religion* 69 (2): 187-207.

Cadge, Wendy, and Christopher Wildeman. 2008. "Facilitators and Advocates: How Mainline Protestant Clergy Respond to Homosexuality." *Sociological Perspectives* 51 (3): 587-603.

Cahill, Sean. 1997. "The Anti-Gay Marriage Movement." In *The Politics of Same-Sex Marriage,* ed. Craig Rimmerman and Clyde Wilcox, 155-92. Chicago: University of Chicago Press.

Campbell, David C., and Carin Robinson. 2007. "Religious Coalitions for and against Gay Marriage: The Culture War Rages On." In *The Politics of Same-Sex Marriage,* ed. Craig A. Rimmerman and Clyde Wilcox, 131-54. Chicago: University of Chicago Press.

Campbell, David E., and J. Quin Monson. 2007a. "The Case of Bush's Reelection: Did Same-Sex Marriage Do It?" In *A Matter of Faith: Religion in the 2004 Presidential Election,* ed. David E. Campbell, 120-41. Washington, DC: Brookings Institution.

–. 2007b. "Dry Kindling: A Political Profile of American Mormons." In *From Pews to Polling Places: Faith and Politics in the American Religious Mosaic,* ed. J.M. Wilson, 105-30. Washington, DC: Georgetown University Press.

–. 2008. "The Religion Card: Gay Marriage and the 2004 Presidential Election." *Public Opinion Quarterly* 72 (3): 399-419.

Campbell, Ernest Q., and Thomas F. Pettigrew. 1959. *Christians in Racial Crisis: A Study of Little Rock's Ministry.* Washington, DC: Public Affairs Press.

Canadian Broadcasting Corporation. 2006. "Canada's Muslims: An International Comparison." http://www.cbc.ca/.

Canadian Conference of Catholic Bishops (CCCB). 2002. "Pastoral Letter by Most Reverend Jacques Berthelet, C.S.V., President of the Canadian Conference of Catholic Bishops, to the Canadian Catholic Community on Marriage," 25 November. http://www.cccb.ca/.

–. 2003a. "Marriage and Legal Recognition of Same-Sex Unions." Presentation by the Canadian Conference of Catholic Bishops to the House of Commons Standing Committee on Justice and Human Rights, 13 February.

–. 2003b. "Marriage and Same-Sex Unions: Statement by the Permanent Council of the Canadian Conference of Catholic Bishops," 19 June. http://www.cccb.ca/.

–. 2003c. "Marriage in the Present Day," 10 September. http://www.cccb.ca/.

–. 2003d. "Presentation by the Canadian Conference of Catholic Bishops to the House of Commons Standing Committee on Justice and Human Rights on the Discussion Paper Marriage and Legal Recognition of Same-Sex Unions," 13 February. http://www.cccb.ca/.

–. 2004a. Factum of the Intervener, Canadian Conference of Catholic Bishops [civil marriage reference]. Supreme Court of Canada, Court File 29866.

–. 2004b. "Statement by the Canadian Conference of Catholic Bishops on the Decision of the Supreme Court of Canada in the Reference of Marriage," 9 December. http://www.cccb.ca/.

–. 2005a. "Bill C-38 and Debate on Marriage: Letter to Members of Parliament and the Senate Concerning Bill C-38," 28 February. http://www.cccb.ca/.

–. 2005b. "Brief by the Canadian Conference of Catholic Bishops to the Special Legislative Committee on Bill C-38," 18 May. http://www.cccb.ca/.

–. 2005c. "Letter to Prime Minister Paul Martin from CCCB President: 'Why Rush the Legislation on Same-Sex Marriage?'" 6 June. http://www.cccb.ca/.

–. 2005d. "Letter to the Honourable Members of the Senate and the Members of the House of Commons: Proposed Changes to the Meaning and Nature of Marriage," 2 June. http://www.cccb.ca/.

–. 2005e. "Pastoral Letter to Catholics in Canada on Redefining Marriage," 9 February. http://www.cccb.ca/.

–. 2005f. "Saving Marriage as a Fundamental Institution Recognized by the State: Brief by the Canadian Conference of Catholic Bishops to the Senate Standing Committee on Constitution and Legal Affairs," 13 July. http://www.cccb.ca/.

Carens, Joseph, and Melissa Williams. 1996. "Muslim Minorities in Liberal Democracies: The Politics of Misrecognition." In *The Challenge of Diversity: Integration and Pluralism in Societies of Immigration*, ed. Rainer Bauböock, Agner Heller, and Aristide R. Zolberg, 157-86. Aldershot: Avebury.

Carpenter, Joel A. 1980. "Fundamentalist Institutions and the Rise of Evangelical Protestantism, 1929-1942." *Church History*, March, 62-75.

–. 1984. "From Fundamentalism to the New Evangelical Coalition." In *Evangelicalism and Modern America*, ed. George Marsden, 3-16. Grand Rapids, MI: William B. Eerdmans Publishing.

–. 2000. "Fundamentalist Institutions and the Rise of Evangelical Protestantism, 1929-1942." In *More Money, More Ministry: Money and Evangelicals in Recent North American History*, ed. Larry Eskridge and Mark A. Noll, 259-73. Grand Rapids, MI: Wm. B. Eerdmans Publishing.

Carty, Ken, William Cross, and Lisa Young. 2000. *Rebuilding Canadian Party Politics*. Vancouver: UBC Press.

Chambers, Simone. 2003. "Deliberative Democratic Theory." *Annual Review of Political Science* 6: 307-26.

Chandler, Marthe A., Elizabeth A. Cook, Ted G. Jelen, and Clyde Wilcox. 1994. "Abortion in the United States and Canada: A Comparative Study of Public Opinion." In *Abortion Politics in the United States and Canada: Studies in Public Opinion*, ed. M.A. Chandler and T.G. Jelen, 131-43. New York: Praeger.

Chase, Steven. 2009. "Veteran Tory Defends Ablonczy over Grant to Gay Pride Event." *Globe and Mail*, 10 July.

Chaves, Mark. 1997. *Ordaining Women: Culture and Conflict in Religious Organizations*. Cambridge, MA: Harvard University Press.

–. 2004. *Congregations in America*. Cambridge, MA: Harvard University Press.

Christian Booksellers Association (CBA). 2007. "Media Information on Christian Retail." http://www.cbaonline.org/.

Christian Coalition. 2008. "Christian Coalition." http://www.cc.org/.

Christie, Nancy, and Michael Gauvreau. 1996. *A Full-Orbed Christianity: The Protestant Churches and Social Welfare in Canada*. Montreal: McGill-Queen's University Press.

Cianciotto, Jason, and Sean Cahill. 2003. *Education Policy: Issues Affecting Lesbian, Gay, Bisexual, and Transgender Youth*. Washington, DC: National Gay and Lesbian Task Force.

Citizenship and Immigration Canada. 2005. "Recent Immigrants in Metropolitan Areas: Canada – A Comparative Profile Based on the 2001 Census." http://www.cic.gc.ca/.

–. 2006. "Facts and Figures 2005." http://www.cic.gc.ca/.

Clark, J. Michael, Joanne C. Brown, and Lorna Hochstein. 1989. "Institutional Religion and Gay/Lesbian Oppression." *Marriage and Family Review* 14: 265-84.

Cloutier, Mario. 2002. "Union civile des personnes de même sexe: Des valeurs qui changent au Québec." *Le Devoir*, 9 février.

Coates, David, ed. 2005. *Varieties of Capitalism: Varieties of Approaches*. New York: Palgrave Macmillan.

Cochran, John K., and Leonard Beeghley. 1991. "The Influence of Religion on Attitudes toward Nonmarital Sexuality: A Preliminary Assessment of Reference Group Therapy." *Journal for the Scientific Study of Religion* 30: 45-62.

Cochrane, Chris. 2007. "The Political Consequences of Value Bundles: Moral and Economic Values in Canada." Paper presented at the Annual Conference of the Canadian Political Science Association, Saskatoon, May-June.

–. 2008. "The Contours of Left-Right Disagreement in Western Europe and Anglo-American Democracies: Right-Wing Fragmentation and Left-Wing Coherence in Comparative Perspective." Paper presented at the annual meeting of the Canadian Political Science Association, Vancouver, May-June.

–. 2009. "Value Change and the Partisan Landscape: An Update." Unpublished research note.

–. 2010. "The Asymmetrical Structure of Left/Right Disagreement." Paper presented at the Annual Meeting of the Canadian Political Science Association, June.

Coffin, Brent. 2005. "Moral Deliberation in Congregations." In *Taking Faith Seriously,* ed. Mary Jo Bane, Brent Coffin, and Richard Higgins, 113-45. Cambridge, MA: Harvard University Press.

Cohen, Adam B., Daniel E. Hall, Harold G. Koenig, and Keith G. Meador. 2005. "Social Versus Individual Motivation: Implications for Normative Definitions of Religious Orientation." *Personality and Social Psychology Review* 9: 48-61.

Cohen, Cathy. 1999. *The Boundaries of Blackness: AIDS and the Breakdown of Black Politics.* Chicago: University of Chicago Press.

Cohen, Naomi. 1992. *Jews in Christian America: The Pursuit of Religious Equality.* New York: Oxford University Press.

Cohen, Steven M. 1983. *American Modernity and Jewish Identity.* New York: Tavistock.

Cohen, Steven M., and Charles S. Liebman. 1997. "American Jewish Liberalism: Unraveling the Strands." *Public Opinion Quarterly* 61: 405-30.

Community of Concern in the United Church. 2006. "Mission Statement." http://www.communityofconcern.org/.

Comstock, Gary D. 1996. *Unrepentant, Self-Affirming, Practicing: Lesbian/Bisexual/Gay People within Organized Religion.* New York: Continuum.

–. 2001. *A Whosoever Church: Welcoming Lesbians and Gay Men into African American Congregations.* Westminster: John Knox Press.

Congregation for Catholic Education (CCE). 2005. "Instruction Concerning the Criteria for the Discernment of Vocations with Regard to Persons with Homosexual Tendencies in View of Their Admission to the Seminary and to Holy Orders," 4 November. http://www.vatican.va/.

Congregation for the Doctrine of the Faith (CDF). 1975. "Declaration on Certain Questions Concerning Sexual Ethics," 29 December. http://www.vatican.va/.

–. 1986. "Letter to the Bishops of the Catholic Church on the Pastoral Care of Homosexual Persons," 1 October. http://www.vatican.va/.

–. 2003a. "Considerations Regarding Proposals to Give Legal Recognition to Unions between Homosexuals," 28 March. http://www.vatican.va/.

–. 2003b. "Doctrinal Note on Some Questions Regarding the Participation of Catholics in Political Life," 16 January. http://www.vatican.va/.

Conover, Pamela Johnston. 1988. "The Role of Social Groups in Political Thinking." *British Journal of Political Science* 18 (1): 51-76.

Cook, Elizabeth Adell, Ted G. Jelen, and Clyde Wilcox. 1992. *Between Two Absolutes: Public Opinion and the Politics of Abortion.* Boulder, CO: Westview.

Côté, Jean-Guy. 2003. "Le nouvel évêque de Québec 'sous surveillance.'" *Fugues,* mars.

Cotten-Huston, Annie, and Bradley M. Waite. 2000. "Anti-Homosexual Attitudes in College Students: Predictors and Classroom Interventions." *Journal of Homosexuality* 38: 117-33.

Crowley, Michael. 2004. "James Dobson: The Religious Right's New Kingmaker." *Slate*, 12 November.

Csillag, Ron. 2006. "Ken Campbell: Christian Crusader 1934-2006." *Globe and Mail*, 23 September.

Curry, Bill, and Gayle MacDonald. 2008. "Evangelist Takes Credit for Film Crackdown." *Globe and Mail*, 29 February.

Cyr, Luc. 2002. "L'union civile." *Le Devoir*, 22 mai.

D'Antonio, William V., James D. Davidson, Dean R. Hoge, and Ruth A. Wallace. 1996. *Laity: American and Catholic – Transforming the Church*. Kansas City: Sheed and Ward.

Davidoff, Judith. 2006. "Conflicted State." *Capital Times*, 26 October.

Davidson, James D., Andrea S. Williams, Richard Lamanna, Jan Stenftenagel, Kathleen Maas Weigert, William J. Whalen, and Patricia Wittberg. 1997. *The Search for Common Ground: What Unites and Divides American Catholics*. Huntington, IN: Our Sunday Visitor.

Davis, James A., Tom W. Smith, and Peter V. Marsden. 2005. "General Social Surveys, 1972-2004" (cumulative file), File ICPSR04295-v1. Produced by National Opinion Research Center, distributed by Roper Center for Public Opinion Research and Inter-University Consortium for Political and Social Research, 2 September.

Dawson, Michael. 1994. *Behind the Mule: Race and Class in African American Politics*. Princeton, NJ: Princeton University Press.

DeBose, Brian. 2004. "Black Caucus Resists Comparison of 'Gay Marriage' to Civil Rights." *Washington Times*, 15 March.

D'Emilio, John, and Estelle Freedman. 1988. *Intimate Matters: A History of Sexuality in America*. Chicago: University of Chicago Press.

DeRogatis, Amy. 2005. "What Would Jesus Do? Sexuality and Salvation in Protestant Evangelical Sex Manuals, 1950s to the Present." *Church History* 74: 97-137.

Diamond, Sara. 1989. *Spiritual Warfare: The Politics of the Christian Right*. Boston: South End Press.

–. 1995. *Roads to Dominion: Right-Wing Movements and Political Power in the United States*. New York: Guilford Press.

Dickey Young, Pamela. 2006. "Same-Sex Marriage and Christian Churches in Canada." *Studies in Religion/Sciences religieuses* 35 (1): 3-23.

Diebel, Linda. 2010. "Pro-Life MPs Flex Muscles, Dig in for Long Fight." *Toronto Star*, 15 May.

Dillon, Michele. 1999. *Catholic Identity: Balancing Reason, Faith, and Power*. New York: Cambridge University Press.

Djupe, Paul A., and Christopher P. Gilbert. 2003. *The Prophetic Pulpit: Clergy, Churches, and Communities in American Politics*. Lanham, MD: Rowman and Littlefield.

–. 2006. "The Resourceful Believer: Generating Civic Skills in Church." *Journal of Politics* 68: 116-27.

–. 2009. *The Political Influence of Churches*. New York: Cambridge University Press.

Djupe, Paul A., and Jacob R. Neiheisel. 2008. "Deliberation on Gay Rights and Homosexuality in Churches." *Polity* 40: 411-35.

Djupe, Paul A., Laura R. Olson, and Christopher P. Gilbert. 2005. "Sources of Support for Denominational Lobbying in Washington." *Review of Religious Research* 47: 86-99.

–. 2006. "Whether to Adopt Statements on Homosexuality in Two Denominations." *Journal for the Scientific Study of Religion* 45: 609-21.

Dobson, James. 2004. *Marriage under Fire: Why We Must Win This Battle.* Sisters, OR: Multnomah Publishers.

Dorff, Elliot N., Daniel S. Nevins, and Avram Reisner. 2006. "Homosexuality, Human Dignity and *Halakhah*: A Combined Responsum for the Committee on Jewish Law and Standards." Prepared for the Rabbinical Assembly. http://www.rabbinicalassembly.org/.

Douglas, Kelly. 1999. *Sexuality and the Black Church: A Womanist Perspective.* Maryknoll, NY: Orbis Books.

Dreher, Christopher. 2006. "In Canada, Faith Takes a Leap to the Right." *Globe and Mail,* 23 September.

Dutwin, David. 2003. "The Character of Deliberation: Equality, Argument, and the Formation of Public Opinion." *International Journal of Public Opinion Research* 15: 239-64.

Duverger, Maurice. 1969. *Political Parties: Their Organization and Activity in the Modern State.* New York: Methuen.

Egale Canada. 2009. *Youth Speak Up about Homophobia and Transphobia: The First National Climate Survey on Homophobia in Canadian Schools, Phase One Report,* March. http://www.egale.ca/.

Egan, Patrick J., Nathaniel Persily, and Kevin Wallsten. 2008. "Gay Rights." *Public Opinion and Constitutional Controversy,* ed. Nathaniel Persily, Jack Citrin, and Patrick J. Egan, 234-66. Oxford: Oxford University Press.

Egan, Patrick, and Kenneth Sherill. 2005. "Neither an In-Law nor an Outlaw Be: Trends in Americans' Attitudes toward Gay People." *Public Opinion Pros,* February. http://www.publicopinionpros.norc.org/.

Eisen, Arnold M., and Steven Martin Cohen. 2000. *The Jew Within: Self, Family, and Community in America.* Bloomington: Indiana University Press.

Ekos Research Associates. 2002. "Public Attitudes toward Same-Sex Marriage," 10 November. http://www.ekos.com/.

Ellingson, Stephen, Nelson Tebbe, Martha Van Haitsma, and Edward Laumann. 2001. "Religion and the Politics of Sexuality." *Journal of Contemporary Ethnography* 30: 3-55.

Ellis, Faron. 2005. *The Limits of Participation: Members and Leaders in Canada's Reform Party.* Calgary: University of Calgary Press.

Ellison, Keith. 2008. "Press Release." http://www.keithellison.org/.

Ellison, Marvin. 2004. *Same-Sex Marriage? A Christian Ethical Analysis.* Cleveland: Pilgrim Press.

English, John, Richard Gwyn, and P. Whitney Lackenbauer. 2004. *The Hidden Pierre Elliott Trudeau: The Faith behind the Politics.* Ottawa: Novalis.

Environics Research. 2003. "Most Canadians Support Gay Marriage: Support Higher among Catholics than among Protestants," 8 July. http://research-environics-net.sitepreview.ca/.

Erzen, Tanya. 2006. *Straight to Jesus: Sexual and Christian Conversions in the Ex-Gay Movement.* Berkeley: University of California Press.

Eskridge, William N., Jr. 1999. *Gaylaw: Challenging the Apartheid of the Closet.* Cambridge, MA: Harvard University Press.

–. 2000. "No Promo Homo: The Sedimentation of Anti-Gay Discourse and the Channeling Effect of Judicial Review." *New York University Law Review* 75: 1327-411.

Evangelical Fellowship of Canada. 2005. "Submission to the Special Legislative Committee on Bill C-38 (CC38) the Civil Marriage Act." http://www.evangelical fellowship.ca/.

Family Research Council. 2008. "Family Research Council." http://www.frc.org/.

Farid, Muhammad. 2008. *Approach to Power: Muslims, Power, Politics and Their Future Role in North America.* Baltimore: Publish America Press.

Farney, Jim. 2008. "The Benefits of Office: Canadian Conservatives, Same-Sex Marriage and the End of the Tory Syndrome." Paper presented at the annual meeting of the Canadian Political Science Association, Vancouver, May-June.

Fatah, Tarek. 2005. "Some Muslims Are Supportive of Same-Sex Marriage." *The Record* (Waterloo region). http://www.muslimcanadiancongress.org/.

Feiguth, Debra. 2004. "The EFC Holds True to Its Roots." *Faith Today*, September-October. http://www.evangelicalfellowship.ca/.

Ferretti, Lucia. 1999. *Brève histoire de l'Église catholique au Québec.* Montréal: Boréal.

Fetner, Tina. 2008. *Fighting the Right: How the Religious Right Changed Lesbian and Gay Activism.* Minneapolis: University of Minnesota Press.

Feuerherd, Joe. 2004. "Joining Forces to Battle Same-Sex Marriage: Bishops' Conference, Religious Right Fund Project that Critics Call an Attack Effort against Gays." *National Catholic Reporter,* 26 March.

Findlay, James F. 1993. *Church People in the Struggle: The National Council of Churches and the Black Freedom Movement, 1950-1970.* New York: Oxford University Press.

Finke, Roger, and Rodney Stark. 1992. *The Churching of America, 1776-1990: Winners and Losers in Our Religious Economy.* New Brunswick, NJ: Rutgers University Press.

Finlay, Barbara, and Carol S. Walther. 2003. "The Relation of Religious Affiliation, Service Attendance, and Other Factors to Homophobic Attitudes among University Students." *Review of Religious Research* 44: 370-93.

Fiorina, Morris P. 2005. *Culture War? The Myth of a Polarized America.* New York: Pearson Longman.

Firebaugh, Glenn. 1997. *Analyzing Repeated Surveys.* Thousand Oaks, CA: Sage Publications.

Fisher, Randy D., Donna Derison, Chester F. Polley III, Jennifer Cadman, and Dana Johnston. 1994. "Religiousness, Religious Orientation, and Attitudes towards Gays and Lesbians." *Journal of Applied Social Psychology* 24: 614-30.

Fishkin, James S. 1995. *The Voice of the People: Public Opinion and Democracy.* New Haven: Yale University Press.

Fishman, Sylvia. 2000. *Jewish Life and American Culture*. Albany, NY: State University of New York Press.

Flanagan, Tom. 2007. *Harper's Team: Behind the Scenes in the Conservative Rise to Power*. Montreal and Kingston: McGill-Queen's University Press.

–. 2010. "'Something Blue ...' Conservative Organization in an Era of Permanent Campaign." Paper presented at the Annual Meeting of the Canadian Political Science Association, June.

Fletcher, Joseph F., and Paul Howe. 2000. "Supreme Court Cases and Court Support: The State of Canadian Public Opinion." *Choices* 6 (3): 30-56.

–. 2001. "Public Opinion and Canada's Courts." In *Judicial Power and Canadian Democracy*, ed. Paul Howe and Peter H. Russell, 255-96. Montreal: McGill-Queen's University Press.

Fletcher, Joseph F., Peter Russell, and Paul Sniderman. 1996. *The Clash of Rights: Liberty, Equality, and Legitimacy*. New Haven: Yale University Press.

Forum André-Naud. 2006. "Dix-neuf prêtres expriment leur perplexité et leur désaccord devant deux interventions ecclésiales, l'une sur le mariage civil des personnes de même sexe, l'autre sur l'accès à la prêtrise des personnes d'orientation homosexuelle." *La Presse*, 6 février.

Foucault, Michel. 1978. *The History of Sexuality*. Vol. 1: *An Introduction*. New York: Pantheon.

Fowler, Robert Booth, Allen D. Hertzke, Laura R. Olson, and Kevin R. den Dulk. 2004. *Religion and Politics in America: Faith, Culture, and Strategic Choices*. 3rd ed. Boulder, CO: Westview Press.

Frankel, Razelle. 1998. "Transformation of Televangelism: Repackaging Christian Family Values." In *Media, Culture, and the Religious Right*, ed. Linda Kintz and Julia Lesage, 163-89. Minneapolis: University of Minnesota Press.

Fraser, Nancy. 2003. *Redistribution or Recognition? A Political-Philosophical Exchange*. London: Verso.

Friedland, Michael B. 1998. *Lift Up Your Voice Like a Trumpet: White Clergy and the Civil Rights and Antiwar Movements, 1954-1973*. Chapel Hill: University of North Carolina Press.

Gallagher, Eugene V. 2004. *The New Religious Movements Experience in America*. Westport, CT: Greenwood.

Gallagher, Sally K. 2003. *Evangelical Identity and Gendered Family Life*. New Brunswick, NJ: Rutgers University Press.

Galloway, Gloria. 2006. "Same-Sex Marriage File Closed for Good, PM Says." *Globe and Mail*, 8 December.

–. 2010. "Ignatieff Vows to Continue Fight for Reproductive Rights." *Globe and Mail*, 25 March.

Gallup Poll. 2009. Gallup poll data, 1982-2008. http://www.gallup.com/.

Gatehouse, Jonathan. 2004. "2004 in Review: The Poll." *Maclean's*, 27 December.

Gay, Lesbian, and Straight Education Network (GLSEN). 2008. *The 2008 National School Climate Survey*. New York: GLSEN.

Gendlin, Eugene T. 1981. *Focusing*. 2nd ed. Toronto: Bantam Books.

General Social Survey (GSS). 2006. *2006*. National Opinion Research Center, University of Chicago, April.

–. 2008. *2008*. National Opinion Research Center, University of Chicago, April.

Gerstmann, Evan. 1999. *The Constitutional Underclass: Gays, Lesbians, and the Failure of Class-Based Equal Protection.* Chicago: University of Chicago Press.

Gidengil, Elisabeth, André Blais, Joanna Everitt, Patrick Fournier, and Neil Nevitte. 2006. "Back to the Future? Making Sense of the 2004 Election outside Quebec." *Canadian Journal of Political Science* 39: 1-25.

Gidengil, Elisabeth, Patrick Fournier, Joanna Everitt, Neil Nevitte, and André Blais. 2009. "Anatomy of a Liberal Defeat." Paper presented to the annual meeting of the Canadian Political Science Association, Carleton University, Ottawa, May 2009.

Giese, Rachel. 2003. "Out of the Koran." *Xtra!* 12 June.

Gilbert, Christopher P. 1993. *The Impact of Churches on Political Behavior: An Empirical Study.* Westport, CT: Greenwood.

Gilgoff, Dan. 2007. *The Jesus Machine: How James Dobson, Focus on the Family, and Evangelical America Are Winning the Culture War.* New York: St. Martin's Press.

Gingras, François-Pierre. 1993. "Divergences ou convergences? Les laïcs anglophones et francophones dans le catholicisme canadien." *Studies in Religion/ Sciences religieuses* 22 (1): 75-92.

Giroux, Serge. 1975. "Homosexualité et morale chrétienne." MA thesis, Université de Montréal.

Glendon, Mary Ann. 1991. *Rights Talk: The Impoverishment of Political Discourse.* New York: Free Press.

Glenmary Research Center. 2000. Mapping data. Nashville, TN: Glenmary Research Center. http://www.glenmary.org/.

Glenn, Norval D., and Charles N. Weaver. 1979. "Attitudes toward Premarital, Extramarital, and Homosexual Relations in the US in the 1970s." *Journal of Sex Research* 15: 108-18.

Goldberg-Hiller, Jonathan. 2002. *The Limits to Union: Same-Sex Marriage and the Politics of Civil Rights.* Ann Arbor: University of Michigan Press.

Goodstein, Laurie. 2006. "Stay Tuned, as Two Churches Struggle with Gay Clergy." *New York Times,* 24 June.

–. 2007a. "Bishops Denounce Writings of a Catholic Theologian." *New York Times,* 23 March.

–. 2007b. "A Divide, and Maybe a Divorce." *New York Times,* 25 February.

–. 2007c. "Episcopal Church Rejects Demand for a Second Leadership." *New York Times,* 22 March.

Grabb, Edward, and James Curtis. 2005. *Regions Apart: The Four Societies of Canada and the United States.* Toronto: Oxford University Press.

Gravel, Raymond. 2003. "Le Vatican erre: L'église catholique n'a aucune crédibilité dans le débat actuel sur la redéfinition du mariage." *La Presse,* 5 août.

Green, John C. 2000. "Antigay: Varieties of Opposition to Gay Rights." In *The Politics of Gay Rights,* ed. Craig Rimmerman, Kenneth D. Wald, and Clyde Wilcox, 121-38. Chicago: University of Chicago Press.

Green, John C., and John S. Jackson. 2007. "Faithful Divides: Party Elites and Religion in 2004." In *A Matter of Faith: Religion in the 2004 Presidential Election*, ed. David E. Campbell, 37-62. Washington, DC: Brookings Institution Press.

Green, John C., Lyman A. Kellstedt, Corwin E. Smidt, and James L. Guth. 2007. "How the Faithful Voted: Religious Communities and the Presidential Vote." In *A Matter of Faith: Religion in the 2004 Presidential Election*, ed. David E. Campbell, 15-36. Washington, DC: Brookings Institution Press.

Greenawalt, Kent. 2006. *Religion and the Constitution.* Vol. 1: *Fairness and Free Exercise.* Princeton: Princeton University Press.

Greenberg, Steven. 2004. *Wrestling with God and Men: Homosexuality in the Jewish Tradition.* Madison: University of Wisconsin Press.

Greenspahn, Frederick E. 2002. "Homosexuality and the Bible." *Central Conference of American Rabbies (CCAR) Journal* (Fall): 38-47.

Greenspon, Edward. 2001. "Covering Campaign 2000." In *The Canadian General Election of 2000*, ed. Jon H. Pammet and Christopher Dornan, 165-90. Toronto: Dundurn.

Grenville, Andrew. 2006. "Church, Conscience, Corruption and the Conservatives." *Faith Today*, March-April.

Gründel, Johannes. 1975. "Natural Law." In *Encyclopedia of Theology: The Concise Sacramentum Mundi*, ed. Karl Rahner, 1017-24. New York: Seabury Press.

Gurin, Patricia, Shirley Hatchett, and James S. Jackson. 1989. *Hope and Independence: Blacks' Response to Electoral and Party Politics.* New York: Russell Sage Foundation.

Guth, James L., and Cleveland R. Fraser. 2001. "Religion and Partisanship in Canada." *Journal for the Scientific Study of Religion* 40 (1): 51-64.

Guth, James L., John C. Green, Corwin E. Smidt, Lyman A. Kellstedt, and Margaret M. Poloma. 1997. *The Bully Pulpit: The Politics of Protestant Clergy.* Lawrence: University Press of Kansas.

Gutmann, Amy. 1992. "Introduction." In *Multiculturalism and the Politics of Recognition*, ed. Charles Taylor, 3-24. Princeton: Princeton University Press.

Gutmann, Amy, and Dennis Thompson. 1996. *Democracy and Disagreement.* Cambridge, MA: Belknap Press.

Hadaway, C.K., P.L. Marler, and M. Chaves. 1993. "What the Polls Don't Show: A Closer Look at US Church Attendance." *American Sociological Review* 56: 741-52.

Haddad, Yvonne Yazbeck. 2002. *Muslims in the West: From Sojourners to Citizens.* Oxford: Oxford University Press.

–. 2004. *Not Quite American? The Shaping of Arab and Muslim Identity in the United States.* Waco, TX: Baylor University Press.

Haddad, Yvonne Yazbeck, and Jane I. Smith. 1994. *Muslim Communities in North America.* Albany, NY: SUNY Press.

Haddad, Yvonne Yazbeck, Jane I. Smith, and John L. Esposito. 2003. *Religion and Immigration: Christian, Jewish, and Muslim Experiences in the United States.* Walnut Creek, CA: AltaMira Press.

Hadden, Jeffrey K. 1969. *The Gathering Storm in the Churches*. Garden City, NY: Doubleday.

Haeberle, Steven H. 1991. "The Role of Religious Organizations in the Gay and Lesbian Rights Movement." In *The Role of Religious Organizations in Social Movements*, ed. Barbara M. Yarnold, 71-90. Westport, CT: Praeger.

—. 1999. "Gay and Lesbian Rights: Emerging Trends in Public Opinion and Voting Behavior." In *Gays and Lesbians in the Democratic Process*, ed. Ellen D.B. Riggle and Barry L. Tadlock, 146-69. New York: Columbia University Press.

Haider-Markel, Donald P., and Kenneth J. Meier. 1996. "The Politics of Gay and Lesbian Rights: Expanding the Scope of the Conflict." *Journal of Politics* 58 (2): 332-49.

Haider-Markel, Donald P., Alana Querze, and Kara Lindaman. 2007. "Lose, Win, or Draw? A Reexamination of Direct Democracy and Minority Rights." *Political Research Quarterly* 60 (2): 304-14.

Hall, Mitchell. 1992. "CALCAV and Religious Opposition to the Vietnam War." In *Give Peace a Chance: Exploring the Vietnam Antiwar Movement*, ed. Melvin Small and William D. Hoover, 35-52. Syracuse, NY: Syracuse University Press.

Hall, Peter A., and David Soskice. 2001. *Varieties of Capitalism: The Institutional Foundations of Comparative Advantage*. Oxford: Oxford University Press.

Hamelin, Jean. 1984. *Histoire du catholicisme québécois: Le xxe siècle. Tome 2: De 1940 à nos jours*. Montréal: Boréal Express.

Hammond, Phillip. 1992. *The Protestant Presence in Twentieth-Century America: Religion and Political Culture*. Albany: State University of New York Press.

Harris, Angelique C. 2008. "Homosexuality and the Black Church." *Journal of African American History* 93: 262-70.

Harris-Lacewell, Melissa. 2004. *Barbershops, Bibles, and BET: Everyday Talk and Black Political Thought*. Princeton: Princeton University Press.

Hartman, Keith. 1996. *Congregations in Conflict: The Battle over Homosexuality*. New Brunswick, NJ: Rutgers University Press.

Hartz, Louis. 1964. *The Founding of New Societies: Studies in the History of the United States, Latin America, South Africa, Canada, and Australia*. New York: Harcourt, Brace and World.

Herek, Gregory M. 1984. "Beyond 'Homophobia': A Social Psychological Perspective on Attitudes toward Lesbians and Gay Men." *Journal of Homosexuality* 10: 1-21.

—. 2002. "Gender Gaps in Public Opinion about Lesbians and Gay Men." *Public Opinion Quarterly* 66: 40-66.

Herek, G.M., and J.P. Capitanio. 1996. "Some of My Best Friends: Intergroup Contact, Concealable Stigma, and Heterosexuals' Attitudes towards Gay Men and Lesbians." *Personality and Social Psychology Bulletin* 55: 178-90.

Herek, Gregory M., and Eric K. Glunt. 1993. "Interpersonal Contact and Heterosexuals' Attitudes toward Gay Men: Results from a National Survey." *Journal of Sex Research* 30: 239-44.

Herman, Didi. 1994. "The Christian Right and the Politics of Morality in Canada." *Parliamentary Affairs* 47 (2): 268-79.

–. 2000. "The Gay Agenda Is the Devil's Agenda: The Christian Right's Vision and the Role of the State." In *The Politics of Gay Rights*, ed. Craig Rimmerman, Kenneth D. Wald, and Clyde Wilcox, 139-60. Chicago: University of Chicago Press.

Hertel, Bradley R., and Michael Hughes. 1987. "Religious Affiliation, Attendance, and Support for 'Pro-Family' Issues in the United States." *Social Forces* 65: 858-82.

Hertzke, Allen D. 1988. *Representing God in Washington: The Role of Religious Lobbies in the American Polity*. Knoxville: University of Tennessee Press.

–. 1991. "An Assessment of the Mainline Churches since 1945." In *The Role of Religion in the Making of Public Policy*, ed. James E. Wood, Jr., and Derek Davis, 43-80. Waco, TX: J.M. Dawson Institute of Church-State Studies.

Hexham, Irving, and Karla Poewe. 1997. *New Religions as Global Cultures: Making the Human Sacred*. Boulder, CO: Westview Press.

Hibbing, John R., and Elizabeth Theiss-Morse. 2002. *Stealth Democracy: Americans' Beliefs about How Government Should Work*. New York: Cambridge University Press.

Hiemstra, Rick. 2007. "Counting Canadian Evangelicals." *Church and Faith Trends* (Evangelical Fellowship of Canada) 1: 1. Available at Centre for Research on Canadian Evangelicalism, Evangelical Fellowship of Canada.

Himmelfarb, Gertrude. 1996. "A De-Moralized Society: The British/American Experience." In *The Essential Neoconservative Reader*, ed. Mark Gerson, 411-33. New York: Addison-Wesley.

Holben, Lawrence Robert. 1999. *What Christians Think about Homosexuality: Six Representative Viewpoints*. North Richland Hills, TX: Bibal Press.

Hoover, Dennis R. 1997. "The Christian Right under Old Glory and the Maple Leaf." In *Sojourners in the Wilderness: The Christian Right in Comparative Perspective*, ed. Corwin E. Smidt and James M. Penning, 193-216. Lanham, MD: Rowman and Littlefield.

Hoover, Dennis R., Michael D. Martinez, Samuel H. Reimer, and Kenneth D. Wald. 2002. "Evangelicalism Meets the Continental Divide: Moral and Economic Conservatism in the United States and Canada." *Political Research Quarterly* 55 (2): 351-74.

"House Passes Gay Hate Bill, White House Threatens Veto." 2007. 365Gay.com. http://www.365gay.com/.

Hout, M., and A.M. Greeley. 1987. "The Center Doesn't Hold: Church Attendance in the United States, 1940-1984." *American Sociological Review* 52: 325-45.

–. 1998. "What Church Official Reports Don't Show: Another Look at Church Attendance Data." *American Sociological Review* 63: 113-19.

Howell, Alison. 2005. "Peaceful, Tolerant and Orderly? A Feminist Analysis of Discourses of 'Canadian Values.'" *Canadian Foreign Policy* 12: 49-69.

Howse, Brannon. 2005. *One Nation under Man? The Worldview War*. Nashville, TN: Broadman and Holman.

Human Rights Campaign (HRC). 2002. "Transgender Poll." Poll conducted by Lake, Snell, Perry, and Associates. http://www.genderadvocates.org/.

Hunter, Albert. 1993. "National Federations: The Role of Voluntary Organizations in Linking Macro and Micro Orders of Society." *Nonprofit and Voluntary Sector Quarterly* 22: 121-36.

Hunter, James Davison. 1983. *American Evangelicalism: Conservative Religion and the Quandary of Modernity.* New Brunswick, NJ: Rutgers University Press.

–. 1987. *Evangelicalism: The Coming Generation.* Chicago: University of Chicago Press.

–. 1991. *Culture Wars: The Struggle to Define America.* New York: Basic Books.

–. 1994. *Before the Shooting Begins: The Rise of Irreconcilable Differences in American Public Life.* New York: Basic Books.

Huntingdon, Samuel P. 1993. "The Clash of Civilizations?" *Foreign Affairs* 72 (3): 22-48.

–. 1996. *The Clash of Civilizations: Remaking of World Order.* New York: Touchstone.

Hussain, Amir. 2001. "The Canadian Face of Islam: Muslim Communities in Toronto." PhD diss., University of Toronto.

–. 2004. "Muslims in Canada: Opportunities and Challenges." *Studies in Religion/ Sciences religieuses* 33: 359-79.

Hutchinson, Don, and Rick Hiemstra. 2009. "Canadian Evangelical Voting Trends by Region, 1996-2008." *Church and Faith Trends* (Evangelical Fellowship of Canada) 2: 3. Available at Centre for Research on Canadian Evangelicalism, Evangelical Fellowship of Canada.

Hutchinson, Roger. 1984. "Towards a 'Pedagogy for Allies of the Oppressed.'" *Studies in Religion/Sciences religieuses* 13 (2): 145-50.

–. 1992. *Prophets, Pastors and Public Choices: Canadian Churches and the Mackenzie Valley Pipeline Debate.* Waterloo, ON: Wilfrid Laurier University.

Iannaccone, Laurence R. 1994. "Why Strict Churches Are Strong." *American Journal of Sociology* 99: 1180-211.

Ibbitson, John. 2010a. "Anti-Contraception Policy Sparks Uproar." *Globe and Mail,* 18 March.

–. 2010b. "Ottawa Changes Course in Wake of Birth-Control Backlash." *Globe and Mail,* 19 March.

–. 2010c. "Placating the Base, Facing the Furor: Tories Deny Division over Census Plan." *Globe and Mail,* 19 July.

–. 2010d. "Placating the Tory Faithful." *Globe and Mail,* 23 July.

Imrie, Robert. 2006. "Churches Reach Out to Faithful to Turn Vote on Gay Marriage." *Associated Press,* 2 November.

Indig, Sheldon. 1979. "Canadian Jewry and Their Struggle for an Exemption in the Federal Lord's Day Act of 1906." *Canadian Jewish Historical Society Journal* 3: 61-114.

Inglehart, Ronald. 1977. *The Silent Revolution: Changing Values and Political Styles among Western Publics.* Princeton: Princeton University Press.

Inglehart, Ronald, and Wayne Baker. 2000. "Modernization, Cultural Change, and the Persistence of Traditional Values." *American Sociological Review* 65: 19-51.

Inglehart, Ronald, Miguel Basáñez, Jaime Díez Medrano, Loek Halman, and Ruud Luijkx. 2004. *Human Beliefs and Values: A Cross-Cultural Sourcebook Based on the 1999-2002 Values Surveys.* México DF: Siglo XXI Editores.

Interfaith Coalition on Marriage and the Family. 1995. "Factum of the Interveners Interfaith Coalition on Marriage and the Family. Supreme Court of Canada." *Egan v. Canada.* [1995], 2 S.C.R. 513 (S.C.C.). Court File No. 23636.

–. 1999. "Factum of the Intervenors the Interfaith Coalition." Supreme Court of Canada. Court File No. 25838.

–. 2003. "Factum of the Intervener, the Interfaith Coalition for Marriage." British Columbia Court of Appeal (Shortt et al., No. CA029048, Court of Appeal Registry: Vancouver No. L002698; Barbeau et al., No. CA029017, Court of Appeal Registry: Vancouver No. L003197).

Irwin, Patrick, and Norman L. Thompson. 1977. "Acceptance of the Rights of Homosexuals: A Social Profile." *Journal of Homosexuality* 3: 107-21.

Ivers, Gregg. 1995. *To Build a Wall: American Jews and the Separation of Church and State.* Charlottesville, VA: University Press of Virginia.

Jalsevac, Steve. 2006. "Opposing Conservatives' Bill C-43 Did Not Cost Lives: Analysis." *Interim.* http://www.lifesite.net/.

Jantz, Harold. 1999. "Welcoming and Yet Not Affirming Homosexuality." *Mennonite Brethren Herald*, 5 November.

Jelen, Ted G. 2000. *To Serve God and Mammon: Church-State Relations in American Politics.* Boulder, CO: Westview Press.

–. 2003. "Catholic Priests and the Political Order: The Political Behavior of Catholic Pastors." *Journal for the Scientific Study of Religion* 42: 591-604.

–. 2005a. "Political Esperanto: Rhetorical Resources and Limitations of the Christian Right in the United States." *Sociology of Religion* 66: 303-21.

–. 2005b. "Roman Catholic Priests." In *Pulpits and Politics: Clergy in American Politics at the Advent of the Millennium,* ed. Corwin E. Smidt and James Penning, 235-46. Waco, TX: Baylor University Press.

–. 2006. "The American Church: Of Being Catholic and American." In *The Catholic Church and the Nation-State: Comparative Perspectives,* ed. Paul Christopher Manuel, Lawrence C. Reardon, and Clyde Wilcox, 69-87. Washington, DC: Georgetown University Press.

–. 2008. "Religion and American Public Opinion: Social Issues." In *Oxford Handbook of Religion and American Politicals,* ed. Corwin E. Smidt, 217-42. New York: Oxford University Press.

Johnson, David K. 2004. *The Lavender Scare: The Cold War Persecution of Gays and Lesbians in the Federal Government.* Chicago: University of Chicago Press.

Johnson, Eithne. 1998. "The Emergence of Christian Video and the Cultivation of Videovangelism." In *Media, Culture, and the Religious Right,* ed. Linda Kintz and Julia Lesage, 191-210. Minneapolis: University of Minnesota Press.

Jourdenais, Manon (avec la collaboration de Jean-Guy Nadeau). 1997. *Maintenant que je ne vais plus mourir: L'expérience spirituelle des homosexuels vivant avec le VIH/Sida – guide pour l'accompagnement.* Montréal: Fides.

Kahn, Y.H. 1989. "Judaism and Homosexuality: The Traditionalist/Progressive Debate." *Journal of Homosexuality* 18: 47-82.

Kaplan, Morris B. 1996. *Sexual Justice: Democratic Citizenship and the Politics of Desire.* New York: Routledge.

Karim, Karim H. 2002. "Crescent Dawn in the Great White North: Muslim Participation in the Canadian Public Sphere." In *Muslims in the West: From Sojourners to Citizens,* ed. Yvonne Yazbeck Haddad, 262-77. Oxford: Oxford University Press.

Keeter, Scott. 2007. "Evangelicals and Moral Values." In *A Matter of Faith: Religion in the 2004 Presidential Election,* ed. David E. Campbell, 80-92. Washington, DC: Brookings Institution.

Kelley, Dean M. 1977. *Why Conservative Churches Are Growing: A Study in Sociology of Religion.* San Francisco: Harper.

Khan, M.A. Muqtedar. 2003. "Constructing the American Muslim Community." In *Religion and Immigration: Christian, Jewish, and Muslim Experiences in the United States,* ed. Yvonne Yazbeck Haddad, Jane I. Smith, and John L. Esposito, 175-98. Walnut Creek, CA: AltaMira Press.

Kim, Andrew E. 1993. "The Absence of Pan-Canadian Civil Religion: Plurality, Duality and Conflict in Symbols of Canadian Culture." *Sociology of Religion* 54 (3): 257-75.

Kinnaman, David, and Gabe Lyons. 2007. *UnChristian: What a New Generation Really Thinks about Christianity ... and Why It Matters.* Grand Rapids: Bakerbooks.

Kirkpatrick, Lee. 1993. "Fundamentalism, Christian Orthodoxy, and Intrinsic Religious Orientation as Predictors of Discriminatory Attitudes." *Journal for the Scientific Study of Religion* 32: 256-68.

Kite, Mary E., and Bernard E. Whitely, Jr. 1996. "Sex Differences in Attitudes toward Homosexual Persons, Behaviors and Civil Rights: A Meta-Analysis." *Personality and Social Psychology Bulletin* 22: 336-53.

Kitschelt, Herbert, and Anthony McGann. 1995. *The Radical Right in Western Europe: A Comparative Analysis.* Ann Arbor: University of Michigan Press.

Knight, Jack, and James Johnson. 1994. "Aggregation and Deliberation: On the Possibility of Democratic Legitimacy." *Political Theory* 22: 277-96.

Kobayashi, Audrey. 2008. "A Research and Policy Agenda for Second Generation Canadians." *Canadian Diversity* 6 (2): 3-6.

Koch, Jerome R., and Evans W. Curry. 2000. "Social Context and the Presbyterian Gay/Lesbian Ordination Debate: Testing Open-Systems Theory." *Review of Religious Research* 42: 206-15.

Kollman, Kelly, and Matthew Waites. 2009. "The Global Politics of Lesbian, Gay, Bisexual, and Transgender Human Rights: An Introduction." *Contemporary Politics* 15 (1): 1-17.

Koussens, David. 2008. "Une pastorale aux frontières de la normativité catholique: Étude d'une église montréalaise *In and Out.*" *Journal of Religion and Culture* 18-19: 158-74.

Kramer, Michael P. 2003. "Beginnings and Ends: The Origins of Jewish American Literary History." In *Cambridge Companion to Jewish American Literature,* ed. Hana Wirth-Nesher and Michael P. Kramer, 12-30. New York: Cambridge University Press.

Kugle, Scott Siraj al-Haqq. 2003. "Sexuality, Diversity and Ethics in the Agenda of Progressive Muslims." In *Progressive Muslims: On Justice, Gender and Pluralism*, ed. Omid Safi, 190-234. Oxford: Oneworld Publications.

Kurland, Philip, and Ralph Lerner. 1987. "Letter of Jonas Phillips to the Constitutional Convention." In *The Founders Constitution*, 638-39. Chicago: University of Chicago Press.

Laghi, Brian, Anthony Reinhart, and Roy MacGregor. 2005. "Harper Uses Same-Sex to Tap into Ethnic Vote." *Globe and Mail*, 12 February.

LaHaye, Tim, and Beverly LaHaye. 1976. *The Act of Marriage: The Beauty of Sexual Love*. Grand Rapids, MI: Zondervan.

Lakoff, George. 2006. "Framing: It's about Values and Ideas." http://www.rockridge institute.org/.

LaMar, Lisa, and Mary Kite. 1998. "Sex Differences in Attitudes toward Gay Men and Lesbians: A Multidimensional Perspective." *Journal of Sex Research* 35 (2): 189-96.

Lapointe, Guy, et Réjean Bisaillon. 1997. "Nouveau regard sur l'homosexualité: Questions d'éthique." Actes du Colloque organisé par la Faculté de théologie de l'Université de Montréal en novembre 1996, Saint-Laurent, Fides.

Laycock, David. 2002. *The New Right and Democracy in Canada: Understanding Reform and the Canadian Alliance*. Toronto: Oxford University Press.

Layman, Geoffrey C. 2001. *The Great Divide: Religious and Cultural Conflict in American Party Politics*. New York: Columbia University Press.

Layman, Geoffrey C., and Thomas M. Carsey. 2002. "Party Polarization and 'Conflict Extension' in the American Electorate." *American Journal of Political Science* 46: 786-802.

Layman, Geoffrey C., and John C. Green. 2006. "Wars and Rumours of Wars: The Contexts of Cultural Conflict in American Political Behaviour." *British Journal of Political Science* 36: 61-89.

Leahy, Kathleen, and Kevin Alderson. 2004. *Same-Sex Marriage: The Personal and the Political*. Toronto: Insomniac Press.

Leblanc, Daniel. 2007. "Tories Target Specific Ethnic Voters." *Globe and Mail*, 16 October.

Leckie, Robert. 2006. "Profane Matrimony." *Canadian Journal of Law and Society/ Review canadienne droit et société* 21 (2): 1-23.

Leclerc, Jean-Claude. 2006. "La lettre des 19 aux évêques du Québec: L'église pourra-t-elle éluder encore longtemps le débat sur l'homosexualité?" *Le Devoir*, 6 March.

Leduc, Lawrence. 2007. "Realignment and Dealignment in Canadian Federal Politics." In *Canadian Parties in Transition*, 3rd ed., ed. Alain-G. Gagnon and A. Brian Tanguay, 163-77. Peterborough, ON: Broadview.

Leege, David C., Kenneth D. Wald, Brian S. Krueger, and Paul D. Mueller. 2002. *Politics of Cultural Differences: Social Change and Voter Mobilization Strategies in the Post-New Deal Period*. Princeton: Princeton University Press.

Lefebvre, Solange. 2004. "Politics and Religion in Quebec." In *The Hidden Pierre Trudeau: The Faith behind the Politics*, ed. John English, Richard Gwyn, and P. Whitney Lackenbauer, 57-64. Ottawa: Novalis.

–. 2006. "Conflicting Interpretations of the Council: The Ratzinger-Kasper Debate." *Concilium* 1: 95-105.

Léger Marketing. 2001a. "Étude sur la perception des Canadiens à l'égard de l'euthanasie," 22 juin. http://www.legermarketing.com/.

–. 2001b. "Opinion des Canadiens à l'égard de l'avortement," septembre. http://www.legermarketing.com/.

–. 2002. "Les Canadiens et la visite du pape au Canada," mai. http://www.leger marketing.com/.

–. 2004. "Les Canadiens et leur tolérance envers l'homosexualité," avril. http://www.legermarketing.com/.

Lemieux, Louis-Guy. 2006. "Les prêtres et l'homosexualité." *Le Soleil*, 28 février.

Leonard, Karen. 2002. "South Asian Leadership of American Muslims." In *Muslims in the West: From Sojourners to Citizens*, ed. Yvonne Yazbeck Haddad, 233-49. Oxford: Oxford University Press.

Levitz, Stephanie. 2003. "Canada's Gay Muslims Unite to Celebrate Their Faith and Their Sexuality." *Canadian Press*, 18 June.

Lewis, Gregory B. 2005. "Same-Sex Marriage and the 2004 Presidential Election." *PS: Political Science and Politics* 38: 195-99.

Liebman, Charles S., and Steven M. Cohen. 1990. *Two Worlds of Judaism: The Israeli and American Experiences*. New Haven: Yale University Press.

Lienesch, Michael. 1993. *Redeeming America: Piety and Politics in the New Christian Right*. Chapel Hill: University of North Carolina Press.

Ligue catholique pour les droits de l'homme et alliance évangélique du Canada. 2003. "Mémoire des appellants." Cour D'Appel, Province de Québec (No. 500-09-012719-027). http://www.evangelicalfellowship.ca/.

Lincoln, Eric C., and Lawrence Mamiya. 1990. *The Black Church in the African American Experience*. Durham, NC: Duke University Press.

Lipset, Seymour Martin. 1964. "Canada and the United States: A Comparative View." *Canadian Review of Sociology and Anthropology* 1: 173-85.

–. 1986. "Historical Traditions and National Characteristics: A Comparative Analysis of Canada and the United States." *Canadian Journal of Sociology/Cahiers canadiens de sociologie* 11: 113-55.

–. 1990. *Continental Divide: The Values and Institutions of the United States and Canada*. New York: Routledge.

–. 1996. *American Exceptionalism: A Double-Edged Sword*. New York: W.W. Norton and Company.

Little, Blake. 2005. "The 25 Most Influential Evangelicals in America." *Time*, 30 January. http://www.time.com/.

Lo, Mbaye. 2004. *Muslims in America: Race, Politics and Community Building*. Beltsville, MD: Amana Publications.

Loftus, Jeni. 2001. "America's Liberalization in Attitudes toward Homosexuality, 1973 to 1998." *American Sociological Review* 66: 762-82.

Long, J. Scott. 2009. "Unbearable Witness: How Western Activists (Mis)recognize Sexuality in Iran." *Contemporary Politics* 15 (1): 119-36.

Lunch, William M. 1995. "Oregon: Identity Politics in the Northeast." In *God at the Grassroots: The Christian Right in the 1994 Election*, ed. M.J. Rozell and C. Wilcox, 227-52. Lanham, MD: Rowman and Littlefield.

Luo, Michael, and Christini Capecchi. 2009. "Lutheran Group Eases Limits on Gay Clergy." *New York Times*, 22 August.

Lutztig, Michael, and J. Matthew Wilson. 2005. "A New Right? Moral Issues and Partisan Change in Canada." *Social Science Quarterly* 86 (1): 109-28.

MacDougall, Bruce. 2002. "A Respectful Distance: Appellate Courts Consider Religious Motivation of Public Figures in Homosexual Equality Discourse – The Cases of *Chamberlain* and *Trinity Western University*." *UBC Law Review* 35: 511-38.

MacFarquhar, Neil. 2008. "For Muslim Students: A Debate on Inclusion." *New York Times*, 21 February.

Mackey, Lloyd. 2005. *The Pilgrimage of Stephen Harper*. Toronto: ECW Press.

Maguire, Daniel. 2000. "Religion and Reproductive Policy." In *God Forbid: Religion and Sex in American Public Life*, ed. Kathleen M. Sands, 185-202. New York: Oxford University Press.

–. 2006. "A Catholic Defense of Same Sex Marriage." http://www.religious consultation.org/.

Maisel, Sandy, and Ira Forman. 2001. *Jews in American Politics: Essays*. Lanham, MD: Rowman and Littlefield.

Makin, Kirk. 2007. "Judges Garner Greater Trust than Politicians, Survey Finds." *Globe and Mail*, 9 April.

Manning, Preston. 2002. *Think Big: My Adventures in Life and Democracy*. Toronto: McClelland and Stewart.

Marler, Penny Long, and C. Kirk Hadaway. 1999. "Testing the Attendance Gap in a Conservative Church." *Sociology of Religion* 60: 175-86.

Marsden, George. 1980. *Fundamentalism and American Culture: The Shaping of Twentieth-Century Evangelicalism, 1870-1925*. New York: Oxford University Press.

Martin, Lawrence. 2010. "The Incredible Shrinking Tory Tent." *Globe and Mail*, 29 July.

Martin, William C. 1991. *A Prophet with Honor: The Billy Graham Story*. New York: William Morrow.

Marty, Martin E. 1970. *Righteous Empire: The Protestant Experience in America*. New York: Dial.

Marzolini, Michael. 2001. "The Politics of Values: Designing the 2000 Liberal Campaign." In *The Canadian General Election of 2000*, ed. Jon H. Pammet and Christopher Dornan, 263-76. Toronto: Dundurn.

Mason, Christopher. 2006. "Gay Marriage Galvanizes Canada's Christian Right." *New York Times*, 16 November.

Matthews, J. Scott. 2005. "The Political Foundations of Support for Same-Sex Marriage in Canada." *Canadian Journal of Political Science* 38: 841-66.

McAdam, Doug. 1982. *Political Process and the Development of Black Insurgency, 1930-1970.* Chicago: University of Chicago Press.

McCarthy, John D., and Mayer N. Zald. 1977. "Resource Mobilization and Social Movements: A Partial Theory." *American Journal of Sociology* 82: 1212-41.

McCloud, Aminah Beverly. 2003. "Islam in America: The Mosaic." In *Religion and Immigration: Christian, Jewish, and Muslim Experiences in the United States,* ed. Yvonne Yazbeck Haddad, Jane I. Smith, and John L. Esposito, 159-74. Walnut Creek, CA: AltaMira Press.

McClurg, Scott D. 2006. "The Electoral Relevance of Political Talk: Examining Disagreement and Expertise Effects in Social Networks on Political Participation." *American Journal of Political Science* 50: 737-54.

McDonald, Marci. 2006. "Stephen Harper and the Theo-Cons: The Religious Right's Mission in Ottawa." *Walrus* (October), 47-49.

–. 2010. *The Armageddon Factor: The Rise of Christian Nationalism in Canada.* Toronto: Random House Canada.

McKenzie, Chris. 2005. *Pro-Family Politics and Fringe Parties in Canada.* Vancouver: UBC Press.

McLain, Melinda V. 1995. "Riding the Waves of Presbyterian Unrest: A Brief History of the Movement for Full Inclusion of Lesbian, Gay, Bisexual, and Transgendered Persons in the Presbyterian Church (PCUSA)." In *Called Out: The Voices and Gifts of Lesbian, Gay, Bisexual, and Transgendered Presbyterians,* ed. Jane Adams Spahr, Kathryn Poethig, Selisse Berry, and Melinda V. McLain, 1-13. Gaithersburg, MD: Chi Rho Press.

McNamara, Patrick H. 1992. *Conscience First, Tradition Second: A Study of Young American Catholics.* Albany, NY: SUNY Press.

Melton, J. Gordon. 1991. *The Churches Speak on Homosexuality: Official Statements from Religious Bodies and Ecumenical Organizations.* New York: Gale Research.

Ménard, Guy. 1978. "Homosexualité et théologie: Jalons pour une théologie de la libération gaie." PhD diss., Université de Montréal.

–, ed. 2003. *Le mariage homosexuel: Les termes du débat (textes choisis).* Montréal: Liber.

Mendelberg, Tali, and John Oleske. 2000. "Race and Public Deliberation." *Political Communication* 17: 169-91.

Meshal, Reem. 2003. "Banners of Faith and Identities in Construct: The Hijab in Canada." In *The Muslim Veil in North America: Issues and Debates,* ed. Sajida Alvi, Homa Hoodfar, and Sheila McDonough, 95-96. Toronto: Women's Press.

Mezey, Susan Gluck. 2007. *Queers in Court: Gay Rights and Public Policy.* Lanham, MD: Rowman and Littlefield.

Michels, Robert. 1966. *Political Parties: A Sociological Study of the Oligarchical Tendencies of Modern Society.* New York: Free Press.

Miles, Margaret. 1990. "Augustine." In *Encyclopedia of Early Christianity,* ed. Everett Ferguson, 354-430. New York: Garland.

Ministère de la Justice du Québec. 2001. *For Equal Treatment: Civil Unions, Consultation Document Regarding the Draft Bill on Same-Sex Civil Unions,* 7 December.

Minter, Shannon Price. 2007. "Banding Together." *Advocate*, 17 October. http://www.advocate.com/.

Minwalla, Omar, B.R. Simon Rosser, Jamie Feldman, and Christine Varga. 2005. "Identity Experience among Progressive Gay Muslims in North America: A Qualitative Study within Al-Fatiha." *Culture, Health and Sexuality* 7: 113-28.

Mockabee, Stephen T. 2007. "The Political Behavior of American Catholics: Change and Continuity." In *From Pews to Polling Places: Faith and Politics in the American Religious Mosaic*, ed. J. Matthew Wilson, 81-104. Washington, DC: Georgetown University Press.

Money, Rachelle. 2007. "Gay Adoption: The Deal Holyrood Cannot Honor." *Daily Herald* (Glasgow), 28 January.

Moon, Dawne. 2004. *God, Sex, and Politics: Homosexuality and Everyday Theologies*. Chicago: University of Chicago Press.

Moon, Richard. 2003. "Liberty, Neutrality and Inclusion: Religious Freedom under the Canadian Charter of Rights and Freedoms." *Brandeis Law Journal* 41 (3): 563-74.

–, ed. 2008. *Law and Religious Pluralism in Canada*. Vancouver: UBC Press.

Mooney, Christopher Z. 1999. "The Politics of Morality Policy." *Policy Studies Journal* 27 (4): 675-80.

–. 2000. "The Decline of Federalism and the Rise of Morality-Policy Conflict in the United States." *Publius* 20: 171-88.

Moore, Robert. 2007. "Political Participation and Tolerance: American Evangelicals in Transition." Paper presented at the Annual Midwest Political Science Association, Chicago, April.

Morone, James A. 2003. *Hellfire Nation: The Politics of Sin in American History*. New Haven: Yale University Press.

Morton, Ted, and Rainer Knopff. 2000. *The Charter Revolution and the Court Party*. Peterborough, ON: Broadview.

Mueller, Carol. 1983. "In Search of a Constituency for the 'New Religious Right.'" *Public Opinion Quarterly* 47: 213-29.

Murdoch, Joyce, and Deb Price. 2001. *Courting Justice: Gay Men and Lesbians vs. the Supreme Court*. New York: Basic Books.

Murray, Stephen O., and Will Roscoe. 1997. *Islamic Homosexualities: Culture, History and Literature*. New York: New York University Press.

Muslim Canadian Congress (MCC). "Muslim Canadian Congress Endorses Same-Sex Marriage Legislation." Press release. http://www.muslimcanadiancongress.org/.

Muslim Public Affairs Council (MPAC). 2008. *Activate 08 Voter's Guide: An Analysis of California's State Propositions*. http://www.mpac.org/.

Mutz, Diana C. 2002. "Cross-Cutting Social Networks: Testing Democratic Theory in Practice." *American Political Science Review* 96: 111-26.

National Gay and Lesbian Task Force (NGLTF). 2010a. "Adoption Laws in the US," 17 September. http://www.thetaskforce.org.

–. 2010b. "Anti-Gay Marriage Measures in the US." http://www.thetaskforce.org/.

–. 2010c. "Second Parent Adoption in the US." http://www.thetaskforce.org/.

National Public Radio (NPR). 2009. "State by State: The Legal Battle over Gay Marriage." Interactive map produced by Maria Godoy/NPR. http://www.npr.org/.

Neiheisel, Jacob R., and Paul A. Djupe. 2008. "Intraorganizational Constraints on Churches' Public Witness." *Journal for the Scientific Study of Religion* 47 (3): 427-41.

Neiheisel, Jacob R., Paul A. Djupe, and Anand E. Sokhey. 2009. "Veni, Vidi, Disseri: Churches and the Promise of Democratic Deliberation." *American Politics Research* 37 (4): 614-43.

Nevitte, Neil. 1996. *The Decline of Deference: Canadian Value Change in Cross-National Perspective.* Peterborough, ON: Broadview.

Nevitte, Neil, and Christopher Cochrane. 2006. "Individualization in Europe and America: Connecting Religious and Moral Values." *Comparative Sociology* 5: 203-30.

Nevitte, Neil, André Blais, Elisabeth Gidengil, Richard Johnston, and Henry Brady. 1998. "The Populist Right in Canada: The Rise of the Reform Party of Canada." In *The New Politics of the Right: Neo-Populist Parties and Movements in Established Democracies*, ed. Hans-Georg Betz and Stefan Immerfall, 172-202. New York: St. Martin's Press.

Niebuhr, H. Richard. 1951. *Christ and Culture.* New York: Harper and Row.

Nimer, Mohamed. 2002. "Muslims in American Public Life." In *Muslims in the West: From Sojourners to Citizens*, ed. Yvonne Yazbeck Haddad, 169-86. Oxford: Oxford University Press.

Noll, Mark. 1997. "Canadian Evangelicalism: A View from the United States." In *Aspects of the Canadian Evangelical Experience*, ed. G.A. Rawlyk, 3-20. Montreal: McGill-Queen's University Press.

Novak, David. 1998. "Religious Communities, Secular Society, and Sexuality: One Jewish Opinion." In *Sexual Orientation and Human Rights in American Religious Discourse*, ed. Saul Olyan and Martha Nussbaum, 11-28. New York: Oxford University Press.

Oldfield, Duane M. 1996. *The Right and the Righteous: The Christian Right Confronts the Republican Party.* Lanham, MD: Rowman and Littlefield.

Oldmixon, Elizabeth. 2005. *Uncompromising Positions: God, Sex and the US House of Representatives.* Washington, DC: Georgetown University Press.

Olson, Daniel V.A., and Jackson W. Carroll. 1992. "Religiously Based Politics: Religious Elites and the Public." *Social Forces* 70: 765-86.

Olson, Daniel V.A., and C. Kirk Hadaway. 1999. "Religious Pluralism and Affiliation among Canadian Counties and Cities." *Journal for the Scientific Study of Religion* 38 (4): 490-508.

Olson, Laura R. 2002. "Mainline Protestant Washington Offices and the Political Lives of Clergy." In *The Quiet Hand of God: Faith-Based Activism and the Public Role of Mainline Protestantism*, ed. Robert Wuthnow and John H. Evans, 54-79. Berkeley: University of California Press.

Olson, Laura R., and Wendy Cadge. 2002. "Talking about Homosexuality: The Views of Mainline Protestant Clergy." *Journal for the Scientific Study of Religion* 41: 153-67.

Olson, Laura R., Wendy Cadge, and James T. Harrison. 2006. "Religion and Public Opinion about Same-Sex Marriage." *Social Science Quarterly* 87: 340-60.

O'Reilly, David. 2006. "Bishops Approve Policy on Gays." *Philadelphia Inquirer,* 15 November.

Ostling, Richard N. 1984. "Evangelical Publishing and Broadcasting." In *Evangelicalism and Modern America,* ed. George Marsden, 46-55. Grand Rapids, MI: William B. Eerdmans Publishing.

Overby, L.M., and J. Barth. 2002. "Contact, Community Context, and Public Attitudes toward Gay Men and Lesbians." *Polity* 34: 433-56.

Overby, L. Marvin, Raymond Tatalovich, and Donley T. Studlar. 1998. "Party and Free Votes in Canada: Abortion in the House of Commons." *Party Politics* 4: 381-92.

Page, Benjamin. 1996. *Who Deliberates? Mass Media in Modern Democracy.* Chicago: University of Chicago Press.

Panebianco, Angelo. 1988. *Political Parties: Organization and Power.* Cambridge: Cambridge University Press.

Park, Jerry, and Samuel Reimer. 2002. "Revisiting the Social Sources of American Christianity, 1972-1998." *Journal for the Scientific Study of Religion* 41: 735-48.

Patten, Steve. 2007. "The Evolution of the Canadian Party System." In *Canadian Parties in Transition,* 3rd ed., ed. Alain-G. Gagnon and A. Brian Tanguay, 55-81. Peterborough, ON: Broadview.

Paulson, Michael. 2006. "Ousted Newton Priest Cheered at Gay Pride Service." *Boston Globe,* 11 June. http://www.boston.com/.

People for the American Way (PFAW). 2006. "Right Wing Organizations: Concerned Women for America." http://www.pfaw.org/.

Pew Forum on Religion and Public Life. 2007. "The Religious Landscape Survey," February. http://www.pewforum.org/.

Pew Research Center for the People and the Press. 2004a. "2004 Annual Religion and Public Life Survey (RLS)," August. http://www.pewresearch.org/.

–. 2004b. "Typology Survey," December. http://www.pewresearch.org/.

–. 2006. "Religion and Public Life Survey," July. http://www.pewresearch.org/.

–. 2007a. "2007 Annual Religion and Public Life Survey," August. http://www.pewresearch.org/.

–. 2007b. *Muslim Americans: Middle Class and Mostly Mainstream,* May. http://www.pewresearch.org/.

–. 2008. "2008 Annual Religion and Public Life Survey," August. http://www.pewresearch.org/.

Pierceson, Jason. 2005. *Courts, Liberalism, and Rights: Gay Law and Politics in the United States and Canada.* Philadelphia: Temple University Press.

Pinello, Daniel R. 2003. *Gay Rights and American Law.* Cambridge: Cambridge University Press.

Piper, John. 1991. "A Vision of Biblical Complementarity: Manhood and Woman-hood Defined According to the Bible." In *Recovering Biblical Manhood and Womanhood: A Response to Evangelical Feminism*, ed. John Piper and Wayne Gordon, 31-59. Wheaton, IL: Crossway Books.

Polikoff, Nancy D. 2000. "Raising Children: Lesbian and Gay Parents Face the Public and the Courts." In *Creating Change: Sexuality, Public Policy, and Civil Rights*, ed. John D'Emilio, William B. Turner, and Urvashi Vaid, 318-19. New York: St. Martin's Press.

Pontifical Council for the Family (PCF). 2000. "Family, Marriage, and 'De Facto' Unions," 21 November. http://www.vatican.va/.

Posner, Michael. 2008. "Ottawa Axes Second Arts Subsidy in Two Weeks." *Globe and Mail*, 11 August.

Powell, Walter W., and Paul J. DiMaggio. 1991. *The New Institutionalism in Organizational Analysis*. Chicago: University of Chicago Press.

Presbyterian Church in Canada. 1996. *Statement on Human Sexuality*. Toronto: Presbyterian Church in Canada.

Presbyterian Church (US). 1999. "Public Role of Presbyterians." Louisville, KY: Presbyterian Church (USA), Research Services.

Preslar, J. Allan. 2006. "Focusing on the Family: Three Reactions." *MinistryWatch. com.* http://www.ministrywatch.com/.

Price, Richard M. 1996. "The Distinctiveness of Early Christian Sexual Ethics." In *Christian Perspectives on Sexuality and Gender*, ed. Elizabeth Stuart and Adrian Thatcher, 14-32. Grand Rapids: Eerdmans.

Public Religion Research. 2008. "The Faith and American Politics Survey," October. http://www.publicreligion.org/.

Pullella, Philip. 2005. "Vatican Reiterates Gay Ban: 'The Church Cannot Admit to Holy Orders Those Who Practice Homosexuality.'" *National Post*, 23 November.

"Quand l'église trahit sa mission." 2005. *Fugues*, July. http://www.fugues.com/.

"Quebec Priests Oppose Vatican Stance on Gay Marriage." 2006. *Associated Press*, 1 March. http://www.foxnews.com/.

Quebedeaux, Richard. 1978. *The Worldly Evangelicals*. San Francisco: Harper and Row.

Quinley, Harold E. 1974. *The Prophetic Clergy: Social Activism among Protestant Ministers*. New York: Wiley.

Rabinove, Samuel. 1990. "How – and Why – American Jews Have Contended for Religious Freedom: The Requirements and Limits of Civility." *Journal of Law and Religion* 8: 131-52.

Radin, Charles A. 2005. "Debate over Gay Clergy Is Testing Many Faiths." *Boston Globe*, 29 November.

Rahman, Momin. 2008. "In Search of My Mother's Garden: Reflections on Migration, Sexuality, and Muslim Identity." *Nebula* 5 (4): 1-25. http://www.noble world.biz/.

Ramji, Rubina. 2008. "Creating a Genuine Islam: Second Generation Muslims Growing Up in Canada." *Canadian Diversity* 6: 104-09.

Rawlyk, George A. 1994. "Who Are These Canadians Who Call Themselves Evangelicals?" *Christian Week*, 15 November.

—. 1996. *Is Jesus Your Personal Saviour? In Search of Canadian Evangelicalism in the 1990s*. Montreal: McGill-Queen's University Press.

Rawlyk, George A., and Mark A. Noll. 1994. *Amazing Grace: Evangelicalism in Australia, Britain, Canada, and the United States*. Montreal: McGill-Queen's University Press.

Rayside, David. 1988. "Gay Rights and Family Values: The Passage of Bill 7 in Ontario." *Studies in Political Economy* 26: 109-47.

—. 1998. *On the Fringe: Gays and Lesbians in Politics*. Ithaca, NY: Cornell University Press.

—. 2008. *Queer Inclusions, Continental Divisions: Public Recognition of Sexual Diversity in Canada and the United States*. Toronto: University of Toronto Press.

—. 2010. "Sex Ed in Ontario: Religious Mobilization and Socio-Cultural Anxiety." Paper presented at the Annual Meeting of the Canadian Political Science Association, June.

Rayside, David, and Scott Bowler. 1988. "Public Opinion and Gay Rights." *Canadian Review of Sociology and Anthropology* 25: 649-60.

Razack, Sherene H. 2008. *Casting Out: The Eviction of Muslims from Western Law and Politics*. Toronto: University of Toronto Press.

Read, Jen'nan Ghazal. 2008. "Are US Muslims Un-American?" Duke University, Office of News and Communications. http://www.news.duke.edu/.

Reed, Paul B., and L. Kevin Selbee. 2000. *Formal and Informal Volunteering and Giving: Regional and Community Patterns in Canada*. Statistics Canada. Catalogue No. 75F0048MIE – No. 05.

Reimer, Samuel H. 2000. "A More Irenic Canadian Evangelicalism? Comparing Evangelicals in Canada and the US." In *Revivals, Baptists, and George Rawlyk: A Memorial Volume*, ed. Daniel C. Goodwin, 153-80. Wolfville, NS: Gaspereau Press.

—. 2003. *Evangelicals and the Continental Divide: The Conservative Protestant Subculture in Canada and the United States*. Montreal: McGill-Queen's University Press.

Reimer, Samuel H., and Jerry Z. Park. 2001. "Tolerant (In)Civility? A Longitudinal Analysis of White Conservative Protestants' Willingness to Grant Civil Liberties." *Journal for the Scientific Study of Religion* 40 (4): 735-45.

Reitz, Jeffrey G., and Raymond Breton. 1994. *The Illusion of Difference: Realities of Ethnicity in Canada and the United States*. Toronto: C.D. Howe Institute.

Richards, David. 2005. *The Case for Gay Rights: From Bowers to Lawrence and Beyond*. Lawrence: University of Kansas Press.

Rimmerman, Craig, and Clyde Wilcox. 2007. "Preface." In *The Politics of Same-Sex Marriage*, ed. Craig Rimmerman and Clyde Wilcox, ix-xv. Chicago: University of Chicago Press.

Rizzo, Helen, Abdel-Hamid Abdel-Latif, and Katherine Meyer. 2007. "The Relationships between Gender Equality and Democracy: A Comparison of Arab versus Non-Arab Muslim Societies." *Sociology* 41: 1151-70.

Roach, Kent. 2001. *The Supreme Court on Trial: Judicial Activism or Democratic Dialogue*. Toronto: Irwin Law.

Robinson, Carin. 2008. "Doctrine, Discussion and Disagreement: Evangelicals and Catholics Together in American Politics." PhD diss., Georgetown University, Washington, DC.

Rodrigue, Isabelle. 2005. "Le mariage gai menace la religion même dans les églises, dit Mgr Ouellet." *Presse Canadienne,* 13 juillet.

Rogers, Jack. 1999. "Biblical Interpretation Regarding Homosexuality in the Recent History of the PCUSA." *Review of Religious Research* 41: 223-38.

Romer, Daniel, Kate Kenski, Kenneth Winneg, Christopher Adasiewicz, and Kathleen Hall Jamieson. 2006. *Capturing Campaign Dynamics, 2000 and 2004.* Philadelphia: University of Pennsylvania Press.

Roof, Wade Clark, and William McKinney. 1987. *American Mainline Religion: Its Changing Shape and Future.* New Brunswick, NJ: Rutgers University Press.

Rosenberg, Gerald. 1991. *The Hollow Hope: Can Courts Bring about Social Change?* Chicago: University of Chicago Press.

Rubin, Gayle S. 1993. "Thinking Sex: Notes for a Radical Theory of the Politics of Sexuality." In *The Lesbian and Gay Studies Reader,* ed. Henry Abelove, Michele Aina Barale, and David M. Halperin, 3-44. New York: Routledge.

Ruether, Rosemary Radford. 2000. "Sex in the Catholic Tradition." In *The Good News of the Body: Sexual Theology and Feminism,* ed. Lisa Isherwood, 35-53. New York: New York University Press.

Safi, Omid. 2003. *Progressive Muslims: On Justice, Gender and Pluralism.* Oxford: Oneworld.

Salaam Toronto. 2003. "First Salaam Canada and the Fourth Al-Fatiha International Conference for Lesbian, Gay, Bisexual, Transgender, Intersex, Questioning Muslims and Their Allies." Toronto. http://www.al-fatiha.org/.

Sandeen, Ernest R. 1978. *The Roots of Fundamentalism: British and American Millenarianism, 1800-1930.* Grand Rapids, MI: Baker Book House.

Schain, Martin, Aristide Zolberg, and Patrick Hossay. 2002. *Shadows over Europe: The Development and Impact of the Extreme Right in Western Europe.* New York: Palgrave Macmillan.

Scheufele, Dietram A., Matthew C. Nisbet, and Dominique Brossard. 2003. "Pathways to Participation? Religion, Communication Contexts, and Mass Media." *International Journal of Public Opinion Research* 15: 300-24.

Schmitt, Arno, and Jehoeda Sofer. 1992. *Sexuality and Eroticism among Males in Moslem Societies.* New York: Haworth Press.

Schoenfeld, Stuart. 1978. "The Jewish Religion in North America: Canadian and American Comparisons." *Canadian Journal of Sociology/Cahiers canadiens de sociologie* 3: 209-31.

Segal, Hugh. 2007. *The Long Road Back: The Conservative Journey in Canada, 1993-2006.* Toronto: HarperCollins.

Seiler, Tamara Palmer. 2000. "Melting Pot and Mosaic: Images and Realities." In *Canada and the United States: Differences that Count,* 2nd ed., ed. David M. Thomas, 97-120. Peterborough, ON: Broadview.

Seow, Choon-Leong. 1996. *Homosexuality and Christian Community.* Louisville, KY: Westminster John Knox Press.

Shallenberger, David. 1996. "Reclaiming the Spirit: The Journeys of Gay Men and Lesbian Women toward Integration." *Qualitative Sociology* 19: 195-215.

Shariff, Shaheen, Roland Case, and Michael Manley-Casimir. 2000. "Balancing Competing Rights in Education: Surrey School Board's Book Ban." *Education and Law Journal* 10: 47-105.

Sherrill, Kenneth, and Patrick J. Egan. 2008. "Lesbians, Gays, Bisexuals and the Electorate." *American Political Science Association*, 4 January. http://www.apsanet.org/.

Shilts, Randy. 1993. *Conduct Unbecoming: Lesbians and Gays in the Military – Vietnam to the Persian Gulf.* New York: St. Martin's.

Siker, Jeffrey. 1994. *Homosexuality in the Church: Both Sides of the Debate.* Louisville, KY: Westminster John Knox Press.

Simpson, John H. 1994. "The Body in Late Capitalism: An Introductory Sketch." In *Abortion Politics in the United States and Canada: Studies in Public Opinion*, ed. Ted G. Jelen and Marthe A. Chandler, 1-14. Westport, CT: Praeger.

Simpson, John H., and Henry G. MacLeod. 1985. "The Politics of Morality in Canada." In *Religious Movements: Genesis, Exodus, Numbers*, ed. Rodney Stark, 221-41. New York: Paragon.

Siraj, Asifa. 2009. "The Construction of the Homosexual 'Other' by British Muslim Heterosexuals." *Contemporary Islam* 3 (1): 41-57.

Smidt, Corwin, and James Penning. 2002. *Evangelicalism: The Next Generation.* Grand Rapids, MI: Baker Academic.

Smith, Christian. 1996. *Resisting Reagan: The US Central America Peace Movement.* Chicago: University of Chicago Press.

–. 2000. *Christian America? What Evangelicals Really Want.* Berkeley: University of California Press.

Smith, Christian, and Robert Faris. 2005. "Socioeconomic Inequality in the American Religious System: An Update and Assessment." *Journal for the Scientific Study of Religion* 44: 95-104.

Smith, Christian (with Michael Emerson, Sally Gallagher, Paul Kennedy, and David Sikkink). 1998. *American Evangelicalism: Embattled and Thriving.* Chicago: University of Chicago Press.

Smith, Jane I. 1999. *Islam in America.* New York: Columbia University Press.

Smith, Miriam. 2005a. "The Politics of Same-Sex Marriage in Canada and the United States." *PS: Political Science and Politics* 38 (2): 225-28.

–. 2005b. "Social Movements and Judicial Empowerment: Courts, Public Policy, and Lesbian and Gay Organizing in Canada." *Politics and Society* 33: 327-53.

–. 2007. "Framing Same-Sex Marriage in Canada and the United States: Goodridge, Halpen and the National Boundaries of Political Discourse." *Social and Legal Studies* 16 (1): 5-26.

–. 2008. *Political Institutions and Lesbian and Gay Rights in the United States and Canada.* New York: Routledge.

Smith, T. Alexander. 1975. *The Comparative Policy Process.* Santa Barbara, CA: CLIO Press.

Smith, T. Alexander, and Raymond Tatalovich. 2003. *Cultures at War: Moral Conflicts in Western Democracies.* Peterborough, ON: Broadview.

Smith, T.W. 1999. "The Religious Right and Anti-Semitism." *Review of Religious Research* 40: 244-58.

Snyder, R. Clare. 2006. *Gay Marriage and Democracy: Equality for All*. Lanham, MD: Rowman and Littlefield.

Soper, J. Christopher. 1994. *Evangelical Christianity in the United States and Great Britain: Religious Beliefs, Political Choices*. London: Macmillan.

Sorauf, Frank J. 1976. *The Wall of Separation: The Constitutional Politics of Church and State*. Princeton: Princeton University Press.

Stackhouse, John, Jr. 1993. *Canadian Evangelicalism in the Twentieth Century: An Introduction to Its Character*. Toronto: University of Toronto Press.

–. 1994. "More than a Hyphen: Twentieth-Century Canadian Evangelicalism in Anglo-American Context." In *Amazing Grace: Evangelicalism in Australia, Britain, Canada, and the United States*, ed. George Rawlyk and Mark Noll, 375-400. Montreal: McGill-Queen's University Press.

–. 1997. "'Who Whom?' Evangelicalism and Canadian Society." In *Aspects of the Canadian Evangelical Experience*, ed. G.A. Rawlyk, 55-70. Montreal: McGill-Queen's University Press.

Stackhouse, Reginald, Jr. 2000. "Bearing Witness: Christian Groups Engage Canadian Politics since the 1960s." In *Rethinking Church, State, and Modernity*, ed. David Lyon and Marguerite Van Die, 113-28. Toronto: University of Toronto Press.

Statistics Canada. 2003. "Ethnic Diversity Survey: Portrait of a Multicultural Society – Content Overview," April. Catalogue No. 89-593-XIE.

Steensland, Brian, Jerry Z. Park, Mark D. Regnerus, Lynn D. Robinson, W. Bradford Wilcox, and Robert D. Woodberry. 2000. "The Measure of American Religion: Toward Improving the State-of-the-Art." *Social Forces* 79: 291-318.

Stokes, Anson Phillips. 1950. *Church and State in the United States*. New York: Harper and Brothers.

Stone, Carol L. "Estimate of Muslims Living in America." In *The Muslims of America*, ed. Yvonne Yazbeck Haddad, 25-36. New York: Oxford University Press.

Studlar, Donley. 2002. *Tobacco Control: Comparative Politics in the United States and Canada*. Peterborough, ON: Broadview.

Sulkin, Tracy, and Adam F. Simon. 2001. "Habermas in the Lab: A Study of Deliberation in an Experimental Setting." *Political Psychology* 22: 809-26.

Sundquist, James L. 1983. *Dynamics of the Party System: Alignment and Realignment of Political Parties in the United States*. Washington, DC: Brookings Institution.

Swindler, Arlene. 1991. *Homosexuality and World Religions*. Valley Forge, PA: Trinity Press International.

Talin, Kristoff. 2006. *Valeurs religieuses et univers politique: Amérique du Nord et Europe*. Québec: Presses de l'Université Laval.

Tatalovich, Raymond. 1997. *The Politics of Abortion in the United States and Canada: A Comparative Study*. Armonk, NY: M.E. Sharpe.

Tate, Katherine. 1994. *From Protest to Politics: The New Black Voters in American Elections*. Cambridge, MA: Harvard University Press.

Taylor, Charles. 1992. *Multiculturalism and the Politics of Recognition.* Princeton: Princeton University Press.

Taylor, Robert Joseph, Linda M. Chatters, Rukmalie Jayakody, and Jeffrey S. Levin. 1996. "Black and White Differences in Religious Participation: A Multisample Comparison." *Journal for the Scientific Study of Religion* 35: 403-10.

Tertullian. 2007. "On the Apparel of Women." Translation on New Advent website. http://www.newadvent.org/.

Thobani, Sunera. 2007. *Exalted Subjects: Studies in the Making of Race and Nation in Canada.* Toronto: University of Toronto Press.

Thomas, Sue, and Clyde Wilcox. 1992. "Religion and Feminist Attitudes among African-American Women: A View from the Nation's Capitol." *Women and Politics* 12: 19-40.

Thumma, Scott. 1991. "Negotiating a Religious Identity: The Case of the Gay Evangelical." *Sociological Analysis* 52 (4): 333-47.

Tocqueville, Alexis de. 2004 [1835]. *Democracy in America.* Vol. 1. New York: Penguin Putnam.

Traditional Values Coalition. 2008. "Traditional Values Coalition." http://www.traditionalvalues.org/.

Trothen, Tracy. 2003. *Linking Sexuality and Gender: Naming Violence against Women in the United Church of Canada.* Waterloo, ON: Wilfrid Laurier University Press.

Turner, Bryan S. 2002. "Sovereignty and Emergency: Political Theology, Islam, and America." *Theory, Culture, and Society* 19: 103-19.

Udis-Kessler, Amanda. 2002. "Lines in the Sand: The Struggle over Lesbian/Gay/Bisexual/Transgender Inclusion in the United Methodist Church." Phd diss., Boston College.

United Church of Canada, Commission on Christian Marriage and Divorce. 1960. *Toward a Christian Understanding of Sex, Love and Marriage: A First Report of the Commission on Christian Marriage and Divorce.* Approved by the Nineteenth General Council of the United Church of Canada, Edmonton, September. Toronto: Board of Christian Education.

–. 1974. *The Permanence of Christian Marriage.* Approved by the Division of Mission in Canada. Toronto: Division of Mission in Canada.

–. 1978. *Marriage Today: An Exploration of Man/Woman Relationship.* Toronto: Division of Mission in Canada.

–. 1988. "Membership, Ministry and Human Sexuality." 32nd General Council of the United Church of Canada. Toronto: General Council of the United Church.

–. 2003a. "In the Matter of an Appeal of Ruling 03-002-R of the General Secretary of the United Church of Canada." http://www.united-church.ca/.

–. 2003b. "Commentary Regarding Same-Sex Marriage from Jim Sinclair and Peter Short". http://www.united-church.ca/.

–. 2003c. "Chronology of Marriage and Equality Rights in the United Church." http://united-church.ca/.

–. 2005a. "Letter to the Moderator" by eight United Church ministers. http://www.united-church.ca/.

–. 2005b. "Marriage: A United Church of Canada Understanding." http://www. united-church.ca/.

United States Conference of Catholic Bishops (USCCB). 2006a. "Married Love and the Gift of Life," 14 November. http://www.usccbpublishing.org/.

–. 2006b. *Ministry to Persons with a Homosexual Inclination: Guidelines for Pastoral Care*, 14 November. http://www.usccbpublishing.org/.

United States Senate, Committee on Expenditures in the Executive Departments. 1950. "Employment of Homosexuals and Other Sex Perverts in the US Government." Report from the Subcommittee on Investigations, by Mr. Hoey. In *We Are Everywhere: A Historical Sourcebook of Gay and Lesbian Politics*, ed. Mark Blasius and Shane Phelan, 241-51. New York: Routledge, 1997.

Vakulenko, Anastasia. 2007. "'Islamic Headscarves' and the European Convention on Human Rights: An Intersectional Perspective." *Social and Legal Studies* 16: 183-99.

Valpy, Michael. 2010. "PM's Push on Census Got Under Way in December." *Globe and Mail*, 26 July.

Valverde, Mariana. 1991. *The Age of Light, Soap and Water: Moral Reform in English Canada, 1885-1925*. Toronto: McClelland and Stewart.

Van Ginkel, Aileen. 2003. "Evangelical Beliefs and Practices: A Summary of the 2003 Ipsos-Reid Survey Results." Evangelical Fellowship of Canada. http://www. evangelicalfellowship.ca/.

Veillette, Martin. 2005. "Pas de précipitation." *Le Nouvelliste*, 4 mars.

Verba, Sidney, Kay Lehman Schlozman, and Henry E. Brady. 1995. *Voice and Equality: Civic Voluntarism in American Politics*. Cambridge, MA: Harvard University Press.

Waaldijk, Kees, and Matteo Bonini-Baraldi. 2006. *Sexual Orientation Discrimination in the European Union: National Laws and the Employment Equality Directive*. The Hague: Asser Press.

Wadsworth, Nancy. 1997. "Reconciliation Politics: Conservative Evangelicals and the New Race Discourse." *Politics and Society* 25: 341-76.

Wadud, Amina. 1999. *Qur'an and Woman: Rereading the Sacred Text from a Woman's Perspective*. New York: Oxford University Press.

Waites, Matthew. 2008. "Analysing Sexualities in the Shadow of War: Islam in Iran, the West, and the Work of Re-Imagining Human Rights." *Sexualities* 11: 64-73.

–. 2009. "Critique of 'Sexual Orientation' and 'Gender Identity' in Human Rights Discourse: Global Queer Politics beyond the Yogyakarta Principles." *Contemporary Politics* 15 (1): 137-56.

Wald, Kenneth D. 1992. "Religious Elites and Public Opinion: The Impact of the Bishops' Peace Pastoral." *Review of Politics* 54: 112-43.

–. 2005. "In the Kingdom of Kindness: American Jews and the Public Role of Religion." In *Taking Religious Pluralism Seriously: Spiritual Politics on America's Sacred Ground*, ed. Barbara McGraw and Jo Renee Formicola, 27-44. Waco, TX: Baylor University Press.

–. 2006. "Toward a Structural Explanation of Jewish-Catholic Political Differences in the United States." In *Jews and Catholics in Dialogue and Confrontation: Religion and Politics since the Second World War*, ed. Eli Lederhendler, 111-31. New York: Oxford University Press.

–. 2009. "Private Religion in the American Public Square." In *Religious Cultures/ Communities of Belief*, ed. Jurgen Gebhardt and David Martin Gebhardt, 195-218. Heidelberg: Universitatsverlag.

Wald, Kenneth D., and Allison Calhoun-Brown. 2006. *Religion and Politics in the United States.* 5th ed. Lanham, MD: Rowman and Littlefield.

Wald, Kenneth D., and Graham Glover. 2007. "Theological Perspectives on Gay Unions: The Uneasy Marriage of Religion and Politics." In *The Politics of Same-Sex Marriage*, ed. Craig Rimmerman and Clyde Wilcox, 105-30. Chicago: University of Chicago Press.

Wald, Kenneth D., and Lee Sigelman. 1997. "Romancing the Jews: The Christian Right in Search of Strange Bedfellows." In *Sojourners in the Wilderness: The Religious Right in Comparative Perspective*, ed. Corwin Smidt and James Penning, 139-68. Lanham, MD: Rowman and Littlefield.

Wald, Kenneth D., and Clyde Wilcox. 2006. "Getting Religion: Has Political Science Rediscovered the Faith Factor?" *American Political Science Review* 100: 523-30.

Wald, Kenneth, James Button, and Barbara Rienzo. 1996. "The Politics of Gay Rights in American Communities: Explaining Anti-Discrimination Ordinances and Policies." *American Journal of Political Science* 40: 1152-78.

Wald, Kenneth D., Dennis Owen, and Samuel Hill. 1988. "Churches as Political Communities." *American Political Science Review* 82: 531-48.

Wallis, Jim. 1996. *Who Speaks for God? An Alternative to the Religious Right – A New Politics of Compassion, Community, and Civility.* New York: Delacorte Press.

Walsh, Edward J. 1981. "Resource Mobilization and Citizen Protest in Communities around Three Mile Island." *Social Problems* 29: 1-21.

Walsh, Katherine Cramer. 2004. *Talking about Politics: Informal Groups and Social Identity in American Life.* Chicago: University of Chicago Press.

Warner, Tom. 2010. *Losing Control: Canada's Social Conservatives in the Age of Rights.* Toronto: Between the Lines.

Weinrib, Lorraine E. 2003. "'Do Justice to Us!' Jews and the Constitution of Canada." In *Not Written in Stone: Jews, Constitutions, and Constitutionalism in Canada*, ed. Daniel J. Elazar, Michael Brown, and Ira Robinson, 33-68. Ottawa: University of Ottawa Press.

Welch, Michael R., and David C. Leege. 1991. "Dual Reference Groups and Political Orientations: An Examination of Evangelically Oriented Catholics." *American Journal of Political Science* 35: 28-56.

Wellman, James K. 1999. "Introduction: The Debate over Homosexual Ordination: Subcultural Identity Theory in American Religious Organizations." *Review of Religious Research* 41: 184-206.

Wen, Patricia. 2006. "Catholic Charities Stun State, End Adoption." *Boston Globe*, 11 March.

Whitaker, Reginald. 1977. *The Government Party: Organizing and Financing the Liberal Party of Canada, 1930-1958*. Toronto: University of Toronto Press.

White, Gayle. 2000. "A Dissident Defrocked." *Atlanta Journal and Constitution*, 29 April.

White, James Boyd. 1985. *Heracles' Bow: Essays on the Rhetoric and Poetics of the Law*. Madison: University of Wisconsin Press.

Wiesner-Hanks, Merry. 2000. *Christianity and Sexuality in the Early Modern World: Regulating Desire, Reforming Practice*. New York: Routledge.

Wilcox, Clyde. 1986. "Fundamentalists and Politics: An Analysis of the Effects of Differing Operational Definitions." *Journal of Politics* 48: 1041-51.

–. 1987. "Popular Backing for the Old Christian Right: Explaining Support for the Christian Anti-Communism Crusade." *Journal of Social History* 21: 117-32.

–. 1991. "Support for Gender Equality in West Europe: A Longitudinal Analysis." *European Journal for Political Research* 20: 127-47.

–. 1992. *God's Warriors: The Christian Right in Twentieth-Century America*. Baltimore: Johns Hopkins University Press.

–. 2007a. Introductory remarks delivered at Religion, Sexuality, and Politics in Canada and the United States, a conference organized by the Mark S. Bonham Centre for Sexual Diversity Studies, University of Toronto, January.

–. 2007b. "Movements and Metaphors." Paper presented at the conference on the Christian Conservative Movement and American Democracy, New York, April.

–. 2010. "The Christian Right and Civic Virtue." In *Religion and American Democracy*, ed. A. Wolfe and I. Katznelson. Princeton: Princeton University Press.

Wilcox, Clyde, and Carin Larson. 2006. *Onward Christian Soldiers: The Christian Right in American Politics*. 3rd ed. Boulder, CO: Westview.

Wilcox, Clyde, and Barbara Norrander. 2002. "Of Moods and Morals: The Dynamics of Opinion on Abortion and Gay Rights." In *Understanding Public Opinion*, 2nd ed., ed. Barbara Norrander and Clyde Wilcox, 121-48. Washington, DC: CQ Press.

Wilcox, Clyde, and Robin Wolpert. 2000. "Gay Rights in the Public Sphere: Public Opinion on Gay and Lesbian Equality." In *The Politics of Gay Rights*, ed. Craig Rimmerman, Kenneth D. Wald, and Clyde Wilcox, 409-32. Chicago: University of Chicago Press.

Wilcox, Clyde, Linda M. Merolla, and David Beer. 2007. "Saving Marriage by Banning Marriage: The Christian Right Finds a New Issue in 2004." In *The Values Campaign: The Christian Right and the 2004 Elections*, ed. John C. Green, Mark J. Rozell, and Clyde Wilcox, 56-75. Washington, DC: Georgetown University Press.

Wilcox, Clyde, Paul R. Brewer, Shauna Shames, and Celinda Lake. 2007. "If I Bend This Far I Will Break? Public Opinion about Same-Sex Marriage." In *The Pol-*

itics of Same-Sex Marriage, ed. Craig A. Rimmerman and Clyde Wilcox, 215-42. Chicago: University of Chicago Press.

Wilcox, W. Bradford. 2004. *Soft Patriarchs and New Men: How Christianity Shapes Fathers and Husbands.* Chicago: University of Chicago Press.

Wildavsky, Aaron. 1987. "Choosing Preferences by Constructing Institutions: A Cultural Theory of Preference Formation." *American Political Science Review* 81: 3-21.

Williams, Rhys H. 1998. *Cultural Wars in American Politics: Critical Reviews of a Popular Myth.* New York: Aldine de Gruyter.

Wilson, Justin T. 2007. "Preservationism, or the Elephant in the Room: How Opponents of Same-Sex Marriage Deceive Us into Establishing Religion." *Duke Journal of Gender Law and Policy* 14: 561-679.

Wintemute, Robert. 2002. "Religion vs. Sexual Orientation Equality: A Clash of Human Rights?" *University of Toronto Journal of Law and Equality* 1: 125-45.

Wintemute, Robert, and Mads Andenaes, eds. 2001. *Legal Recognition of Same-Sex Partnerships: A Study of National, European and International Law.* Oxford: Hart Publishing.

Witte, John, Jr. 1998. "Between Sacrament and Contract: Marriage as Governance in John Calvin's Geneva." *Calvin Theological Journal* 33: 9-75.

Wolfe, Alan. 1998. *One Nation, After All: What Americans Really Think about God, Country, Family, Racism, Welfare, Immigration, Homosexuality, Work, the Right, the Left, and Each Other.* New York: Viking.

Wood, James R. 2000. *Where the Spirit Leads: The Evolving Views of United Methodists on Homosexuality.* Nashville: Abington Press.

Wood, James, and Jon Bloch. 1995. "The Role of Church Assemblies: The Case of the United Methodist General Conference's Debate on Homosexuality." *Sociology of Religion* 56: 121-36.

World Values Survey. 2009a. "1995-2000 World Value Survey Data." http://www.worldvaluessurvey.org/.

—. 2009b. "Official Aggregate of Data from 1981-2008." http://www.worldvaluessurvey.org/.

Wright, Robert A. 1990. "The Canadian Protestant Tradition 1914-1945." In *The Canadian Protestant Experience, 1760-1990*, ed. G.A. Rawlyk, 139-97. Burlington: Welch Publishing Company.

Wuthnow, Robert. 1988. *The Restructuring of American Religion: Society and Faith since World War II.* Princeton: Princeton University Press.

—. 1993. *Christianity in the 21st Century: Reflections on the Challenges Ahead.* New York: Oxford University Press.

—. 1996. *The Crisis in the Churches: Spiritual Malaise, Fiscal Woe.* New York: Oxford University Press.

—. 2000a. "The Moral Minority." *American Prospect*, 22 May, 31-34.

—. 2000b. "Religion and Politics Survey." Data available at the Association of Religion Data Archives. http://thearda.com/.

–. 2007. *After the Baby Boomers: How Twenty and Thirty-Somethings Are Shaping the Future of American Religion.* Princeton: Princeton University Press.

Wuthnow, Robert, and John H. Evans. 2002. *The Quiet Hand of God: Faith-Based Activism and the Public Role of Mainline Protestantism.* Berkeley: University of California Press.

Yang, Alan S. 1997. "Attitudes toward Homosexuality." *Public Opinion Quarterly* 61: 477-507.

–. 1999. "From Wrongs to Rights: Public Opinion on Gay and Lesbian Americans Moves toward Equality." *National Gay and Lesbian Task Force.* http://www.the taskforce.org/.

Yip, Andrew Kam-Tuck. 2005. "Religion and the Politics of Spirituality/Sexuality: Reflections on Researching British Lesbian, Gay, and Bisexual Christians and Muslims." *Fieldwork in Religion* 1 (3): 271-89.

–. 2007. "Changing Religion, Changing Faith: Reflections on the Transformative Strategies of Lesbian, Gay, and Bisexual Christians and Muslims." *Journal of Faith, Spirituality and Social Change* 1 (1). http://www.fssconference.org.uk/.

–. 2008a. "The Quest for Intimate/Sexual Citizenship: Lived Experiences of Lesbian and Bisexual Muslim Women." *Contemporary Islam* 2 (2): 99-117.

–. 2008b. "Researching Lesbian, Gay, and Bisexual Christians and Muslims: Some Thematic Reflections." *Sociological Research Online* 13 (1). http://www.socres online.org.uk/.

–. 2009. "Introduction to the Special Issue on Islam and Sexuality." *Contemporary Islam* 3 (1): 1-5.

Zamiska, Nicholas. 2003. "Clergy Coalition Offers Support for Same-Sex Marriage." *Boston Globe,* 6 June.

Zuckerman, Phil. 1999. *Strife in the Sanctuary: Religious Schism in a Jewish Community.* Walnut Creek, CA: Alta Mira.

LEGAL CASES CITED

Boutilier v. INS, 387 U.S. 118 (1967).

Bowers v. Hardwick, 478 U.S. (1986).

Boy Scouts of America v. Dale, 530 U.S. 640 (2000); 160 N.J. 562 (1999).

B(R) v. Children's Aid Society of Metropolitan Toronto, [1995] 1 S.C.R. 315.

Caldwell v. St. Thomas Aquinas High School, [1984] 2 S.C.R. 603.

Chamberlain v. Surrey School District #36 (2002), 221 D.L.R. (4th) 156 (S.C.C.).

Conaway v. Deane, 401 Md. 219 (2007).

Doe v. Commonwealth's Attorney, 425 U.S. 901 (1976).

Egan v. Canada, [1995] 2 S.C.R. 513.

Goodridge v. Department of Public Health, 440 Mass 309 (2003).

Halpern et al. v. Canada (Attorney General), [2003] O.J. No. 2268.

Hurley v. Irish-American Gay, Lesbian, and Bisexual Group of Boston, 515 U.S. 557 (1995).

Kempling v. BCCT, [2005] B.C.J. No. 1288 (B.C.C.A.).

Lawrence v. Texas, 539 U.S. 1 (2003).

M. v. H., [1999] 2 S.C.R. 3.

Norton v. Macy, 417 F.2d 1161 (D.C.Cir. 1969).

One v. Olesen, 355 U.S. 772 (1958).

Ontario (Human Rights Commission) v. Brillinger, [2002] O.J. No. 2375.

Owens v. Saskatchewan (Human Rights Commission), [2006] S.J. No. 221 (Sask C.A.).

Powell v. Georgia, 278 Ga. 327 (1998).

Re Guardianship of Kowalski, 478 N.W.2d 790 (Minn. Ct. App. 1991).

Romer v. Evans, 517 U.S. 620 (1996).

Rosenberger v. The Rectors and Visitors of the University of Virginia, 515 U.S. 819 (1995).

Ross v. New Brunswick School District No. 15, [1996] 1 S.C.R. 825.

Roth v. US, 354 U.S. 476 (1957).

Scott v. Macy, 349 F.2d 182 (C.A.D.C. 1965).

Smith and Chymyshyn v. Knights of Columbus, 2005 BCHRT 544.

Trinity Western University v. British Columbia College of Teachers, [2001] 1 S.C.R. 772.

Zylberberg v. Sudbury School Bd. (1988), 52 D.L.R. (4th) 577 (ON C.A.).

Contributors

Jean-François Breton is a PhD candidate in sciences of religion at the Université de Montréal, currently preparing a dissertation entitled "To Be Gay/Lesbian and Catholic in Quebec Today: A Socio-Religious Analysis of Identities."

Wendy Cadge is an associate professor of political science at Clemson University in South Carolina. She is the author, co-author, or co-editor of nine books, including *Religion and Politics in America: Faith, Culture, and Strategic Choices* (Westview Press 2010) and *Women with a Mission: Religion, Gender, and the Politics of Women Clergy* (University of Alabama Press 2005).

Daniel Cox is the research director and co-founder of Public Religion Research Institute, a non-profit, independent research and education organization specializing in work at the intersection of religion, values, and public life. His work at the institute, and before that at the Pew Forum on Religion and Public Life, has appeared in numerous national news and religious publications. He is a PhD candidate in American government at Georgetown University, Washington, DC.

Paul Djupe is an associate professor of political science at Denison University in Granville, Ohio, and is co-author of *The Political Influence of Churches*

(Cambridge University Press 2009) and *The Prophetic Pulpit* (Rowman and Littlefield 2003)

Tina Fetner is an associate professor of sociology at McMaster University in Ontario. She has authored *How the Religious Right Shaped Lesbian and Gay Activism* (University of Minnesota Press 2008) as well as articles in such journals as *Social Problems, Public Opinion Quarterly,* and the *American Journal of Political Science.*

John C. Green is distinguished professor of political science and director of the Ray C. Bliss Institute of Applied Politics at the University of Akron in Ohio. He has authored *The Faith Factor: How Religion Influences American Elections* (Praeger 2007), co-edited *The State of the Parties* (Rowman and Littlefield 2007), and published numerous articles and book chapters on religion and politics and party politics in the United States.

Amir Hussain, a Canadian Muslim, is a professor of theological studies at Loyola Marymount University, the Jesuit university in Los Angeles. He is author of *Oil and Water: Two Faiths, One God* (Wood Lake 2006), which discusses Islam and Christianity, and *World Religions: Western Traditions,* 3rd ed. (Oxford University Press 2010). From 2011 to 2015 he will be serving as editor of the *Journal of the American Academy of Religion.*

Roger Hutchinson was the principal of, and now is a professor emeritus at, Emmanuel College of Victoria University at the University of Toronto. He has authored *Ethical Choices in a Pluralistic World* (Chester Ronning Centre for the Study of Religion and Public Life 2009) and numerous articles and book chapters on environmental ethics, debates over same-sex marriage, and ecumenical social action.

Rentaro Iida is a PhD candidate in political science at Georgetown University in Washington, DC. He has published chapters on interest groups in elections and is currently researching networks of activists and groups in the US abortion debate as well as networks of groups that file *amicus curae* briefs before the US Supreme Court.

Ted G. Jelen is a professor of political science at the University of Nevada, Las Vegas. The most recent of his numerous books is the 2nd edition of *To Serve God and Mammon: Church-State Relations in American Politics*

(Westview 2010). He is co-editor of the journal *Politics and Religion* and former editor of the *Journal for the Scientific Study of Religion.*

Robert P. Jones is the founder and CEO of Public Religion Research Institute, a non-profit, non-partisan, independent research and education organization working at the intersection of religion, values, and public life. He is the author of *Progressive and Religious* (Rowman and Littlefield 2008), *Liberalism's Troubled Search for Equality* (University of Notre Dame Press 2007), and numerous articles on religion, ethics, and politics.

Didi Kuo is a PhD candidate in the Department of Government at Harvard University. Her research interests include democratization, political party development, clientelism, and the effects of reforming electoral systems.

Amy Langstaff is an independent writer and consultant. Her contribution to this volume emerges from her previous research on social values and public affairs at Environics Research Group, a major public opinion research firm in Canada.

Solange Lefebvre is a professor in the Faculté de théologie et de sciences des religions; holds the chair in religion, culture, and society; and was the founder of the Centre d'étude des religions at the Université de Montréal. She has authored *Cultures et spiritualités des jeunes* (Bellarmin 2008) and edited or co-edited *Le patrimoine religieux du Québec* (Presses de l'Université Laval 2009), *Migration in a Global World* (SCM Press 2008), and *Stages of Life and Christian Experience* (SCM Press 2007).

Katherine Levine is a PhD candidate in government and social policy at Harvard University. Her research interests include political behaviour, public opinion, urban politics, and social policy.

Jonathan Malloy is an associate professor of political science and public policy and administration at Carleton University in Ottawa. His research focuses on Canadian political institutions, social movement links to those institutions, and the role of evangelical Christians in politics, and his articles appear in *Canadian Public Administration, Governance,* the *Canadian Journal of Political Science,* and the *Journal of Legislative Studies.*

Richard Moon is a professor in the Faculty of Law at the University of Windsor in Ontario. He is author of *The Constitutional Protection of Freedom of Expression* (University of Toronto Press 2000), editor of *Law and Religious Pluralism in Canada* (UBC Press 2008), and contributing editor to *Canadian Constitutional Law*, 4th ed. (Emond Montgomery Press 2010).

Laura R. Olson is a professor of political science at Clemson University in South Carolina. She is author, co-author, or co-editor of nine books, including *Religion and Politics in America: Faith, Culture, and Strategic Choices* (Westview 2010) and *Women with a Mission: Religion, Gender, and the Politics of Women Clergy* (University of Alabama Press 2005).

Jason Pierceson is an associate professor of political science and legal studies and chair of political science at the University of Illinois Springfield. He has authored *Courts, Liberalism, and Rights: Gay Law and Politics in the United States and Canada* (Temple University Press 2005) and co-edited *Moral Argument, Religion, and Same-Sex Marriage* (Lexington Books 2009) and *Same-Sex Marriage in the Americas* (Lexington Books 2010).

Momin Rahman teaches sociology at Trent University in Peterborough, Ontario. He is the author of *Sexuality and Democracy: Identities and Strategies in Lesbian and Gay Politics* (Edinburgh University Press 2000), *Gender and Sexuality: Sociological Approaches* (2010), and articles on LGBT politics, cultural representations, and theory.

David Rayside is a professor of political science and former director of the Mark S. Bonham Centre for Sexual Diversity Studies at the University of Toronto. He has authored *Queer Inclusions, Continental Divisions: Public Recognition of Sexual Diversity in Canada and the United States* (University of Toronto Press 2008), *On the Fringe: Gays and Lesbians in Politics* (Cornell University Press 1998), and articles and book chapters on LGBT rights and activism in North America and Europe.

Samuel Reimer is a professor of sociology at Crandall University in Moncton, New Brunswick. He is the author of *Evangelicals and the Continental Divide* (McGill-Queen's University Press 2003) and numerous articles and book chapters on the sociology of religion and, in particular, on Canada-US differences.

Carrie B. Sanders is an assistant professor of criminology at Wilfrid Laurier University, Brantford, Ontario. She is an interpretive theorist who studies social problems, policing, science, and technology.

Shauna L. Shames is a PhD candidate in American government at Harvard University. She has published articles, reports, and book chapters on women as electoral candidates, comparative child care policy, work-family conflict, abortion, feminism in the United States and internationally, public opinion, and gay and lesbian rights.

Kenneth D. Wald is distinguished professor of political science at the University of Florida. He is a specialist in the study of religion and politics in the United States and has also published extensively on the conflict between advocates of gay rights and their religiously inspired opponents. He is the author, co-author, and co-editor of numerous books, including *Religion and Politics* (Rowman and Littlefield 2010), now in its sixth edition.

Clyde Wilcox is a professor of political science at Georgetown University in Washington, DC, and has authored, co-authored, or co-edited numerous books on US electoral politics, gender politics, religion and politics, and the role of religion in shaping attitudes towards sexual diversity. Among these are *Onward Christian Soldiers: The Christian Right in American Politics*, 4th ed. (Westview 2010); *The Values Campaign? The Christian Right in the 2004 Elections* (Georgetown University Press 2006); and *The Politics of Same-Sex Marriage* (University of Chicago Press 2007).

Pamela Dickey Young is professor of religion and culture in the School of Religion at Queen's University in Kingston, Ontario, and has published on the intersections of religion, sex, gender, and public policy. Her recent publications include *Women and Religious Traditions*, 2nd ed. (Oxford University Press 2010), which she co-edited, as well as articles and book chapters on debates over sexual diversity.

Index